Hard Press

George Gissing

In the Year of Jubilee

Part I: Miss. Lord

CHAPTER 1

At eight o'clock on Sunday morning, Arthur Peachey unlocked his front door, and quietly went forth. He had not ventured to ask that early breakfast should be prepared for him. Enough that he was leaving home for a summer holiday—the first he had allowed himself since his marriage three years ago.

It was a house in De Crespigny Park; unattached, double-fronted, with half-sunk basement, and a flight of steps to the stucco pillars at the entrance. De Crespigny Park, a thoroughfare connecting Grove Lane, Camberwell, with Denmark Hill, presents a double row of similar dwellings; its clean breadth, with foliage of trees and shrubs in front gardens, makes it pleasant to the eye that finds pleasure in suburban London. In point of respectability, it has claims only to be appreciated by the ambitious middle-class of Camberwell. Each house seems to remind its neighbour, with all the complacence expressible in buff brick, that in this locality lodgings are *not* to let.

For an hour after Peachey's departure, the silence of the house was unbroken. Then a bedroom door opened, and a lady in a morning gown of the fashionable heliotrope came downstairs. She had acute features; eyes which seemed to indicate the concentration of her thoughts upon a difficult problem, and cheeks of singular bloom. Her name was Beatrice French; her years numbered six and twenty.

She entered the dining-room and drew up the blind. Though the furniture was less than a year old, and by no means of the cheapest description, slovenly housekeeping had dulled the brightness of every surface. On a chair lay a broken toy, one of those elaborate and costly playthings which serve no purpose but to stunt a child's imagination. Though the time was midsummer, not a flower appeared among the pretentious ornaments. The pictures were a strange medley —autotypes of some artistic value hanging side by side with hideous oleographs framed in ponderous gilding. Miss. then violently rang the bell. When the summons had been twice French looked about her with an expression of strong disgust, repeated, there appeared a young woman whose features told of long and placid slumbers.

'Well? what does this mean?'

'The cook doesn't feel well, miss; she can't get up.

'Then get breakfast yourself, and look sharp about it.'

Beatrice spoke with vehemence; her cheeks showed a circle of richer hue around the unchanging rose. The domestic made insolent reply, and there began a war of words. At this moment another step sounded on the stairs, and as it drew near, a female voice was raised in song.

2

'And a penny in his pocket, la-de-da, la-de-da,—and a penny in his pocket, la-de-da!'

A younger girl, this, of much slighter build; with a frisky gait, a jaunty pose of the head; pretty, but thin-featured, and shallow-eyed; a long neck, no chin to speak of, a low forehead with the hair of washed-out flaxen fluffed all over it. Her dress was showy, and in a taste that set the teeth on edge. Fanny French, her name.

'What's up? Another row?' she asked, entering the room as the servant went out.

'I've known a good many fools,' said Beatrice, 'but Ada's the biggest I've come across yet.'

'Is she? Well, I shouldn't wonder,' Fanny admitted impartially. And with a skip she took up her song again. *'A penny paper collar round his neck, la-de-da—'*

'Are you going to church this morning?' asked her sister.

'Yes. Are you?'

'Come for a walk instead. There's something I want to talk to you about.'

'Won't it do afterwards? I've got an appointment.'

'With Lord?'

Fanny laughed and nodded.

Interrupted by the reappearance of the servant, who brought a tray and began to lay the table, they crossed the hall to the drawing-room. In half-an-hour's time a sluttish meal was prepared for them, and whilst they were satisfying their hunger, the door opened to admit Mrs. Peachey. Ada presented herself in a costume which, at any season but high summer, would have been inconveniently cool. Beneath a loose thin dressing-gown her feet, in felt slippers, showed stockingless, her neck was bare almost to the bosom, and the tresses of pale yellow, upon which she especially prided herself, lay raggedly pinned together on the top of her flat head. She was about twenty-eight years old, but at present looked more than thirty. Her features resembled Fanny's, but had a much less amiable expression, and betokened, if the thing were possible, an inferior intellect. Fresh from the morning basin, her cheeks displayed that peculiar colourlessness which results from the habitual use of paints and powders; her pale pink lips, thin and sullen, were curiously wrinkled; she had eyes of slate colour, with lids so elevated that she always seemed to be staring in silly wonder.

'So you've got breakfast, have you?' were her first words, in a thin and rather nasal voice. 'You may think yourselves lucky.'

'You have a cheek of your own,' replied Beatrice. 'Whose place is it to see that we get meals?'

'And what can any one do with servants like I've got?' retorted the married sister.

'It's your own fault. You should get better; and when you've got them, you should manage them. But that's just what you can't do.'

'Oh, *you*'d be a wonderful housekeeper, we know all about that. If you're not satisfied, you'd better find board and lodging somewhere else, as I've told you often enough. You're not likely to get it as cheap.'

They squabbled for some minutes, Fanny looking on with ingenuous amusement, and putting in a word, now for this side, now for that.

'And what am I going to have for breakfast?' demanded Mrs. Peachey at length, surveying the table. 'You've taken jolly good care of yourselves, it seems to me.'

She jumped up, and rang the bell. When a minute's interval brought no reply, she rang again. Beatrice thought it probable that the bell might be rung without effect, 'till all was blue.'

'We'll see about that,' answered her sister, and forthwith invaded the lower parts of the house. Thence, presently, her voice became audible, rising gradually to shrillness; with it there blended the rougher accents of the housemaid, now in reckless revolt. Beatrice listened for a minute or two in the hall, then passed on into the drawing-room with a contemptuous laugh. Fanny, to whom the uproar seemed to bring a renewal of appetite, cut herself a slice of bread and butter, and ate it as she stood at the window.

'Dirty cat! beast! swine!'

The mistress of the house, fairly beaten away by superior force of vocabulary, reappeared with these and other exclamations, her face livid, her foolish eyes starting from their sockets. Fanny, a sort of Mother Cary's chicken, revelled in the row, and screamed her merriment.

It was long before the domestic uproar wholly subsided, but towards eleven o'clock the sisters found themselves together in the drawing-room. Ada sprawled limply on a sofa; Beatrice sat with legs crossed in the most comfortable chair; and Fanny twirled about on a music stool.

The only books in the room were a few show-volumes, which belonged to Arthur Peachey, and half-a-dozen novels of the meaner kind, wherewith Ada sometimes beguiled her infinite leisure. But on tables and chairs lay scattered a multitude of papers: illustrated weeklies, journals of society, cheap miscellanies, penny novelettes, and the like. At the end of the week, when new numbers came in, Ada Peachey passed many hours upon her sofa, reading instalments of a dozen serial stories, paragraphs relating to fashion, sport, the theatre, answers to correspondents (wherein she especially delighted), columns of facetiae, and gossip about notorious people. Through a great deal of this matter Beatrice followed her, and read much besides in which Ada took no interest; she studied a daily newspaper, with special note of law suits, police intelligence, wills, bankruptcies, and any concern, great or small, wherein money played a part. She understood the nature of investments, and liked to talk about stocks and shares with her male acquaintances.

They were the daughters of a Camberwell builder, lately deceased; to each of them had fallen a patrimony just sufficient for their support in elegant leisure. Ada's money, united with a small capital in her husband's possession, went to purchase a share in the business of Messrs. Ducker, Blunt & Co., manufacturers of disinfectants; Arthur Peachey, previously a clerk to the firm, became a junior partner, with the result that most of the hard work was thrown upon his shoulders. At their marriage, the happy pair first of all established themselves in a modest house near Camberwell Road; two years later, growing prosperity brought about their removal to De Crespigny Park, where they had now resided for some twelve months. Unlike their elder sister, Beatrice and Fanny had learnt to support themselves, Beatrice in the postal service, and Fanny, sweet blossom! by mingling her fragrance with that of a florist's shop in Brixton; but on their father's death both forsook their employment, and came to live with Mrs. Peachey. Between them, these two were the owners of house-property, which produced L140 a year. They disbursed, together, a weekly sum of twenty-four shillings for board and lodging, and spent or saved the rest as their impulses dictated.

CHAPTER 2

Ada brooded over her wrongs; Beatrice glanced over *The Referee*. Fanny, after twirling awhile in maiden meditation, turned to the piano and jingled a melody from 'The Mikado.' She broke off suddenly, and, without looking round, addressed her companions.

'You can give the third seat at the Jubilee to somebody else. I'm provided for.'

'Who are you going with?' asked Ada.

'My masher,' the girl replied with a giggle.

'Where?'

'Shop-windows in the Strand, I think.'

She resumed her jingling; it was now 'Queen of my Heart.' Beatrice, dropping her paper, looked fixedly at the girl's profile, with an eyelid droop which signified calculation.

'How much is he really getting?' she inquired all at once.

'Seventy-five pounds a year. "*Oh where, oh where, is my leetle dog gone?*"'

'Does he say,' asked Mrs. Peachey, 'that his governor will stump up?'

They spoke a peculiar tongue, the product of sham education and mock refinement grafted upon a stock of robust vulgarity. One and all would have been moved to indignant surprise if accused of ignorance or defective breeding. Ada had frequented an 'establishment for young ladies' up to the close of her seventeenth year; the other two had pursued culture at a still more pretentious institute until they were eighteen. All could 'play the piano;' all declared—and believed—that they 'knew French.' Beatrice had 'done' Political Economy; Fanny had 'been through' Inorganic Chemistry and Botany. The truth was, of course, that their minds, characters, propensities had remained absolutely proof against such educational influence as had been brought to bear upon them. That they used a finer accent than their servants, signified only that they had grown up amid falsities, and were enabled, by the help of money, to dwell above-stairs, instead of with their spiritual kindred below.

Anticipating Fanny's reply, Beatrice observed, with her air of sagacity:

'If you think you're going to get anything out of an old screw like Lord, you'll jolly soon find your mistake.'

'Don't you go and make a fool of yourself, Fanny,' said Mrs. Peachey. 'Why, he can't be more than twenty-one, is he?'

'He's turned twenty-two.'

The others laughed scornfully.

'Can't I have who I like for a masher?' cried Fanny, reddening a little. 'Who said I was going to marry him? I'm in no particular hurry to get married. You think everybody's like yourselves.'

'If there was any chance of old Lord turning up his toes,' said Beatrice thoughtfully. 'I dare say he'll leave a tidy handful behind him, but then he may live another ten years or more.'

'And there's Nancy,' exclaimed Ada. 'Won't she get half the plunder?'

'May be plenty, even then,' said Beatrice, her head aside. 'The piano business isn't a bad line. I shouldn't wonder if he leaves ten or fifteen thousand.'

'Haven't you got anything out of Horace?' asked Ada of Fanny. 'What has he told you?'

'He doesn't know much, that's the fact.'

'Silly! There you are. His father treats him like a boy; if he talked about marrying, he'd get a cuff on the ear. Oh, I know all about old Lord,' Ada proceeded. 'He's a regular old tyrant. Why, you've only to look at him. And he thinks no small beer of himself, either, for all he lives in that grubby little house; I shouldn't wonder if he thinks us beneath him.'

She stared at her sisters, inviting their comment on this_ ludicrous state of things.

'I quite believe Nancy does,' said Fanny, with a point of malice.

'She's a stuck-up thing,' declared Mrs. Peachey. 'And she gets worse as she gets older. I shall never invite her again; it's three times she has made an excuse—all lies, of course.'

'Who will *she* marry?' asked Beatrice, in a tone of disinterested speculation.

Mrs. Peachey answered with a sneer:

'She's going to the Jubilee to pick up a fancy Prince.'

'As it happens,' objected Fanny, 'she isn't going to the Jubilee at all. At least she says she isn't. She's above it—so her brother told me.'

'I know who *wants* to marry her,' Ada remarked, with a sour smile.

'Who is that?' came from the others.

'Mr. Crewe.'

With a significant giggle, Fanny glanced at the more sober of her sisters; she, the while, touched her upper lip with the point of her tongue, and looked towards the window.

'Does he?' Fanny asked of the ceiling.

'He wants money to float his teetotal drink,' said Beatrice. 'Hasn't he been at Arthur about it?'

'Not that I know,' answered the wife.

'He tried to get round me, but I—'

A scream of incredulity from Fanny, and a chuckle from Mrs. Peachey, covered the rest of the sentence. Beatrice gazed at them defiantly.

'Well, idiots! What's up now?'

'Oh, nothing.'

'There's nobody knows Luckworth Crewe better than I do,' Beatrice pursued disdainfully, 'and I think he knows *me* pretty well. He'll make a fool of himself when he marries; I've told him so, and he as good as said I was right. If it wasn't for that, I should feel a respect for him. He'll have money one of these days.'

'And he'll marry Nancy Lord,' said Ada tauntingly.

'Not just yet.'

Ada rolled herself from the sofa, and stood yawning.

'Well, I shall go and dress. What are you people going to do? You needn't expect any dinner. I shall have mine at a restaurant.'

'Who have you to meet?' asked Fanny, with a grimace.

Her sister disregarded the question, yawned again, and turned to Beatrice.

'Who shall we ask to take Fan's place on Tuesday? Whoever it 15, they'll have to pay. Those seats are selling for three guineas, somebody told me.'

Conversation lingered about this point for a few minutes, till Mrs. Peachey went upstairs. When the door was open, a child's crying could be heard, but it excited no remark. Presently the other two retired, to make themselves ready for going out. Fanny was the first to reappear, and, whilst waiting for her sister, she tapped out a new music-hall melody on the piano.

As they left the house, Beatrice remarked that Ada really meant to have her dinner at Gatti's or some such place; perhaps they had better indulge themselves in the same way.

'Suppose you give Horace Lord a hint that we've no dinner at home? He might take us, and stand treat.'

Fanny shook her head.

'I don't think he could get away. The guv'nor expects him home to dinner on Sundays.'

The other laughed her contempt.

'You see! What good is he? Look here, Fan, you just wait a bit, and you'll do much better than that. Old Lord would cut up rough as soon as ever such a thing was mentioned; I know he would. There's something I have had in my mind for a long time. Suppose I could show you a way of making a heap of money—no end of money—? Shouldn't you like it better,—to live as you pleased, and be independent?'

The listener's face confessed curiosity, yet was dubious.

'What do you say to going into business with me?' pursued Miss French. 'We've only to raise a little money on the houses, and m a year or two we might be making thousands.'

'Business? What sort of business?'

'Suppose somebody came to you and said: Pay me a sovereign, and I'll make you a member of an association that supplies fashionable clothing at about half the ordinary price,—wouldn't you jump at it?'

'If I thought it wasn't a swindle,' Fanny replied ingenuously.

'Of course. But you'd be made to see it wasn't. And suppose they went on to say: Take a ten-pound share, and you shall have a big interest on it, as well as your dresses for next to nothing. How would you like that?'

'Can it be done?'

'I've got a notion it can, and I think I know two or three people who would help to set the thing going. But we must have some capital to show. Have you the pluck to join in?'

'And suppose I lose my money?'

'I'll guarantee you the same income you're getting now—if that will satisfy you. I've been looking round, and making inquiries, and I've got to know a bit about the profits of big dressmakers. We should start in Camberwell, or somewhere about there, and fish in all the women who want to do the heavy on very little. There are thousands and thousands of them, and most of them'—she lowered her voice—-'know as much about cut and material as they do about stockbroking. Do you twig? People like Mrs. Middlemist and Mrs. Murch. They spend, most likely, thirty or forty pounds a year on their things, and we could dress them a good deal more smartly for half the money. Of course we should make out that a dress we sold them for five guineas was worth ten in the shops, and the real cost would be two. See? The thing is to persuade them that they're getting an article cheap, and at the same time making money out of other people.'

Thus, and at much greater length, did Miss. French discourse to her attentive sister. Forgetful of the time, Fanny found at length that it would be impossible to meet Horace Lord as he came out of church; but it did not distress her.

CHAPTER 3

Nancy Lord stood at the front-room window, a hand grasping each side of her waist, her look vaguely directed upon the limetree opposite and the house which it in part concealed. She was a well-grown girl of three and twenty, with the complexion and the mould of form which indicate, whatever else, habitual nourishment on good and plenteous food. In her ripe lips and softlyrounded cheeks the current of life ran warm. She had hair of a fine auburn, and her mode of wearing it, in a plaited diadem, answered the purpose of completing a figure which, without being tall, had some stateliness and promised more. Her gown, trimmed with a collar of lace, left the neck free; the maiden cincture at her waist did no violence to natural proportion.

This afternoon—it was Monday—she could not occupy or amuse herself in any of the familiar ways. Perhaps the atmosphere of national Jubilee had a disturbing effect upon her,—in spite of her professed disregard for the gathering tumult of popular enthusiasm. She had not left home to-day, and the brilliant weather did not tempt her forth. On the table lay a new volume from the circulating library,—something about Evolution—but she had no mind to read it; it would have made her too conscious of the insincerity with which she approached such profound subjects. For a quarter of an hour and more she had stood at the window, regarding a prospect, now as always, utterly wearisome and depressing to her.

Grove Lane is a long acclivity, which starts from Camberwell suburban dwellings. The houses vary considerably in size and Green, and, after passing a few mean shops, becomes a road of aspect, also in date,—with the result of a certain picturesqueness, enhanced by the growth of fine trees on either side. Architectural grace can nowhere be discovered, but the contract-builder of today has not yet been permitted to work his will; age and irregularity, even though the edifices be but so many illustrations of the ungainly, the insipid, and the frankly hideous, have a pleasanter effect than that of new streets built to one pattern by the mile. There are small cottages overgrown with creepers, relics of Camberwell's rusticity; rows of tall and of squat dwellings that lie behind grassy plots, railed from the road; larger houses that stand in their own gardens, hidden by walls. Narrow passages connect the Lane with its more formal neighbour Camberwell Grove; on the other side are ways leading towards Denmark Hill, quiet, leafy. From the top of the Lane, where Champion Hill enjoys an aristocratic seclusion, is obtainable a glimpse of open fields and of a wooded horizon southward.

It is a neighbourhood in decay, a bit of London which does not keep pace with the times. And Nancy hated it. She would have preferred to live even in a poor and grimy street which neighboured the main track of business and pleasure.

Here she had spent as much of her life as she remembered, from the end of her third year. Mr. Lord never willingly talked of days gone by, but by questioning him she had learnt that her birthplace was a vaguely indicated part of northern London; there, it seemed, her mother had died, a year or so after the birth of her brother Horace. The relatives of whom she knew were all on her father's side, and lived scattered about England. When she sought information concerning her mother, Mr. Lord became evasive and presently silent; she had seen no portrait of the dead parent. Of late years this obscure point of the family history had often occupied her thoughts.

Nancy deemed herself a highly educated young woman,—'cultured' was the word she would have used. Her studies at a day-school which was reputed 'modern' terminated only when she herself chose to withdraw in her eighteenth year; and since then she had pursued 'courses' of independent reading, had attended lectures, had thought of preparing for examinations—only thought of it. Her father never suggested that she should use these acquirements for the earning of money; little as she knew of his affairs, it was obviously to be taken for granted that he could ensure her life-long independence. Satisfactory, this; but latterly it had become a question with her how the independence was to be used, and no intelligible aim as yet presented itself to her roving mind. All she knew was, that she wished to live, and not merely to vegetate. Now there are so many ways of living, and Nancy felt no distinct vocation for any one of them.

 She was haunted by an uneasy sense of doubtfulness as to her social position. Mr. Lord followed the calling of a dealer in pianos; a respectable business, to be sure, but, it appeared, not lucrative enough to put her above caring how his money was made. She knew that one's father may be anything whatever, yet suffer no social disability, provided he reap profit enough from the pursuit. But Stephen Lord, whilst resorting daily to his warehouse in Camberwell Road—not a locality that one would care to talk about in 'cultured' circles—continued, after twenty years, to occupy this small and ugly dwelling in Grove Lane. Possibly, owing to an imperfect education, he failed to appreciate his daughter's needs, and saw no reason why she should not be happy in the old surroundings.

On the other hand, perhaps he cared very little about her. Undoubtedly his favourite was Horace, and in Horace he had suffered a disappointment. The boy, in spite of good schooling, had proved unequal to his father's hope that he would choose some professional career, by preference the law; he idled away his schooldays, failed at examinations, and ultimately had to be sent into 'business.' Mr Lord obtained a place for him in a large shipping agency; but it still seemed doubtful whether he would make any progress there, notwithstanding the advantage of his start; at two-and-twenty he was remunerated with a mere thirty shillings a week, a nominal salary,' his employers called it. Nancy often felt angry with her brother for his lack of energy and ambition; he might so easily, she thought, have helped to establish, by his professional dignity, her own social status at the level she desired.

There came into view a familiar figure, crossing from the other side of the way. Nancy started, waved her hand, and went to open the door. Her look had wholly altered; she was bright, mirthful, overflowing with affectionate welcome.

This friend of hers, Jessica Morgan by name, had few personal attractions. She looked overwrought and low-spirited; a very plain and slightly-made summer gown exhibited her meagre frame with undue frankness; her face might have been pretty if

12

health had filled and coloured the flesh, but as it was she looked a ghost of girlhood, a dolorous image of frustrate sex. In her cotton-gloved hand she carried several volumes and notebooks.

'I'm so glad you're in,' was her first utterance, between pants after hasty walking and the jerks of a nervous little laugh. 'I want to ask you something about Geometrical Progression. You remember that formula—'

'How can I remember what I never knew?' exclaimed Nancy. 'I always hated those formulas; I couldn't learn them to save my life.'

'Oh, that's nonsense! You were much better at mathematics than I was. Do just look at what I mean.'

She threw her books down upon a chair, and opened some pages of scrawled manuscript, talking hurriedly in a thin falsetto.

Her family, a large one, had fallen of late years from a position of moderate comfort into sheer struggle for subsistence. Jessica, armed with certificates of examinational prowess, got work as a visiting governess. At the same time, she nourished ambitions, discernible perhaps in the singular light of her deep-set eyes and a something of hysteric determination about her lips. Her aim, at present, was to become graduate of London University; she was toiling in her leisure hours—the hours of exhaustion, that is to say—to prepare herself for matriculation, which she hoped to achieve in the coming winter. Of her intimate acquaintances only one could lay claim to intellectual superiority, and even she, Nancy Lord to wit, shrank from the ordeals of Burlington House. To become B.A., to have her name in the newspapers, to be regarded as one of the clever, the uncommon women—for this Jessica was willing to labour early and late, regardless of failing health, regardless even of ruined complexion and hair that grew thin beneath the comb.

She talked only of the 'exam,' of her chances in this or that 'paper,' of the likelihood that this or the other question would be 'set.' Her brain was becoming a mere receptacle for dates and definitions, vocabularies and rules syntactic, for thrice-boiled essence of history, ragged scraps of science, quotations at fifth hand, and all the heterogeneous rubbish of a 'crammer's' shop. When away from her books, she carried scraps of paper, with jottings to be committed to memory. Beside her plate at meals lay formulae and tabulations. She went to bed with a manual and got up with a compendium.

Nancy, whose pursuit of 'culture' followed a less exhausting track, regarded the girl with a little envy and some compassion. Esteeming herself in every respect Jessica's superior, she could not help a slight condescension in the tone she used to her; yet their friendship had much sincerity on both sides, and each was the other's only confidante. As soon as the mathematical difficulty could be set aside, Nancy began to speak of her private troubles.

'The Prophet was here last night,' she said, with a girlish grimace. 'He's beginning again. I can see it coming. I shall have to snub him awfully next time.'

'Oh, what a worry he is!'

'Yes, but there's something worse. I suspected that the Pasha knew of it; now I feel sure he's encouraging him.'

By this oriental style Nancy signified her father. The Prophet was her father's partner in business, Mr. Samuel Bennett Barmby.

'I feel sure now that they talked it over when the Prophet was taken into partnership. I was thrown in as a "consideration."'

'But how could your father possibly think—?'

'It's hard to say what he *does* think about me. I'm afraid I shall have to have a talk with him. If so, it will be a long talk, and a very serious talk. But he isn't well just now, and I must put it off.'

'He isn't well?'

'A touch of gout, he says. Two days last week he didn't go to business, and his temper was *that 'orrible!*' Nancy had a habit of facetiously quoting vulgarities; this from an acquaintance of theirs who often supplied them with mirth. 'I suppose the gout does make one bad-tempered.'

'Has he been coming often?—Mr. Barmby, I mean.'

'Pretty well. I think I must turn matchmaker, and get him married to some one. It oughtn't to be difficult. The Prophet "has points."'

'I dare say some people would think him handsome,' assented Miss Morgan, nibbling a finger which showed an ink-stain, and laughing shyly.

'And his powers of conversation!—Don't you know any one that would do for him?'

They jested on this theme until Nancy chose to become serious again.

'Have you any lessons to-morrow?'

'No. Thank goodness every one is going to see the procession, or the decorations, or the illuminations, and all the rest of the nonsense,' Jessica replied. 'I shall have a good long day of work; except that I've promised to go in the afternoon, and have tea with the little girls at Champion Hill. I wish you'd come too; they'd be delighted to see you, and there'll be nobody except the governess.'

Nancy looked up in doubt.

'Are you sure? Won't the dowager be at home?'

'She hasn't left her room for three weeks.'

They exchanged a look of some special significance.

'Then I suppose,' said Nancy, with a peculiar smile, 'that's why Mr Tarrant has been calling?'

'Has he? How do you know?'

Again they looked at each other, and Nancy laughed.

'I have happened to meet him twice, the last few days.' She spoke in an off-hand way. 'The first time, it was just at the top of the lane; he was coming away. The second time, I was walking along Champion Hill, and he came up behind me, going to the house.'

'Did he talk?'

Nancy gave a nod.

'Yes, both times. But he didn't tell me that the dowager was worse.'

'High and mighty?' asked Jessica.

'Not quite so majestic as usual, I thought. I didn't feel quite so much of a shrimp before him. And decidedly he was in better spirits. Perhaps the dowager's death would be important to him?'

'Very likely. Will you come to-morrow?'

Miss. Lord hesitated—then, with a sudden frankness:

'To tell you the truth, I'm afraid he might be there.'

'Oh, I don't think so, not on Jubilee Day.'

'But that's the very reason. He may come to be out of the uproar.'

15

'I meant he was more likely to be out of town altogether.'

Nancy, still leaning over the table, propped her chin on her hands, and reflected.

'Where does he go, I wonder?'

'Oh, all sorts of places, no doubt. Men of that kind are always travelling. I suppose he goes shooting and fishing—'

Nancy's laugh made an interruption.

'No, no, he doesn't! He told me once that he didn't care for that sort of thing.'

'Oh, well, you know much more about him than I do,' said Miss Morgan, with a smile.

'I've often meant to ask you—have they anything to do with Tarrant's black-lead?'

Jessica declared that she had never heard of it.

'Never heard of it? nonsense! A few years ago it used to be posted up everywhere, and I see it sometimes even now, but other kinds seem to have driven it out of the market. Now that's just like you! Pray, did you ever hear of Pears' Soap?'

'Of course.'

'Really? Oh, there's hope of you. You'll be a woman of the world some day.'

'Don't tease, Nancy. And what would it matter if he *was* there to-morrow?'

'Oh! I don't know. But I shouldn't particularly like his lordship to imagine that I went in the hope of paying my respects to him, and having the reward of a gracious smile.'

'One can't always be thinking about what other people think,' said Jessica impatiently. 'You're too sensitive. Any one else in your position would have lots of such friends.'

'In my position! What *is* my position?'

'Culture is everything now-a-days,' observed Miss. Morgan, with the air of one who feels herself abundantly possessed of that qualification.

But Nancy laughed.

16

'You may depend upon it, Mr. Tarrant doesn't think so.'

'He calls himself a democrat.'

'And talks like one: doesn't he?'

'Oh! that's only his way, I think. He doesn't really mean to be haughty, and—and so on.'

'I wish I knew if he had any connection with Tarrant's blacklead,' said Miss. Lord mischievously.

'Why not ask him?'

They laughed merrily, Jessica's thin note contrasting with the mellow timbre of her friend's voice.

'I will some day.'

'You would never dare to!'

'I daren't? Then I will!'

'It would be dreadfully rude.'

'I don't mind being thought rude,' replied Nancy, with a movement of the head, 'if it teaches people that I consider myself as good as they are.'

'Well, will you come to-morrow?'

'Ye-es; if you'll go somewhere else with me in the evening.'

'Where to?'

'To walk about the streets after dark, and see the crowds and the illuminations.'

Nancy uttered this with a sly mirthfulness. Her friend was astonished.

'Nonsense! you don't mean it.'

'I do. I want to go for the fun of the thing. I should feel ashamed of myself if I ran to stare at Royalties, but it's a different thing at night. It'll be wonderful, all the traffic stopped, and the streets crammed with people, and blazing with lights. Won't you go?'

'But the time, the time! I can't afford it. I'm getting on so wretchedly with my Greek and my chemistry.'

'You've time enough,' said Nancy. 'And, you know, after all it's a historical event. In the year 3000 it will be 'set' in an examination paper, and poor wretches will get plucked because they don't know the date.'

This was quite a new aspect of the matter to Jessica Morgan. She pondered it, and smiled.

'Yes, I suppose it will. But we should have to be out so late.'

'Why not, for once? It needn't be later than half-past eleven.' Nancy broke off and gesticulated. 'That's just why I want to go! I should like to walk about all night, as lots of people will. The public-houses are going to be kept open till two o'clock.'

'Do you want to go into public-houses?' asked Jessica, laughing.

'Why not? I should like to. It's horrible to be tied up as we are; we're not children. Why can't we go about as men do?'

'Won't your father make any objection?' asked Jessica.

'We shall take Horace with us. Your people wouldn't interfere, would they?'

'I think not. Father is away in Yorkshire, and will be till the end of the week. Poor mother has her rheumatism. The house is so dreadfully damp. We ought never to have taken it. The difference of rent will all go in doctors' bills.—I don't think mother would mind; but I must be back before twelve, of course.'

'I don't see the "of course,"' Nancy returned impatiently, 'but we could manage that. I'll speak to the Pasha to-night, and either come, or let you have a note, to-morrow morning. If there's any objection, I'm not sure that I shan't make it the opportunity for setting up my standard of revolt. But I don't like to do that whilst the Pasha is out of sorts—it might make him worse.'

'You could reason with him quietly.'

'Reason with the Pasha—How innocent you are, Jess! How unworldly! It always refreshes me to hear you talk.'

18

CHAPTER 4

Only twelve months ago Stephen Lord had renewed the lease of his house for a period of seven years. Nancy, had she been aware of this transaction, would assuredly have found courage to enter a protest, but Mr. Lord consulted neither son nor daughter on any point of business; but for this habit of acting silently, he would have seemed to his children a still more arbitrary ruler than they actually thought him.

The dwelling consisted of but eight rooms, one of which, situated at the rear of the entrance passage, served Mr. Lord as sitting-room and bed-chamber; it overlooked a small garden, and afforded a side glimpse of the kitchen with its outer appurtenances. In the front room the family took meals. Of the chambers in the storey above, one was Nancy's, one her brother's; the third had, until six years ago, been known as 'Grandmother's room,' and here its occupant, Stephen Lord's mother, died at the age of seventy-eight. Wife of a Norfolk farmer, and mother of nine children, she was one of the old-world women whose thoughts found abundant occupation in the cares and pleasures of home. Hardship she had never known, nor yet luxury; the old religion, the old views of sex and of society, endured with her to the end.

After her death the room was converted into a parlour, used almost exclusively by the young people. At the top of the house slept two servants, each in her own well-furnished retreat; one of them was a girl, the other a woman of about forty, named Mary Woodruff. Mary had been in the house for twenty years; she enjoyed her master's confidence, and, since old Mrs. Lord's death, exercised practical control in the humbler domestic affairs.

With one exception, all parts of the abode presented much the same appearance as when Stephen Lord first established himself antiquated, and in primitive taste. Nancy's bedroom alone here. The furniture was old, solid, homely; the ornaments were displayed the influence of modern ideas. On her twentieth birthday, the girl received permission to dress henceforth as she chose (a strict sumptuary law having previously been in force), and at the same time was allowed to refurnish her chamber. Nancy pleaded for modern reforms throughout the house, but in vain; even the drawing-room kept its uninviting aspect, not very different, save for the removal of the bed, from that it had presented when the ancient lady slept here. In her own little domain, Miss. Lord made a clean sweep of rude appointments, and at small expense surrounded herself with pretty things. The woodwork and the furniture were in white enamel; the paper had a pattern of wild-rose. A choice chintz, rose-leaf and flower on a white ground, served for curtains and for bed-hangings. Her carpet was of green felt, matching in shade the foliage of the chintz. On suspended shelves stood the books which she desired to have near her, and round about the walls hung prints, photographs, chromolithographs, selected in an honest spirit of admiration, which on the whole did no discredit to Nancy's sensibilities.

To the best of Nancy's belief, her father had never seen this room. On its completion she invited him to inspect it, but Mr. Lord coldly declined, saying that he knew nothing, and cared nothing, about upholstery.

His return to-day was earlier than usual. Shortly after five o'clock Nancy heard the familiar heavy step in the passage, and went downstairs.

'Will you have a cup of tea, father?' she asked, standing by the door of the back room, which was ajar.

'If it's ready,' replied a deep voice.

She entered the dining-room, and rang the bell. In a few minutes Mary Woodruff appeared, bringing tea and biscuits. She was a neat, quiet, plain-featured woman, of strong physique, and with set lips, which rarely parted save for necessary speech. Her eyes had a singular expression of inquietude, of sadness. A smile seldom appeared on her face, but, when it did, the effect was unlooked for: it touched the somewhat harsh lineaments with a gentleness so pleasing that she became almost comely.

Having set down the tray, she went to Mr. Lord's door, gave a soft tap, and withdrew into the kitchen.

Nancy, seated at the table, turned to greet her father. In early life, Stephen Lord must have been handsome; his face was now rugged, of unhealthy tone, and creased with lines betokening a moody habit. He looked much older than his years, which were fifty-seven. Dressed with excessive carelessness, he had the appearance rather of one at odds with fortune than of a substantial man of business. His short beard was raggedly trimmed; his grizzled hair began to show the scalp. Judging from the contour of his visage, one might have credited him with a forcible and commanding character; his voice favoured that impression; but the countenance had a despondent cast, the eyes seemed to shun observation, the lips suggested a sullen pride, indicative of some defect or vice of will.

Yet in the look which he cast upon her, Nancy detected a sign of more amiability than she had found in him of late. She addressed him with confidence.

'Early to-day, father.'

'Yes.'

The monosyllable sounded gruff, but again Nancy felt satisfaction. Mr. Lord, who disliked to seat himself unless he were going to keep his position for some time, took the offered beverage from his daughter's hand, and stood with it before the fireplace, casting glances about the room.

20

'How have you felt, father?'

'Nothing to complain of.'

His pronunciation fell short of refinement, but was not vulgar. Something of country accent could still be detected in it. He talked like a man who could strike a softer note if he cared to, but despises the effort.

'I suppose you will have a rest to-morrow?'

'I suppose so. If your grandmother had lived,' he added thoughtfully, 'she would have been eighty-four this week on Thursday.'

'The 23rd of June. Yes, I remember.'

Mr. Lord swallowed his tea at two draughts, and put down the cup. Seemingly refreshed, he looked about him with a half smile, and said quietly:

'I've had the pleasure of punishing a scoundrel to-day. That's worth more than the Jubilee.'

Nancy waited for an explanation, but it was not vouchsafed.

'A scoundrel?' she asked.

Her father nodded—the nod which signified his pleasure that the subject should not be pursued. Nancy could only infer that he spoke of some incident in the course of business, as indeed was the case.

He had no particular aptitude for trade, and that by which he lived (he had entered upon it thirty years ago rather by accident than choice) was thoroughly distasteful to him. As a dealer in pianofortes, he came into contact with a class of people who inspired him with a savage contempt, and of late years his business had suffered considerably from the competition of tradesmen who knew nothing of such conflicts between sentiment and interest. A majority of his customers obtained their pianos on the 'hire-purchase system,' and oftener than not, they were persons of very small or very precarious income, who, rabid in the pursuit of gentility, signed agreements they had little chance of fulfilling; when in pecuniary straits, they either raised money upon the instruments, or allowed them to fall into the hands of distraining creditors. Inquiry into the circumstances of a would-be customer sometimes had ludicrous results; a newly-married couple, for instance, would be found tenanting two top-floor rooms, the furnishing whereof seemed to them incomplete without the piano of which their friends and relatives boasted. Not a few professional swindlers came to the office; confederate rogues, vouching for each other's respectability, got possession of pianos merely to pawn or sell them, having paid no more than the first month's charge. It was Mr Lord's experience that year by year the recklessness of

21

the vulgar became more glaring, and deliberate fraud more artful. To-day he had successfully prosecuted a man who seemed to have lived for some time on the hirepurchase system, and it made him unusually cheerful.

'You don't think of going to see the Queen to-morrow?' said his daughter, smiling.

'What have I to do with the Queen? Do you wish to go?'

'Not to see Her Majesty. I care as little about her as you do. But I thought of having a walk in the evening.'

Nancy phrased it thus with intention. She wished to intimate that, at her age, it could hardly be necessary to ask permission. But her father looked surprised.

'In the evening? Where?'

'Oh, about the main streets—to see the people and the illuminations.'

Her voice was not quite firm.

'But,' said her father, 'there'll be such a swarm of blackguards as never was known. How can you go into such a crowd? It's astonishing that you should think of it.'

'The blackguards will be outnumbered by the decent people, father.'

'You suppose that's possible?' he returned gloomily.

'Oh, I think so,' Nancy laughed. 'At all events, there'll be a great majority of people who pretend to be decent. I have asked Jessica Morgan to go with me.'

'What right had you to ask her, without first finding out whether you could go or not?'

It was spoken rather gravely than severely. Mr. Lord never looked fixedly at his daughter, and even a glance at her face was unusual; but at this juncture he met her eyes for an instant. The nervous motion with which he immediately turned aside had been marked by Nancy on previous occasions, and she had understood it as a sign of his lack of affection for her.

'I am twenty-three years old, father,' she replied, without aggressiveness.

'That would be something of an answer if you were a man,' observed the father, his eyes cast down.

'Because I am a woman, you despise me?'

22

Stephen was startled at this unfamiliar mode of address. He moved uneasily.

'If I despised you, Nancy, I shouldn't care very much what you did. I suppose you must do as you like, but you won't go with my permission.'

There was a silence, then the girl said:

'I meant to ask Horace to go with us.'

'Horace—pooh!'

Again a silence. Mr. Lord laid down his cup, moved a few steps away, and turned back.

'I didn't think this kind of thing was in your way,' he said gruffly. 'I thought you were above it.'

Nancy defended herself as she had done to Jessica, but without the playfulness. In listening, her father seemed to weigh the merits of the case conscientiously with wrinkled brows. At length he spoke.

'Horace is no good. But if Samuel Barmby will go with you, I make no objection.'

A movement of annoyance was Nancy's first reply. She drummed with her fingers on the table, looking fixedly before her.

'I certainly can't ask Mr. Barmby to come with us,' she said, with an effort at self-control.

'Well, you needn't. I'll speak about it myself.'

He waited, and again it chanced that their eyes met. Nancy, on the point of speaking, checked herself. A full minute passed, and Stephen stood waiting patiently.

'If you insist upon it,' said Nancy, rising from her chair, 'we will take Mr. Barmby with us.'

Without comment, Mr. Lord left the room, and his own door closed rather loudly behind him.

Not long afterwards Nancy heard a new foot in the passage, and her brother made his appearance. Horace had good looks, but his face showed already some of the unpleasant characteristics which time had developed on that of Stephen Lord, and from which the daughter was entirely free; one judged him slow of intellect and weakly self-willed. His hair was of pale chestnut, the silky pencillings of his moustache considerably darker. His cheek, delicately pink and easily changing to a warmer hue, his bright-coloured lips, and the limpid glistening of his eyes, showed him of frail constitution; he was very slim, and narrow across the shoulders. The fashion of his attire tended to a dandiacal extreme,—modish silk hat, lavender necktie, white waistcoat, gaiters over his patent-leather shoes, gloves crushed together in one hand, and in the other a bamboo cane. For the last year or two he had been progressing in this direction, despite his father's scornful remarks and his sister's good-natured mockery.

'Father in yet?' he asked at the door of the dining-room, in subdued voice.

Nancy nodded, and the young man withdrew to lay aside his outdoor equipments.

'What sort of temper?' was his question when he returned.

'Pretty good—until I spoilt it.'

Horace exhibited a pettish annoyance.

'What on earth did you do that for? I want to have a talk with him to-night.'

'About what?'

'Oh, never mind; I'll tell you after.'

Both kept their voices low, as if afraid of being overheard in the next room. Horace began to nibble at a biscuit; the hour of his return made it unnecessary for him, as a rule, to take anything before dinner, but at present he seemed in a nervous condition, and acted mechanically.

'Come out into the garden, will you?' he said, after receiving a brief explanation of what had passed between Nancy and her father. 'I've something to tell you.'

His sister carelessly assented, and with heads uncovered they went through the house into the open air. The garden was but a strip of ground, bounded by walls of four feet high; in the midst stood a laburnum, now heavy with golden bloom, and at the end grew a holly-bush, flanked with laurels; a border flower-bed displayed Stephen Lord's taste and industry. Nancy seated herself on a rustic bench in the shadow of the laburnum, and Horace stood before her, one of the branches in his hand.

'I promised Fanny to take her to-morrow night,' he began awkwardly.

'Oh, you have?'

'And we're going together in the morning, you know.'

24

'I know now. I didn't before,' Nancy replied.

'Of course we can make a party in the evening.'

'Of course.'

Horace looked up at the ugly house-backs, and hesitated before proceeding.

'That isn't what I wanted to talk about,' he said at length. 'A very queer thing has happened, a thing I can't make out at all.'

The listener looked her curiosity.

'I promised to say nothing about it, but there's no harm in telling you, you know. You remember I was away last Saturday afternoon? Well, just when it was time to leave the office, that day, the porter came to say that a lady wished to see me—a lady in a carriage outside. Of course I couldn't make it out at all, but I went down as quickly as possible, and saw the carriage waiting there,—a brougham,—and marched up to the door. Inside there was a lady—a great swell, smiling at me as if we were friends. I took off my hat, and said that I was Mr. Lord. "Yes," she said, "I see you are;" and she asked if I could spare her an hour or two, as she wished to speak to me of something important. Well, of course I could only say that I had nothing particular to do,—that I was just going home. "Then will you do me the pleasure," she said, "to come and have lunch with me? I live in Weymouth Street, Portland Place."

The young man paused to watch the effect of his narrative, especially of the last words. Nancy returned his gaze with frank astonishment.

'What sort of lady was it?' she asked.

'Oh, a great swell. Somebody in the best society—you could see that at once.'

'But how old?'

'Well, I couldn't tell exactly; about forty, I should think.'

'Oh!—Go on.'

'One couldn't refuse, you know; I was only too glad to go to a house in the West End. She opened the carriage-door from the inside, and I got in, and off we drove. I felt awkward, of course, but after all I was decently dressed, and I suppose I can behave like a gentleman, and—well, she sat looking at me and smiling, and I could only smile back. Then she said she must apologise for behaving so strangely, but I was very young, and she was an old woman,—one couldn't call her that, though,—

and she had taken this way of renewing her acquaintance with me. Renewing? But I didn't remember to have ever met her before, I said. "Oh, yes, we have met before, but you were a little child, a baby in fact, and there's no wonder you don't remember me?" And then she said, "I knew your mother very well."

Nancy leaned forward, her lips apart.

'Queer, wasn't it? Then she went on to say that her name was Mrs. Damerel; had I ever heard it? No, I couldn't remember the name at all. She was a widow, she said, and had lived mostly abroad for a great many years; now she was come back to settle in England. She hadn't a house of her own yet, but lived at a boarding-house; she didn't know whether to take a house in London, or somewhere just out in the country. Then she began to ask about father, and about you; and it seemed to amuse her when I looked puzzled. She's a jolly sort of person, always laughing.'

'Did she say anything more about our mother?'

'I'll tell you about that presently. We got to the house, and went in, and she took me upstairs to her own private sitting-room, where the table was laid for two. She said that she usually had her meals with the other people, but it would be better for us to be alone, so that we could talk.'

'How did she know where to find you?' Nancy inquired.

'Of course I wondered about that, but I didn't like to ask. Well, she went away for a few minutes, and then we had lunch. Everything was A-1 of course; first-rate wines to choose from, and a rattling good cigar afterwards—for me, I mean. She brought out a box; said they were her husband's, and had a laugh about it.'

'How long has she been a widow?' asked Nancy.

'I don't know. She didn't wear colours, I noticed; perhaps it was a fashionable sort of mourning. We talked about all sorts of things; I soon made myself quite at home. And at last she began to explain. She was a friend of mother's, years and years ago, and father was the cause of their parting, a quarrel about something, she didn't say exactly what. And it had suddenly struck her that she would like to know how we were getting on. Then she asked me to promise that I would tell no one.'

'She knew about mother's death, I suppose?'

'Oh yes, she knew about that. It happened not very long after the affair that parted them. She asked a good many questions about you. And she wanted to know how father had got on in his business.'

'What did you say?'

'Oh, I told her I really didn't know much about it, and she laughed at that.'

'How long did you stay there?'

'Till about four. But there's something else. Before I went away she gave me an invitation for next Saturday. She wants me to meet her at Portland Road Station, and go out to Richmond, and have dinner there.'

'Shall you go?'

'Well, it's very awkward. I want to go somewhere else on Saturday, with Fanny. But I didn't see how to refuse.'

Nancy wore a look of grave reflection, and kept silence.

'It isn't a bad thing, you know,' pursued her brother, 'to have a friend of that sort. There's no knowing what use she might be, especially just now.'

His tone caused Nancy to look up.

'Why just now?'

'I'll tell you after I've had a talk with father to-night,' Horace replied, setting his countenance to a show of energetic resolve.

'Shall I guess what you're going to talk about?'

'If you like.'

She gazed at him.

'You're surely not so silly as to tell father about all that nonsense?'

'What nonsense?' exclaimed the other indignantly.

'Why, with Fanny French.'

'You'll find that it's anything but nonsense,' Horace replied, raising his brows, and gazing straight before him, with expanded nostrils.

'All right. Let me know the result. It's time to go in.'

Horace sat alone for a minute or two, his legs at full length, his feet crossed, and the upper part of his body bent forward. He smiled to himself, a smile of singular fatuity, and began to hum a popular tune.

CHAPTER 5

When they assembled at table, Mr. Lord had recovered his moderate cheerfulness. Essentially, he was anything but ill-tempered; Horace and Nancy were far from regarding him with that resentful bitterness which is produced in the victims of a really harsh parent. Ten years ago, as they well remembered, anger was a rare thing in his behaviour to them, and kindness the rule. Affectionate he had never shown himself; reserve and austerity had always distinguished him. Even now-a-days, it was generally safe to anticipate mildness from him at the evening meal. In the matter of eating and drinking his prudence notably contradicted his precepts. He loved strong meats, dishes highly flavoured, and partook of them without moderation. At table his beverage was ale; for wine—unless it were very sweet port—he cared little; but in the privacy of his own room, whilst smoking numberless pipes of rank tobacco, he indulged freely in spirits. The habit was unknown to his children, but for some years he had seldom gone to bed in a condition that merited the name of sobriety.

When the repast was nearly over, Mr. Lord glanced at his son and said unconcernedly:

'You have heard that Nancy wants to mix with the rag-tag and bobtail to-morrow night?'

'I shall take care of her,' Horace replied, starting from his reverie.

'Doesn't it seem to you rather a come-down for an educated young lady?'

'Oh, there'll be lots of them about.'

'Will there? Then I can't see much difference between them and the servant girls.'

Nancy put in a word.

'That shows you don't in the least understand me, father.'

'We won't argue about it. But bear in mind, Horace, that you bring your sister back not later than half-past eleven. You are to be here by half-past eleven.'

'That's rather early,' replied the young man, though in a submissive tone.

'It's the hour I appoint. Samuel Barmby will be with you, and he will know the arrangement; but I tell you now, so that there may be no misunderstanding.'

Nancy sat in a very upright position, displeasure plain upon her countenance. But she made no remark. Horace, who had his reasons for desiring to preserve a genial tone, affected acquiescence. Presently he and his sister went upstairs to the drawing-room, where they sat down at a distance apart—Nancy by the window, gazing at the warm clouds above the roofs opposite, the young man in a corner which the dusk already shadowed. Some time passed before either spoke, and it was Horace's voice which first made itself heard.

'Nancy, don't you think it's about time we began to behave firmly?'

'It depends what you mean by firmness,' she answered in an absent tone.

'We're old enough to judge for ourselves.'

'I am, no doubt. But I'm not so sure about you.'

'Oh, all right. Then we won't talk about it.'

Another quarter of an hour went by. The room was in twilight. There came a knock at the door, and Mary Woodruff, a wax-taper in her hand, entered to light the gas. Having drawn the blind, and given a glance round to see that everything was in order, she addressed Nancy, her tone perfectly respectful, though she used no formality.

'Martha has been asking me whether she can go out to-morrow night for an hour or two.'

'You don't wish to go yourself?' Miss. Lord returned, her voice significant of life-long familiarity.

'Oh no!'

And Mary showed one of her infrequent smiles.

'She may go immediately after dinner, and be away till half-past ten.'

The servant bent her head, and withdrew. As soon as she was gone, Horace laughed.

'There you are! What did father say?'

Nancy was silent.

'Well, I'm going to have a word with him,' continued the young man, sauntering towards the door with his hands in his pockets. He looked exceedingly nervous. 'When I come back, I may have something to tell you.'

30

'Very likely,' remarked his sister in a dry tone, and seated herself under the chandelier with a book.

Horace slowly descended the stairs. At the foot he stood for a moment, then moved towards his father's door. Another hesitancy, though briefer, and he knocked for admission, which was at once granted. Mr. Lord sat in his round-backed chair, smoking a pipe, on his knees an evening paper. He looked at Horace from under his eyebrows, but with good humour.

'Coming to report progress?'

'Yes, father,—and to talk over things in general.'

The slim youth—he could hardly be deemed more than a lad tried to assume an easy position, with his elbow on the corner of the mantelpiece; but his feet shuffled, and his eyes strayed vacantly. It cost him an effort to begin his customary account of how things were going with him at the shipping-office. In truth, there was nothing particular to report; there never was anything particular; but Horace always endeavoured to show that he had made headway, and to-night he spoke with a very pronounced optimism.

'Very well, my boy,' said his father. 'If you are satisfied, I shalltry to be the same. Have you your pipe with you?—At your age I hadn't begun to smoke, and I should advise you to be moderate; but we'll have a whiff together, if you like.'

'I'll go and fetch it,' Horace replied impulsively.

He came back with a rather expensive meerschaum, recently purchased.

'Hollo! luxuries!' exclaimed his father.

'It kept catching my eye in a window,—and at last I couldn't resist. Tobacco's quite a different thing out of a pipe like this, you know.'

No one, seeing them thus together, could have doubted of the affectionate feeling which Stephen Lord entertained for his son. It appeared in his frequent glances, in the relaxation of his features, in a certain abandonment of his whole frame, as though he had only just begun to enjoy the evening's repose.

'I've something rather important to speak about, father,' Horace began, when he had puffed for a few minutes in silence.

'Oh? What's that?'

'You remember telling me, when I was one and twenty, that you wished me to work my way up, and win an income of my own, but that I could look to you for help, if ever there was need of it—?'

Yes, Stephen remembered. He had frequently called it to mind, and wondered whether it was wisely said, the youth's character considered.

'What of that?' he returned, still genially. 'Do you think of starting a new line of ocean steamships?'

'Well, not just yet,' Horace answered, with an uncertain laugh. 'I have something more moderate in view. I may start a competition with the P. and O. presently.'

'Let's hear about it.'

'I dare say it will surprise you a little. The fact is, I—I am thinking of getting married.'

The father did not move, but smoke ceased to issue from his lips, and his eyes, fixed upon Horace, widened a little in puzzled amusement.

'Thinking of it, are you?' he said, in an undertone, as one speaks of some trifle. 'No harm in thinking. Too many people do it without thinking at all.'

'I'm not one of that kind,' said Horace, with an air of maturity which was meant to rebuke his father's jest. 'I know what I'm about. I've thought it over thoroughly. You don't think it too soon, I hope?'

Horace's pipe was going out; he held it against his knee and regarded it with unconscious eyes.

'I dare say it won't be,' said Mr. Lord, 'when you have found a suitable wife.'

'Oh, but you misunderstand me. I mean that I have decided to marry a particular person.'

'And who may that be?'

'The younger Miss. French—Fanny.'

His voice quivered over the name; at the end he gave a gasp and a gulp. Of a sudden his lips and tongue were very dry, and he felt a disagreeable chill running down his back. For the listener's face had altered noticeably; it was dark, stern, and something worse. But Mr. Lord could still speak with self-control.

32

'You have asked her to marry you?'

'Yes, I have; and she has consented.'

Horace felt his courage returning, like the so-called 'second wind' of a runner. It seemed to him that he had gone through the worst. The disclosure was made, and had resulted in no outbreak of fury; now he could begin to plead his cause. Imagination, excited by nervous stress, brought before him a clear picture of the beloved Fanny, with fluffy hair upon her forehead and a laugh on her never-closed lips. He spoke without effort.

'I thought that there would be no harm in asking you to help us. We should be quite content to start on a couple of hundred a year— quite. That is only about fifty pounds more than we have.'

Calf-love inspires many an audacity. To Horace there seemed nothing outrageous in this suggestion. He had talked it over with Fanny French several times, and they had agreed that his father could not in decency offer them *less* than a hundred a year. He began to shake out the ashes from his pipe, with a vague intention of relighting it.

'You really imagine,' said his father, 'that I should give you money to enable you to marry that idiot?'

Evidently he put a severe restraint upon himself. The veins of his temples were congested; his nostrils grew wide; and he spoke rather hoarsely. Horace straightened his back, and, though in great fear, strung himself for conflict.

'I don't see—what right—to insult the young lady.'

His father took him up sternly.

'Young lady? What do you mean by "young lady"? After all your education, haven't you learnt to distinguish a lady from a dressed-up kitchen wench? *I* had none of your advantages. There was —there would have been some excuse for *me*, if I had made such a fool of myself. What were you doing all those years at school, if it wasn't learning the difference between real and sham, getting to understand things better than poor folks' children? You disappointed me, and a good deal more than I ever told you. I had hoped you would come from school better able to make a place in the world than your father was. I made up my mind long ago that you should never go into my business; you were to be something a good deal better. But after all you couldn't, or wouldn't, do what I wanted. Never mind—I said to myself—- never mind; at all events, he has learnt to *think* in a better way than if I had sent him to common schools, and after all that's the main thing. But here you come to me and talk of marrying a low-bred, low-minded creature, who wouldn't be good enough for the meanest clerk!'

'How do you know that, father? What—what right have you to say such things, without knowing more of her than you do?'

There was a brief silence before Mr. Lord spoke again.

'You are very young,' he said, with less vehement contempt. 'I must remember that. At your age, a lad has a sort of devil in him, that's always driving him out of the path of common sense, whether he will or no. I'll try my best to talk quietly with you. Does your sister know what has been going on?'

'I daresay she does. I haven't told her in so many words.'

'I never thought of it,' pursued Mr. Lord gloomily. 'I took it for granted that everybody must see those people as I myself did. I have wondered now and then why Nancy kept up any kind of acquaintance with them, but she spoke of them in the rational way, and that seemed enough. I may have thought that they might get some sort of good out of *her*, and I felt sure she had too much sense to get harm from *them*. If it hadn't been so, I should have forbidden her to know them at all. What have you to say for yourself? I don't want to think worse of you than I need. I can make allowance for your age, as I said. What do you see in that girl? Just talk to me freely and plainly.'

'After all you have said,' replied Horace, his voice still shaky, 'what's the use? You seem to be convinced that there isn't a single good quality in her.'

'So I am. What I want to know is, what good *you* have found.'

'A great deal, else I shouldn't have asked her to marry me.'

A vein of stubbornness, unmistakable inheritance from Stephen Lord, had begun to appear in the youth's speech and bearing. He kept his head bent, and moved it a little from side to side.

'Do you think her an exception in the family, then?'

'She's a great deal better in every way than her sisters. But I don't think as badly of them as you do.'

Mr. Lord stepped to the door, and out into the passage, where he shouted in his deep voice 'Nancy!' The girl quickly appeared.

'Shut the door, please,' said her father. All three were now standing about the room. 'Your brother has brought me a piece of news. It ought to interest you, I should think. He wants to marry, and out of all the world, he has chosen Miss. French—the youngest.' Horace's position was trying. He did not know what to do with his hands, and he kept balancing now on one foot, now on the other. Nancy had her eyes averted from him, but she met her father's look gravely.

'Now, I want to ask you,' Mr. Lord proceeded, 'whether you consider Miss. French a suitable wife for your brother? Just give me a plain yes or no.'

'I certainly don't,' replied the girl, barely subduing the tremor of her voice.

'Both my children are not fools, thank Heaven! Now tell me, if you can, what fault you have to find with the "young lady," as your brother calls her?'

'For one thing, I don't think her Horace's equal. She can't really be called a lady.'

'You are listening?'

Horace bit his lip in mortification, and again his head swung doggedly from side to side.

'We might pass over that,' added Mr. Lord. 'What about her character? Is there any good point in her?'

'I don't think she means any harm. But she's silly, and I've often thought her selfish.'

'You are listening?'

Horace lost patience.

'Then why do you pretend to be friends with her?' he demanded almost fiercely.

'I don't,' replied his sister, with a note of disdain. 'We knew each other at school, and we haven't altogether broken off, that's all.'

'It isn't all!' shouted the young man on a high key. 'If you're not friendly with her and her sisters, you've been a great hypocrite. It's only just lately you have begun to think yourself too good for them. They used to come here, and you went to them; and you talked just like friends would do. It's abominable to turn round like this, for the sake of taking father's side against me!'

Mr. Lord regarded his son contemptuously. There was a rather long silence; he spoke at length with severe deliberation.

'When you are ten years older, you'll know a good deal more about young women as they're turned out in these times. You'll have heard the talk of men who have been fools enough to marry choice specimens. When common sense has a chance of getting in a word with you, you'll understand what I now tell you. Wherever you look now-a-days there's sham and rottenness; but the most worthless creature living is one of these trashy, flashy girls,—the kind of girl you see everywhere, high and low,—calling themselves "ladies,"—thinking themselves too good for any honest, womanly work. Town and country, it's all the same. They're educated; oh yes, they're educated! What sort of wives do they make, with their education? What sort of mothers are they? Before long, there'll be no such thing as a home. They don't know what the word means. They'd like to live in hotels, and trollop about the streets day and night. There won't be any servants much longer; you're lucky if you find one of the old sort, who knows how to light a fire or wash a dish. Go into the houses of men with small incomes; what do you find but filth and disorder, quarrelling and misery? Young men are bad enough, I know that; they want to begin where their fathers left off, and if they can't do it honestly, they'll embezzle or forge. But you'll often find there's a worthless wife at the bottom of it, —worrying and nagging because she has a smaller house than some other woman, because she can't get silks and furs, and wants to ride in a cab instead of an omnibus. It is astounding to me that they don't get their necks wrung. Only wait a bit; we shall come to that presently!'

It was a rare thing for Stephen Lord to talk at such length. He ceased with a bitter laugh, and sat down again in his chair. Horace and his sister waited.

'I've no more to say,' fell from their father at length. 'Go and talk about it together, if you like.'

Horace moved sullenly towards the door, and with a glance at his sister went out. Nancy, after lingering for a moment, spoke.

'I don't think you need have any fear of it, father.'

'Perhaps not. But if it isn't that one, it'll be another like her. There's not much choice for a lad like Horace.'

Nancy changed her purpose of leaving the room, and drew a step nearer.

'Don't you think there *might* have been?'

Mr. Lord turned to look at her.

'How? What do you mean?'

'I don't want to make you angry with me—'

'Say what you've got to say,' broke in her father impatiently.

36

'It isn't easy, when you so soon lose your temper.'

'My girl,'—for once he gazed at her directly,—'if you knew all I have gone through in life, you wouldn't wonder at my temper being spoilt.—What do you mean? What could I have done?'

She stood before him, and spoke with diffidence.

'Don't you think that if we had lived in a different way, Horace and I might have had friends of a better kind?'

'A different way?—I understand. You mean I ought to have had a big house, and made a show. Isn't that it?'

'You gave us a good education,' replied Nancy, still in the same tone, 'and we might have associated with very different people from those you have been speaking of; but education alone isn't enough. One must live as the better people do.'

'Exactly. That's your way of thinking. And how do you know that I could afford it, to begin with?'

'Perhaps I oughtn't to have taken that for granted.'

'Perhaps not. Young women take a good deal for granted now a-days. But supposing you were right, are you silly enough to think that richer people are better people, as a matter of course?'

'Not as a matter of course,' said Nancy. 'But I'm quite sure—I know from what I've seen—that there's more chance of meeting nice people among them.'

'What do you mean by "nice"?' Mr. Lord was lying back in his chair, and spoke thickly, as if wearied. 'People who can talk so that you forget they're only using words they've learnt like parrots?'

'No. Just the contrary. People who have something to say worth listening to.'

'If you take my advice, you'll pay less attention to what people say, and more to what they do. What's the good of a friend who won't come to see you because you live in a small house? That's the plain English of it. If I had done as I thought right, I should never have sent you to school at all. I should have had you taught at home all that's necessary to make a good girl and an honest woman, and have done my best to keep you away from the kind of life that I hate. But I hadn't the courage to act as I believed. I knew how the times were changing, and I was weak enough to be afraid I might do you an injustice. I did give you the chance of making friends among better people than your father. Didn't I use to talk to you about your school friends, and encourage you when they seemed of the right kind? And now you tell me that they don't care for your society because you live in a decent, unpretending way. I should think you're better without such friends.'

Nancy reflected, seemed about to prolong the argument, but spoke at length in another voice.

'Well, I will say good-night, father.'

It was not usual for them to see each other after dinner, so that a good-night could seldom be exchanged. The girl, drawing away, expected a response; she saw her father nod, but he said nothing.

'Good-night, father,' she repeated from a distance.

'Good-night, Nancy, good-night,' came in impatient reply.

CHAPTER 6

On Tuesday afternoon, when, beneath a cloudless sky, the great London highways reeked and roared in celebration of Jubilee, Nancy and her friend Miss. Morgan walked up Grove Lane to Champion Hill. Here and there a house had decked itself with colours of loyalty; otherwise the Lane was as quiet as usual.

Champion Hill is a gravel byway, overhung with trees; large houses and spacious gardens on either hand. Here the heat of the sun was tempered. A carriage rolled softly along; a nurse with well-dressed children loitered in the shade. One might have imagined it a country road, so profound the stillness and so leafy the prospect.

A year ago, Jessica Morgan had obtained a three months' engagement as governess to two little girls, who were sent under her care to the house of their grandmother at Teignmouth. Their father, Mr Vawdrey of Champion Hill, had recently lost his wife through an illness contracted at a horse-race, where the lady sat in wind and rain for some hours. The children knew little of what is learnt from books, but were surprisingly well informed on matters of which they ought to have known nothing; they talked of theatres and race-courses, of 'the new murderer' at Tussaud's, of police-news, of notorious spendthrifts and demi-reps; discussed their grown-up acquaintances with precocious understanding, and repeated scandalous insinuations which could have no meaning for them. Jessica was supposed to teach them for two hours daily; she found it an impossibility. Nevertheless a liking grew up between her and her charges, and, save by their refusal to study, the children gave her no trouble; they were abundantly good-natured, they laughed and sported all day long, and did their best to put life into the pale, overworked governess.

Whilst living thus at the seaside, Jessica was delighted by the arrival of Nancy Lord, who came to Teignmouth for a summer holiday. With her came Mary Woodruff. The faithful servant had been ill; Mr Lord sent her down into Devon to make a complete recovery, and to act as Nancy's humble chaperon. Nancy's stay was for three weeks. The friends saw a great deal of each other, and Miss. Lord had the honour of being presented to Mrs. Tarrant, the old lady with whom Jessica lived, Mr. Vawdrey's mother-in-law. At the age of three score and ten, Mrs. Tarrant still led an active life, and talked with great volubility, chiefly of herself; Nancy learnt from her that she had been married at seventeen, and had had two children, a son and a daughter, both deceased; of relatives there remained to her only Mr Vawdrey and his family, and a grandson, Lionel Tarrant.

One evening, as Jessica returned from a ramble with the children, they encountered a young man who was greeted, without much fervour, as 'cousin Lionel.' Mr. Tarrant professed himself merely a passing visitant; he had come to inquire after the health of his grandmother, and in a day or two must keep an appointment with friends elsewhere. Notwithstanding this announcement, he remained at Teignmouth for a fortnight, exhibiting a pious assiduity in his attendance upon the old lady. Naturally, he made acquaintance with Miss. Lord, whom his cousins regarded as a great acquisition, so vivacious was she, so ready to take part in any kind of lively amusement. Mr. Tarrant had been at Oxford; his speech was marked with the University accent; he talked little, and seemed to prefer his own society. In conversation with Nancy, though scrupulously courteous and perfectly good-natured, he never forgot that she was the friend of his cousins' governess, that their intercourse must be viewed as an irregular sort of thing, and that it behoved him to support his dignity whilst condescending to a social inferior. So, at all events, it struck Miss. Lord, very sensitive in such matters. Fond of fitting people with nicknames, she called this young man sometimes 'His Royal Highness,' sometimes 'His Majesty.'

Of Mr. Tarrant's station in life nothing was discovered. His grandmother, though seemingly in possession of ample means, betrayed an indifferent education, and in her flow of gossip never referred to ancestral dignities, never made mention of the calling her husband had pursued. Mr. Vawdrey was known to be 'in business,'—a business which must be tolerably lucrative.

On their return to London, the children passed from Miss. Morgan's care into that of Mrs. Baker, who kept house for the widower at Champion Hill; but Jessica did not wholly lose sight of them, and, at their request, she persuaded Nancy Lord to make an occasional call with her. Mrs. Baker (relict, it was understood, of a military officer who had fallen in Eastern warfare) behaved to the young ladies with much friendliness. They did not meet Mr. Vawdrey.

Early in the following year, old Mrs. Tarrant, forsaking Teignmouth, came to live under her son-in-law's roof; the winter had tried her health, and henceforth she seldom left home.

To-day, as on former occasions (only two or three in all), Nancy was reluctant to approach the big house; its imposing front made her feel that she came only on sufferance; probably even Mrs. Baker did not regard her as having a right to call here on terms of equality. Yet the place touched her curiosity and her imagination; she liked to study the luxurious appointments within, and to walk about the neglected but pleasant garden, quiet and secluded as if whole counties divided it from Camberwell. In the hall she and Jessica were at once welcomed by the children, who first informed them that tea would be served out of doors, and next made known that 'cousin Lionel' was here, in Mrs. Tarrant's drawing-room. The second piece of news vexed Nancy; she resolved never to come again, unless on formal invitation.

Mrs. Baker, an agreeable woman, received them as if she were the mistress of the house. With Jessica she chatted about matters examinational, which she seemed thoroughly to understand; with Miss Lord she talked of wider subjects, in a tone not unpleasing to Nancy, seeing that it presumed, on her part, some knowledge of the polite world. It was observable that Mr. Vawdrey's daughters had benefited by the superintendence of this lady; they no longer gossiped loudly about murders and scandals, but demeaned themselves more as became their years.

On the arrival of other ladies to call upon Mrs. Baker, the children drew their friends away into the garden, where tea now awaited them. Amid the trees and flowers time passed not unpleasantly, until, on happening to turn her head, Nancy perceived at a distance the approaching figure of Mr. Lionel Tarrant. He sauntered over the grass with easy, indolent step; his straw hat and light lounge costume (excellent tailoring) suited the season and the place. Jessica, who regarded the young man with something of awe, stood up to shake hands, but Miss. Lord kept her place in the garden chair.

'Did you see the procession?' Tarrant inquired. 'Ah, then I can give you very important news—thrilling news. I know the colour of the Queen's bonnet, and of her parasol.'

'Please don't keep us in suspense,' said Nancy.

'They were of pale primrose. Touching, don't you think?'

He had seated himself crosswise on a camp-stool, and seemed to be admiring the contour of his brown boots. Lionel's age was not more than seven-and-twenty; he enjoyed sound health, and his face signified contentment with the scheme of things as it concerned himself; but a chronic languor possessed him. It might be sheer laziness, possibly a result of that mental habit, discernible In his look, whereby he had come to regard his own judgment as the criterion of all matters in heaven and earth. Yet the conceit which relaxed his muscles was in the main amiable; it never repelled as does the conceit of a fop or a weakling or a vulgar person; he could laugh heartily, even with his own affectations for a source of amusement. Of personal vanity he had little, though women esteemed him good-looking; his steady, indolent gaze made denial of such preoccupation. Nor could he be regarded as emasculate; his movements merely disguised the natural vigour of a manly frame, and his conversational trifling hinted an intellectual reserve, a latent power of mind, obvious enough in the lines of his countenance.

Nancy was excusable for supposing that he viewed her slightingly. He spoke as one who did not expect to be quite understood by such a hearer, addressing her, without the familiarity, much as he addressed his young cousins. To her, his careful observance of formalities seemed the reverse of flattering; she felt sure that with young women in his own circle he would allow himself much more freedom. Whether the disparagement applied to her intellect or to her social status might be a question; Nancy could not decide which of the two she would prefer. Today an especial uneasiness troubled her from the first moment of his appearance; she felt a stronger prompting than hitherto to assert herself, and, if possible, to surprise Mr. Tarrant. But, as if he understood her thought, his manner became only more bland, his calm aloofness more pronounced.

The children, who were never at ease in their cousin's presence, succeeded in drawing Jessica apart, and chattered to her about the educational methods imposed by Mrs. Baker, airing many grievances. They nourished a hope that Miss. Morgan might again become their governess; lessons down at Teignmouth had been nothing like so oppressive as here at Champion Hill.

Tarrant, meanwhile, having drunk a cup of tea, and touched his moustache with a silk handkerchief, transferred himself from the camp-stool to the basket chair vacated by Jessica. He was now further from Nancy, but facing her.

'I have been talking with Mrs. Bellamy,' fell from him, in the same tone of idle good nature. 'Do you know her? She has but one subject of conversation; an engrossing topic, to be sure; namely, her servants. Do you give much thought to the great servant question? I have my own modest view of the matter. It may not be novel, but my mind has worked upon it in the night watches.'

Nancy, resolved not to smile, found herself smiling. Not so much at what he said, as at the manner of it. Her resentment was falling away; she felt the influence of this imperturbable geniality.

'Shall I tell you my theory?'

He talked with less reserve than on the last occasion when they had sat together. The mellow sunlight, the garden odours, the warm, still air, favoured a growth of intimacy.

'By all means,' was Nancy's reply.

'We must begin by admitting that the ordinary woman hates nothing so much as to have another woman set in authority over her.' He paused, and laughed lazily. 'Now, before the triumph of glorious Democracy, only those women kept servants who were capable of rule,—who had by birth the instinct of authority. They knew themselves the natural superiors of their domestics, and went through an education fitting them to rule. Things worked very well; no servant-difficulty existed. Now-a-days, every woman who can afford it must have another woman to wait upon her, no matter how silly, or vulgar, or depraved she may be; the result, of course, is a spirit of rebellion in the kitchen. Who could have expected anything else?'

Nancy played with a dandelion she had plucked, and gave sign neither of assent nor disagreement.

'Mrs. Bellamy,' continued the young man, 'marvels that servants revolt against her. What could be more natural? The servants have learnt that splendid doctrine that every one is as good as everybody else, and Mrs. Bellamy is by no means the person to make them see things differently. And this kind of thing is going on in numberless houses—an utterly incompetent mistress and a democratic maid in spirited revolt. The incompetents, being in so vast a majority, will sooner or later spoil all the servants in the country.'

'You should make an article of it,' said Nancy, 'and send it to *The Nineteenth Century*.'

'So I might.' He paused, and added casually, 'You read *The Nineteenth Century*?'

'Now and then.'

Nancy felt herself an impostor, for of leading reviews she knew little more than the names. And Tarrant's look, so steady, yet so good-tempered, disturbed her conscience with the fear that he saw through her. She was coming wretchedly out of this dialogue, in which she had meant to make a figure.

He changed the subject; was it merely to spare her?

'Shall you go to Teignmouth again this year?'

'I don't know yet. I think not.'

Silence followed. Tarrant, to judge from his face, was absorbed in pleasant thought; Nancy, on the other hand, felt so ill at ease that she was on the point of rising, when his voice checked her.

'I have an idea'—he spoke dreamily—'of going to spend next winter in the Bahamas.'

'Why the Bahamas?'

Speaking with all the carelessness she could command, Nancy shivered a little. Spite of her 'culture,' she had but the vaguest notion where the Bahamas were. To betray ignorance would be dreadful. A suspicion awoke in her that Tarrant, surprised by her seeming familiarity with current literature, was craftily testing the actual quality of her education. Upon the shiver followed a glow, and, in fear lest her cheeks would redden, she grew angry.

He was replying.

'Partly because it is a delightful winter climate; partly because I have a friend there; partly because the islands are interesting. A man I knew at Oxford has gone out there, and is likely to stay. His father owns nearly the whole of an island; and as he's in very bad health, my friend may soon come into possession. When he does, he's going to astonish the natives.'

'How?'

A vision of savages flashed before Nancy's mind. She breathed more freely, thinking the danger past.

'Simply by making a fortune out of an estate that is lying all but barren. Before the emancipation of the niggers, the Bahamas flourished wonderfully; now they are fallen to decay, and ruled, so far as I understand it, by a particularly contemptible crew of native whites, who ought all to be kicked into the sea. My friend's father is a man of no energy; he calls himself magistrate, coroner, superintendent of the customs, and a dozen other things, but seems to have spent his time for years in lying about, smoking and imbibing. His son, I'm afraid, waits impatiently for the old man's removal to a better world. He believes there are immense possibilities of trade.'

Trying hard to recollect her geography, Miss. Lord affected but a slight interest.

'There's no direct way of getting there,' Tarrant pursued. 'What route should you suggest?'

She was right, after all. He wished to convict her of ignorance. Her cheeks were now burning, beyond a doubt, and she felt revengeful.

'I advise you to make inquiries at a shipping-office,' was her distant reply.

'It seems'—he was smiling at Nancy—'I shall have to go to New York, and then take the Cuba mail.'

'Are you going to join your friend in business?'

'Business, I fear, is hardly my vocation.'

There was a tremor on Nancy's lips, and about her eyelids. She said abruptly:

'I thought you were perhaps in business?'

'Did you? What suggested it?'

Tarrant looked fixedly at her; in his expression, as in his voice, she detected a slight disdain, and that decided her to the utterance of the next words.

'Oh'—she had assumed an ingenuous air—'there's the Black Lead that bears your name. Haven't you something to do with it?'

She durst not watch him, but a change of his countenance was distinctly perceptible, and for the moment caused her a keen gratification. His eyes had widened, his lips had set themselves; he looked at once startled and mortified.

44

'Black lead?' The words fell slowly, in a voice unlike that she had been hearing. 'No. I have nothing to do with it.'

The silence was dreadful. Nancy endeavoured to rise, but her limbs would not do their office. Then, her eyes fixed on the grass, she became aware that Tarrant himself had stood up.

'Where are the children?' he was saying absently.

He descried them afar off with Miss. Morgan, and began to saunter in that direction. As soon as his back was turned, Nancy rose and began to walk towards the house. In a few moments Jessica and the girls were with her.

'I think we must go,' she said.

They entered, and took leave of Mrs. Baker, who sat alone in the drawing-room.

'Did you say good-bye to Mr. Tarrant?' Jessica asked, as they came forth again.

'Yes.'

'I didn't. But I suppose it doesn't matter.'

Nancy had thought of telling her friend what she had done, of boasting that she had asked the impossible question. But now she felt ashamed of herself, and something more than ashamed. Never again could she enter this garden. And it seemed to her that, by a piece of outrageous, of wanton, folly, she had for ever excluded herself from the society of all 'superior' people.

CHAPTER 7

'Now, *I* look at it in this way. It's to celebrate the fiftieth year of the reign of Queen Victoria—yes: but at the same time, and far more, it's to celebrate the completion of fifty years of Progress. National Progress, without precedent in the history of mankind! One may say, indeed, Progress of the Human Race. Only think what has been done in this half-century: only think of it! Compare England now, compare the world, with what it was in 1837. It takes away one's breath!'

Thus Mr. Samuel Bennett Barmby, as he stood swaying forward upon his toes, his boots creaking. Nancy and Jessica listened to him. They were ready to start on the evening's expedition, but Horace had not yet come home, and on the chance of his arrival they would wait a few minutes longer.

'I shall make this the subject of a paper for our Society next winter—the Age of Progress. And with special reference to one particular—the Press. Only think now, of the difference between our newspapers, all our periodicals of to-day, and those fifty years ago. Did you ever really consider, Miss. Morgan, what a marvellous thing one of our great newspapers really is? Printed in another way it would make a volume—absolutely; a positive volume; packed with thought and information. And all for the ridiculous price of one penny!'

He laughed; a high, chuckling, crowing laugh; the laugh of triumphant optimism. Of the man's sincerity there could be no question; it beamed from his shining forehead, his pointed nose; glistened in his prominent eyes. He had a tall, lank figure, irreproachably clad in a suit of grey: frock coat, and waistcoat revealing an expanse of white shirt. His cuffs were magnificent, and the hands worthy of them. A stand-up collar, of remarkable stiffness, kept his head at the proper level of self-respect.

'By the bye, Miss. Lord, are you aware that the Chinese Empire, with four *hundred* MILLION inhabitants, has only *ten* daily papers? Positively; only ten.'

'How do you know?' asked Nancy.

'I saw it stated in a paper. That helps one to *grasp* the difference between civilisation and barbarism. One doesn't think clearly enough of common things. Now that's one of the benefits one gets from Carlyle. Carlyle teaches one to see the marvellous in everyday life. Of course in many things I don't agree with him, but I shall never lose an opportunity of expressing my gratitude to Carlyle. Carlyle and Gurty! Yes, Carlyle and Gurty; those two authors are an education in themselves.'

He uttered a long 'Ah!' and moved his lips as if savouring a delicious morsel.

'Now here's an interesting thing. If all the cabs in London were put end to end,'—he paused between the words, gravely,—'what do you think, Miss. Morgan, would be the total length?'

'Oh, I have no idea, Mr. Barmby.'

'Forty miles—positively! Forty miles of cabs!'

'How do you know?' asked Nancy.

'I saw it stated in a paper.'

The girls glanced at each other, and smiled. Barmby beamed upon them with the benevolence of a man who knew his advantages, personal and social.

And at this moment Horace Lord came in. He had not the fresh appearance which usually distinguished him; his face was stained with perspiration, his collar had become limp, the flower at his buttonhole hung faded.

'Well, here I am. Are you going?'

'I suppose you know you have kept us waiting,' said his sister.

'Awf'ly sorry. Couldn't get here before.'

He spoke as if he had not altogether the command of his tongue, and with a fixed meaningless smile.

'We had better not delay,' said Barmby, taking up his hat. 'Seven o'clock. We ought to be at Charing Cross before eight; that will allow us about three hours.'

They set forth at once. By private agreement between the girls, Jessica Morgan attached herself to Mr. Barmby, allowing Nancy to follow with her brother, as they walked rapidly towards Camberwell Green. Horace kept humming popular airs; his hat had fallen a little to the side, and he swung his cane carelessly. His sister asked him what he had been doing all day.

'Oh, going about. I met some fellows after the procession. We had a splendid view, up there on the top of Waterloo House.'

'Did Fanny go home?'

'We met her sisters, and had some lunch at a restaurant. Look here; you don't want me to-night. You won't mind if I get lost in the crowd? Barmby will be quite enough to take care of you.'

'You are going to meet her again, I suppose?'

Horace nodded.

'We had better agree on a rendezvous at a certain time. I say, Barmby, just a moment; if any of us should get separated, we had better know where to meet, for coming home.'

'Oh, there's no fear of that.'

'All the same, it *might* happen. There'll be a tremendous crush, you know. Suppose we say the place where the trams stop, south of Westminster Bridge, and the time a quarter to eleven?'

This was agreed upon.

At Camberwell Green they mingled with a confused rush of hilarious crowds, amid a clattering of cabs and omnibuses, a jingling of tram-car bells. Public-houses sent forth their alcoholic odours upon the hot air. Samuel Barmby, joyous in his protectorship of two young ladies, for he regarded Horace as a mere boy, bustled about them whilst they stood waiting for the arrival of the Westminster car.

'It'll have to be a gallant rush! You would rather be outside, wouldn't you, Miss. Lord? Here it comes: charge!'

But the charge was ineffectual for their purpose. A throng of far more resolute and more sinewy people swept them aside, and seized every vacant place on the top of the vehicle. Only with much struggle did they obtain places within. In an ordinary mood, Nancy would have resented this hustling of her person by the profane public; as it was, she half enjoyed the tumult, and looked forward to get more of it along the packed streets, with a sense that she might as well amuse herself in vulgar ways, since nothing better was attainable. This did not, however, modify her contempt of Samuel Barmby; it seemed never to have occurred to him that the rough-and-tumble might be avoided, and time gained, by the simple expedient of taking a cab.

Sitting opposite to Samuel, she avoided his persistent glances by reading the rows of advertisements above his head. Somebody's 'Blue;' somebody's 'Soap;' somebody's 'High-class Jams;' and behold, inserted between the Soap and the Jam—'God so loved the world, that He gave His only-begotten Son, that whoso believeth in Him should not perish, but have everlasting life.' Nancy perused the passage without perception of incongruity, without emotion of any kind. Her religion had long since fallen to pieces, and universal defilement of Scriptural phrase by the associations of the market-place had in this respect blunted her sensibilities.

Barmby was talking to Jessica Morgan. She caught his words now and then.

'Can you tell me what is the smallest tree in the world?—No, it's the Greenland birch. Its full-grown height is only three inches— positively! But it spreads over several feet.'

48

Nancy was tempted to lean forward and say, 'How do you know?' But the jest seemed to involve her in too much familiarity with Mr Barmby; for her own peace it was better to treat him with all possible coldness.

A woman near her talked loudly about the procession, with special reference to a personage whom she called 'Prince of Wiles.' This enthusiast declared with pride that she had stood at a certain street corner for seven hours, accompanied by a child of five years old, the same who now sat on her lap, nodding in utter weariness; together they were going to see the illuminations, and walk about, with intervals devoted to refreshments, for several hours more. Beyond sat a working-man, overtaken with liquor, who railed vehemently at the Jubilee, and in no measured terms gave his opinion of our Sovereign Lady; the whole thing was a 'lay,' an occasion for filling the Royal pocket, and it had succeeded to the tune of something like half a million of money, wheedled, most of it, from the imbecile poor. 'Shut up!' roared a loyalist, whose patience could endure no longer. 'We're not going to let a boozing blackguard like you talk in that way about 'er Majesty!' Thereupon, retort of insult, challenge to combat, clamour from many throats, deep and shrill. Nancy laughed, and would rather have enjoyed it if the men had fought.

At Westminster Bridge all jumped confusedly into the street and ran for the pavement. It was still broad daylight; the sun—a potentate who keeps no Jubilee—dropping westward amid the hues of summer eventide, was unmarked, for all his splendour, by the roaring multitudes.

'Where are you going to leave us?' Nancy inquired of her brother.

'Charing Cross, or somewhere about there.'

'Keep by me till then.'

Barmby was endeavouring to secure her companionship. He began to cross the bridge at her side, but Nancy turned and bade him attend upon Miss. Morgan, saying that she wished to talk with her brother. In this order they moved towards Parliament Street, where the crowd began to thicken.

'Now let us decide upon our route,' exclaimed Barmby, with the air of a popular leader planning a great demonstration. 'Miss. Lord, we will be directed by your wishes. Where would you like to be when the lighting-up begins?'

'I don't care. What does it matter? Let us go straight on and see whatever comes in our way.'

'That's the right spirit! Let us give ourselves up to the occasion! We can't be wrong in making for Trafalgar Square. Advance!'

They followed upon a group of reeling lads and girls, who yelled in chorus the popular song of the day, a sentimental one as it happened—

'Do not forget me, Do not forget me, Think sometimes of me still'—

Nancy was working herself into a nervous, excited state. She felt it impossible to walk on and on under Barmby's protection, listening to his atrocious commonplaces, his enthusiasms of the Young Men's Debating Society. The glow of midsummer had entered into her blood; she resolved to taste independence, to mingle with the limitless crowd as one of its units, borne in whatever direction. That song of the streets pleased her, made sympathetic appeal to her; she would have liked to join in it.

Just behind her—it was on the broad pavement at Whitehall—some one spoke her name.

'Miss. Lord! Why, who would have expected to see you here? Shouldn't have dared to think of such a thing; upon my word, I shouldn't!'

A man of about thirty, dressed without much care, middle-sized, wiry, ruddy of cheek, and his coarse but strong features vivid with festive energy, held a hand to her. Luckworth Crewe was his name. Nancy had come to know him at the house of Mrs. Peachey, where from time to time she had met various people unrecognised in her own home. His tongue bewrayed him for a native of some northern county; his manner had no polish, but a genuine heartiness which would have atoned for many defects. Horace, who also knew him, offered a friendly greeting; but Samuel Barmby, when the voice caught his ear, regarded this intruder with cold surprise.

'May I walk on with you?' Crewe asked, when he saw that Miss. Lord felt no distaste for his company.

Nancy deigned not even a glance at her nominal protector.

'If you are going our way,' she replied.

Barmby, his dignity unobserved, strode on with Miss. Morgan, of whom he sought information concerning the loud-voiced man. Crewe talked away.

'So you've come out to have a look at it, after all. I saw the Miss Frenches last Sunday, and they told me you cared no more for the Jubilee than for a dog-fight. Of course I wasn't surprised; you've other things to think about. But it's worth seeing, that's my opinion. Were you out this morning?'

'No. I don't care for Royalties.'

'No more do I. Expensive humbugs, that's what I call 'em. But I had a look at them, for all that. The Crown Prince was worth seeing; yes, he really was. I'm not so prejudiced as to deny that. He's the kind of chap I should like to get hold of, and have a bit of a talk with, and ask him what he thought about things in general. It's been a big affair, hasn't it? I know a chap who made a Jubilee Perfume, and he's netting something like a hundred pounds a day.'

'Have you any Jubilee speculation on hand?'

'Don't ask me! It makes me mad. I had a really big thing,—a Jubilee Drink,—a teetotal beverage; the kind of thing that would have sold itself, this weather. A friend of mine hit on it, a clerk in a City warehouse, one of the cleverest chaps I ever knew. It really was *the* drink; I've never tasted anything like it. Why, there's the biggest fortune on record waiting for the man who can supply *the* drink for total-abstainers. And this friend of mine had it. He gave me some to taste one night, about a month ago, and I roared with delight. It was all arranged. I undertook to find enough capital to start with, and to manage the concern. I would have given up my work with Bullock and Freeman. I'd have gone in, tooth and nail, for that drink! I sat up all one night trying to find a name for it; but couldn't hit on the right one. A name is just as important as the stuff itself that you want to sell. Next morning— it was Sunday—I went round to my friend's lodgings, and'—he slapped his thigh—- 'I'm blest if the chap hadn't cut his throat!'

'Why?'

'Betting and forgery. He would have been arrested next day. But the worst of it was that his beverage perished with him. I hadn't a notion how it was made; he wouldn't tell me till I planked down money to start with; and not a drop of it could be found anywhere. And to think that he had absolutely struck oil, as they say; had nothing to do but sit down and count the money as it came in! That's the third man I've known go wrong in less than a year. Betting and embezzlement; betting and burglary; betting and forgery. I'll tell you some time about the chap who went in for burglary. One of the best fellows I ever knew; when he comes out, I must give him a hand. But ten to one he'll burgle again; they always do; burglary grows on a man, like drink.'

His laughter rang across the street; Barmby, who kept looking back, surprised and indignant that this acquaintance of Miss. Lord's was not presented to him, paused for a moment, but Nancy waved to him commandingly, 'Straight on!'

They reached Charing Cross. Horace, who took no part in the conversation, and had dropped behind, at this point found an opportunity of stealing away. It was Crewe who first remarked his absence.

'Hollo! where's your brother?'

'Gone, evidently.—Hush! Don't say anything. Will you do something for me, Mr. Crewe?'

'Of course I will. What is it?'

Nancy pursued in a low voice.

'He's gone to meet Fanny French. At least, he told me so; but I want to know whether it is really Fanny, or some one else. He said they were to meet in front of the Haymarket Theatre. Will you go as quickly as you can, and see if Fanny is there?'

Crewe laughed.

'Like a bird!—But how am I to meet you again?'

'We'll be at the top of Regent Street at nine o'clock,—by Peter Robinson's. Don't lose time.'

He struck off in the westerly direction, and Barmby, looking round at that moment, saw him go. Engrossed in thought of Nancy, Samuel did not yet perceive that her brother had vanished.

'Your friend isn't coming any further?' he said, in a tone of forbearance.

'No.'

'But where's Mr. Lord?' exclaimed Jessica.

Nancy pretended to look back for him, and for a minute or two they waited. Barmby, glad to be delivered from both male companions, made light of the matter; Horace could take care of himself; they had the appointment for a quarter to eleven;—on! And he now fixed himself resolutely at Nancy's side.

She, delighted with the success of her stratagem, and careless of what might result from it, behaved more companionably. To Luckworth Crewe's society she had no objection; indeed, she rather liked him; but his presence would have hindered the escape for which she was preparing. Poor Jessica might feel it something of a hardship to pass hours alone with 'the Prophet,' but that could not be helped. Nancy would be free to-night, if never again. They turned into the Strand, and Barmby voiced his opinion of the public decorations.

'There's very little of what can be called Art,—very little indeed. I'm afraid we haven't made much progress in Art.—Now what would Ruskin say to this kind of thing? The popular taste wants educating. My idea is that we ought to get a few leading men Burne Jones and—and William Morris—and people of that kind, you know, Miss. Lord,—to give lectures in a big hall on the elements of Art. A great deal might be done in that way, don't you think so, Miss. Morgan?'

'I have no faith in anything popular,' Jessica replied loftily.

'No, no. But, after all, the people have got the upper hand now-a-days, and we who enjoy advantages of education, of culture, ought not to allow them to remain in darkness. It isn't for our own interest, most decidedly it isn't.'

'Did your sisters go to see the procession?' Nancy asked.

'Oh, they were afraid of the crowd. The old gentleman took them out to Tooting Common this afternoon, and they enjoyed themselves. Perhaps I should have been wiser if I had imitated their example; I mean this morning; of course I wouldn't have missed this evening for anything whatever. But somehow, one feels it a sort of duty to see something of these great public holidays. I caught a glimpse of the procession. In its way it was imposing—yes, really. After all, the Monarchy is a great *fact*—as Gurty would have said. I like to keep my mind open to facts.'

The sun had set, and with approach of dusk the crowds grew denser. Nancy proposed a return westwards; the clubs of Pall Mall and of St James's Street would make a display worth seeing, and they must not miss Piccadilly.

'A little later,' said their escort, with an air of liberality, 'we must think of some light refreshment. We shall be passing a respectable restaurant, no doubt.'

Twilight began to obscure the distance. Here and there a house-front slowly marked itself with points of flame, shaping to wreath, festoon, or initials of Royalty. Nancy looked eagerly about her, impatient for the dark, wishing the throng would sweep her away. In Pall Mall, Barmby felt it incumbent upon him to name the several clubs, a task for which he was inadequately prepared. As he stood staring in doubt at one of the coldly insolent façades, Jessica gazing in the same direction, Nancy saw that her moment had come. She darted off, struggled through a moving crowd, and reached the opposite pavement. All she had now to do was to press onward with the people around her; save by chance, she could not possibly be discovered.

Alarm at her daring troubled her for a few minutes. As a matter of course Barmby would report this incident to her father,—unless she plainly asked him not to do so, for which she had no mind. Yet what did it matter? She had escaped to enjoy herself, and the sense of freedom soon overcame anxieties. No one observed her solitary state; she was one of millions walking about the streets because it was Jubilee Day, and every moment packed her more tightly among the tramping populace. A procession, this, greatly more significant than that of Royal personages earlier in the day. Along the main thoroughfares of mid-London, wheel-traffic was now suspended; between the houses moved a double current of humanity, this way and that, filling the whole space, so that no vehicle could possibly have made its way on the wonted track. At junctions, pickets of police directed progress; the slowly advancing masses wheeled to left or right at word of command, carelessly obedient. But for an occasional bellow of hilarious blackguardism, or for a song uplifted by strident voices, or a cheer at some flaring symbol that pleased the passers, there was little noise; only a thud, thud of footfalls numberless, and the low, unvarying sound that suggested some huge beast purring to itself in stupid contentment.

Nancy forgot her identity, lost sight of herself as an individual. Her blood was heated by close air and physical contact. She did not think, and her emotions differed little from those of any shop-girl let loose. The 'culture,' to which she laid claim, evanesced in this atmosphere of exhalations. Could she have seen her face, its look of vulgar abandonment would have horrified her.

Some one trod violently on her heel, and she turned with a half-angry laugh, protesting. 'Beg your pardon, miss,' said a young fellow of the clerkly order. 'A push be'ind made me do it.' He thrust himself to a place beside her, and Nancy conversed with him unrestrainedly, as though it were a matter of course. The young man, scrutinising her with much freedom, shaped clerkly compliments, and, in his fashion, grew lyrical; until, at a certain remark which he permitted himself, Nancy felt it time to shake him off. Her next encounter was more noteworthy. Of a sudden she felt an arm round her waist, and a man, whose breath declared the source of his inspiration, began singing close to her ear the operatic ditty, 'Queen of my Heart.' He had, moreover, a good tenor voice, and belonged, vaguely, to some stratum of educated society.

'I think you had better leave me alone,' said Nancy, looking him severely in the face.

'Well, if you really think so,'—he seemed struck by her manner of speech,—'of course I will: but I'd much rather not.'

'I might find it necessary to speak to a policeman at the next corner.'

'Oh, in that case.'—He raised his hat, and fell aside. And Nancy felt that, after all, the adventure had been amusing.

She was now in Regent Street, and it came to her recollection that she had made an appointment with Luckworth Crewe for nine o'clock. Without any intention of keeping it; but why not do so? Her lively acquaintance would be excellent company for the next hour, until she chose to bring the escapade to an end. And indeed, save by a disagreeable struggle, she could hardly change the direction of her steps. It was probably past nine; Crewe might have got tired of waiting, or have found it impossible to keep a position on the pavement. Drawing near to the top of Regent Street, she hoped he might be there. And there he was, jovially perspiring; he saw her between crowded heads, and crushed through to her side.

54

CHAPTER 8

'Where are your friends?'

'That's more than I can tell you.'

They laughed together.

'It's a miracle we've been able to meet,' said Crewe. 'I had to thrash a fellow five minutes ago, and was precious near getting run in. Shall we go the Tottenham Court Road way? Look out! You'd better hold on to my arm. These big crossings are like whirlpools; you might go round and round, and never get anywhere. Don't be afraid; if any one runs up against you, I'll knock him down.'

'There wouldn't be room for him to fall,' said Nancy, wild with merriment, as they swayed amid the uproar. For the first time she understood how perilous such a crowd might be. A band of roisterers, linked arm in arm, were trying to break up the orderly march of thousands into a chaotic fight. The point for which Crewe made was unattainable; just in front of him a woman began shrieking hysterically; another fainted, and dropped into her neighbour's arms.

'Don't get frightened!'

'Not I! I like it. It's good fun.'

'You're the right sort, you are. But we must get out of this. It's worse than the pit-door on the first night of a pantomime. I must hold you up; don't mind.'

His arm encircled her body, and for a moment now and then he carried rather than led her. They were safe at length, in the right part of Oxford Street, and moving with the stream.

'I couldn't find your brother,' Crewe had leisure to say; 'and I didn't see Fanny French. There weren't many people about just then, either. They must have gone off before I came.'

'Yes, they must. It doesn't matter.'

'You have some life in you.' He gazed at her admiringly. 'You're worth half a million of the girls that squeak and wobble when there's a bit of rough play going on.'

'I hope so. Did you set me down as one of that kind?'

Nancy found that her tongue had achieved a liberty suitable to the occasion. She spoke without forethought, and found pleasure in her boldness.

'Not I,' Crewe answered. 'But I never had a chance before now of telling you what I thought.'

Some one in front of them ignited a Bengal light and threw it into the air; the flame flashed across Nancy's features, and fell upon the hat of a man near her.

'How do you mean to get home?' asked Crewe presently. Nancy explained that all her party were to meet on the other side of the river.

'Oh, then, there's plenty of time. When you've had enough of this kind of thing we can strike off into the quiet streets. If you were a man, which I'm glad you're not, I should say I was choking for a glass of beer.'

'Say it, and look for a place where you can quench your thirst.'

'It must be a place, then, where you can come in as well. You don't drink beer, of course, but we can get lemonade and that kind of thing. No wonder we get thirsty; look up there.'

Following the direction of his eyes, Nancy saw above the heads of the multitude a waving dust-canopy, sent up by myriad tramplings on the sun-scorched streets. Glare of gas illumined it in the foreground; beyond, it dimmed all radiance like a thin fog.

'We might cut across through Soho,' he pursued, 'and get among the restaurants. Take my arm again. Only a bit of cross-fighting, and we shall be in the crowd going the other way. Did you do physics at school? Remember about the resultant of forces? Now *we*'re a force tending to the right, and the crowd is a force making for straight on; to find the—'

His hat was knocked over his eyes, and the statement of the problem ended in laughter.

With a good deal of difficulty they reached one of the southward byways; and thenceforth walking was unimpeded.

'You know that I call myself Luckworth Crewe,' resumed Nancy's companion after a short silence.

'Of course I do.'

'Well, the fact is, I've no right to either of the names. I thought I'd just tell you, for the fun of the thing; I shouldn't talk about it to any one else that I know. They tell me I was picked up on a doorstep in Leeds, and the wife of a mill-hand adopted me. Their name was Crewe. They called me Tom, but somehow it isn't a name I care for, and when I was grown up I met a man called Luckworth, who was as kind as a father to me, and so I took his name in place of Tom. That's the long and short of it.'

Nancy looked a trifle disconcerted.

'You won't think any worse of me, because I haven't a name of my own?'

'Why should I? It isn't your fault.'

'No. But I'm not the kind of man to knuckle under. I think myself just as good as anybody else I'll knock the man down that sneers at me; and I won't thank anybody for pitying me; that's the sort of chap I am. And I'm going to have a big fortune one of these days. It's down in the books. I know I shall live to be a rich man, just as well as I know that I'm walking down Dean Street with Miss. Lord.'

'I should think it very possible,' his companion remarked.

'It hasn't begun yet. I can only lay my hand on a few hundred pounds, one way and another. And I'm turned thirty. But the next ten years are going to do it. Do you know what I did last Saturday? I got fifteen hundred pounds' worth of advertising for our people, from a chap that's never yet put a penny into the hands of an agent. I went down and talked to him like a father. He was the hardest nut I ever had to crack, but in thirty-five minutes I'd got him—like a roach on a hook. And it'll be to his advantage, mind you. That fifteen hundred 'll bring him in more business than he's had for ten years past. I got him to confess he was going down the hill. "Of course," I said, "because you don't know how to advertise, and won't let anybody else know for you?" In a few minutes he was telling me he'd dropped more than a thousand on a patent that was out of date before it got fairly going. "All right," said I. "Here's your new cooking-stove. You've dropped a thousand on the other thing; give your advertising to us, and I'll guarantee you shall come home on the cooking-stove."'

'Come home on it?' Nancy inquired, in astonishment.

'Oh, it's our way of talking,' said the other, with his hearty laugh. 'It means to make up one's loss. And he'll do it. And when he has, he'll think no end of me.'

'I daresay.'

'Not long ago, I boxed a chap for his advertising. A fair turn-up with the gloves. Do you suppose I licked him? Not I; though I could have done it with one hand. I just let him knock me out of time, and two minutes after he put all his business into my hands.'

'Oh, you'll get rich,' declared Nancy, laughing. 'No doubt about it.'

'There was a spot down the South Western Railway where we wanted to stick up a board, a great big board, as ugly as they make 'em. It was in a man's garden; a certain particular place, where the trains slow, and folks have time to read the advertisement and meditate on it. That chap wouldn't listen. What! spoil his garden with our da——with our confounded board! not for five hundred a year! Well, I went down, and I talked to him—'

'Like a father,' put in Nancy.

'Just so, like a father. "Look here," said I, "my dear sir, you're impeding the progress of civilisation. How could we have become what we are without the modern science and art of advertising? Till advertising sprang up, the world was barbarous. Do you suppose people kept themselves clean before they were reminded at every corner of the benefits of soap? Do you suppose they were healthy before every wall and hoarding told them what medicine to take for their ailments? Not they indeed! Why, a man like you—an enlightened man, I see it in your face (he was as ugly as Ben's bull-dog), ought to be proud of helping on the age." And I made him downright ashamed of himself. He asked me to have a bit of dinner, and we came to terms over the cheese.'

In this strain did Luckworth Crewe continue to talk across the gloomy solitudes of Soho. And Nancy would on no account have had him cease. She was fascinated by his rough vigour and by his visions of golden prosperity. It seemed to her that they reached very quickly the restaurant he had in view. With keen enjoyment of the novelty, she followed him between tables where people were eating, drinking, smoking, and took a place beside him on a cushioned seat at the end of the room.

'I know you're tired,' he said. 'There's nearly half-an-hour before you need move.'

Nancy hesitated in her choice of a refreshment. She wished to have something unusual, something that fitted an occasion so remarkable, yet, as Crewe would of course pay, she did not like to propose anything expensive.

'Now let me choose for you,' her companion requested. 'After all that rough work, you want something more than a drop of lemonade. I'm going to order a nice little bottle of champagne out of the ice, and a pretty little sandwich made of whatever you like.'

'Champagne—?'

It had been in her thoughts, a sparkling audacity. Good; champagne let it be. And she leaned back in defiant satisfaction.

'I didn't expect much from Jubilee Day,' observed the man of business, 'but that only shows how things turn out—always better or worse than you think for. I'm not likely to forget it; it's the best day I've had in my life yet, and I leave you to guess who I owe *that* to.'

'I think this is good wine,' remarked Nancy, as if she had not heard him.

'Not bad. You wouldn't suppose a fellow of my sort would know anything about it. But I do. I've drunk plenty of good champagne, and I shall drink better.'

Nancy ate her sandwich and smiled. The one glass sufficed her; Crewe drank three. Presently, looking at her with his head propped on his hand, he said gravely:

'I wonder whether this is the last walk we shall have together?'

'Who can say?' she answered in a light tone.

'Some one ought to be able to say.'

'I never make prophecies, and never believe other people's.'

'Shows your good sense. But *I* make wishes, and plenty of them.'

'So do I,' said Nancy.

'Then let us both make a wish to ourselves,' proposed Crewe, regarding her with eyes that had an uncommon light in them.

His companion laughed, then both were quiet for a moment.

They allowed themselves plenty of time to battle their way as far as Westminster Bridge. At one point police and crowd were in brief conflict; the burly guardians of order dealt thwacking blows, right and left, sound fisticuffs, backed with hearty oaths. The night was young; by magisterial providence, hours of steady drinking lay before the hardier jubilants. Thwacks and curses would be no rarity in another hour or two.

At the foot of Parliament Street, Nancy came face to face with Samuel Barmby, on whose arm hung the wearied Jessica. Without heeding their exclamations, she turned to her protector and bade him a hearty good-night. Crewe accepted his dismissal. He made survey of Barmby, and moved off singing to himself, '*Do not forget me—do not forget me—*'

Part II: Nature's Graduate

CHAPTER 1

The disorder which Stephen Lord masked as a 'touch of gout' had in truth a much more disagreeable name. It was now twelve months since his doctor's first warning, directed against the savoury meats and ardent beverages which constituted his diet; Stephen resolved upon a change of habits, but the flesh held him in bondage, and medical prophecy was justified by the event. All through Jubilee Day he suffered acutely; for the rest of the week he remained at home, sometimes sitting in the garden, but generally keeping his room, where he lay on a couch.

A man of method and routine, sedentary, with a strong dislike of unfamiliar surroundings, he could not be persuaded to try change of air. The disease intensified his native stubbornness, made him by turns fretful and furious, disposed him to a sullen solitude. He would accept no tendance but that of Mary Woodruff; to her, as to his children, he kept up the pretence of gout. He was visited only by Samuel Barmby, with whom he discussed details of business, and by Mr. Barmby, senior, his friend of thirty years, the one man to whom he unbosomed himself.

His effort to follow the regimen medically prescribed to him was even now futile. At the end of a week's time, imagining himself somewhat better, he resumed his daily walk to Camberwell Road, but remained at the warehouse only till two or three o'clock, then returned and sat alone in his room. On one of the first days of July, when the weather was oppressively hot, he entered the house about noon, and in a few minutes rang his bell. Mary Woodruff came to him. He was sitting on the couch, pale, wet with perspiration, and exhausted.

'I want something to drink,' he said wearily, without raising his eyes.

'Will you have the lime-water, sir?'

'Yes—what you like.'

Mary brought it to him, and he drank two large glasses, with no pause.

'Where is Nancy?'

'In town, sir. She said she would be back about four.'

He made an angry movement.

'What's she doing in town? She said nothing to me. Why doesn't she come back to lunch? Where does she go to for all these hours?'

'I don't know, sir.'

The servant spoke in a low, respectful voice, looking at her master with eyes that seemed to compassionate him.

'Well, it doesn't matter.' He waved a hand, as if in dismissal. 'Wait—if I'm to be alone, I might as well have lunch now. I feel hungry, as if I hadn't eaten anything for twenty-four hours. Get me something, Mary.'

Later in the afternoon his bell again sounded, and Mary answered it. As he did not speak at once,—he was standing by the window with his hands behind him,—she asked him his pleasure.

'Bring me some water, Mary, plain drinking-water.'

She returned with a jug and glass, and he took a long draught.

'No, don't go yet. I want to—to talk to you about things. Sit down there for a minute.'

He pointed to the couch, and Mary, with an anxious look, obeyed him.

'I'm thinking of leaving this house, and going to live in the country. There's no reason why I shouldn't. My partner can look after the business well enough.'

'It might be the best thing you could do, sir. The best for your health.'

'Yes, it might. I'm not satisfied with things. I want to make a decided change, in every way.'

His face had grown more haggard during the last few days, and his eyes wandered, expressing fretfulness or fear; he spoke with effort, and seemed unable to find the words that would convey his meaning.

'Now I want you to tell me plainly, what do you think of Nancy?'

'Think of her, sir?'

'No, no—don't speak in that way. I don't want you to call me 'sir'; it isn't necessary; we've known each other so long, and I think of you as a friend, a very good friend. Think of me in the same way, and speak naturally. I want to know your opinion of Nancy.'

The listener had a face of grave attention: it signified no surprise, no vulgar self-consciousness, but perhaps a just perceptible pleasure. And in replying she looked steadily at her master for a moment.

'I really don't feel I can judge her, Mr. Lord. It's true, in a way, I ought to know her very well, as I've seen her day by day since she was a little thing. But now she's a well-educated and clever young lady, and she has got far beyond me—'

'Ay, there it is, there it is!' Stephen interrupted with bitterness. 'She's got beyond us—beyond me as well as you. And she isn't what I meant her to be, very far from it. I haven't brought them up as I wished. I don't know—I'm sure I don't know why. It was in own hands. When they were little children, I said to myself: hey shall grow up plain, good, honest girl and boy. I said that I wouldn't educate them very much; I saw little good that came of it, in our rank of life. I meant them to be simple-minded. I hoped Nancy would marry a plain countryman, like the men I used to know when I was a boy; a farmer, or something of that kind. But see how it's come about. It wasn't that I altered my mind about what was best. But I seemed to have no choice. For one thing, I made more money at business than I had expected, and so—and so it seemed that they ought to be educated above me and mine. There was my mother, did a better woman ever live? She had no education but that of home. She could have brought up Nancy in the good, old-fashioned way, if I had let her. I wish I had, yes, I wish I had.'

'I don't think you could have felt satisfied,' said the listener, with intelligent sympathy.

'Why not? If she had been as good and useful a woman as *you* are—'

'Ah, you mustn't think in that way, Mr. Lord. I was born and bred to service. Your daughter had a mind given her at her birth, that would never have been content with humble things. She was meant for education and a higher place.'

'What higher place is there for her? She thinks herself too good for the life she leads here, and yet I don't believe she'll ever find a place among people of a higher class. She has told me herself it's my fault. She says I ought to have had a big house for her, so that she might make friends among the rich. Perhaps she's right. I have made her neither one thing nor another. Mary, if I had never come to London, I might have lived happily. My place was away there, in the old home. I've known that for many a year. I've thought: wait till I've made a little more money, and I'll go back. But it was never done; and now it looks to me as if I had spoilt the lives of my children, as well as my own. I can't trust Nancy, that's the worst of it. You don't know what she did on Jubilee night. She wasn't with Mr. Barmby and the others—Barmby told me about it; she pretended to lose them, and went off somewhere to meet a man she's never spoken to me about. Is that how a good girl would act? I didn't speak to her about it; what use? Very likely she wouldn't tell me the truth. She takes it for granted I can't understand her. She thinks her education puts her above all plain folk and their ways— that's it.'

Mary's eyes had fallen, and she kept silence.

'Suppose anything happened to me, and they were left to themselves. I have money to leave between them, and of course they know it. How could it do them anything but harm? Do you know that Horace wants to marry that girl Fanny French—a grinning, chattering fool—if not worse. He has told me he shall do as he likes. Whether or no it was right to educate Nancy, I am very sure that I ought to have done with *him* as I meant at first. He hasn't the brains to take a good position. When his schooling went on year after year, I thought at last to make of him something better than his father—a doctor, or a lawyer. But he hadn't the brains: he disappointed me bitterly. And what use can he make of my money, when I'm in my grave? If I die soon he'll marry, and ruin his life. And won't it be the same with Nancy? Some plotting, greedy fellow—the kind of man you see everywhere now-a-days, will fool her for the money's sake.'

'We must hope they'll be much older and wiser before they have to act for themselves,' said Mary, looking into her master's troubled face.

'Yes!' He came nearer to her, with a sudden hopefulness. 'And whether I live much longer or not, I can do something to guard them against their folly. They needn't have the money as soon as I am gone.'

He seated himself in front of his companion.

'I want to ask you something, Mary. If they were left alone, would you be willing to live here still, as you do now, for a few more years?'

'I shall do whatever you wish—whatever you bid me, Mr. Lord,' answered the woman, in a voice of heartfelt loyalty.

'You would stay on, and keep house for them?'

'But would they go on living here?'

'I could make them do so. I could put it down as a condition, in my will. At all events, I would make Nancy stay. Horace might live where he liked—though not with money to throw about. They have no relatives that could be of any use to them. I should wish Nancy to go on living here, and you with her; and she would only have just a sufficient income, paid by my old friend Barmby, or by his son. And that till she was—what? I have thought of six-and-twenty. By that time she would either have learnt wisdom, or she never would. She must be free sooner or later.'

'But she couldn't live by herself, Mr. Lord.'

'You tell me you would stay,' he exclaimed impulsively.

'Oh, but I am only her servant. That wouldn't be enough.'

64

'It would be. Your position shall be changed. There's no one living to whom I could trust her as I could to you. There's no woman I respect so much. For twenty years you have proved yourself worthy of respect—and it shall be paid to you.'

His vehemence would brook no opposition.

'You said you would do as I wished. I wish you to have a new position in this house. You shall no longer be called a servant; you shall be our housekeeper, and our friend. I will have it, I tell you!' he cried angrily. 'You shall sit at table with us, and live with us. Nancy still has sense enough to acknowledge that this is only your just reward; from her, I know, there won't be a word of objection. What can you have to say against it?'

The woman was pale with emotion. Her reserve and sensibility shrank from what seemed to her an invidious honour, yet she durst not irritate the sick man by opposition.

'It will make Nancy think,' he pursued, with emphasis. 'It will help her, perhaps, to see the difference between worthless women who put themselves forward, and the women of real value who make no pretences. Perhaps it isn't too late to set good examples before her. I've never found her ill-natured, though she's wilful; it isn't her heart that's wrong—I hope and think not—only her mind, that's got stuffed with foolish ideas. Since her grandmother's death she's had no guidance. You shall talk to her as a woman can; not all at once, but when she's used to thinking of you in this new way.'

'You are forgetting her friends,' Mary said at length, with eyes of earnest appeal.

'Her friends? She's better without such friends. There's one thing I used to hope, but I've given it up. I thought once that she might have come to a liking for Samuel Barmby, but now I don't think she ever will, and I believe it's her friends that are to blame for it. One thing I know, that she'll never meet with any one who will make her so good a husband as he would. We don't think alike in every way; he's a young man, and has the new ideas; but I've known him since he was a boy, and I respect his character. He has a conscience, which is no common thing now-a-days. He lives a clean, homely life—and you won't find many of his age who do. Nancy thinks herself a thousand times too good for him; I only hope he mayn't prove a great deal too good for *her*. But I've given up that thought. I've never spoken to her about it, and I never shall; no good comes of forcing a girl's inclination. I only tell you of it, Mary, because I want you to understand what has been going on.'

They heard a bell ring; that of the front door.

'It'll be Miss. Nancy,' said Mary, rising.

'Go to the door then. If it's Nancy, tell her I want to speak to her, and come back yourself.'

'Mr. Lord—'

'Do as I tell you—at once!'

All the latent force of Stephen's character now declared itself. He stood upright, his face stern and dignified. In a few moments, Nancy entered the room, and Mary followed her at a distance.

'Nancy,' said the father, 'I want to tell you of a change in the house. You know that Mary has been with us for twenty years. You know that for a long time we haven't thought of her as a servant, but as a friend, and one of the best possible. It's time now to show our gratitude. Mary will continue to help us as before, but henceforth she is one of our family. She will eat with us and sit with us; and I look to you, my girl, to make the change an easy and pleasant one for her.'

As soon as she understood the drift of her father's speech, Nancy experienced a shock, and could not conceal it. But when silence came, she had commanded herself. An instant's pause; then, with her brightest smile, she turned to Mary and spoke in a voice of kindness.

'Father is quite right. Your place is with us. I am glad, very glad.'

Mary looked from Mr. Lord to his daughter, tried vainly to speak, and left the room.

CHAPTER 2

His father's contemptuous wrath had an ill effect upon Horace. Of an amiable disposition, and without independence of character, he might have been guided by a judicious parent through all the perils of his calf-love for Fanny French; thrown upon his own feeble resources, he regarded himself as a victim of the traditional struggle between prosaic age and nobly passionate youth, and resolved at all hazards to follow the heroic course—which meant, first of all, a cold taciturnity towards his father, and, as to his future conduct, a total disregard of the domestic restraints which he had hitherto accepted. In a day or two he sat down and wrote his father a long letter, of small merit as a composition, and otherwise illustrating the profitless nature of the education for which Stephen Lord had hopefully paid. It began with a declaration of rights. He was a man; he could no longer submit to childish trammels. A man must not be put to inconvenience by the necessity of coming home at early hours. A man could not brook cross-examination on the subject of his intimacies, his expenditure, and so forth. Above all, a man was answerable to no one but himself for his relations with the other sex, for the sacred hopes he cherished, for his emotions and aspirations which transcended even a man's vocabulary.—With much more of like tenor.

To this epistle, delivered by post, Mr. Lord made no answer.

Horace flattered himself that he had gained a victory. There was nothing like 'firmness,' and that evening, about nine, he went to De Crespigny Park. As usual, he had to ring the bell two or three times before any one came; the lively notes of a piano sounded from the drawing-room, intimating, no doubt, that Mrs. Peachey had guests. The door at length opened, and he bade the servant let Miss. Fanny know that he was here; he would wait in the dining-room.

It was not yet dark, but objects could only just be distinguished; the gloom supplied Horace with a suggestion at which he laughed to himself. He had laid down his hat and cane, when a voice surprised him.

'Who's that?' asked some one from the back of the room.

'Oh, are *you* there, Mr. Peachey?—I've come to see Fanny. I didn't care to go among the people.'

'All right. We'd better light the gas.'

With annoyance, Horace saw the master of the house come forward, and strike a match. Remains of dinner were still on the table. The two exchanged glances.

'How is your father?' Peachey inquired. He had a dull, depressed look, and moved languidly to draw down the blind.

67

'Oh, he isn't quite up to the mark. But it's nothing serious, I think.'

'Miss. Lord quite well?—We haven't seen much of her lately.'

'I don't know why, I'm sure.—Nobody can depend upon her very much.'

'Well, I'll leave you,' said the other, with a dreary look about the room. 'The table ought to have been cleared by now—but that's nothing new.'

'Confounded servants,' muttered Horace.

'Oh yes, the servants,' was Peachey's ironical reply.

As soon as he was left alone, Horace turned out the gas. Then he stood near the door, trembling with amorous anticipation. But minutes went by; his impatience grew intolerable; he stamped, and twisted his fingers together. Then of a sudden the door opened.

'Why, it's dark, there's nobody here.'

Fanny discovered her mistake. She was seized and lifted off her feet.

'Oh! Do you want to eat me? I'll hit you as hard as I can, I will! You're spoiling my dress?'

The last remonstrance was in a note that Horace did not venture to disregard.

'Strike a light, silly! I know you've done something to my dress.'

Horace pleaded abjectly to be forgiven, and that the room might remain shadowed; but Fanny was disturbed in temper.

'If you don't light the gas, I'll go at once.'

'I haven't any matches, darling.'

'Oh, just like you! You never have anything. I thought every man carried matches.'

She broke from him, and ran out. Wretched in the fear that she might not return, Horace waited on the threshold. In the drawing-room some one was singing 'The Maid of the Mill.' It came to an end, and there sounded voices, which the tormented listener strove to recognise. For at least ten minutes he waited, and was all but frantic, when the girl made her appearance, coming downstairs.

'Never do that again,' she said viciously. 'I've had to unfasten my things, and put them straight. What a nuisance you are!'

He stood cowed before her, limp and tremulous.

'There, light the gas. Why couldn't you come into the drawing-room, like other people do?'

'Who is there?' asked the young man, when he had obeyed her.

'Go and see for yourself.'

'Don't be angry, Fanny.' He followed her, like a dog, as she walked round the table to look at herself in the mirror over the fireplace. 'It was only because I'm so fond of you.'

'Oh, what a silly you are!' she laughed, seating herself on the arm of an easy-chair. 'Go ahead! What's the latest?'

'Well, for one thing, I've had a very clear understanding with the gov'nor about my independence. I showed him that I meant having my own way, and he might bully as much as he liked.'

It was not thus that Horace would naturally have spoken, not thus that he thought of his father. Fanny had subdued him to her own level, poisoned him with the desires excited by her presence. And he knew his baseness; he was not ignorant of the girl's ignoble nature. Only the fury of a virgin passion enabled him to talk, and sometimes think, as though he were in love with ideal purity.

'I didn't think you had the pluck,' said Fanny, swinging one of her feet as she tittered.

'That shows you haven't done me justice.'

'And you're going to stay out late at night?'

'As late as I like,' Horace answered, crossing his arms.

'Then where will you take me to-morrow?'

It happened that Horace was in funds just now; he had received his quarter's salary. Board and lodging were no expense to him; he provided his own clothing, but, with this exception, had to meet no serious claim. So, in reply to Fanny's characteristic question, he jingled coins.

'Wherever you like.—"Dorothy," "Ruddigore—"'

Delighted with his assent, she became more gracious, permitted a modest caress, and presently allowed herself to be drawn on to her lover's knee. She was passive, unconcerned; no second year graduate of the pavement could have preserved a completer equanimity; it did not appear that her pulse quickened ever so slightly, nor had her eyelid the suspicion of a droop. She hummed 'Queen of my Heart,' and grew absent in speculative thought, whilst Horace burned and panted at the proximity of her white flesh.

'Oh, how I do love you, Fanny!'

She trod playfully on his toe.

'You haven't told the old gentleman yet?'

'I—I'm thinking about it. But, Fanny, suppose he was to—to refuse to do anything for us. Would it make any difference? There are lots of people who marry on a hundred and fifty a year—oh lots!'

The maiden arched her brows, and puckered her lips. Hitherto it had been taken for granted that Mr. Lord would be ready with subsidy; Horace, in a large, vague way, had hinted that assurance long ago. Fanny's disinclination to plight her troth—she still deemed herself absolutely free—had alone interfered between the young man and a definite project of marriage.

'What kind of people?' she asked coldly.

'Oh—respectable, educated people, like ourselves.'

'And live in apartments? Thank you; I don't quite see myself. There isn't a bit of hurry, dear boy. Wait a bit.' She began to sing 'Wait till the clouds roll by.'

'If you thought as much of me as I do of you—'

Tired of her position, Fanny jumped up and took a spoonful of sweet jelly from a dish on the table.

'Have some?'

'Come here again. I've something more to tell you. Something very important.'

She could only be prevailed upon to take a seat near him. Horace, beset with doubts as to his prudence, but unable to keep the secret, began to recount the story of his meeting with Mrs. Damerel, whom he had now seen for the second time. Fanny's

70

curiosity, instantly awakened, grew eager as he proceeded. She questioned with skill and pertinacity, and elicited many more details than Nancy Lord had been able to gather.

'You'll promise me not to say a word to any one?' pleaded Horace.

'I won't open my lips. But you're quite sure she's as old as you say?'

'Old enough to be my mother, I assure you.'

The girl's suspicions were not wholly set at rest, but she made no further display of them.

'Now just think what an advantage it might be to you, to know her,' Horace pursued. 'She'd introduce you at once to fashionable society, really tip-top people. How would you like that?'

'Not bad,' was the judicial reply.

'She must have no end of money, and who knows what she might do for me!'

'It's a jolly queer thing,' mused the maiden.

'There's no denying that. We must keep it close, whatever we do.'

'You haven't told anybody else?'

'Not a soul!' Horace lied stoutly.

They were surprised by the sudden opening of the door; a servant appeared to clear the table. Fanny reprimanded her for neglecting to knock.

'We may as well go into the drawing-room. There's nobody particular. Only Mrs. Middlemist, and Mr. Crewe, and—'

In the hall they encountered Crewe himself, who stood there conversing with Beatrice. A few words were exchanged by the two men, and Horace followed his enchantress into the drawing-room, where he found, seated in conversation with Mrs. Peachey, two persons whom he had occasionally met here. One of them, Mrs. Middlemist, was a stout, coarse, high-coloured woman, with fingers much bejewelled. Until a year or two ago she had adorned the private bar of a public-house kept by her husband; retired from this honourable post, she now devoted herself to society and the domestic virtues. The other guest, Mrs. Murch by name, proclaimed herself, at a glance, of less prosperous condition, though no less sumptuously arrayed. Her face had a hungry, spiteful, leering expression; she spoke in a shrill, peevish tone, and wriggled nervously on her chair. In eleven years of married life, Mrs. Murch had borne six children, all of whom died before they were six months old. She lived apart from her husband, who had something to do with the manufacture of an Infants' Food.

Fanny was requested to sing. She sat down at the piano, rattled a prelude, and gave forth an echo of the music-halls:

'It's all up with poor Tommy now.
I shall never more be happy, I vow.
It's just a week to-day
Since my Sairey went away,
And it's all up with poor Tommy now.'

Mrs. Middlemist, who prided herself upon serious vocal powers, remarked that comic singing should be confined to men.

'You haven't a bad voice, my dear, if you would only take pains with it. Now sing us "For Ever and for Ever."'

This song being the speaker's peculiar glory, she was of course requested to sing it herself, and, after entreaty, consented. Her eyes turned upward, her fat figure rolling from side to side, her mouth very wide open, Mrs. Middlemist did full justice to the erotic passion of this great lyric:

'Perchawnce if we 'ad never met,
We 'ad been spared this mad regret,
This hendless striving to forget—
For hever—hand—for he-e-e-ver!'

Mrs. Murch let her head droop sentimentally. Horace glanced at Fanny, who, however, seemed absorbed in reflections as unsentimental as could be.

In the meanwhile, on a garden seat under the calm but misty sky, sat Luckworth Crewe and Beatrice French. Crewe smoked a cigar placidly; Beatrice was laying before him the suggestion of her great commercial scheme, already confided to Fanny.

'How does it strike you?' she asked at length.

'Not bad, old chap. There's something in it, if you're clever enough to carry it through. And I shouldn't wonder if you are.' 'Will you help to set it going?'

'Can't help with money,' Crewe replied.

'Very well; will you help in other ways? Practical hints, and so on?'

'Of course I will. Always ready to encourage merit in the money-making line. What capital are you prepared to put into it?'

'Not much. The public must supply the capital.'

'A sound principle,' Crewe laughed. 'But I shouldn't go on the old lines. You didn't think of starting a limited company? You'd find difficulties. Now what you want to start is a—let us call it the South London Dress Supply Association, or something of that kind. But you won't get to that all at once. You ought to have premises to begin with.'

'I'm aware of it.'

'Can you raise a thousand or so?'

'Yes, I could—if I chose.'

'Now, look here. Your notion of the Fashion Club is a deuced good one, and I don't see why it shouldn't be pretty easily started. Out of every five hundred women, you can reckon on four hundred and ninety-nine being fools; and there isn't a female fool who wouldn't read and think about a circular which promised her fashionable dresses for an unfashionable price. That's a great and sound basis to start on. What I advise is, that you should first of all advertise for a dress-making concern that would admit a partner with a small capital. You'll have between ten and twelve hundred replies, but don't be staggered; go through them carefully, and select a shop that's well situated, and doing a respectable trade. Get hold of these people, and induce them to make changes in their business to suit your idea. Then blaze away with circulars, headed "South London Fashion Club;" send them round the whole district, addressed to women. Every idiot of them will, at all events, come and look at the shop; that can be depended upon; in itself no bad advertisement. Arrange to have a special department—special entrance, if possible—with "The Club" painted up. Yes, by jingo! Have a big room, with comfortable chairs, and the women's weekly papers lying about, and smart dresses displayed on what-d'ye-call-'ems, like they have in windows. Make the subscription very low at first, and give rattling good value; never mind if you lose by it. Then, when you've got hold of a lot of likely people, try them with the share project. By-the-bye, if you lose no time, you can bring in the Jubilee somehow. Yes, start with the "Jubilee Fashion Club." I wonder nobody's done it already.'

Beatrice was growing elated.

'The public has to wait for its benefactors,' she replied.

'I'll tell you what, would you like me to sketch you out a prospectus of the Club?'

73

'Yes, you might do that if you like. You won't expect to be paid?'

'Hang it! what do you take me for?'

'Business is business,' Miss. French remarked coldly.

'So it is. And friendship is friendship. Got a match?' He laughed. 'No, I suppose you haven't.'

'I'll go and get you one if you like.'

'There's a good fellow. I'll think in the meantime.'

Beatrice rose lazily, and was absent for several minutes. When she returned, Crewe re-lit his cigar.

'Why shouldn't I start the shop on my own account?' Beatrice asked.

'You haven't capital enough. A little place wouldn't do.'

'I think I can get Fanny to join me.'

'Can you? What will young Lord have to say to that?'

'Psh! That's all fooling. It'll never come to anything. Unless, of course, the old man turned up his toes, and left the boy a tidy sum. But he won't just yet. I've told Fanny that if she'll raise something on her houses, I'll guarantee her the same income she has now.'

'Take my advice,' said Crewe weightily, 'and hook on to an established business. Of course, you can change the name if you like; and there'd have to be alterations, and painting up, to give a new look.'

'It's risky, dealing with strangers. How if they got hold of my idea, and then refused to take me in?'

'Well now, look here. After all, I'll make a bargain with you, old chap. If I can introduce you to the right people, and get you safely started, will you give me all your advertising, on the usual commission?'

'You mean, give it to Bullock and Freeman?'

'No, I don't. It's a secret just yet, but I'm going to start for myself.'

74

Beatrice was silent. They exchanged a look in the gloom, and Crewe nodded, in confirmation of his announcement.

'How much have you got?' Miss. French inquired carelessly.

'Not much. Most of the capital is here.' He touched his forehead. 'Same as with you.'

The young woman glanced at him again, and said in a lower voice:

'You'd have had more by now, if—'

Crewe waited, puffing his cigar, but she did not finish.

'Maybe,' he replied impartially. 'Maybe not.'

'Don't think I'm sorry,' Beatrice hastened to add. 'It was an idea, like any other.'

'Not half a bad idea. But there were obstacles.'

After a pause, Beatrice inquired:

'Do you still think the same about women with money?'

'Just the same,' Crewe replied at once, though with less than his usual directness; the question seemed to make him meditative. 'Just the same. Every man looks at it in his own way, of course. I'm not the sort of chap to knuckle under to my wife; and there isn't one woman in a thousand, if she gave her husband a start, could help reminding him of it. It's the wrong way about. Let women be as independent as they like as long as they're not married. I never think the worse of them, whatever they do that's honest. But a wife must play second fiddle, and think her husband a small god almighty —that's my way of looking at the question.'

Beatrice laughed scornfully.

'All right. We shall see.—When do you start business?'

'This side Christmas. End of September, perhaps.'

'You think to snatch a good deal from B. & F., I daresay?'

Crewe nodded and smiled.

'Then you'll look after this affair for me?' said Beatrice, with a return to the tone of strict business.

'Without loss of time. You shall be advised of progress. Of course I must debit you with exes.'

'All right. Mind you charge for all the penny stamps.'

'Every one—don't you forget it.'

He stood up, tilted forward on his toes, and stretched himself.

'I'll be trotting homewards. It'll be time for by-by when I get to Kennington.'

CHAPTER 3

Nancy was undisturbed by the promotion of Mary Woodruff. A short time ago it would have offended her; she would have thought her dignity, her social prospects, imperilled. She was now careless on that score, and felt it a relief to cast off the show of domestic authority. Henceforth her position would be like that of Horace. All she now desired was perfect freedom from responsibility,—to be, as it were, a mere lodger in the house, to come and go unquestioned and unrestrained by duties.

Thus, by aid of circumstance, had she put herself into complete accord with the spirit of her time. Abundant privilege; no obligation. A reference of all things to her sovereign will and pleasure. Withal, a defiant rather than a hopeful mood; resentment of the undisguisable fact that her will was sovereign only in a poor little sphere which she would gladly have transcended.

Now-a-days she never went in the direction of Champion Hill, formerly her favourite walk. If Jessica Morgan spoke of her acquaintances there, she turned abruptly to another subject. She thought of the place as an abode of arrogance and snobbery. She recalled with malicious satisfaction her ill-mannered remark to Lionel Tarrant. Let him think of her as he would; at all events he could no longer imagine her overawed by his social prestige. The probability was that she had hurt him in a sensitive spot; it might be hoped that the wound would rankle for a long time.

Her personal demeanour showed a change. So careful hitherto of feminine grace and decorum, she began to affect a mannishness of bearing, a bluntness of speech, such as found favour at De Crespigny Park. In a few weeks she had resumed friendly intercourse with Mrs. Peachey and her sisters, and spent an occasional evening at their house. Her father asked no questions; she rarely saw him except at meals. A stranger must have observed the signs of progressive malady in Mr. Lord's face, but Nancy was aware of nothing to cause uneasiness; she thought of him as suffering a little from 'gout;' elderly people were of course subject to such disorders. On most days he went to business; if he remained at home, Mary attended him assiduously, and he would accept no other ministration.

Nancy was no longer inclined to study, and cared little for reading of any sort. That new book on Evolution, which she had brought from the library just before Jubilee Day, was still lying about; a dozen times she had looked at it with impatience, and reminded herself that it must be returned. Evolution! She already knew all about Darwinism, all she needed to know. If necessary she could talk about it—oh, with an air. But who wanted to talk about such things? After all, only priggish people,—— the kind of people who lived at Champion Hill. Or idiots like Samuel Bennett Barmby, who bothered about the future of the world. What was it to *her*—the future of the world? She wanted to live in the present, to enjoy her youth. An evening like that she had spent in the huge crowd, with a man like Crewe to amuse her with his talk, was worth whole oceans of 'culture.'

'Culture' she already possessed, abundance of it. The heap of books she had read! Last winter she had attended a course of lectures, delivered by 'a young University gentleman with a tone of bland omniscience, on 'The History of Hellenic Civilisation;' her written answers to the little 'test papers' had been marked 'very satisfactory.' Was it not a proof of culture achieved? Education must not encroach upon the years of maturity. Nature marked the time when a woman should begin to live.

There was poor Jessica. As July drew on, Jessica began to look cadaverous, ghostly. She would assuredly break down long before the time of her examination. What a wretched, what an absurd existence! Her home, too, was so miserable. Mrs. Morgan lay ill, unable to attend to anything; if she could not have a change of air, it must soon be all over with her. But they had no money, no chance of going to the seaside.

It happened at length that Mr. Lord saw Jessica one evening, when she had come to spend an hour in Grove Lane. After her departure, he asked Nancy what was the matter with the girl, and Nancy explained the situation.

'Well, why not take her with you, when you go away?'

'I didn't know that I was going away, father. Nothing has been said of it.'

'It's your own business. I leave you to make what plans you like.'

Nancy reflected.

'*You* ought to have a change,' she said considerately. 'It would do you good. Suppose we all go to Teignmouth? I should think that would suit you.'

'Why Teignmouth?'

'I enjoyed it last year. And the lodgings were comfortable. We could have the same, from the first week in August.'

'How do you know?'

'I wrote the other day, and asked,' Nancy replied with a smile.

But Mr. Lord declined to leave home. Mary Woodruff did her best to persuade him, until he angrily imposed silence. In a day or two he said to Nancy:

'If you wish to go to Teignmouth, take Jessica and her mother. People mustn't die for want of a five-pound note. Make your arrangements, and let me know what money you'll need.'

'It's very kind of you, father.'

Mr. Lord turned away. His daughter noticed that he walked feebly, and she felt a moment's compunction.

'Father—you are not so well to-day.'

Without looking round, he replied that he would be well enough if left alone; and Nancy did not venture to say more.

A few days later, she called in De Crespigny Park after dinnertime. Mrs. Peachey and Fanny were at Brighton; Beatrice had preferred to stay in London, being very busy with her great project. Whilst she talked of it with Nancy, Peachey and Luckworth Crewe came in together. There was sprightly conversation, in which the host, obviously glad of his wife's absence, took a moderate part. Presently, Miss. Lord and he found themselves gossiping alone; the other two had moved aside, and, as a look informed Nancy, were deep in confidential dialogue.

'What do you think of that business?' she asked her companion in an undertone.

'I shouldn't wonder if it answers,' said the young man, speaking as usual, with a soft, amiable voice. 'Our friend is helping, and he generally knows what he's about.'

Crewe remained only for half-an-hour; on shaking hands with him, Nancy made known that she was going to the seaside next Monday for a few weeks, and the man of business answered only with 'I hope you'll enjoy yourself.' Soon afterwards, she took leave. At the junction of De Crespigny Park and Grove Lane, some one approached her, and with no great surprise Nancy saw that it was Crewe.

'Been waiting for you,' he said. 'You remember you promised me another walk.'

'Oh, it's much too late.'

'Of course it is. I didn't mean now. But to-morrow.'

'Impossible.' She moved on, in the direction away from her home. 'I shall be with friends in the evening, the Morgans.'

'Confound it! I had made up my mind to ask you for last Saturday, but some country people nabbed me for the whole of that day. I took them up the Monument, and up St Paul's.'

'I've never been up the Monument,' said Nancy.

'Never? Come to-morrow afternoon then. You can spare the afternoon. Let's meet early somewhere. Take a bus to London Bridge. I'll be at the north end of London Bridge at three o'clock.'

'All right; I'll be there,' Nancy replied off-hand.

'You really will? Three, sharp. I was never late at an appointment, business or pleasure.'

'Which do you consider this?' asked his companion, with a shrewd glance.

'Now that's unkind. I came here to-night on business, though. You quite understand that, didn't you? I shouldn't like you to make any mistake. Business, pure and simple.'

'Why, of course,' replied Nancy, with an ingenuous air. 'What else could it be?' And she added, 'Don't come any further. Ta-ta!'

Crewe went off into the darkness.

The next afternoon, Nancy alighted at London Bridge a full quarter of an hour late. It had been raining at intervals through the day, and clouds still cast a gloom over the wet streets. Crewe, quite insensible to atmospheric influence, came forward with his wonted brisk step and animated visage. At Miss. Lord's side he looked rather more plebeian than when walking by himself; his high-hat, not of the newest, utterly misbecame his head, and was always at an unconventional angle, generally tilting back; his clothes, of no fashionable cut, bore the traces of perpetual hurry and multifarious impact. But he carried a perfectly new and expensive umbrella, to which, as soon as he had shaken hands with her, he drew Nancy's attention.

'A present this morning, from a friend of mine in the business. I ran into his shop to get shelter. Upon my word, I had no intention; didn't think anything about it. However, he owed me an acknowledgment; I've sent him three customers from our office since I saw him last. By-the-bye, I shall have half a day at the seaside on Monday. There's a sale of building-plots down at Whitsand. The estate agents run a complimentary special train for people going down to bid, and give a lunch before the auction begins. Not bad business.'

'Are *you* going to bid?' asked Nancy.

'I'm going to have a look, at all events; and if I see anything that takes my fancy—. Ever been to Whitsand? I'm told it's a growing place. I should like to get hold of a few advertising stations.— Where is it you are going to on Monday? Teignmouth? I don't know that part of the country. Wish I could run down, but I shan't have time. I've got my work cut out for August and September. Would you like to come and see the place where I think of opening shop?'

'Is it far?'

'No. We'll walk round when we've been up the Monument. You don't often go about the City, I daresay. Nothing doing, of course, on a Saturday afternoon.'

Nancy made him moderate his pace, which was too quick for her. Part of the pleasure she found in Crewe's society came from her sense of being so undeniably his superior; she liked to give him a sharp command, and observe his ready obedience. To his talk she listened with a good-natured, condescending smile, occasionally making a remark which implied a more liberal view, a larger intelligence, than his. Thus, as they stood for a moment to look down at the steamboat wharf, and Crewe made some remark about the value of a cargo just being discharged, she said carelessly:

'I suppose that's the view you take of everything? You rate everything at market price.'

'Marketable things, of course. But you know me well enough to understand that I'm not always thinking of the shop. Wait till I've made money.—Now then, clumsy!'

A man, leaning over the parapet by Nancy's side, had pushed against her. Thus addressed he glared at the speaker, but encountered a bellicose look which kept him quiet.

'I shall live in a big way,' Crewe continued, as they walked on towards Fish Street Hill. 'Not for the swagger of it; I don't care about that, but because I've a taste for luxury. I shall have a country house, and keep good horses. And I should like to have a little farm of my own, a model farm; make my own butter and cheese, and know that I ate the real thing. I shall buy pictures. Haven't I told you I like pictures? Oh yes. I shall go round among the artists, and encourage talent that hasn't made itself known.'

'Can you recognise it?' asked Nancy.

'Well, I shall learn to. And I shall have my wife's portrait painted by some first-rate chap, never mind what it costs, and hung in the Academy. That's a great idea of mine—to see my wife's portrait in the Academy.'

His companion laughed.

'Take care, then, that your wife is ornamental.'

'I'll take precious good care of that!' Crewe exclaimed merrily. 'Do you suppose I should dream of marrying a woman who wasn't good-looking?'

'Don't shout, please. People can hear you.'

'I beg your pardon.' His voice sank to humility. 'That's a bad habit of mine. But I was going to say—I went to the Academy this year just to look at the portraits of men's wives. There was nothing particular in that line. Not a woman I should have felt particularly proud of. Tastes differ, of course. Mine has altered a good deal in the last ten years. A man can't trust himself about women till he's thirty or near it.'

'Talk of something else,' Nancy commanded.

'Certainly. There's the sun coming out. You see, I was afraid it would keep on raining, and you would have an excuse for staying at home.'

'I needed no excuse,' said Nancy. 'If I hadn't wished to come, you may be sure I should have said so.'

Crewe flashed a look at her.

'Ah, that's how I like to hear you speak! That does one good. Well, here we are. People used to be fond of going up, they say, just to pitch themselves down. A good deal of needless trouble, it seems to me. Perhaps they gave themselves the off-chance of changing their minds before they got to the top.'

'Or wanted to see if life looked any better from up there,' suggested Nancy.

'Or hoped somebody would catch them by the coat-tails, and settle a pension on them out of pity.'

Thus jesting, they began the ascent. Crewe, whose spirits were at high pressure, talked all the way up the winding stairs; on issuing into daylight, he became silent, and they stood side by side, mute before the vision of London's immensity. Nancy began to move round the platform. The strong west wind lashed her cheeks to a glowing colour; excitement added brilliancy to her eyes. As soon as she had recovered from the first impression, this spectacle of a world's wonder served only to exhilarate her; she was not awed by what she looked upon. In her conceit of self-importance, she stood there, above the battling millions of men, proof against mystery and dread, untouched by the voices of the past, and in the present seeing only common things, though from an odd point of view. Here her senses seemed to make literal the assumption by which her mind had always been directed: that she—Nancy Lord—was the mid point of the universe. No humility awoke in her; she felt the stirring of envies, avidities, unavowable passions, and let them flourish unrebuked.

Crewe had his eyes fixed upon her; his lips parted hungrily.

'Now *that's* how I should like to see you painted,' he said all at once. 'Just like that! I never saw you looking so well. I believe you're the most beautiful girl to be found anywhere in this London!'

There was genuine emotion in his voice, and his sweeping gesture suited the mood of vehemence. Nancy, having seen that the two or three other people on the platform were not within hearing, gave an answer of which the frankness surprised even herself.

'Portraits for the Academy cost a great deal, you know.'

'I know. But that's what I'm working for. There are not many men down yonder,' he pointed over the City, 'have a better head for money-making than I have.'

'Well, prove it,' replied Nancy, and laughed as the wind caught her breath.

'How long will you give me?'

She made no answer, but walked to the side whence she could look westward. Crewe followed close, his features still set in the hungry look, his eyes never moving from her warm cheek and full lips.

'What it must be,' she said, 'to have about twenty thousand a year!'

The man of business gave a gasp. In the same moment he had to clutch at his hat, lest it should be blown away.

'Twenty thousand a year?' he echoed. 'Well, it isn't impossible. Men get beyond that, and a good deal beyond it. But it's a large order.'

'Of course it is. But what was it you said? The most beautiful girl in all London? That's a large order, too, isn't it? How much is she worth?'

'You're talking for the joke now,' said Crewe. 'I don't like to hear that kind of thing, either. You never think in that way.'

'My thoughts are my own. I may think as I choose.'

'Yes. But you have thoughts above money.'

'Have I? How kind of you to say so.—I've had enough of this wind; we'll go down.'

She led the way, and neither of them spoke till they were in the street again. Nancy felt her hair.

'Am I blown to pieces?' she asked.

'No, no; you're all right. Now, will you walk through the City?'

'Where's the place you spoke of?'

'Farringdon Street. That'll bring you round to Blackfriars Bridge, when you want to go home. But there's plenty of time yet.'

So they rambled aimlessly by the great thoroughfares, and by hidden streets of which Nancy had never heard, talking or silent as the mood dictated. Crewe had stories to tell of this and that thriving firm, of others struggling in obscurity or falling from high estate; to him the streets of London were so many chapters of romance, but a romance always of to-day, for he neither knew nor cared about historic associations. Vast sums sounded perpetually on his lips; he glowed with envious delight in telling of speculations that had built up great fortunes. He knew the fabulous rents that were paid for sites that looked insignificant; he repeated anecdotes of calls made from Somerset House upon men of business, who had been too modest in returning the statement of their income; he revived legends of dire financial disaster, and of catastrophe barely averted by strange expedients. To all this Nancy listened with only moderate interest; as often as not, she failed to understand the details which should have excited her wonder. None the less, she received an impression of knowledge, acuteness, power, in the speaker; and this was decidedly pleasant.

'Here's the place where I think of starting for myself,' said Crewe, as he paused at length before a huge building in Farringdon Street.

'This?—Can you afford such a rent?'

Her companion burst into laughter.

'I don't mean the whole building. Two or three rooms, that's all, somewhere upstairs.'

Nancy made a jest of her mistake.

'An advertising agent doesn't want much space,' said Crewe. 'I know a chap who's doing a pretty big business in one room, not far from here.—Well, we've had a long walk; now you must rest a bit, and have a cup of tea.'

'I thought you were going to propose champagne.'

'Oh—if you like—'

84

They went to a restaurant in Fleet Street, and sat for half an hour over the milder beverage. Crewe talked of his projects, his prospects; and Nancy, whom the afternoon had in truth fatigued a little, though her mind was still excited, listened without remark.

'Well,' he said at length, leaning towards her, 'how long do you give me?'

She looked away, and kept silence.

'Two years:—just to make a solid start; to show that something worth talking 'about is to come?'

'I'll think about it.'

He kept his position, and gazed at her.

'I know it isn't money that would tempt you.' He spoke in a very low voice, though no one was within earshot. 'Don't think I make any mistake about *that*! But I have to show you that there's something in me. I wouldn't marry any woman that thought I made love to her out of interest.'

Nancy began to draw on her gloves, and smiled, just biting her lower lip.

'Will you give me a couple of years, from to-day? I won't bother you. It's honour bright!'

'I'll think about it,' Nancy repeated.

'Whilst you're away?'

'Yes, whilst I'm away at Teignmouth.'

'And tell me when you come back?'

'Tell you—how long. Yes.'

And she rose.

CHAPTER 4

From the mouth of Exe to the mouth of Teign the coast is uninteresting. Such beauty as it once possessed has been destroyed by the railway. Cliffs of red sandstone drop to the narrow beach, warm between the blue of sky and sea, but without grandeur, and robbed of their native grace by navvy-hewing, which for the most part makes of them a mere embankment: their verdure stripped away, their juttings tunnelled, along their base the steel parallels of smoky traffic. Dawlish and Teignmouth have in themselves no charm; hotel and lodging-house, shamed by the soft pure light that falls about them, look blankly seaward, hiding what remains of farm or cottage in the older parts. Ebb-tide uncovers no fair stretch of sand, and at flood the breakers are thwarted on a bulwark of piled stone, which supports the railway, or protects a promenade.

But inland these discontents are soon forgotten; there amid tilth and pasture, gentle hills and leafy hollows of rural Devon, the eye rests and the mind is soothed. By lanes innumerable, deep between banks of fern and flower; by paths along the bramble-edge of scented meadows; by the secret windings of copse and brake and stream-worn valley—a way lies upward to the long ridge of Haldon, where breezes sing among the pines, or sweep rustling through gorse and bracken. Mile after mile of rustic loveliness, ever and anon the sea-limits blue beyond grassy slopes. White farms dozing beneath their thatch in harvest sunshine; hamlets forsaken save by women and children, by dogs and cats and poultry, the labourers afield. Here grow the tall foxgloves, bending a purple head in the heat of noon; here the great bells of the convolvulus hang thick from lofty hedges, massing their pink and white against dark green leafage; here amid shadowed undergrowth trail the long fronds of lustrous hartstongue; wherever the eye falls, profusion of summer's glory. Here, in many a nook carpeted with softest turf, canopied with tangle of leaf and bloom, solitude is safe from all intrusion— unless it be that of flitting bird, or of some timid wild thing that rustles for a moment and is gone. From dawn to midnight, as from midnight to dawn, one who would be alone with nature might count upon the security of these bosks and dells.

By Nancy Lord and her companions such pleasures were unregarded. For the first few days after their arrival at Teignmouth, they sat or walked on the promenade, walked or sat on the pier, sat or walked on the Den—a long, wide lawn, decked about with shrubs and flower-beds, between sea-fronting houses and the beach. Nancy had no wish to exert herself, for the weather was hot; after her morning bathe with Jessica, she found amusement enough in watching the people—most of whom were here simply to look at each other, or in listening to the band, which played selections from Sullivan varied with dance music, or in reading a novel from the book-lender's,— that is to say, gazing idly at the page, and letting such significance as it possessed float upon her thoughts.

She was pleasantly conscious that the loungers who passed by, male and female, gave something of attention to her face and costume. Without attempting to rival the masterpieces of fashion which invited envy or wonder from all observers, she

86

thought herself nicely dressed, and had in fact, as always, made good use of her father's liberality. Her taste in garments had a certain timidity that served her well; by avoiding the extremes of mode, and in virtue of her admirable figure, she took the eye of those who looked for refinement rather than for extravagance. The unconsidered grace of her bearing might be recognised by all whom such things concerned; it by no means suggested that she came from a small house in Camberwell. In her companions, to be sure, she was unfortunate; but the over-modest attire and unimpressive persons of Mrs. Morgan and Jessica at least did her the office of relief by contrast.

Nancy had made this reflection; she was not above it. Yet her actual goodness of heart saved her from ever feeling ashamed of the Morgans. It gratified her to think that she was doing them a substantial kindness; but for her, they would have dragged through a wretched summer in their unwholesome, jimcrack house, without a breath of pure air, without a sight of the free heaven. And to both of them that would probably have meant a grave illness.

Mrs. Morgan was a thin, tremulous woman, with watery eyes and a singular redness about the prominent part of her face, which seemed to indicate a determination of blood to the nose. All her married life had been spent in a cheerless struggle to maintain the externals of gentility. Not that she was vain or frivolous—indeed her natural tendencies made for homeliness in everything—but, by birth and by marriage connected with genteel people, she felt it impossible to abandon that mode of living which is supposed to distinguish the educated class from all beneath it. She had brought into the world three sons and three daughters; of the former, two were dead, and of the latter, one,—in each case, poverty of diet having proved fatal to a weak constitution. For close upon thirty years the family had lived in houses of which the rent was out of all reasonable proportion to their means; at present, with a total income of one hundred and sixty pounds (Mr. Morgan called himself a commission agent, and seldom had anything to do), they paid in rent and rates a matter of fifty-five, and bemoaned the fate which neighboured them with people only by courtesy to be called gentlefolk. Of course they kept a servant,—her wages nine pounds a year. Whilst the mother and elder daughter were at Teignmouth, Mr Morgan, his son, and the younger girl felt themselves justified in making up for lack of holiday by an extra supply of butcher's meat.

Well-meaning, but with as little discretion in this as in other things, Mrs. Morgan allowed scarce an hour of the day to pass without uttering her gratitude to Nancy Lord for the benefit she was enjoying. To escape these oppressive thanks, Nancy did her best never to be alone with the poor lady; but a *tete-a-tete* was occasionally unavoidable, as, for instance, on the third or fourth day after their arrival, when Mrs. Morgan had begged Nancy's company for a walk on the Den, whilst Jessica wrote letters. At the end of a tedious hour Jessica joined them, and her face had an unwonted expression. She beckoned her friend apart.

'You'll be surprised. Who do you think is here?'

'No one that will bore us, I hope.'

'Mr. Tarrant. I met him near the post-office, and he stopped me.'

Nancy frowned.

'Are they all here again?'

'No; he says he's alone.—One minute, mamma; please excuse us.'

'He was surprised to see you?' said Nancy, after reflecting.

'He said so. But—I forgot to tell you—in a letter to Mrs. Baker I spoke of our plans. She had written to me to propose a pupil for after the holidays.—Perhaps she didn't mention it to Mr. Tarrant.'

'Evidently not!' Nancy exclaimed, with some impatience. 'Why should you doubt his word?'

'I can't help thinking'—Jessica smiled archly—'that he has come just to meet—somebody.'

'Somebody? Who do you mean?' asked her friend, with a look of sincere astonishment.

'I may be mistaken'—a glance completed the suggestion.

'Rubbish!'

For the rest of that day the subject was unmentioned. Nancy kept rather to herself, and seemed meditative. Next morning she was in the same mood. The tide served for a bathe at eleven o'clock; afterwards, as the girls walked briskly to and fro near the seat where Mrs. Morgan had established herself with a volume of Browning, —- Jessica insisted on her reading Browning, though the poor mother protested that she scarcely understood a word,—they came full upon the unmistakable presence of Mr. Lionel Tarrant. Miss. Morgan, in acknowledging his salute, offered her hand; it was by her that the young man had stopped. Miss. Lord only bent her head, and that slightly. Tarrant expected more, but his half-raised hand dropped in time, and he directed his speech to Jessica. He had nothing to say but what seemed natural and civil; the dialogue—Nancy remained mute—occupied but a few minutes, and Tarrant went his way, sauntering landwards.

As Mrs. Morgan had observed the meeting, it was necessary to offer her an explanation. But Jessica gave only the barest facts concerning their acquaintance, and Nancy spoke as though she hardly knew him.

88

The weather was oppressively hot; in doors or out, little could be done but sit or lie in enervated attitudes, a state of things accordant with Nancy's mood. Till late at night she watched the blue starry sky from her open window, seeming to reflect, but in reality wafted on a stream of fancies and emotions. Jessica's explanation of the arrival of Lionel Tarrant had strangely startled her; no such suggestion would have occurred to her own mind. Yet now, she only feared that it might not be true. A debilitating climate and absolute indolence favoured that impulse of lawless imagination which had first possessed her on the evening of Jubilee Day. With luxurious heedlessness she cast aside every thought that might have sobered her; even as she at length cast off all her garments, and lay in the warm midnight naked upon her bed.

The physical attraction of which she had always been conscious in Tarrant's presence seemed to have grown stronger since she had dismissed him from her mind. Comparing him with Luckworth Crewe, she felt only a contemptuous distaste for the coarse vitality and vigour, whereto she had half surrendered herself, when hopeless of the more ambitious desire.

Rising early, she went out before breakfast, and found that a little rain had fallen. Grass and flowers were freshened; the air had an exquisite clearness, and a coolness which struck delightfully on the face, after the close atmosphere within doors. She had paused to watch a fishing-boat off shore, when a cheery voice bade her 'good-morning,' and Tarrant stepped to her side.

'You are fond of this place,' he said.

'Not particularly.'

'Then why do you choose it?'

'It does for a holiday as well as any other.'

He was gazing at her, and with the look which Nancy resented, the look which made her feel his social superiority. He seemed to observe her features with a condescending gratification. Though totally ignorant of his life and habits, she felt a conviction that he had often bestowed this look upon girls of a class below his own.

'How do you like those advertisements of soaps and pills along the pier?' he asked carelessly.

'I see no harm in them.'

Perversity prompted her answer, but at once she remembered Crewe, and turned away in annoyance. Tarrant was only the more good-humoured.

'You like the world as it is? There's wisdom in that. Better be in harmony with one's time, advertisements and all.' He added, 'Are you reading for an exam?'

'I? You are confusing me with Miss. Morgan.'

'Oh, not for a moment! I couldn't possibly confuse you with any one else. I know Miss. Morgan is studying professionally; but I thought you were reading for your own satisfaction, as so many women do now-a-days.'

The distinction was flattering. Nancy yielded to the charm of his voice and conversed freely. It began to seem not impossible that he found some pleasure in her society. Now and then he dropped a word that made her pulses flutter; his eyes were constantly upon her face.

'Don't you go off into the country sometimes?' he inquired, when she had turned homewards.

'We are thinking of having a drive to-day.'

'And I shall most likely have a ride; we may meet.'

Nancy ordered a carriage for the afternoon, and with her friends drove up the Teign valley; but they did not meet Tarrant. But next morning he joined them on the pier, and this time Jessica had no choice but to present him to her mother. Nancy felt annoyed that this should have come about; Tarrant, she supposed, would regard poor Mrs. Morgan with secret ridicule. Yet, if that were his disposition, he concealed it perfectly; no one could have behaved with more finished courtesy. He seated himself by Mrs. Morgan, and talked with her of the simplest things in a pleasant, kindly humour. Yesterday, so he made known, he had ridden to Torquay and back, returning after sunset. This afternoon he was going by train to Exeter, to buy some books.

Again he strolled about with Nancy, and talked of idle things with an almost excessive amiability. As the girl listened, a languor crept upon her, a soft and delicious subdual of the will to dreamy luxury. Her eyes were fixed on the shadows cast by her own figure and that of her companion. The black patches by chance touched. She moved so as to part them, and then changed her position so that they touched again—so that they blended.

CHAPTER 5

Nancy had written to her father, a short letter but affectionate, begging him to let her know whether the improvement in his health, of which he had spoken before she left home, still continued. The answer came without delay. On the whole, said Mr. Lord, he was doing well enough; no need whatever to trouble about him. He wrote only a few lines, but closed with 'love to you, my dear child,' an unwonted effusiveness.

At the same time there came a letter from Horace.

'You will be surprised,' it began, 'at the address I write from. As you know, I had planned to go to Brighton; but on the day before my holiday commenced I heard from F. F., saying that she and Mrs. Peachey had had a quarrel, and she was tired of Brighton, and was coming home. So I waited a day or two, and then, as I had half promised, I went to see Mrs. D. We had a long talk, and it ended in my telling her about F., and all the row there's been. Perhaps you will think I had better have kept it to myself, but Mrs. D. and I are on first-rate terms, and she seems to understand me better than any one I ever met. We talked about my holiday, and she persuaded me to come to Scarborough, where she herself was going for a week or two. It's rather an expensive affair, but worth the money. Of course I have lodgings of my own. Mrs. D. is at a big hotel, where friends of hers are staying. I have been introduced to two or three people, great swells, and I've had lunch with Mrs. D. at the hotel twice. This kind of life suits me exactly. I don't think I get on badly with the swells. Of course I say not a word about my position, and of course nobody would think of asking questions. You would like this place; I rather wish you were here. Of course father thinks I have come on my own hook. It's very awkward having to keep a secret of this kind; I must try and persuade Mrs. D. to have a talk with father. But one thing I can tell you,—I feel pretty sure that she will get me, somehow or other, out of that beastly City life; she's always talking of things I might do. But not a word to any one about all this—be sure.'

This news caused Nancy to ponder for a long time. The greater part of the morning she spent at home, and in her own room; after lunch, she sat idly on the promenade, little disposed for conversation.

It was the second day since Tarrant had told her that he was going to Exeter, and they had not again met; the Morgans had not seen him either. The next morning, however, as all three were sitting in one of their favourite places, Tarrant approached them. Mrs. Morgan, who was fluttered by the natural supposition of a love affair between Miss. Lord and the interesting young man, made it easy for them to talk together.

'Did you get your books?' Nancy asked, when silence followed on trivialities.

'Yes, and spent half a day with them in a favourite retreat of mine, inland. It's a very beautiful spot. I should like you to see it. Indeed, you ought to.'

Nancy turned her eyes to the sea.

'We might walk over there one afternoon,' he added.

'Mrs. Morgan can't walk far.'

'Why should we trouble her? Are you obliged to remain under Mrs. Morgan's wing?'

It was said jestingly, but Nancy felt piqued.

'Certainly not. I am quite independent.'

'So I should have supposed. Then why not come?'

He seemed perfectly self-possessed, but the voice was not quite his own. To Nancy, her eyes still looking straight forward, it sounded as though from a distance; it had an effect upon her nerves similar to that she had experienced three days ago, when they were walking about the pier. Her hands fell idly; she leaned back more heavily on the seat; a weight was on her tongue.

'A country ramble of an hour or two,' pursued the voice, which itself had become languorous. 'Surely you are sometimes alone? It isn't necessary to give a detailed account of your time?'

She answered impatiently. 'Of course not.' In this moment her thoughts had turned to Luckworth Crewe, and she was asking herself why this invitation of Tarrant's affected her so very differently from anything she had felt when Crewe begged her to meet him in London. With him she could go anywhere, enjoying a genuine independence, a complete self-confidence, thinking her unconventional behaviour merely good fun. Tarrant's proposal startled her. She was not mistress of the situation, as when trifling with Crewe. A sense of peril caused her heart to beat quickly.

'This afternoon, then,' the voice was murmuring.

She answered mechanically. 'It's going to rain, I think.'

'I think not. But, if so, to-morrow.'

'To-morrow is Sunday.'

92

'Yes. Monday, then.'

Nancy heard him smother a laugh. She wished to look at him, but could not.

'It won't rain,' he continued, still with the ease of one who speaks of everyday matters. 'We shall see, at all events. Perhaps you will want to change your book at the library.' A novel lay on her lap. 'We'll leave it an open possibility—to meet there about three o'clock.'

Nancy pointed out to sea, and asked where the steamer just passing might be bound for. Her companion readily turned to this subject.

The rain—she half hoped for it—did not come. By luncheon-time every doubtful cloud had vanished. Before sitting down to table, she observed the sky at the open window.

'Lovely weather!' sighed Mrs. Morgan behind her. 'But for you, dear Nancy, I should have been dreaming and wishing—oh, how vainly!— in the stifling town.'

'We'll have another drive this afternoon,' Nancy declared.

'Oh, how delightful! But pray, pray, not on our account—'

'Jessica,'—Nancy turned to her friend, who had just entered the room,—'we'll have the carriage at three. And a better horse than last time; I'll take good care of that. Pen, ink, and paper!' she cried joyously. 'The note shall go round at once.'

'You're a magnificent sort of person,' said Jessica. 'Some day, no doubt, you'll keep a carriage and pair of your own.'

'Shan't I, just! And drive you down to Burlington House, for your exams. By-the-bye, does a female Bachelor of Arts lose her degree if she gets married?'

Nancy was sprightlier than of late. Her mood maintained itself throughout the first half of the drive, then she seemed to be overcome by a sudden weariness, ceased to talk, and gave only a listless look at things which interested her companions. By when they reached home again, she had a pale troubled countenance. Until dinner nothing more was seen of her, and after the meal she soon excused herself on the plea of a headache.

Again there passed two days, Sunday and Monday, without Tarrant's appearing. Mrs. Morgan and Jessica privately talked much of the circumstance. Sentimental souls, they found this topic inexhaustible; Jessica, having her mind thus drawn away from Burlington House, benefited not a little by the mystery of her friend's position; she thought, however, that Nancy might have practised a less severe reticence. To

Mrs. Morgan it never occurred that so self-reliant a young woman as Miss. Lord stood in need of matronly counsel, of strict chaperonage; she would have deemed it an impertinence to allow herself the most innocent remark implying such a supposition.

On Wednesday afternoon, about three o'clock, Nancy walked alone to the library. There, looking at books and photographs in the window, stood Lionel Tarrant. He greeted her as usual, seemed not to remark the hot colour in her cheeks, and stepped with her into the shop. She had meant to choose a novel, but, with Tarrant looking on, felt constrained to exhibit her capacity for severe reading. The choice of grave works was not large, and she found it difficult to command her thoughts even for the perusal of titles; however, she ultimately discovered a book that promised anything but frivolity, Helmholtz's 'Lectures on Scientific Subjects,' and at this she clutched.

Two loudly-dressed women were at the same time searching the shelves.

'I wonder whether this is a pretty book?' said one to the other, taking down a trio of volumes.

'Oh, it looks as if it might be pretty,' returned her friend, examining the cover.

They faced to the person behind the counter.

'Is this a pretty book?' one of them inquired loftily.

'Oh yes, madam, that's a very pretty book—very pretty.'

Nancy exchanged a glance with her companion and smiled. When they were outside again Tarrant asked:

'Have you found a pretty book?'

She showed the title of her choice.

'Merciful heavens! You mean to read that? The girls of to-day! What mere man is worthy of them? But—I must rise to the occasion. We'll have a chapter as we rest.'

Insensibly, Nancy had followed the direction he chose. His words took for granted that she was going into the country with him.

'My friends are on the pier,' she said, abruptly stopping.

'Where doubtless they will enjoy themselves. Let me carry your book, please. Helmholtz is rather heavy.'

94

'Thanks, I can carry it very well. I shall turn this way.'

'No, no. My way this afternoon.'

Nancy stood still, looking up the street that led towards the sea. She was still bright-coloured; her lips had a pathetic expression, a child-like pouting.

'There was an understanding,' said Tarrant, with playful firmness.

'Not for to-day.'

'No. For the day when you disappointed me. The day after, I didn't think it worth while to come here; yesterday I came, but felt no surprise that I didn't meet you. To-day I had a sort of hope. This way.'

She followed, and they walked for several minutes in silence.

'Will you let me look at Helmholtz?' said the young man at length. 'Most excellent book, of course. "Physiological Causes of Harmony in Music," "Interaction of Natural Forces," "Conservation of Force."— You enjoy this kind of thing?'

'One must know something about it.'

'I suppose so. I used to grind at science because everybody talked science. In reality I loathed it, and now I read only what I like. Life's too short for intellectual make-believe. It is too short for anything but enjoyment. Tell me what you read for pure pleasure. Poetry?'

They had left the streets, and were pursuing a road bordered with gardens, gardens of glowing colour, sheltered amid great laurels, shadowed by stately trees; the air was laden with warm scents of flower and leaf. On an instinct of resistance, Nancy pretended that the exact sciences were her favourite study. She said it in the tone of superiority which habit had made natural to her in speaking of intellectual things. And Tarrant appeared to accept her declaration without scepticism; but, a moment after, he turned the talk upon novels.

Thus, for half an hour and more, they strolled on by upward ways, until Teignmouth lay beneath them, and the stillness of meadows all about. Presently Tarrant led from the beaten road into a lane all but overgrown with grass. He began to gather flowers, and offered them to Nancy. Personal conversation seemed at an end; they were enjoying the brilliant sky and the peaceful loveliness of earth. They exchanged simple, natural thoughts, or idle words in which was no thought at all.

Before long, they came to an old broken gate, half open; it was the entrance to a narrow cartway, now unused, which descended windingly between high thick hedges. Ruts of a foot in depth, baked hard by summer, showed how miry the track must be in the season of rain.

'This is our way,' said Tarrant, his hand on the lichened wood. 'Better than the pier or the promenade, don't you think?'

'But we have gone far enough.'

Nancy drew back into the lane, looked at her flowers, and then shaded her eyes with them to gaze upward.

'Almost. Another five minutes, and you will see the place I told you of. You can't imagine how beautiful it is.'

'Another day—'

'We are all but there—'

He seemed regretfully to yield; and Nancy yielded in her turn. She felt a sudden shame in the thought of having perhaps betrayed timidity. Without speaking, she passed the gate.

The hedge on either side was of hazel and dwarf oak, of hawthorn and blackthorn, all intertwined with giant brambles, and with briers which here and there met overhead. High and low, blackberries hung in multitudes, swelling to purple ripeness. Numberless the trailing and climbing plants. Nancy's skirts rustled among the greenery; her cheeks were touched, as if with a caress, by many a drooping branchlet; in places, Tarrant had to hold the tangle above her while she stooped to pass.

And from this they emerged into a small circular space, where the cartway made a turn at right angles and disappeared behind thickets. They were in the midst of a plantation; on every side trees closed about them, with a low and irregular hedge to mark the borders of the grassy road. Nancy's eyes fell at once upon a cluster of magnificent foxgloves, growing upon a bank which rose to the foot of an old elm; beside the foxgloves lay a short-hewn trunk, bedded in the ground, thickly overgrown with mosses, lichens, and small fungi.

'Have I misled you?' said Tarrant, watching her face with frank pleasure.

'No, indeed you haven't. This is very beautiful!'

'I discovered it last year, and spent hours here alone. I couldn't ask you to come and see it then,' he added, laughing.

'It is delightful!'

'Here's your seat,—who knows how many years it has waited for you?'

She sat down upon the old trunk. About the roots of the elm above grew masses of fern, and beneath it a rough bit of the bank was clothed with pennywort, the green discs and yellowing fruity spires making an exquisite patch of colour. In the shadow of bushes near at hand hartstongue abounded, with fronds hanging to the length of an arm.

'Now,' said Tarrant, gaily, 'you shall have some blackberries. And he went to gather them, returning in a few minutes with a large leaf full. He saw that Nancy, meanwhile, had taken up the book from where he dropped it to the ground; it lay open on her lap.

'Helmholtz! Away with him!'

'No; I have opened at something interesting.'

She spoke as though possession of the book were of vital importance to her. Nevertheless, the fruit was accepted, and she drew off her gloves to eat it. Tarrant seated himself on the ground, near her, and gradually fell into a half-recumbent attitude.

'Won't you have any?' Nancy asked, without looking at him.

'One or two, if you will give me them.'

She chose a fine blackberry, and held it out. Tarrant let it fall into his palm, and murmured, 'You have a beautiful hand.' When, a moment after, he glanced at her, she seemed to be reading Helmholtz.

The calm of the golden afternoon could not have been more profound. Birds twittered softly in the wood, and if a leaf rustled, it was only at the touch of wings. Earth breathed its many perfumes upon the slumberous air.

'You know,' said Tarrant, after a long pause, and speaking as though he feared to break the hush, 'that Keats once stayed at Teignmouth.'

Nancy did not know it, but said 'Yes.' The name of Keats was familiar to her, but of his life she knew hardly anything, of his poetry very little. Her education had been chiefly concerned with names.

'Will you read me a paragraph of Helmholtz?' continued the other, looking at her with a smile. 'Any paragraph, the one before you.'

She hesitated, but read at length, in an unsteady voice, something about the Conservation of Force. It ended in a nervous laugh.

'Now I'll read something to you,' said Tarrant. And he began to repeat, slowly, musically, lines of verse which his companion had never heard:

'*O what can ail thee, Knight-at-arms,*
Alone and palely loitering?
The sedge has wither'd from the lake,
And no birds sing.'

He went through the poem; Nancy the while did not stir. It was as though he murmured melody for his own pleasure, rather than recited to a listener; but no word was inaudible. Nancy knew that his eyes rested upon her; she wished to smile, yet could not. And when he ceased, the silence held her motionless.

'Isn't it better?' said Tarrant, drawing slightly nearer to her.

'Of course it is.'

'I used to know thousands of verses by heart.'

'Did you ever write any?'

'Half-a-dozen epics or so, when I was about seventeen. Yet, I don't come of a poetical family. My father—'

He stopped abruptly, looked into Nancy's face with a smile, and said in a tone of playfulness:

'Do you remember asking me whether I had anything to do with—'

Nancy, flushing over all her features, exclaimed, 'Don't! please don't! I'm ashamed of myself!'

'I didn't like it. But we know each other better now. You were quite right. That was how my grandfather made his money. My father, I believe, got through most of it, and gave no particular thought to me. His mother—the old lady whom you know—had plenty of her own—to be mine, she tells me, some day. Do you wish to be forgiven for hurting my pride?' he added.

'I don't know what made me say such a thing—'

She faltered the words; she felt her will subdued. Tarrant reached a hand, and took one of hers, and kissed it; then allowed her to draw it away.

98

'Now will you give me another blackberry?'

The girl was trembling; a light shone in her eyes. She offered the leaf with fruit in it; Tarrant, whilst choosing, touched the blue veins of her wrist with his lips.

'What are you going to do?' she asked presently. 'I mean, what do you aim at in life?'

'Enjoyment. Why should I trouble about anything else. I should be content if life were all like this: to look at a beautiful face, and listen to a voice that charms me, and touch a hand that makes me thrill with such pleasure as I never knew.'

'It's waste of time.'

'Oh, never time was spent so well! Look at me again like that— with the eyes half-closed, and the lips half-mocking. Oh, the exquisite lips! If I might—if I might—'

He did not stir from his posture of languid ease, but Nancy, with a quick movement, drew a little away from him, then rose.

'It's time to go back,' she said absently.

'No, no; not yet. Let me look at you for a few minutes more!'

She began to walk slowly, head bent.

'Well then, to-morrow, or the day after. The place will be just as beautiful, and you even more. The sea-air makes you lovelier from day to day.'

Nancy looked back for an instant. Tarrant followed, and in the deep leafy way he again helped her to pass the briers. But their hands never touched, and the silence was unbroken until they had issued into the open lane.

CHAPTER 6

The lodgings were taken for three weeks, and more than half the time had now elapsed.

Jessica, who declared herself quite well and strong again, though her face did not bear out the assertion, was beginning to talk of matters examinational once more. Notwithstanding protests, she brought forth from their hiding-place sundry arid little manuals and black-covered notebooks; her thoughts were divided between algebraic formulae and Nancy's relations with Lionel Tarrant. Perhaps because no secret was confided to her, she affected more appetite for the arid little books than she really felt. Nancy would neither speak of examinations, nor give ear when they were talked about; she, whether consciously or not, was making haste to graduate in quite another school.

On the morning after her long walk with Tarrant, she woke before sunrise, and before seven o'clock had left the house. A high wind and hurrying clouds made the weather prospects uncertain. She strayed about the Den, never losing sight for more than a minute or two of the sea-fronting house where Tarrant lived. But no familiar form approached her, and she had to return to breakfast unrewarded for early rising.

Through the day she was restless and silent, kept alone as much as possible, and wore a look which, as the hours went on, darkened from anxiety to ill-humour. She went to bed much earlier than usual.

At eleven next morning, having lingered behind her friends, she found Tarrant in conversation with Mrs. Morgan and Jessica on the pier. His greeting astonished her; it had precisely the gracious formality of a year ago; a word or two about the weather, and he resumed his talk with Miss. Morgan—its subject, the educational value of the classics. Obliged to listen, Nancy suffered an anguish of resentful passion. For a quarter of an hour she kept silence, then saw the young man take leave and saunter away with that air which, in satire, she had formerly styled majestic.

And then passed three whole days, during which Lionel was not seen.

The evening of the fourth, between eight and nine o'clock, found Nancy at the door of the house which her thoughts had a thousand times visited. A servant, in reply to inquiry, told her that Mr Tarrant was in London; he would probably return to-morrow.

She walked idly away—and, at less than a hundred yards' distance, met Tarrant himself. His costume showed that he had just come from the railway station. Nancy would gladly have walked straight past him, but the tone in which he addressed her was a new surprise, and she stood in helpless confusion. He had been to London—called away on sudden business.

'I thought of writing—nay, I did write, but after all didn't post the letter. For a very simple reason—I couldn't remember your address.'

And he laughed so naturally, that the captive walked on by his side, unresisting. Their conversation lasted only a few minutes, then Nancy resolutely bade him good-night, no appointment made for the morrow.

A day of showers, then a day of excessive heat. They saw each other several times, but nothing of moment passed. The morning after they met before breakfast.

'To-morrow is our last day,' said Nancy.

'Yes, Mrs. Morgan told me.' Nancy herself had never spoken of departure. 'This afternoon we'll go up the hill again.'

'I don't think I shall care to walk so far. Look at the mist; it's going to be dreadfully hot again.'

Tarrant was in a mood of careless gaiety; his companion appeared to struggle against listlessness, and her cheek had lost its wonted colour.

'You have tea at four or five, I suppose. Let us go after that, when the heat of the day is over.'

To this, after various objections, Nancy consented. Through the hours of glaring sunshine she stayed at home, lying inert, by an open window. Over the tea-cups she was amiable, but dreamy. When ready to go out, she just looked into the sitting-room, where Jessica bent over books, and said cheerfully:

'I may be a little late for dinner. On no account wait—I forbid it!'

And so, without listening to the answer, she hurried away.

In the upward climbing lanes, no breeze yet tempered the still air; the sky of misted sapphire showed not a cloud from verge to verge. Tarrant, as if to make up for his companion's silence, talked ceaselessly, and always in light vein. Sunshine, he said, was indispensable to his life; he never passed the winter in London; if he were the poorest of mortals, he would, at all events, beg his bread in a sunny clime.

'Are you going to the Bahamas this winter?' Nancy asked, mentioning the matter for the first time since she heard of it at Champion Hill.

'I don't know. Everything is uncertain.'

And he put the question aside as if it were of no importance.

They passed the old gate, and breathed with relief in the never-broken shadow of tangled foliage. Whilst pushing a bramble aside, Tarrant let his free arm fall lightly on Nancy's waist. At once she sprang forward, but without appearing to notice what had happened.

'Stay—did you ever see such ivy as this?'

It was a mass of large, lustrous leaves, concealing a rotten trunk. Whilst Nancy looked on, Tarrant pulled at a long stem, and tried to break it away.

'I must cut it.'

'Why?'

'You shall see.'

He wove three stems into a wreath.

'There now, take off your hat, and let me crown you. Have I made it too large for the little head?'

Nancy, after a moment's reluctance, unfastened her hat, and stood bareheaded, blushing and laughing.

'You do your hair in the right way—the Greek way. A diadem on the top—the only way when the hair and the head are beautiful. It leaves the outline free—the exquisite curve that unites neck and head. Now the ivy wreath; and how will you look?'

She wore a dress of thin, creamy material, which, whilst seeming to cumber her as little as garments could, yet fitted closely enough to declare the healthy beauty of her form. The dark green garland, for which she bent a little, became her admirably.

'I pictured it in my letter,' said Tarrant, 'the letter you never got.'

'Where is it?'

'Oh, I burnt it.'

'Tell me what was in it.'

'All sorts of things—a long letter.'

'I think that's all nonsense about forgetting my address.'

'Mere truth. In fact, I never knew it.'

'Be so good as to tell me,' she spoke as she walked on before him, 'what you meant by your behaviour that morning before you went to London.'

'But how did I behave?'

'Very strangely.'

Tarrant affected not to understand; but, when she again turned, Nancy saw a mischievous smile on his face.

'A bit of nonsense.—Shall I tell you?' He stepped near, and suddenly caught both her hands,—one of them was trailing her sunshade. 'Forgive me in advance—will you?'

'I don't know about that.' And she tried, though faintly, to get free.

'But I will make you—now, refuse!'

His lips had just touched hers, just touched and no more. Rosy red, she trembled before him with drooping eyelids.

'It meant nothing at all, really,' he pursued, his voice at its softest. 'A sham trial—to see whether I was hopelessly conquered or not. Of course I was.'

Nancy shook her head.

'You dare to doubt it?—I understand now what the old poet meant, when he talked of bees seeking honey on his lady's lips. That fancy isn't so artificial as it seemed.'

'That's all very pretty'—she spoke between quick breaths, and tried to laugh—'but you have thrown my hat on the ground. Give it me, and take the ivy for yourself.'

'I am no Bacchus.' He tossed the wreath aside. 'Take the hat; I like you in it just as well.—You shall have a girdle of woodbine, instead.'

'I don't believe your explanation,' said Nancy.

'Not believe me?'

With feigned indignation, he moved to capture her again; but Nancy escaped. Her hat in her hand, she darted forward. A minute's run brought her into the open space, and there, with an exclamation of surprise, she stopped. Tarrant, but a step or two behind her, saw at almost the same moment the spectacle which had arrested her flight. Before them stood two little donkeys munching eagerly at a crop of rosy-headed thistles. They—the human beings—looked at each other; Tarrant burst into extravagant laughter, and Nancy joined him. Neither's mirth was spontaneous; Nancy's had a note of nervous tension, a ring of something like recklessness.

'Where can they come from?' she asked.

'They must have strayed a long way. I haven't seen any farm or cottage.—But perhaps some one is with them. Wait, I'll go on a little, and see if some boy is hanging about.'

He turned the sharp corner, and disappeared. For two or three minutes Nancy stood alone, watching the patient little grey beasts, whose pendent ears, with many a turn and twitch, expressed their joy in the feast of thistles. She watched them in seeming only; her eyes beheld nothing.

A voice sounded from behind her—'Nancy!' Startled, she saw Tarrant standing high up, in a gap of the hedge, on the bank which bordered the wood.

'How did you get there?'

'Went round.' He showed the direction with his hand. 'I can see no one, but somebody may come. It's wonderful here, among the trees. Come over.'

'How can I?—We will drive the donkeys away.'

'No; it's much better here; a wild wood, full of wonderful things. The bank isn't too steep. Give me your hand, and you can step up easily, just at this place.'

She drew near.

'Your sunshade first.'

'Oh, it's too much trouble,' she said languidly, all but plaintively. 'I'd rather be here.'

'Obey!—Your sunshade—'

She gave it.

'Now, your hand.'

He was kneeling on the top of the bank. With very little exertion, Nancy found herself beside him. Then he at once leapt down among the brushwood, a descent of some three feet.

'We shall be trespassing,' said Nancy.

'What do I care? Now, jump!'

'As if you could catch me!' Again she uttered her nervous laugh. 'I am heavy.'

'Obey! Jump!' he cried impatiently, his eyes afire.

She knelt, seated herself, dropped forward. Tarrant caught her in his arms.

'You heavy! a feather weight! Why, I can carry you; I could run with you.'

And he did carry her through the brushwood, away into the shadow of the trees.

At dinner-time, Mrs. Morgan and her daughter were alone. They agreed to wait a quarter of an hour, and sat silent, pretending each to be engaged with a book. At length their eyes met.

'What does it mean, Jessica?' asked the mother timidly.

'I'm sure I don't know. It doesn't concern us. She didn't mean to be back, by what she said.'

'But—isn't it rather—?'

'Oh, Nancy is all right. I suppose she'll have something to tell you, to-night or to-morrow. We must have dinner; I'm hungry.'

'So am I, dear.—Oh, I'm quite afraid to think of the appetites we're taking back. Poor Milly will be terrified.'

Eight o'clock, nine o'clock. The two conversed in subdued voices; Mrs. Morgan was anxious, all but distressed. Half-past nine. 'What *can* it mean, Jessica? I can't help feeling a responsibility. After all, Nancy is quite a young girl; and I've sometimes thought she might be steadier.'

'Hush! That was a knock.'

They waited. In a minute or two the door was opened a few inches, and a voice called 'Jessica!'

She responded. Nancy was standing in the gloom.

'Come into my room,' she said curtly.

Arrived there, she did not strike a light. She closed the door, and took hold of her friend's arm.

'We can't go back the day after to-morrow, Jessica. We must wait a day longer, till the afternoon of Friday.'

'Why? What's the matter, Nancy?'

'Nothing serious. Don't be frightened, I'm tired, and I shall go to bed.'

'But why must we wait?'

'Listen: will you promise me faithfully—as friend to friend, faith fully—not to tell the reason even to your mother?'

'I will, faithfully.'

'Then, it's this. On Friday morning I shall be married to Mr Tarrant.'

'Gracious!'

'I may tell you more, before then; but perhaps not. We shall be married by licence, and it needs one day between getting the licence and the marriage. You may tell your mother, if you like, that I want to stay longer on *his* account. I don't care; of course she suspects something. But not a syllable to hint at the truth. I have been your best friend for a long time, and I trust you.'

She spoke in a passionate whisper, and Jessica felt her trembling.

'You needn't have the least fear of me, dear.'

'I believe it. Kiss me, and good-night!'

Part III: Into Bontage

CHAPTER 1

During his daughter's absence, Stephen Lord led a miserable life. The wasting disease had firm hold upon him; day by day it consumed his flesh, darkened his mind. The more need he had of nursing and restraint, the less could he tolerate interference with his habits, invasion of his gloomy solitude. The doctor's visits availed nothing; he listened to advice, or seemed to listen, but with a smile of obstinate suspicion on his furrowed face which conveyed too plain a meaning to the adviser.

On one point Mary had prevailed with him. After some days' resistance, he allowed her to transform the cabin-like arrangements of his room, and give it the appearance of a comfortable bed-chamber. But he would not take to his bed, and the suggestion of professional nursing excited his wrath.

'Do you write to Nancy?' he asked one morning of his faithful attendant, with scowling suspicion.

'No.'

'You are telling me the truth?'

'I never write to any one.'

'Understand plainly that I won't have a word said to her about me.'

This was when Horace had gone away to Scarborough, believing, on his father's assurance, that there was no ground whatever for anxiety. Sometimes Mr. Lord sat hour after hour in an unchanging position, his dull eyes scarcely moving from one point. At others he paced his room, or wandered about the house, or made an attempt at gardening —which soon ended in pain and exhaustion. Towards night he became feverish, his hollow cheeks glowing with an ominous tint. In the morning he occasionally prepared himself as if to start for his place of business; he left the house, and walked for perhaps a couple of hundred yards, then slackened his pace, stopped, looked about him in an agony of indecision, and at length returned. After this futile endeavour, he had recourse to the bottles in his cupboard, and presently fell into a troubled sleep.

At the end of the second week, early one evening, three persons came to him by appointment: his partner Samuel Barmby, Mr. Barmby, senior, and a well-dressed gentleman whom Mary—she opened the door to them—had never seen before. They sat together in the drawing-room for more than an hour; then the well-dressed gentleman took his leave, the others remaining for some time longer.

The promoted servant, at Mr. Lord's bidding, had made a change in her dress; during the latter part of the day she presented the appearance of a gentlewoman, and sat, generally with needlework, sometimes with a book, alone in the dining-room. On a Sunday, whilst Nancy and her brother were away, the Barmby family—father, son, and two daughters—came to take tea and spend the evening, Mary doing the honours of the house; she bore herself without awkwardness, talked simply, and altogether justified Mr. Lord's opinion of her. When the guests were gone, Stephen made no remark, but, in saying good-night to her, smiled for an instant—the first smile seen upon his face for many days.

Mary remained ignorant of the disease from which he was suffering; in the matter of his diet, she consulted and obeyed him, though often enough it seemed to her that his choice suited little with the state of an invalid. He ate at irregular times, and frequently like a starving man. Mary suspected that, on the occasions when he went out for half-an-hour after dark, he brought back food with him: she had seen him enter with something concealed beneath his coat. All his doings were to her a subject of ceaseless anxiety, of a profound distress which, in his presence, she was obliged to conceal. If she regarded him sadly, the sufferer grew petulant or irate. He would not endure a question concerning his health.

On the day which was understood to be Nancy's last at Teignmouth, he brightened a little, and talked with pleasure, as it seemed, of her return on the morrow. Horace had written that he would be home this evening, but Mr. Lord spoke only of his daughter. At about six o'clock he was sitting in the garden, and Mary brought him a letter just delivered; he looked at the envelope with a smile.

'To tell us the train she's coming by, no doubt.'

Mary waited. When Mr. Lord had read the brief note, his face darkened, first with disappointment, then with anger.

'Here, look at it,' he said harshly. 'What else was to be expected?'

'Dearest Father,' wrote Nancy, 'I am sorry that our return must be put off; we hope to get back on Friday evening. Of course this will make no difference to you.—With best love, dear father, and hoping I shall find you much better—'

'What does she mean by behaving in this way?' resumed the angry voice, before Mary had read to the end. 'What does she mean by it? Who gave her leave to stay longer? Not a word of explanation. How does she know it will make no difference to me? What does she mean by it?'

'The fine weather has tempted them,' replied Mary. 'I daresay they want to go somewhere.'

'What right has she to make the change at a moment's notice?' vociferated the father, his voice suddenly recovering its old power, his cheeks and neck suffused with red wrath. 'And hopes she will find me better. What does *she* care whether she finds me alive or dead?'

'Oh, don't say that! You wouldn't let her know that you were worse.'

'What does it mean? I hate this deceitful behaviour! She knew before, of course she knew; and she left it to the last moment, so that I couldn't write and prevent her from staying. As if I should have wished to! As if I cared a brass farthing how long she stays, or, for that matter, whether I ever see her again!'

He checked the course of his furious speech, and stood staring at the letter.

'What did you say?' He spoke now in a hoarse undertone. 'You thought they were going somewhere?'

'Last year there used to be steamers that went to places on certain days—'

'Nonsense! She wouldn't alter all their plans for that. It's something I am not to know—of course it is. She's deceitful— like all women.'

He met Mary's eye, suddenly turned upon him. His own fell before it, and without speaking again he went into the house.

In half-an-hour's time his bell rang, and not Mary, but the young servant responded. According to her directions, she knocked at the door, and, without opening it, asked her master's pleasure. Mr. Lord said that he was going out, and would not require a meal till late in the evening.

It was nearly ten o'clock when he returned. Mary, sitting in the front room, rose at his entrance.

'I want nothing,' he said. 'I've been to the Barmbys'.' Voice and movements proved how the effort had taxed him. In sitting down, he trembled; fever was in his eyes, and pain in every line of his countenance.

Mary handed him a letter; it came from Horace, and was an intimation that the young gentleman would not return to-night, but to-morrow. When Mr. Lord had read it, he jerked a contemptuous laugh, and threw the sheet of note-paper across the table.

'There you are. Not much to choose between daughter and son. He's due at business in the morning; but what does that matter? It doesn't suit his lordship to keep time.'

He laughed again, his emphasis on 'lordship' showing that he consciously played with the family name.

110

'But I was a fool to be angry. Let them come when they will.'

For a few minutes he lay back in the chair, gazing at vacancy.

'Has the girl gone to bed?'

'I'll tell her she can go.'

Mary soon returned, and took up the book with which she had been engaged. In a low voice, and as if speaking without much thought, Stephen asked her what she was reading. It was a volume of an old magazine, bought by Mr. Lord many years ago.

'Yes, yes. Nancy laughs at it—calls it old rubbish. These young people are so clever.'

His companion made no remark. Unobserved, he scrutinised her face for a long time, and said at length:

'Don't let *us* fall out, Mary. You're not pleased with me, and I know why. I said all women were deceitful, and you took it too seriously. You ought to know me better. There's something comes on me every now and then, and makes me say the worst I can no matter who it hurts. Could I be such a fool as to think ill of *you*?'

'It did hurt me,' replied the other, still bent over her book. 'But it was only the sound of it. I knew you said more than you meant.'

'I'm a fool, and I've been a fool all my life. Is it likely I should have wise children? When I went off to the Barmbys', I thought of sending Samuel down to Teignmouth, to find out what they were at. But I altered my mind before I got there. What good would it have done? All I *can* do I've done already. I made my will the other day; it's signed and witnessed. I've made it as I told you I should. I'm not much longer for this world, but I've saved the girl from foolishness till she's six-and-twenty. After that she must take care of herself.'

They sat silent whilst the clock on the mantelpiece ticked away a few more minutes. Mr. Lord's features betrayed the working of turbid thought, a stern resentment their prevailing expression. When reverie released him, he again looked at his companion.

'Mary, did you ever ask yourself what sort of woman Nancy's mother may have been?'

The listener started, like one in whom a secret has been surprised. She tried to answer, but after all did not speak.

'I'll tell you,' Stephen pursued. 'Yes, I'll tell you. You must know it. Not a year after the boy's birth, she left me. And I made myself free of her—I divorced her.'

Their eyes just met.

'You needn't think that it cost me any suffering. Not on her account; not because I had lost my wife. I never felt so glad, before or since, as on the day when it was all over, and I found myself a free man again. I suffered only in thinking how I had fooled away some of the best years of my life for a woman who despised me from the first, and was as heartless as the stones of the street. I found her in beggary, or close upon it. I made myself her slave—it's only the worthless women who accept from a man, who expect from him, such slavish worship as she had from me. I gave her clothing; she scarcely thanked me, but I thought myself happy. I gave her a comfortable home, such as she hadn't known for years; for a reward she mocked at my plain tastes and quiet ways—but I thought no ill of it—could see nothing in it but a girlish, lighthearted sort of way that seemed one of her merits. As long as we lived together, she pretended to be an affectionate wife; I should think no one ever matched her in hypocrisy. But the first chance she had—husband, children, home, all flung aside in a moment. Then I saw her in the true light, and understood all at once what a blind fool I had been.'

He breathed quickly and painfully. Mary sat without a movement.

'I thought I had done a great thing in marrying a wife that was born above me. Her father had been a country gentleman; horse-racing and such things had brought him down, and from her twelfth year his daughter lived—I never quite knew how, but on charity of some kind. She grew up without trying to earn her own living; she thought herself too good for that, thought she had a claim to be supported, because as a child she was waited upon by servants. When I asked her once if she couldn't have done something, she stared at me and laughed in my face. For all that she was glad enough to marry a man of my sort—rough and uneducated as I was. She always reminded me of it, though—that I had no education; I believe she thought that she had a perfect right to throw over such a husband, whenever she chose. Afterwards, I saw very well that *her* education didn't amount to much. How could it, when she learnt nothing after she was twelve? She was living with very poor people who came from my part of the country—that's how I met her. The father led some sort of blackguard life in London, but had no money for her, nor yet for his other girl, who went into service, I was told, and perhaps made herself a useful, honest woman. He died in a hospital, and he was buried at my expense—not three months before his daughter went off and left me.'

'You will never tell your children,' said Mary, when there had been a long pause.

'I've often thought it would only be right if I told them. I've often thought, the last year or two, that Nancy ought to know. It might make her think, and do her good.'

'No, no,' returned the other hurriedly. 'Never let her know of it— never. It might do her much harm.'

'You know now, Mary, why I look at the girl so anxiously. She's not like her mother; not much like her in face, and I can't think she's like her in heart. But you know what her faults are as well as I do. Whether I've been right or wrong in giving her a good education, I shall never know. Wrong, I fear—but I've told you all about that.'

'You don't know whether she's alive or not?' asked Mary, when once more it was left to her to break silence.

'What do I care? How should I know?'

'Don't be tempted to tell them—either of them!' said the other earnestly.

'My friend Barmby knows. Whether he's told his son, I can't say; it's twenty years since we spoke about it. If he *did* ever mention it to Samuel, then it might somehow get known to Horace or the girl, when I'm gone.—I won't give up the hope that young Barmby may be her husband. She'll have time to think about it. But if ever she should come to you and ask questions—I mean, if she's been told what happened—you'll set me right in her eyes? You'll tell her what I've told you?'

'I hope it may never—'

'So do I,' Stephen interrupted, his voice husky with fatigue. 'But I count on you to make my girl think rightly of me, if ever there's occasion. I count on you. When I'm dead, I won't have her think that I was to blame for her mother's ill-doing. That's why I've told you. You believe me, don't you?'

And Mary, lifting her eyes, met his look of appeal with more than a friend's confidence.

CHAPTER 2

From chambers in Staple Inn, Lionel Tarrant looked forth upon the laborious world with a dainty enjoyment of his own limitless leisure. The old gables fronting upon Holborn pleased his fancy; he liked to pass under the time-worn archway, and so, at a step, estrange himself from commercial tumult,—to be in the midst of modern life, yet breathe an atmosphere of ancient repose.

He belonged to an informal club of young men who called themselves, facetiously, the Hodiernals. *Vixi hodie*! The motto, suggested by some one or other after a fifth tumbler of whisky punch, might bear more than a single interpretation. Harvey Munden, the one member of this genial brotherhood who lived by the sweat of his brow, proposed as a more suitable title, Les Faineants; that, however, was judged pedantic, not to say offensive. For these sons of the Day would not confess to indolence; each deemed himself, after his own fashion, a pioneer in art, letters, civilisation. They had money of their own, or were supported by some one who could afford that privilege; most of them had, ostensibly, some profession in view; for the present, they contented themselves with living, and the weaker brethren read in their hodiernity an obligation to be 'up to date.'

Tarrant professed himself critical of To-day, apprehensive of To-morrow; he cast a backward eye. None the less, his avowed principle was to savour the passing hour. When night grew mellow, and the god of whisky inspired his soul, he shone in a lyrical egoism which had but slight correspondence with the sincerities of his solitude. His view of woman—the Hodiernals talked much of woman—differed considerably from his thoughts of the individual women with whom he associated; protesting oriental sympathies, he nourished in truth the chivalry appropriate to his years and to his education, and imaged an ideal of female excellence whereof the prime features were moral and intellectual.

He had no money of his own. What could be saved for him from his father's squandered estate—the will established him sole inheritor—went in the costs of a liberal education, his grandmother giving him assurance that he should not go forth into the world penniless. This promise Mrs. Tarrant had kept, though not exactly in the manner her grandson desired. Instead of making him a fixed allowance, the old lady supplied him with funds at uncertain intervals; with the unpleasant result that it was sometimes necessary for him to call to her mind his dependent condition. The cheques he received varied greatly in amount,—from handsome remittances of a hundred pounds or so, down to minim gifts which made the young man feel uncomfortable when he received them. Still, he was provided for, and it could not be long before this dependency came to an end.

He believed in his own abilities. Should it ever be needful, he could turn to journalism, for which, undoubtedly, he had some aptitude. But why do anything at all, in the sense of working for money? Every year he felt less disposed for that kind of exertion, and had a greater relish of his leisurely life. Mrs. Tarrant never rebuked him; indeed she had long since ceased to make inquiry about his professional views.

114

Perhaps she felt it something of a dignity to have a grandson who lived as gentleman at large.

But now, in the latter days of August, the gentleman found himself, in one most important particular, at large no longer. On returning from Teignmouth to Staple Inn he entered his rooms with a confused, disagreeable sense that things were not as they had been, that his freedom had suffered a violation, that he could not sit down among his books with the old self-centred ease, that his prospects were completely, indescribably changed, perchance much for the worse. In brief, Tarrant had gone forth a bachelor, and came back a married man.

Could it be sober fact? Had he in very deed committed so gross an absurdity?

He had purposed no such thing. Miss. Nancy Lord was not by any means the kind of person that entered his thoughts when they turned to marriage. He regarded her as in every respect his inferior. She belonged to the social rank only just above that of wage-earners; her father had a small business in Camberwell; she dressed and talked rather above her station, but so, now-a-days, did every daughter of petty tradesfolk. From the first he had amused himself with her affectation of intellectual superiority. Miss. Lord represented a type; to study her as a sample of the pretentious half-educated class was interesting; this sort of girl was turned out in thousands every year, from so-called High Schools; if they managed to pass some examination or other, their conceit grew boundless. Craftily, he had tested her knowledge; it seemed all sham. She would marry some hapless clerk, and bring him to bankruptcy by the exigencies of her 'refinement.'

So had he thought of Nancy till a few months ago. But in the spring-time, when his emotions blossomed with the blossoming year, he met the girl after a long interval, and saw her with changed eyes. She had something more than prettiness; her looks undeniably improved. It seemed, too, that she bore herself more gracefully, and even talked with, at times, an approximation to the speech of a lady. These admissions signified much in a man of Tarrant's social prejudice—so strong that it exercised an appreciable effect upon his every-day morals. He began to muse about Miss. Lord, and the upshot of his musing was that, having learnt of her departure for Teignmouth, he idly betook himself in the same direction.

But as for marriage, he would as soon have contemplated taking to wife a barmaid. Between Miss. Lord and the young lady who dispenses refreshment there were distinctions, doubtless, but none of the first importance. Then arose the question, in what spirit, with what purpose, did he seek her intimacy? The answer he simply postponed.

And postponed it very late indeed. Until the choice was no longer between making love in idleness, and conscientiously holding aloof; but between acting like a frank blackguard, and making the amends of an honest man.

The girl's fault, to be sure. He had not credited himself with this power of fascination, and certainly not with the violence of passion which recklessly pursues indulgence. Still, the girl's fault; she had behaved—well, as a half-educated girl of her class might be expected to behave. Ignorance she could not plead; that were preposterous. Utter subjugation by first love; that, perhaps; she affirmed it, and possibly with truth; a flattering assumption, at all events. But, all said and done, the issue had been of her own seeking. Why, then, accuse himself of blackguardly conduct, if he had turned a deaf ear to her pleading? Not one word of marriage had previously escaped his lips, nor anything that could imply a promise.

Well, there was the awkward and unaccountable fact that he *felt* himself obliged to marry her; that, when he seemed to be preparing resistance, downright shame rendered it impossible. Her face—her face when she looked at him and spoke! The truth was, that he had not hesitated at all; there was but one course open to him. He gave glances in the other direction; he wished to escape; he reviled himself for his folly; he saw the difficulties and discontents that lay before him; but choice he had none.

Love, in that sense of the word which Tarrant respected, could not be said to influence him. He had uttered the word; yes, of course he had uttered it; as a man will who is goaded by his raging blood. But he was as far as ever from loving Nancy Lord. Her beauty, and a certain growing charm in her companionship, had lured him on; his habitual idleness, and the vagueness of his principles, made him guilty at last of what a moralist would call very deliberate rascality. He himself was inclined to see his behaviour in that light; yet why had Nancy so smoothed the path of temptation?

That *her* love was love indeed, he might take for granted. To a certain point, it excused her. But she seemed so thoroughly able to protect herself; the time of her green girlhood had so long gone by. For explanation, he must fall back again on the circumstances of her origin and training. Perhaps she illustrated a social peril, the outcome of modern follies. Yes, that was how he would look at it. A result of charlatan 'education' operating upon crude character.

Who could say what the girl had been reading, what cheap philosophies had unsettled her mind? Is not a little knowledge a dangerous thing?

Thus far had he progressed in the four and twenty hours which followed his—or Nancy's—conquest. Meanwhile he had visited the office of the registrar, had made his application for a marriage licence, a proceeding which did not tend to soothe him. Later, when he saw Nancy again, he experienced a revival of that humaner mood which accompanied his pledge to marry her, the mood of regret, but also of tenderness, of compassion. A tenderness that did not go very deep, a half-slighting compassion. His character, and the features of the case, at present allowed no more; but he preferred the kindlier attitude.

Of course he preferred it. Was he not essentially good-natured? Would he not, at any ordinary season, go out of his way to do a kindness? Did not his soul revolt against every form of injustice? Whom had he ever injured? For his humanity, no less than for his urbanity, he claimed a noteworthy distinction among young men of the time.

And there lay the pity of it. But for Nancy's self-abandonment, he might have come to love her in good earnest. As it was, the growth of their intimacy had been marked with singular, unanticipated impulses on his side, impulses quite inconsistent with heartless scheming. In the compunctious visitings which interrupted his love-making at least twice, there was more than a revolt of mere honesty, as he recognised during his brief flight to London. Had she exercised but the common prudence of womanhood!

Why, that she did not, might tell both for and against her. Granting that she lacked true dignity, native refinement, might it not have been expected that artfulness would supply their place? Artful fencing would have stamped her of coarse nature. But coarseness she had never betrayed; he had never judged her worse than intellectually shallow. Her self-surrender might, then, indicate a trait worthy of admiration. Her subsequent behaviour undeniably pleaded for respect. She acquainted him with the circumstances of her home life, very modestly, perhaps pathetically. He learnt that her father was not ill to do, heard of her domestic and social troubles, that her mother had been long dead, things weighing in her favour, to be sure.

If only she had loved him less!

It was all over; he was married. In acting honourably, it seemed probable that he had spoilt his life. He must be prepared for anything. Nancy said that she should not, could not, tell her father, yet awhile; but that resolution was of doubtful stability. For his own part, he thought it clearly advisable that the fact should not become known at Champion Hill; but could he believe Nancy's assurance that Miss. Morgan remained in the dark? Upon one catastrophe, others might naturally follow.

Here, Saturday at noon, came a letter of Nancy's writing. A long letter, and by no means a bad one; superior, in fact, to anything he thought she could have written. It moved him somewhat, but would have moved him more, had he not been legally bound to the writer. On Sunday she could not come to see him; but on Monday, early in the afternoon—

Well, there were consolations. A wise man makes the best of the inevitable.

CHAPTER 3

Since his return he had seen no one, and none of his friends knew where he had been. A call from some stray Hodiernal would be very unseasonable this Monday afternoon; but probably they were all enjoying their elegant leisure in regions remote from town. As the hour of Nancy's arrival drew near, he sat trying to compose himself —with indifferent success. At one moment his thoughts found utterance, and he murmured in a strange, bewildered tone—'My wife.' Astonishing words! He laughed at their effect upon him, but unmirthfully. And his next murmur was—'The devil!' A mere ejaculation, betokening his state of mind.

He reached several times for his pipe, and remembered when he had touched it that the lips with which he greeted Nancy ought not to be redolent of tobacco. In outward respect, at all events, he would not fall short.

Just when his nervousness was becoming intolerable, there sounded a knock. The knock he had anticipated—timid, brief. He stepped hastily from the room, and opened. Nancy hardly looked at him, and neither of them spoke till the closing of two doors had assured their privacy.

'Well, you had no difficulty in finding the place?'

'No—none at all.'

They stood apart, and spoke with constraint. Nancy's bosom heaved, as though she had been hastening overmuch; her face was deeply coloured; her eyes had an unwonted appearance, resembling those of a night-watcher at weary dawn. She cast quick glances about the room, but with the diffidence of an intruder. Her attitude was marked by the same characteristic; she seemed to shrink, to be ashamed.

'Come and sit down,' said Tarrant cheerfully, as he wheeled a chair.

She obeyed him, and he, stooping beside her, offered his lips. Nancy kissed him, closing her eyes for the moment, then dropping them again.

'It seems a long time, Nancy—doesn't it?'

'Yes—a very long time.'

'You couldn't come on Sunday?'

'I found my father very ill. I didn't like to leave home till to-day.'

'Your father ill?—You said nothing of it in your letter.'

118

'No—I didn't like to—with the other things.'

A singular delicacy this; Tarrant understood it, and looked at her thoughtfully. Again she was examining the room with hurried glance; upon him her eyes did not turn. He asked questions about Mr. Lord. Nancy could not explain the nature of his illness; he had spoken of gout, but she feared it must be something worse; the change in him since she went away was incredible and most alarming. This she said in short, quick sentences, her voice low. Tarrant thought to himself that in her too, a very short time had made a very notable change; he tried to read its significance, but could reach no certainty.

'I'm sorry to hear all this—very sorry. You must tell me more about your father. Take off your hat, dear, and your gloves.'

Her gloves she removed first, and laid them on her lap; Tarrant took them away. Then her hat; this too he placed on the table. Having done so, he softly touched the plaits of her hair. And, for the first time, Nancy looked up at him.

'Are you glad to see me?' she asked, in a voice that seemed subdued by doubt of the answer.

'I am—very glad.'

His hand fell to her shoulder. With a quick movement, a stifled exclamation, the girl rose and flung her arms about him.

'Are you really glad?—Do you really love me?'

'Never doubt it, dear girl.'

'Ah, but I can't help. I have hardly slept at night, in trying to get rid of the doubt. When you opened the door, I felt you didn't welcome me. Don't you think of me as a burden? I can't help wondering why I am here.'

He took hold of her left hand, and looked at it, then said playfully:

'Of course you wonder. What business has a wife to come and see her husband without the ring on her finger?'

Nancy turned from him, opened the front of her dress, unknotted a string of silk, and showed her finger bright with the golden circlet.

'That's how I must wear it, except when I am with you. I keep touching—to make sure it's there.'

Tarrant kissed her fingers.

'Dear,'—she had her face against him—'make me certain that you love me. Speak to me like you did before. Oh, I never knew in my life what it was to feel ashamed!'

'Ashamed? Because you are married, Nancy?'

'Am I really married? That seems impossible. It's like having dreamt that I was married to you. I can hardly remember a thing that happened.'

'The registry at Teignmouth remembers,' he answered with a laugh. 'Those books have a long memory.'

She raised her eyes.

'But wouldn't you undo it if you could?—No, no, I don't mean that. Only that if it had never happened—if we had said good-bye before those last days—wouldn't you have been glad now?'

'Why, that's a difficult question to answer,' he returned gently. 'It all depends on your own feeling.'

For whatever reason, these words so overcame Nancy that she burst into tears. Tarrant, at once more lover-like, soothed and fondled her, and drew her to sit on his knee.

'You're not like your old self, dear girl. Of course, I can understand it. And your father's illness. But you mustn't think of it in this way. I do love you, Nancy. I couldn't unsay a word I said to you—I don't wish anything undone.'

'Make me believe that. I think I should be quite happy then. It's the hateful thought that perhaps you never wanted me for your wife; it *will* come, again and again, and it makes me feel as if I would rather have died.'

'Send such thoughts packing. Tell them your husband wants all your heart and mind for himself.'

'But will you never think ill of me?'

She whispered the words, close-clinging.

'I should be a contemptible sort of brute.'

'No. I ought to have—. If we had spoken of our love to each other, and waited.'

120

'A very proper twelvemonth's engagement,—meetings at five o'clock tea,—fifty thousand love-letters,—and all that kind of thing. Oh, we chose a better way. Our wedding was among the leaves and flowers. You remember the glow of evening sunlight between the red pine and the silver birch? I hope that place may remain as it is all our lives; we will go there—'

'Never! Never ask me to go there. I want to forget—I hope some day I may forget.'

'If you hope so, then I will hope the same.'

'And you love me—with real, husband's love—love that will last?'

'Why should *I* answer all the questions?' He took her face between his hands. What if the wife's love should fail first?'

'You can say that lightly, because you know—'

'What do I know?'

'You know that I am *all* love of you. As long as I am myself, I must love you. It was because I had no will of my own left, because I lived only in the thought of you day and night—'

Their lips met in a long silence.

'I mustn't stay past four o'clock,' were Nancy's next words. 'I don't like to be away long from the house. Father won't ask me anything, but he knows I'm away somewhere, and I'm afraid it makes him angry with me.' She examined the room. 'How comfortable you are here! what a delightful old place to live in!'

'Will you look at the other rooms?'

'Not to-day—when I come again. I must say good-bye very soon— oh, see how the time goes! What a large library you have! You must let me look at all the books, when I have time.'

'Let you? They are yours as much as mine.'

Her face brightened.

'I should like to live here; howl should enjoy it after that hateful Grove Lane! Shall I live here with you some day?'

'There wouldn't be room for two. Why, your dresses would fill the whole place.'

She went and stood before the shelves.

'But how dusty you are! Who cleans for you?'

'No one. A very rickety old woman draws a certain number of shillings each week, on pretence of cleaning.'

'What a shame! She neglects you disgracefully. You shall go away some afternoon, and leave me here with a great pile of dusters.'

'You can do that kind of thing? It never occurred to me to ask you: are you a domestic person?'

She answered with something of the old confident air.

'That was an oversight, wasn't it? After all, how little you know about me!'

'Do you know much more of me?'

Her countenance fell.

'You are going to tell me—everything. How long have you lived here?'

'Two years and a half.'

'And your friends come to see you here? Of course they do. I meant, have you many friends?'

'Friends, no. A good many acquaintances.'

'Men, like yourself?'

'Mostly men, fellows who talk about art and literature.'

'And women?' Nancy faltered, half turning away.

'Oh, magnificent creatures—Greek scholars—mathematicians— all that is most advanced!'

'That's the right answer to a silly question,' said Nancy humbly.

Whereat, Tarrant fixed his gaze upon her.

'I begin to think that—'

He checked himself awkwardly. Nancy insisted on the completion of his thought.

'That of all the women I know, you have the most sense.'

'I had rather hear you say that than have a great fortune.' She blushed with joy. 'Perhaps you will love me some day, as I wish to be loved.'

'How?'

'I'll tell you another time. If it weren't for my father's illness, I think I could go home feeling almost happy. But how am I to know what you are doing?'

'What do you wish me to do?'

'Just tell me how you live. What shall you do now, when I'm gone?'

'Sit disconsolate,'—he came nearer—'thinking you were just a little unkind.'

'No, don't say that.' Nancy was flurried. 'I have told you the real reason. Our housekeeper says that father was disappointed and angry because I put off my return from Teignmouth. He spoke to me very coldly, and I have hardly seen him since. He won't let me wait upon him; and I have thought, since I know how ill he really is, that I must seem heartless. I will come for longer next time.'

To make amends for the reproach he had uttered in spite of himself, Tarrant began to relate in full the events of his ordinary day.

'I get my own breakfast—the only meal I have at home. Look, here's the kitchen, queer old place. And here's the dining-room. Cupboards everywhere, you see; we boast of our cupboards. The green paint is *de rigueur*; duck's egg colour; I've got to like it. That door leads into the bedroom. Well, after breakfast, about eleven o'clock that's to say, I light up—look at my pipe-rack—and read newspapers. Then, if it's fine, I walk about the streets, and see what new follies men are perpetrating. And then—'

He told of his favourite restaurants, of his unfashionable club, of a few houses where, at long intervals, he called or dined, of the Hodiernals, of a dozen other small matters.

'What a life,' sighed the listener, 'compared with mine!'

'We'll remedy that, some day.'

'When?' she asked absently.

'Wait just a little.—You don't wish to tell your father?'

'I daren't tell him. I doubt whether I shall ever dare to tell him face to face.'

'Don't think about it. Leave it to me.'

'I must have letters from you—but how? Perhaps, if you could promise always to send them for the first post—I generally go to the letter-box, and I could do so always—whilst father is ill.'

This was agreed upon. Nancy, whilst they were talking, took her hat from the table; at the same moment, Tarrant's hand moved towards it. Their eyes met, and the hand that would have checked her was drawn back. Quickly, secretly, she drew the ring from her finger, hid it somewhere, and took her gloves.

'Did you come by the back way?' Tarrant asked, when he had bitten his lips for a sulky minute.

'Yes, as you told me.'

He said he would walk with her into Chancery Lane; there could be no risk in it.

'You shall go out first. Any one passing will suppose you had business with the solicitor underneath. I'll overtake you at Southampton Buildings.'

Impatient to be gone, she lingered minute after minute, and broke hurriedly from his restraining arms at last. The second outer door, which Tarrant had closed on her entrance, surprised her by its prison-like massiveness. In the wooden staircase she stopped timidly, but at the exit her eyes turned to an inscription above, which she had just glanced at when arriving: *Surrexit e flammis*, and a date. Nancy had no Latin, but guessed an interpretation from the last word. Through the little court, with its leafy plane-trees and white-worn cobble-stones, she walked with bent head, hearing the roar of Holborn through the front archway, and breathing more freely when she gained the quiet garden at the back of the Inn.

Tarrant's step sounded behind her. Looking up she asked the meaning of the inscription she had seen.

'You don't know Latin? Well, why should you? *Surrexit e flammis*, "It rose again from the flames."'

'I thought it might be something like that. You will be patient with my ignorance?'

A strange word upon Nancy's lips. No mortal ere this had heard her confess to ignorance.

124

'But you know the modern languages?' said Tarrant, smiling.

'Yes. That is, a little French and German—a very little German.'

Tarrant mused, seemingly with no dissatisfaction.

CHAPTER 4

In her brother's looks and speech Nancy detected something mysterious. Undoubtedly he was keeping a secret from her, and there could be just as little doubt that he would not keep it long. Whenever she questioned him about the holiday at Scarborough, he put on a smile unlike any she had ever seen on his face, so profoundly thoughtful was it, so loftily reserved. On the subject of Mrs. Damerel he did not choose to be very communicative; Nancy gathered little more than she had learnt from his letter. But very plainly the young man held himself in higher esteem than hitherto; very plainly he had learnt to think of 'the office' as a burden or degradation, from which he would soon escape. Prompted by her own tormenting conscience, his sister wondered whether Fanny French had anything to do with the mystery; but this seemed improbable. She mentioned Fanny's name one evening.

'Do you see much of her?'

'Not much,' was the dreamy reply. 'When are you going to call?'

'Oh, not at present,' said Nancy.

'You've altered again, then?'

She vouchsafed no answer.

'There's something I think I ought to tell you,' said Horace, speaking as though he were the elder and felt a responsibility. 'People have been talking about you and Mr. Crewe.'

'What!' She flashed into excessive anger. 'Who has been talking?'

'The people over there. Of course I know it's all nonsense. At least'—he raised his eyebrows—'I suppose it is.'

'*I* should suppose so,' said Nancy, with vehement scorn.

Their father's illness imposed a restraint upon trifling conversation. Mary Woodruff, now attending upon Mr. Lord under the doctor's directions, had held grave talk with Nancy. The Barmbys, father and son, called frequently, and went away with gloomy faces. Nancy and her brother were summoned, separately, to the invalid's room at uncertain times, but neither was allowed to perform any service for him; their sympathy, more often than not, excited irritation; the sufferer always seemed desirous of saying more than the few and insignificant words which actually passed his lips, and generally, after a long silence, he gave the young people an abrupt dismissal. With his daughter he spoke at length, in language which awed her by its solemnity; Nancy could only understand him as meaning that his end drew near. He had been reviewing, he said, the course of her life, and trying to forecast her future.

'I give you no more advice; it would only be repeating what I have said hundreds of times. All I can *do* for your good, I have done. You will understand me better if you live a few more years, and I think, in the end, you will be grateful to me.'

Nancy, sitting by the bedside, laid a hand upon her father's and sobbed. She entreated him to believe that even now she understood how wisely he had guided her.

'Tried to, Nancy; tried to, my dear. Guidance isn't for young people now-a-days. Don't let us shirk the truth. I have never been satisfied with you, but I have loved you—'

'And I you, dear father—I have! I have!—I know better now how good your advice was. I wish—far, far more sincerely than you think—that I had kept more control upon myself—thought less of myself in every way—'

Whilst she spoke through her tears, the yellow, wrinkled face upon the pillow, with its sunken eyes and wasted lips, kept sternly motionless.

'If you won't mock at me,' Stephen pursued, 'I will show you an example you would do well to imitate. It is our old servant, now my kindest, truest friend. If I could hope that you will let her be *your* friend, it would help to put my mind at rest. Don't look down upon her,—that's such a poor way of thinking. Of all the women I have known, she is the best. Don't be too proud to learn from her, Nancy. In all these twenty years that she has been in my house, whatever she undertook to do, she did well;—nothing too hard or too humble for her, if she thought it her duty. I know what that means; I myself have been a poor, weak creature, compared with her. Don't be offended because I ask you to take pattern by her. I know her value now better than I ever knew it before. I owe her a debt I can't pay.'

Nancy left the room burdened with strange and distressful thoughts. When she saw Mary she looked at her with new feelings, and spoke to her less familiarly than of wont. Mary was very silent in these days; her face had the dignity of a profound unspoken grief.

To his son, Mr. Lord talked only of practical things, urging sound advice, and refraining, now, from any mention of their differences. Horace, absorbed in preoccupations, had never dreamt that this illness might prove fatal; on finding Nancy in tears, he was astonished.

'Do you think it's dangerous?' he asked.

'I'm afraid he will never get well.'

It was Sunday morning. The young man went apart and pondered. After the midday meal, having heard from Mary that his father was no worse, he left home without remark to any one, and from Camberwell Green took a cab to Trafalgar Square. At the Hotel Metropole he inquired for Mrs. Damerel; her rooms were high up, and he ascended by the lift. Sunk in a deep chair, her feet extended upon a hassock, Mrs. Damerel was amusing herself with a comic paper; she rose briskly, though with the effort of a person who is no longer slim.

'Here I am, you see!—up in the clouds. Now, *did* you get my letter?'

'No letter, but a telegram.'

'There, I thought so. Isn't that just like me? As soon as I had sent out the letter to post, I said to myself that I had written the wrong address. What address it *was*, I couldn't tell you, to save my life, but I shall see when it comes back from the post-office. I rather suspect it's gone to Gunnersbury; just then I was thinking about somebody at Gunnersbury—or somebody at Hampstead, I can't be sure which. What a good thing I wired!—Oh, now, Horace, I *don't* like that, I don't really!'

The young man looked at her in bewilderment.

'What don't you like?'

'Why, that tie. It won't do at all. Your taste is generally very good, but that tie! I'll choose one for you to-morrow, and let you have it the next time you come. Do you know, I've been thinking that it might be well if you parted your hair in the middle. I don't care for it as a rule; but in your case, with your soft, beautiful hair, I think it would look well. Shall we try? Wait a minute; I'll run for a comb.'

'But suppose some one came—'

'Nobody will come, my dear boy. Hardly any one knows I'm here. I like to get away from people now and then; that's why I've taken refuge in this cock-loft.'

She disappeared, and came back with a comb of tortoise-shell.

'Sit down there. Oh, what hair it is, to be sure! Almost as fine as my own. I think you'll have a delicious moustache.'

Her personal appearance was quite in keeping with this vivacity. Rather short, and inclining—but as yet only inclining—to rotundity of figure, with a peculiarly soft and clear complexion, Mrs. Damerel made a gallant battle against the hostile years. Her bright eye, her moist lips, the admirable smoothness of brow and cheek and throat, bore witness to sound health; as did the rows of teeth, incontestably her own, which she exhibited in her frequent mirth. A handsome woman still, though not of the type that commands a reverent admiration. Her frivolity did not exclude a suggestion of shrewdness, nor yet of capacity for emotion, but it was difficult to imagine wise or elevated thought behind that narrow brow. She was elaborately dressed, with only the most fashionable symbols of widowhood; rings adorned her podgy little hand, and a bracelet her white wrist. Refinement she possessed only in the society-journal sense, but her intonation was that of the idle class, and her grammar did not limp.

'There—let me look. Oh, I think that's an improvement—more *distingue*. And now tell me the news. How is your father?'

'Very bad, I'm afraid,' said Horace, when he had regarded himself in a mirror with something of doubtfulness. 'Nancy says that she's afraid he won't get well.'

'Oh, you don't say that! Oh, how very sad! But let us hope. I can't think it's so bad as that.'

Horace sat in thought. Mrs. Damerel, her bright eyes subduing their gaiety to a keen reflectiveness, put several questions regarding the invalid, then for a moment meditated.

'Well, we must hope for the best. Let me know to-morrow how he gets on—be sure you let me know. And if anything *should* happen— oh, but that's too sad; we won't talk about it.'

Again she meditated, tapping the floor, and, as it seemed, trying not to smile.

'Don't be downcast, my dear boy. Never meet sorrow half-way—if you knew how useful I have found it to remember that maxim. I have gone through sad, sad things—ah! But now tell me of your own affairs. Have you seen *la petite*?'

'I just saw her the other evening,' he answered uneasily.

'Just? What does that mean, I wonder? Now you don't look anything like so well as when you were at Scarborough. You're worrying; yes, I know you are. It's your nervous constitution, my poor boy. So you just saw her? No more imprudences?'

She examined his face attentively, her lips set with tolerable firmness.

'It's a very difficult position, you know,' said Horace, wriggling in his chair. 'I can't get out of it all at once. And the truth is, I'm not sure that I wish to.'

Mrs. Damerel drew her eyebrows together, and gave a loud tap on the floor.

'Oh, that's weak—that's very weak! After promising me! Now listen; listen seriously.' She raised a finger. 'If it goes on, I have nothing—more—whatever to do with you. It would distress me very, very much; but I can't interest myself in a young man who makes love to a girl so very far beneath him. Be led by me, Horace, and your future will be brilliant. Prefer this young lady of Camberwell, and lose everything.'

Horace leaned forward and drooped his head.

'I don't think you form anything like a right idea of her,' he said.

The other moved impatiently.

'My dear boy, I know her as well as if I'd lived with her for years. Oh, how silly you are! But then you are so young, so very young.'

With the vexation on her face there blended, as she looked at him, a tenderness unmistakably genuine.

'Now, I'll tell you what. I have really no objection to make Fanny's acquaintance. Suppose, after all, you bring her to see me one of these days. Not just yet. You must wait till I am in the mood for it. But before very long.'

Horace looked up with pleasure and gratitude.

'Now, that's really kind of you!'

'Really? And all the rest is only pretended kindness? Silly boy! Some day you will know better. Now, think, Horace; suppose you were so unhappy as to lose your father. Could you, as soon as he was gone, do something that you know would have pained him deeply?'

The pathetic note was a little strained; putting her head aside, Mrs. Damerel looked rather like a sentimental picture in an advertisement. Horace did not reply.

'You surely wouldn't,' pursued the lady, with emphasis, watching him closely; 'you surely wouldn't and couldn't marry this girl as soon as your poor father was in his grave?'

'Oh, of course not.'

Mrs. Damerel seemed relieved, but pursued her questioning.

'You couldn't think of marrying for at least half a year?'

'Fanny wouldn't wish it.'

130

'No, of course not,—well now, I think I must make her acquaintance. But how weak you are, Horace! Oh, those nerves! All finely, delicately organised people, like you, make such blunders in life. Your sense of honour is such a tyrant over you. Now, mind, I don't say for a moment that Fanny isn't fond of you,—how could she help being, my dear boy? But I do insist that she will be very much happier if you let her marry some one of her own class. You, Horace, belong to a social sphere so far, far above her. If I could only impress that upon your modesty. You are made to associate with people of the highest refinement. How deplorable to think that a place in society is waiting for you, and you keep longing for Camberwell!'

The listener's face wavered between pleasure in such flattery and the impulse of resistance.

'Remember, Horace, if anything *should* happen at home, you are your own master. I could introduce you freely to people of wealth and fashion. Of course you could give up the office at once. I shall be taking a house in the West-end, or a flat, at all events. I shall entertain a good deal—and think of your opportunities! My dear boy, I assure you that, with personal advantages such as yours, you might end by marrying an heiress. Nothing more probable! And you can talk of such a girl as Fanny French—for shame!

'I mustn't propose any gaieties just now,' she said, when they had been together for an hour. 'And I shall wait so anxiously for news of your father. If anything *did* happen, what would your sister do, I wonder?'

'I'm sure I don't know—except that she'd get away from Camberwell. Nancy hates it.'

'Who knows? I may be able to be of use to her. But, you say she is such a grave and learned young lady? I am afraid we should bore each other.'

To this, Horace could venture only an uncertain reply. He had not much hope of mutual understanding between his sister and Mrs. Damerel.

At half-past five he was home again, and there followed a cheerless evening. Nancy was in her own room until nine o'clock. She came down for supper, but had no appetite; her eyes showed redness from weeping; Horace could say nothing for her comfort. After the meal, they went up together to the drawing-room, and sat unoccupied.

'If we lose father,' said Nancy, in a dull voice very unlike her ordinary tones, 'we shall have not a single relative left, that is anything to us.'

Her brother kept silence.

'Has Mrs. Damerel,' she continued, 'ever said anything to you about mother's family?'

After hesitation, Horace answered, 'Yes,' and his countenance showed that the affirmative had special meaning. Nancy waited with an inquiring look.

'I haven't told you,' he added, 'because—we have had other things to think about. But Mrs. Damerel is mother's sister, our aunt.'

'How long have you known that?'

'She told me at Scarborough.'

'But why didn't she tell you so at first?'

'That's what I can't understand. She says she was afraid I might mention it; but I don't believe that's the real reason.'

Nancy's questioning elicited all that was to be learnt from her brother, little more than she had heard already; the same story of a disagreement between Mrs. Damerel and their father, of long absences from England, and a revival of interest in her relatives, following upon Mrs. Damerel's widowhood.

'She would be glad to see you, if you liked. But I doubt whether you would get on very well.'

'Why?'

'She doesn't care about the same things that you do. She's a woman of society, you know.'

'But if she's mother's sister. Yes, I should like to know her.' Nancy spoke with increasing earnestness. 'It makes everything quite different. I must see her.'

'Well, as I said, she's quite willing. But you remember that I'm supposed not to have spoken about her at all. I should have to get her to send you a message, or something of that kind. Of course, we have often talked about you.'

'I can't form an idea of her,' said Nancy impatiently. 'Is she good? Is she really kind? Couldn't you get her portrait to show me?'

'I should be afraid to ask, unless she had given me leave to speak to you.'

'She really lives in good society?'

'Haven't I told you the sort of people she knows? She must be very well off; there can't be a doubt of it.'

I don't care so much about that,' said Nancy in a brooding voice. 'It's herself,—— whether she's kind and good and wishes well to us.

The next day there was no change in Mr. Lord's condition; a deep silence possessed the house. In the afternoon Nancy went to pass an hour with Jessica Morgan; on her return she met Samuel Barmby, who was just leaving after a visit to the sick man. Samuel bore himself with portentous gravity, but spoke only a few commonplaces, affecting hope; he bestowed upon Nancy's hand a fervent pressure, and strode away with the air of an undertaker who had called on business.

Two more days of deepening gloom, then a night through which Nancy sat with Mary Woodruff by her father's bed. Mr. Lord was unconscious, but from time to time a syllable or a phrase fell from his lips, meaningless to the watchers. At dawn, Nancy went to her chamber, pallid, exhausted. Mary, whose strength seemed proof against fatigue, moved about the room, preparing for a new day; every few minutes she stood with eyes fixed on the dying face, and the tears she had restrained in Nancy's presence flowed silently.

When the sun made a golden glimmer upon the wall, Mary withdrew, and was absent for a quarter of an hour. On returning, she bent at once over the bed; her eyes were met by a grave, wondering look.

'Do you know me?' she whispered.

The lips moved; she bent lower, but could distinguish no word. He was speaking; the murmur continued; but she gathered no sense.

'You can trust me, I will do all I can.'

He seemed to understand her, and smiled. As the smile faded away, passing into an austere calm, Mary pressed her lips upon his forehead.

CHAPTER 5

After breakfast, and before Arthur Peachey's departure for business, there had been a scene of violent quarrel between him and his wife. It took place in the bed-room, where, as usual save on Sunday morning, Ada consumed her strong tea and heavily buttered toast; the state of her health—she had frequent ailments, more or less genuine, such as afflict the indolent and brainless type of woman— made it necessary for her to repose till a late hour. Peachey did not often lose self-control, though sorely tried; the one occasion that unchained his wrath was when Ada's heedlessness or ill-temper affected the well-being of his child. This morning it had been announced to him that the nurse-girl, Emma, could no longer be tolerated; she was making herself offensive to her mistress, had spoken insolently, disobeyed orders, and worst of all, defended herself by alleging orders from Mr. Peachey. Hence the outbreak of strife, signalled by furious shrill voices, audible to Beatrice and Fanny as they sat in the room beneath.

Ada came down at half-past ten, and found Beatrice writing letters. She announced what any who did not know her would have taken for a final resolve.

'I'm going—I won't put up with that beast any longer. I shall go and live at Brighton.'

Her sister paid not the slightest heed; she was intent upon a business letter of much moment.

'Do you hear what I say? I'm going by the first train this afternoon.'

'All right,' remarked Beatrice placidly. 'Don't interrupt me just now.

The result of this was fury directed against Beatrice, who found herself accused of every domestic vice compatible with her position. She was a sordid creature, living at other people's expense,—a selfish, scheming, envious wretch—

'If I were your husband,' remarked the other without looking up, 'I should long since have turned you into the street—if I hadn't broken your neck first.'

Exercise in quarrel only made Ada's voice the clearer and more shrill. It rose now to the highest points of a not inconsiderable compass. But Beatrice continued to write, and by resolute silence put a limit to her sister's railing. A pause had just come about, when the door was thrown open, and in rushed Fanny, hatted and gloved from a walk.

'He's dead!' she said excitedly. 'He's dead!'

Beatrice turned with a look of interest. 'Who? Mr. Lord?'

134

'Yes. The blinds are all down. He must have died in the night.'

Her cheeks glowed and her eyes sparkled, as though she had brought the most exhilarating news.

'What do I care?' said Mrs. Peachey, to whom her sister had addressed the last remark.

'Just as much as I care about your affairs, no doubt,' returned Fanny, with genial frankness.

'Don't be in too great a hurry,' remarked Beatrice, who showed the calculating wrinkle at the corner of her eye. 'Because he's dead, that doesn't say that your masher comes in for money.'

'Who'll get it, then?'

'There may be nothing worth speaking of to get, for all we know.'

Beatrice had not as yet gained Fanny's co-operation in the commercial scheme now being elaborated; though of far more amiable nature than Mrs. Peachey, she heartily hoped that the girl might be disappointed in her expectations from Mr. Lord's will. An hour later, she walked along Grove Lane, and saw for herself that Fanny's announcement was accurate; the close-drawn blinds could mean but one thing.

To-day there was little likelihood of learning particulars, but on the morrow Fanny might perchance hear something from Horace Lord. However, the evening brought a note, hand-delivered by some stranger. Horace wrote only a line or two, informing Fanny that his father had died about eight o'clock that morning, and adding: 'Please be at home to-morrow at twelve.'

At twelve next day Fanny received her lover alone in the drawing-room. He entered with the exaggerated solemnity of a very young man who knows for the first time a grave bereavement, and feels the momentary importance it confers upon him. Fanny, trying to regard him without a smile, grimaced; decorous behaviour was at all times impossible to her, for she neither understood its nature nor felt its obligation. In a few minutes she smiled unrestrainedly, and spoke the things that rose to her lips.

'I've been keeping a secret from you,' said Horace, in the low voice which had to express his sorrow,—for he could not preserve a gloomy countenance with Fanny before him. 'But I can tell you now.'

'A secret? And what business had you to keep secrets from me?'

'It's about Mrs. Damerel. When I was at the seaside she told me who she really is. She's my aunt—my mother's sister. Queer, isn't it? Of course that makes everything different. And she's going to ask you to come and see her. It'll have to be put off a little—now; but not very long, I dare say, as she's a relative. You'll have to do your best to please her.'

'I'm sure I shan't put myself out of the way. People must take me as they find me.'

'Now don't talk like that, Fanny. It isn't very kind—just now. I thought you'd be different to-day.'

'All right.—Have you anything else to tell me?'

Horace understood her significant glance, and shook his head.

'I'll let you know everything as soon as I know myself.'

Having learnt the day and hour of Mr. Lord's funeral, Ada and Fanny made a point of walking out to get a glimpse of it. The procession of vehicles in Grove Lane excited their contempt, so far was it from the splendour they had anticipated.

'There you are!' said Ada; 'I shouldn't wonder if it's going to be a jolly good take in for you, after all. If he'd died worth much, they wouldn't have buried him like that.'

Fanny's heart sank. She could conceive no other explanation of a simple burial save lack of means, or resentment in the survivors at the disposition made of his property by the deceased. When, on the morrow, Horace told her that his father had strictly charged Mr Barmby to have him buried in the simplest mode compatible with decency, she put it down to the old man's excessive meanness.

On this occasion she learnt the contents of Mr. Lord's will, and having learnt them, got rid of Horace as soon as possible that she might astonish her sisters with the report.

In the afternoon of that day, Beatrice had an appointment with Luckworth Crewe. She was to meet him at the office he had just taken in Farringdon Street, whence they would repair to a solicitor's in the same neighbourhood, for the discussion of legal business connected with Miss. French's enterprise. She climbed the staircase of a big building, and was directed to the right door by the sound of Crewe's voice, loudly and jocularly discoursing. He stood with two men in the open doorway, and at the sight of Beatrice waved a hand to her.

'Take your hook, you fellows; I have an engagement.' The men, glancing at Miss. French facetiously, went their way. 'How do, old chum? It's all in a mess yet; hold your skirts together. Come along this way.'

Through glue-pots and shavings and an overpowering smell of paint, Beatrice followed to inspect the premises, which consisted of three rooms; one, very much the smallest, about ten feet square. Three workmen were busy, and one, fitting up shelves, whistled a melody with ear-piercing shrillness.

'Stop that damned noise!' shouted Crewe. 'I've told you once already. Try it on again, my lad, and I'll drop you down the well of the staircase—you've too much breath, you have.'

The other workmen laughed. It was evident that Crewe had made friends with them all.

'Won't be bad, when we get the decks cleared,' he remarked to Beatrice. 'Plenty of room to make twenty thousand a year or so.'

He checked himself, and asked in a subdued voice, 'Seen anything of the Lords?'

Beatrice nodded with a smile. 'And heard about the will. Have you?'

'No, I haven't. Come into this little room.'

He closed the door behind them, and looked at his companion with curiosity, but without show of eagerness.

'Well, it's a joke,' said Miss. French.

'Is it? How?'

'Fanny's that mad about it! She'd got it into her silly noddle that Horace Lord would drop in for a fortune at once. As it is, he gets nothing at all for two years, except what the Barmbys choose to give him. And if he marries before he's four-and-twenty, he loses everything—every cent!'

Crewe whistled a bar of a street-melody, then burst into laughter.

'That's how the old joker has done them, is it? Quite right too. The lad doesn't know his own mind yet. Let Fanny wait if she really wants him—and if she can keep hold of him. But what are the figures?'

'Nothing startling. Of course I don't know all the ins and outs of it, but Horace Lord will get seven thousand pounds, and a sixth share in the piano business. Old Barmby and his son are trustees. They may let Horace have just what they think fit during the next two years. If he wants money to go into business with, they may advance what they like. But for two years he's simply in their hands, to be looked after. And if he marries—pop goes the weasel!'

'And Miss. Lord?' asked Crewe carelessly.

Beatrice pointed a finger at him.

'You want to know badly, don't you? Well, it's pretty much the same as the other. To begin with, if she marries before the age of six-and-twenty, she gets nothing whatever. If she doesn't marry, there's two hundred a year to live on and to keep up the house.— Oh, I was forgetting; she must not only keep single to twenty-six, but continue to live where she does now, with that old servant of theirs for companion. At six-and-twenty she takes the same as her brother, about seven thousand, and a sixth share in Lord and Barmby.'

Again Crewe whistled.

'That's about three years still to live in Grove Lane,' he said thoughtfully. 'Well, the old joker has pinned them, and no mistake. I thought he had more to leave.'

'Of course you did,' remarked Beatrice significantly.

'Look here, old fellow, don't talk to me like that,' he replied good-humouredly, but with a reproof not to be mistaken. 'I thought nothing about it in the way that *you* mean. But it isn't much, after living as he has done. I suppose you don't know how the money lies?'

'I have it all from Fanny, and it's a wonder she remembered as much as she did.'

'Oh, Fanny's pretty smart in L. s. d. But did she say what becomes of the money if either of them break the terms?'

'Goes to a girl's orphanage, somewhere in the old man's country. But there's more than I've accounted for yet. Young Barmby's sisters get legacies—a hundred and fifty apiece. And, last of all, the old servant has an annuity of two hundred. He made her a sort of housekeeper not long ago, H. L. says; thought no end of her.'

'Don't know anything about her,' said Crewe absently. 'I should like to know the business details. What arrangement was made, I wonder, when he took Barmby into partnership?'

'I shouldn't be surprised if he simply gave him a share. Old Barmby and Lord were great chums. Then, you see, Samuel Barmby has a third of his profits to pay over, eventually.'

Beatrice went on to speak of the mysterious Mrs. Damerel, concerning whom she had heard from Fanny. The man of business gave particular ear to this story, and asked many questions. Of a sudden, as if dismissing matters which hardly concerned him, he said mirthfully:

'You've heard about the row at Lillie Bridge yesterday?'

'I saw something about it in the paper.'

'Well, I was there. Pure chance; haven't been at that kind of place for a year and more. It was a match for the Sprint Championship and a hundred pounds. Timed for six o'clock, but at a quarter past the chaps hadn't come forward. I heard men talking, and guessed there was something wrong; they thought it a put-up job. When it got round that there'd be no race, the excitement broke out, and then—I'd have given something for you to see it! First of all there was a rush for the gate-money; a shilling a piece, you know, we'd all paid. There were a whole lot of North-of-England chaps, fellow countrymen of mine, and I heard some of them begin to send up a roar that sounded dangerous. I was tumbling along with the crowd, quite ready for a scrimmage—I rather enjoy a fight now and then,—and all at once some chap sang out just in front, 'Let's burst up the blooming show!'—only he used a stronger word. And a lot of us yelled hooray, and to it we went. I don't mean I had a hand in the pillaging and smashing,—it wouldn't have done for a man just starting in business to be up at the police-court,—but I looked on and laughed—laughed till I could hardly stand! They set to work on the refreshment place. It was a scene if you like! Fellows knocking off the heads of bottles, and drinking all they could, then pouring the rest on the ground. Glasses and decanters flying right and left,—sandwiches and buns, and I don't know what, pelting about. They splintered all the small wood they could lay their hands on, and set fire to it, and before you could say Jack Robinson the whole place was blazing. The bobbies got it pretty warm—bottles and stones and logs of wood; I saw one poor chap with the side of his face cut clean open. It does one good, a real stirring-up like that; I feel better to-day than for the last month. And the swearing that went on! It's a long time since I heard such downright, hearty, solid swearing. There was one chap I kept near, and he swore for a full hour without stopping, except when he had a bottle at his mouth; he only stopped when he was speechless with liquor.'

'I wish I'd been there,' said Miss. French gaily. 'It must have been no end of fun.'

'A right down good spree. And it wasn't over till about eight o'clock. I stayed till the police had cleared the grounds, and then came home, laughing all the way. It did me good, I tell you!'

'Well, shall we go and see the lawyer?' suggested Beatrice.

'Right you are.—Have a drink first? Nice quiet place round in Fleet Street—glass of wine. No? As you please, old chum.—Think this shop 'll do, don't you? You must come round when it's finished. But I daresay you'll be here many a time—on biz.'

'Oh, I daresay.'

And as they went down the stairs, Crewe laughed again at his recollections of yesterday's sport.

CHAPTER 6

Gusts of an October evening swept about the square of the old Inn, and made rushes at the windows; all the more cosy seemed it here in Tarrant's room, where a big fire, fed into smokeless placidity, purred and crackled. Pipe in mouth, Tarrant lay back in his big chair, gracefully indolent as ever. Opposite him, lamp-light illuminating her face on one side, and fire-gloom on the other, Nancy turned over an illustrated volume, her husband's gift today. Many were the presents he had bestowed upon her, costly some of them, all flattering the recipient by a presumption of taste and intelligence.

She had been here since early in the afternoon, it was now near seven o'clock.

Nancy looked at the pictures, but inattentively, her brows slightly knitted, and her lips often on the point of speech that concerned some other matter. Since the summer holiday she had grown a trifle thinner in face; her beauty was no longer allied with perfect health; a heaviness appeared on her eyelids. Of course she wore the garb of mourning, and its effect was to emphasise the maturing change manifest in her features.

For several minutes there had passed no word; but Tarrant's face, no less than his companion's, signalled discussion in suspense. No unfriendly discussion, yet one that excited emotional activity in both of them. The young man, his pipe-hand falling to his knee, first broke silence.

'I look at it in this way. We ought to regard ourselves as married people living under exceptionally favourable circumstances. One has to bear in mind the brutal fact that man and wife, as a rule, see a great deal too much of each other—thence most of the ills of married life: squabblings, discontents, small or great disgusts, leading often enough to *altri guai* People get to think themselves victims of incompatibility, when they are merely suffering from a foolish custom—the habit of being perpetually together. In fact, it's an immoral custom. What does immorality mean but anything that tends to kill love, to harden hearts? The common practice of man and wife occupying the same room is monstrous, gross; it's astounding that women of any sensitiveness endure it. In fact, their sensitiveness is destroyed. Even an ordinary honeymoon generally ends in quarrel—as it certainly ought to. You and I escape all that. Each of us lives a separate life, with the result that we like each other better as time goes on; I speak for myself, at all events. I look forward to our meetings. I open the door to you with as fresh a feeling of pleasure as when you came first. If we had been ceaselessly together day and night—well, you know the result as well as I do.'

He spoke with indulgent gravity, in the tone of kindness to which his voice was naturally attuned. And Nancy's reply, though it expressed a stronger feeling, struck the same harmonious note.

'I can agree with all that. But it applies to people married in the ordinary way. I was speaking of ourselves, placed as we are.'

'I don't pretend to like the concealment,' said Tarrant. 'For one thing, there's a suggestion of dishonour about it. We've gone over all that—'

'Oh, I don't mean that for a moment. It isn't really dishonourable. My father could never have objected to *you* for my husband. He only wanted to guard me—Mary says so, and he told her everything. He thought me a silly, flighty girl, and was afraid I should be trapped for the sake of my money. I wish—oh how I wish I had had the courage to tell him! He would have seen you, and liked and trusted you—how could he help?'

'It might have been better—but who knows whether he would have seen me with your eyes, Nancy?'

'Yes, yes. But I was going to say——'

She hesitated.

'Say on.'

'There are so many difficulties before us, dear.'

'Not if we continue to think of each other as we do now. Do you mean it might be discovered?'

'Yes, through no fault of ours.'

She hesitated again.

'Quite sure you haven't told anybody?'

'No one.'

Tarrant had a doubt on this point. He strongly suspected that Jessica Morgan knew the truth, but he shrank from pressing Nancy to an avowal of repeated falsehood.

'Then it's very unlikely we should be found out. Who would dream of tracking you here, for instance? And suppose we were seen together in the street or in the country, who would suspect anything more than love-making? and that is not forbidden you.'

'No. But—'

142

'But?'

'But suppose I—'

She rose, crossed to him, seated herself on his knee and put an arm about his neck. Before she had spoken another word, Tarrant understood; the smile on his face lost its spontaneity; a bitter taste seemed to distort his lips.

'You think—you are afraid—'

He heard a monosyllable, and sat silent. This indeed had not entered into his calculations; but why not? He could hardly say; he had ignored the not unimportant detail, as it lurked among possibilities. Perhaps had willingly ignored it, as introducing a complication oppressive to his indolence, to his hodiernal philosophy. And now he arraigned mother-nature, the very divinity whom hitherto he had called upon to justify him. All at once he grew cold to Nancy. The lulled objections to matrimony awoke in him again; again he felt that he had made a fool of himself. Nancy was better than he had thought; he either loved her, or felt something towards her, not easily distinguishable from love. His inferior she remained, but not in the sense he had formerly attributed to the word. Her mind and heart excelled the idle conception he had formed of them. But Nancy was not his wife, as the world understands that relation; merely his mistress, and as a mistress he found her charming, lovable. What she now hinted at, would shatter the situation. Tarrant thought not of the peril to her material prospects; on that score he was indifferent, save in so far as Mr Lord's will helped to maintain their mutual independence. But he feared for his liberty, in the first place, and in the second, abhorred the change that must come over Nancy herself. Nancy a mother—he repelled the image, as though it degraded her.

Delicacy, however, constrained him to a disguise of these emotions. He recognised the human sentiments that should have weighed with him; like a man of cultivated intelligence, he admitted their force, their beauty. None the less, a syllable on Nancy's lips had arrested the current of his feelings, and made him wish again that he had been either more or less a man of honour down at Teignmouth.

'And yet,' he said to himself, 'could I have resisted an appeal for marriage *now*? That comes of being so confoundedly humane. It's a marvel that I didn't find myself married to some sheer demirep long ago.'

Nancy was speaking.

'Will it make you love me less?'

'I have always refused to prophesy about love,' he answered, with forced playfulness.

'But you wouldn't—you wouldn't?'

'We should find ourselves in a very awkward position.'

'I know,' said Nancy hurriedly. 'I can't see what would be done. But you seem colder to me all at once, Lionel. Surely it oughtn't to— to turn you away from me. Perhaps I am mistaken.'

This referred to the alarming possibility, and Tarrant caught at hope. Yes, she might be mistaken; they wouldn't talk about it; he shook it away.

'Let me fill my pipe again. Yes, you can do it for me. That reminds me of a story Harvey Munden tells. A man he knew, a doctor, got married, and there was nothing his wife wouldn't do for him. As he sat with her one evening, smoking, a patient called him into the consulting-room. He had only just lighted a fresh pipe, and laid it down regretfully. 'I'll keep it in for you,' said his wife. And she did so, with dainty and fearful puffs, at long intervals. But the doctor was detained, and when he came back—well, the poor wife had succumbed to her devotion. She never kept in his pipe again.

Nancy tried to laugh. She was in her own chair again, and sat resting her cheek upon her hand, gazing at the fire.

'How is it, Lionel, that no one ever knocks at your door when I'm here.'

'Oh, very simple. I sport the oak—as you know.'

'But don't you think some friend of yours might see a light in your window, and come up?'

'If so, *il respecte la consigne.*'

'No, no; I don't like you when you begin to use French words. I think it reminds me of once when you did it a long time ago,—and I thought you—never mind.'

Tarrant laughed.

'Weren't they strange—those meetings of ours at Champion Hill? What did you think me? Arrogant? Insolent? That is my tendency with strangers, I admit.'

'But I was asking you a question,' said Nancy. 'You mean that no one would knock, if he saw your outer door closed. But what would they think?'

'No doubt—that I was working. I am supposed to be secretly engaged on some immortal composition.'

144

Nancy pondered.

'I do hope no one that knows you will ever see me coming or going.'

'What could it matter? They wouldn't know who you were.'

'But to have such things thought. I should feel it just as if they knew me. I believe I could never come again.'

'Why, what's the matter with you?' Tarrant asked. 'You have tears in your eyes. You're not well to-day.' He checked himself on an unwelcome thought, and proceeded more carelessly. 'Do you suppose for a moment that any friend of mine is ass enough to think with condemnation of a girl who should come to my rooms—-whatever the circumstances? You must get rid of that provincialism—let us call it Camberwellism.'

'They wouldn't think it any harm—even if—?'

'My dear girl, we have outgrown those ancestral prejudices.' Tarrant's humour never quite deserted him, least of all when he echoed the talk of his world; but his listener kept a grave face. 'We have nothing to do with Mrs. Grundy's morals.'

'But you believe in a morality of some kind?' she pursued with diffidence. 'You used the word "immoral" just now.'

Nancy felt no consciousness of the gulf that yawned between herself as she spoke now and the old self which had claimed 'superiority.' Her mind was so completely unsettled that she never tried to connect its present state with its earlier phases. For the most part, her sensations and her reflections were concerned with the crude elements of life; the exceptional moments she spent in a world of vague joys and fears, wherein thought, properly speaking, had no share. Before she could outlive the shock of passion which seemed at once to destroy and to re-create her, she was confronted with the second supreme crisis of woman's existence,—its natural effects complicated with the trials of her peculiar position. Tarrant's reception of her disclosure came as a new disturbance—she felt bewildered and helpless.

He, preoccupied with the anxiety he affected to dismiss, had no inclination to debate ethical problems. For a while he talked jestingly, and at length fell into a mood of silence. Nancy did not stay much longer; they parted without mention of the subject uppermost in their thoughts.

They had no stated times of meeting. Tarrant sent an invitation whenever it pleased him. When the next arrived, in about a week, Nancy made reply that she did not feel well enough to leave home. It was the briefest letter Tarrant had yet received from her, and the least affectionate. He kept silence for a few days, and wrote again. This time Nancy responded as usual, and came.

To the involuntary question in his eyes, hers answered unmistakably. For the first few minutes they said very little to each other. Tarrant was struggling with repulsions and solicitudes of which he felt more than half ashamed; Nancy, reticent for many reasons, not the least of them a resentful pride, which for the moment overcame her fondness, endeavoured to speak of trivial things. They kept apart, and at length the embarrassment of the situation held them both mute.

With a nervous movement, the young man pushed forward the chair on which Nancy usually sat.

'I see that you don't look well.'

Nancy turned to the window. She had unbuttoned her jacket, and taken off her gloves, but went no further in the process of preparing herself for the ordinary stay of some hours.

'Did something in my letter displease you?' inquired her husband.

'You mean—because I didn't come? No; I really didn't feel well enough.'

Tarrant hesitated, but the softer feeling prevailed with him. He helped to remove her jacket, seated her by the fire, and led her to talk.

'So there's no doubt of it?'

Her silence made answer.

'Then of course there's just as little doubt as to what we must do.'

His voice had not a convincing sincerity; he waited for the reply.

'You mean that we can't keep the secret?'

'How is it possible?'

'But you are vexed about it. You don't speak to me as you used to. I don't think you ever will again.'

'It will make no change in *me*,' said Tarrant, with resolute good humour. 'All I want to be sure of is that you are quite prepared for the change in your prospects.'

'Are *you*, dear?'

Her tone and look deprived the inquiry of unpleasant implication. He answered her with a laugh.

146

'You know exactly how I regard it. In one way I should feel relief. Of course I don't like the thought that I shall have caused you to suffer such a loss.'

'I should never have that thought. But are you quite sure about the result to yourself? You remember saying that you couldn't be certain how—'

'How it will be taken at Champion Hill? I was going to tell you the latest report from there. It is very doubtful whether I should ever have to break the news.'

They did not look at each other.

'Everything, in that quarter, must be long since settled. Pray remember that I have no vast expectations. Quite certainly, it won't be a large fortune; very likely not more than your own. But enough to live on, no doubt. I know the value of money—no man better. It would be pleasant enough to play with thousands a year. But I don't grumble so long as I have a competency.'

Nancy meditated, and sighed.

'Oh, it's a pity. Father never meant me to be penniless if I married wisely.'

'I suppose not.'

'Of course not!'

They both meditated.

'It wouldn't be possible—would it?'

'Why,' he answered with a laugh, 'last time you were here you spoke in quite the other way. You were utterly miserable at the thought of living through it alone.'

'Yes—I don't know whether I could—even if—'

'What are you thinking of?'

'I've been talking with Mary,' she replied, after an uneasy pause. 'She has lived with us so long; and since father's death it seems quite natural to make a friend of her. No one could be more devoted to me than she is. I believe there's nothing she wouldn't do. I believe I might trust her with any secret.'

The obvious suggestion demanded thought.

'By-the-bye,' said Tarrant, looking up, 'have you seen your aunt again?'

Nancy's face changed to a cold expression.

'No. And I don't think I shall.'

'Probably you were as little sympathetic to her as she to you.'

'I don't like her,' was the brief reply.

'I've had curious thoughts about that lady,' said Tarrant, smiling. 'The mystery, it seems to me, is by no means solved. You think she really *is* your aunt?'

'Impossible to doubt it. Any one could see her likeness to Horace at once.'

'Ah, you didn't mention that. I had a fear that she might be simply an adventuress, with an eye to your brother's money.'

'She is what she says, I'm sure. But I shall never ask her to come and see me again, and I don't think she'll want to. That would be fortunate if—if we wished—'

Tarrant nodded. At the same moment they heard a sound that startled them.

'That's a knock at the door,' said Nancy, rising as if to escape.

'So it is. Banging with a stick. Let him bang. It must be a stranger, or he'd respect the oak.'

They sat listening. The knock sounded again, loud and prolonged. Tarrant joked about it; but a third time came the summons.

'I may as well go and see who it is.'

'Oh—you won't let any one—'

'Of course not. Sit quietly.'

He went out, closing the room-door behind him, and opened the heavy door which should have ensured his privacy. For five minutes he was absent, then returned with a face portending news.

'It was Vawdrey. He knew my habit of sporting the oak, and wouldn't go away till he had made sure. My grandmother is dying. They telegraphed to Vawdrey in the City, and he came here at once to tell me. I must go. Perhaps I shall be too late.'

'What did he think of your keeping him outside?'

148

'I made some sort of excuse. He's a good-natured fellow; it didn't matter. Stay a little after I'm gone; stay as long as you like, In fact. You can pull to the inner door when you go.'

'What did the telegram say?'

'Mrs. Tarrant sinking. Come immediately.' Of course we expected it. It's raining hard: wait and see if it stops; you must take care of yourself.'

For this, Nancy was not slow in exhibiting her gratitude, which served as mask of the pleasure she could not decently betray. When her husband had hastened off, she sat for a few minutes in thought; then, alone here for the first time, she began to walk about the rooms, and to make herself more intimately acquainted with their contents.

CHAPTER 7

Whilst she was thus occupied, darkness came on. She did not care to light the lamp, so made herself ready, and stole forth.

The rain had ceased. Walking alone at night was a pleasure in which she now indulged herself pretty frequently; at such times Mary Woodruff believed her in the company of Miss. Morgan. The marked sobriety of her demeanour since Mr. Lord's death, and the friendliness, even the affection, she evinced in their common life at home, had set Mary's mind at ease concerning her. No murmur at her father's will had escaped Nancy, in this respect very unlike her brother, who, when grief was forgotten, declared himself ill-used; she seemed perfectly content with the conditions laid upon her, and the sincerity of her mourning could not be doubted. Anxious to conciliate the girl in every honest way, Mary behaved to her with the same external respect as ever, and without a hint of express guardianship. The two were on excellent terms. It seemed likely that before long they would have the house to themselves; already Horace had spoken of taking lodgings in a part of London more congruous with the social aspirations encouraged by his aunt, Mrs. Damerel.

From Chancery Lane she passed into Fleet Street, and sauntered along with observation of shop-windows. She was unspeakably relieved by the events of the afternoon; it would now depend upon her own choice whether she preserved her secret, or declared herself a married woman. Her husband had proved himself generous as well as loving; yes, she repeated to herself, generous and loving; her fears and suspicions had been baseless. Mrs. Tarrant's death freed them from all sordid considerations. A short time, perhaps a day or two, might put an end to irregularities, and enable her to hold up her head once more.

Feeling hungry, she entered a restaurant, and dined. Not carelessly, but with fastidious choice of viands. This was enjoyable; she began to look more like herself of a few months ago.

She would return to Camberwell by train from Ludgate Hill. At the circus, crowding traffic held her back for a minute or two; just as she ran forward, a familiar voice caused her to stop again. She became flurried, lost her head, stood still amid a tumult of omnibuses, cabs and carts; but a hand grasped her by the arm, and led her safely to the opposite pavement.

'What do you mean by shouting at me in the street?' were her first words.

The person addressed was Luckworth Crewe; he had by no means anticipated such wrathful greeting, and stood in confusion.

'I beg your pardon, Miss. Lord. I didn't think I shouted. I only meant to call your attention.'

'Why should you call my attention?' Her cheeks were flushed with anger; she regarded him as though he were a stranger guilty of mere insolence. 'I don't wish to speak to you.'

With astonishment, Crewe found himself alone. But a rebuff such as this, so irrational as he thought it, so entirely out of keeping with Miss. Lord's behaviour, he could by no means accept. Nancy was walking towards the railway-station; he followed. He watched her as she took a ticket, then put himself in her way, with all the humility of countenance he could command.

'I'm so sorry I offended you. It wasn't the right thing to do; I ought to have waited till you were across. I'm a blundering sort of fellow in those things. Do let me beg your pardon, and forgive me.'

She was calmer now, though still tremulous. But for the attack of nervousness, she would have met Crewe with nothing worse than a slight reserve, to mark a change in their relations. Very soon after her father's death he had written a becoming letter, though it smacked of commercial phraseology. To the hope expressed in it, that he might be allowed to call upon her in a few weeks' time, Nancy made no reply. A fortnight later he wrote again, this time reminding her, with modest propriety, of what had occurred between them before she left town in August. Nancy responded, and in grave, friendly language, begged him to think of her no more; he must not base the slightest hope upon anything she might have said. To her surprise, Crewe held his peace, and she saw him now for the first time since their ascent of the Monument.

'I'm ashamed that I lost my temper, Mr. Crewe. I am in a hurry to get home.'

In the booking-office at Ludgate Hill it is not easy to detain, by chivalrous discourse, a lady bent on escaping; but Crewe attempted it. He subdued his voice, spoke rapidly and with emotion, implored that he might be heard for a moment. Would she not permit him to call upon her? He had waited, respecting her seclusion. He asked for nothing whatever but permission to call, as any acquaintance might.

'Have you heard I have opened an office in Farringdon Street? I should so like to tell you all about it—what I'm doing—'

'No one calls to see me,' said Nancy, with firmness. 'I wish to live quite alone. I'm very sorry to seem unfriendly.'

'Is it anything I've done?'

'No—nothing whatever. I assure you, nothing. Let us say good-bye; I can't stop another moment.'

They shook hands and so parted.

'You're back early,' said Mary, when Nancy entered the drawing-room.

'Yes. I left Jessica to her books sooner than usual. The examination draws near.'

Quiet, sad, diligent ever, Mary kept unchanged the old domestic routine. There was the same perfect order, the same wholesome economy, as when she worked under the master's eyes. Nancy had nothing to do but enjoy the admirable care with which she was surrounded; she took it all as a matter of course, never having considered the difference between her own home and those of her acquaintances.

Horace had dined, and was gone out again. They talked of him; Mary said that he had spoken of moving into lodgings very soon.

'Of course he doesn't tell us everything,' said Nancy. 'I feel pretty sure that he's going to leave the office, but how he means to live I don't understand. Perhaps Mrs. Damerel will give him money, or lend it him. I only hope she may break it off between him and Fanny.'

'Hasn't he told you that Fanny is often with Mrs. Damerel?'

'With her?' Nancy exclaimed. 'He never said a word of it to me.'

'He said so to me this evening, and laughed when I looked surprised.'

'Well then, I don't pretend to understand what's going on. We can't do anything.'

About nine o'clock the servant entered the room, bringing Miss. Lord a note, which had just been left by a cab-driver. Nancy, seeing that the address was in Tarrant's hand, opened it with a flutter of joy; such a proceeding as this, openly sending a note by a messenger, could only mean that her husband no longer cared to preserve secrecy. To her astonishment, the envelope contained but a hurried line.

'Not a word yet to any one. Without fail, come to-morrow afternoon, at four.'

With what show of calmness she could command, she looked up at her companion.

'The idea of his sending in this way! It's that Mr. Crewe I've told you of. I met him as I was coming home, and had to speak to him rather sharply to get rid of him. Here comes his apology, foolish man!'

Living in perpetual falsehood, Nancy felt no shame at a fiction such as this. Mere truth-telling had never seemed to her a weighty matter of the law. And she was now grown expert in lies. But Tarrant's message disturbed her gravely. Something unforeseen must have happened—something, perhaps, calamitous. She passed a miserable night.

When she ascended the stairs at Staple Inn, next afternoon, it wanted ten minutes to four. As usual at her coming, the outer door stood open, exposing the door with the knocker. She had just raised her hand, when, with a sound of voices from inside, the door opened, and Tarrant appeared in company with a stranger. Terror-stricken, she stepped back. Tarrant, after a glance, paid no attention to her.

'All right,' he was saying to his friend, 'I shall see you in a day or two. Good-bye, old man.'

The stranger had observed Nancy, but withheld his eyes from her, and quickly vanished down the stairs.

'Who was that?' she whispered.

'I told you four o'clock.'

'It is four.'

'No—ten minutes to at least. It doesn't matter, but if you had been punctual you wouldn't have had a fright.'

Nancy had dropped into a chair, white and shaking. Tarrant's voice, abruptly reproachful, affected her scarcely less than the preceding shock. In the struggle to recover herself she sobbed and choked, and at length burst into tears. Tarrant spoke impatiently.

'What's the matter? Surely you are not so childish'—

She stood up, and went into the bedroom, where she remained for several minutes, returning at length without her jacket, but with her hat still on.

'I couldn't help it; and you shouldn't speak to me in that way. I have felt ill all the morning.'

Looking at her, the young man said to himself, that love was one thing, wedded life another. He could make allowance for Nancy's weakness—but it was beyond his power to summon the old warmth and tenderness. If henceforth he loved her, it must be with husband's love—a phrase which signified to him something as distinct as possible from the ardour he had known; a moral attachment instead of a passionate desire.

And there was another reason for his intolerant mood.

'You hadn't spoken to any one before you got my note?'

'No.—Why are you treating me like this? Are you ashamed that your friend saw me?'

'Ashamed? not at all.'

'Who did he think I was?'

'I don't know. He doesn't know anything about you, at all events. As you may guess, I have something not very pleasant to tell. I didn't mean to be unkind; it was only the surprise at seeing you when I opened the door. I had calculated the exact time. But never mind. You look cold; warm yourself at the fire. You shall drink a glass of wine; it will put your nerves right again.'

'No, I want nothing. Tell me at once what it is.'

But Tarrant quietly brought a bottle and glass from his cupboard. Nancy again refused, pettishly.

'Until you have drunk,' he said, with a smile of self-will, 'I shall tell you nothing.'

'I don't know what I've done to make you like this.'

Her sobs and tears returned. After a moment of impatience, Tarrant went up to her with the glass, laid a hand upon her shoulder, and kissed her.

'Now, come, be reasonable. We have uncommonly serious things to talk about.'

'What did your friend think of me?'

'That you were one of the prettiest girls he had ever been privileged to see, and that I was an enviable fellow to have such a visitor. There now, another sip, and let us have some colour back into your cheeks. There's bad news, Nancy; confoundedly bad news, dear girl. My grandmother was dead when I got there. Well, the foolish old woman has been muddling her affairs for a long time, speculating here and there without taking any one's advice, and so on; and the result is that she leaves nothing at all.'

Nancy was mute.

'Less than nothing, indeed. She owed a few hundreds that she had no means of paying. The joke of the thing is, that she has left an elaborate will, with legacies to half-a-dozen people, myself first of all. If she had been so good as to die two years ago, I should have come in for a thousand a year or so. No one suspected what was going on; she never allowed Vawdrey, the one man who could have been useful to her, to have an inkling of the affair. An advertising broker got her in his clutches.

154

Vawdrey's lawyer has been going through her papers, and finds everything quite intelligible. The money has gone in lumps, good after bad. Swindling, of course, but perfectly legal swindling, nothing to be done about it. A minute or two before her death she gasped out some words of revelation to the nurse, enough to set Vawdrey on the track, when he was told.'

Still the listener said nothing.

'Well, I had a talk with Vawdrey. He's a blackguard, but not a bad fellow. Wished he could help me, but didn't quite see how, unless I would go into business. However, he had a suggestion to make.'

For Nancy, the pause was charged with apprehensions. She seemed to discover in her husband's face a purpose which he knew would excite her resistance.

'He and I have often talked about my friend Sutherland, in the Bahamas, and Vawdrey has an idea that there'll be a profitable opening in that quarter, before long. Sutherland has written to me lately that he thinks of bestirring himself in the projects I've told you about; he has got the old man's consent to borrow money on the property. Now Vawdrey, naturally enough, would like Sutherland to join him in starting a company; the thoughts of such men run only on companies. So he offers, if I will go out to the Bahamas for a month or two, and look about me, and put myself in a position to make some kind of report—he offers to pay my expenses. Of course if the idea came to anything, and a company got floated, I should have shares.'

Again he paused. The listener had wide, miserable eyes.

'Well, I told him at once that I would accept the proposal. I have no right to refuse. All I possess in the world, at this moment, is about sixty pounds. If I sold all my books and furniture, they might bring another sixty or so. What, then, is to become of me? I must set to work at something, and here's the first work that comes to hand. But,' his voice softened, 'this puts us face to face with a very grave question; doesn't it? Are we to relinquish your money, and be both of us penniless? Or is there any possibility of saving it?'

'How *can* we? How could the secret be kept?'

Voice and countenance joined in utter dismay.

'It doesn't seem to me,' said Tarrant slowly, 'a downright impossibility. It *might* be managed, with the help of your friend Mary, and granting that you yourself have the courage. But'—he made a large gesture—'of course I can't exact any such thing of you. It must seem practicable to you yourself.'

'What are we to do if my money is lost?'

155

'Don't say *we*.' He smiled generously, perhaps too generously. 'A man must support his wife. I shall arrange it somehow, of course, so that *you* have no anxiety. But—'

His voice dropped.

'Lionel!' She sprang up and approached him as he stood by the fireplace. 'You won't leave me, dear? How can you think of going so far away—for months—and leaving me as I am now? Oh, you won't leave me!'

He arched his eyebrows, and smiled gently.

'If that's how you look at it—well, I must stay.'

'You can do something here,' Nancy continued, with rapid pleading. 'You can write for the papers. You always said you could—yes, you did say so. We don't need very much to live upon—at first. I shall be content—'

'A moment. You mean that the money must be abandoned.'

She had meant it, but under his look her confused thoughts took a new direction.

'No. We needn't lose it. Only stay near me, and I will keep the secret, through everything. You will only need, then, just to support yourself, and that is so easy. I will tell Mary how it is. She can be trusted, I am sure she can. She would do anything for me. She knows that father was not thinking of a man such as you. It would be cruelly wrong if I lost everything. I will tell her, and she will help me. Scarcely any one comes to the house, as it is; and I will pretend to have bad health, and shut myself up. And then, when the time comes, Mary will go away with me, and—and the child shall be taken care of by some people we can trust to be kind to it. Horace is going to live in lodgings; and Mrs. Damerel, I am sure, won't come to see me again; and I can get rid of other people. The Barmbys shall think I am sulking about the will; I'm sure they think already that I dislike them because of it. Let them think it; I will refuse, presently, to see them at all. It's only a few months. If I tell people I'm not well, nobody will feel surprised if I go away for a month or two—now—soon. Mary would go with me, of course. I might go for December and January. Father didn't mean I was never to have change of air. Then there would be February and March at home. And then I might go away again till near the end of May. I'm sure we can manage it.'

She stopped, breathless. Tarrant, who had listened with averted face, turned and spoke judicially.

'There's one thing you're forgetting, Nancy. Do you propose that we shall never acknowledge the child? Remember that even if you were bold enough, after our

156

second marriage, to acknowledge it in the face of scandal—that wouldn't be safe. Any one, if suspicion is aroused, can find out when we were actually married.'

'We can't think of that. The child may not live.'

Tarrant moved, and the movement startled Nancy. It meant that she had pained him, perhaps made him think of her with repugnance.

'I hardly know what I am saying. You know I don't wish that. But all I can think of now is to keep you near me. I can't bear to be separated from you. I love you so much more than you love me.'

'Let me just tell you what I had in mind, Nancy. Supposing the secret can be kept, we must eventually live abroad, that is to say, if our child is not to grow up a stranger to us, which neither you nor I could wish. Now, at Nassau, the capital of the Bahamas, a lot of Americans always spend the winter. If I made acquaintances among them, it might be a very useful step, it would be preparing for the future.'

To Nancy this sounded far from convincing. She argued against it in a perfectly natural way, and as any one else would have done who knew Tarrant. More than once he had declared to her that he would rather die than drag out his life in one of the new countries, that he could not breathe in an atmosphere of commercialism unrelieved by historic associations. Nancy urged that it would be better to make a home on the continent, whither they could go, at any moment, without a sense of exile.

'So it comes to this,' he interrupted, with an air of resignation. 'I must refuse Vawdrey's offer, and, in doing so, refuse an excellent chance of providing for our future, if—what is by no means improbable the secret should be discovered. I must turn to journalism, or be a clerk. Well and good. My wife decrees it.'

And he began to hum an air, as if the matter were dismissed. There was a long silence.

'How long would you be away?' murmured Nancy, at length.

'I suppose two months at most.'

'November—December.'

'The second of those months you might be spending, as you said, away from London. Down in Devon, perhaps. I can't blame your thoughts about it; but it seems—doesn't it?—a trifle inconsiderate, when you think what may result from my journey.'

'Would you promise me to be back by the end of the year?'

'Not promise, Nancy. But do my best. Letters take fourteen days, that's all. You should hear by every mail.'

'Why not promise?'

'Because I can't foresee how much I may have to do there, and how long it will take me. But you may be very sure that Vawdrey won't pay expenses for longer than he can help. It has occurred to me that I might get materials for some magazine articles. That would help to float me with the editors, you know, if it's necessary.'

Nancy sighed.

'If I consented—if I did my best not to stand in your way— would you love me better when you came back?'

The answer was a pleased laugh.

'Why, there,' he cried, 'you've given in a nutshell the whole duty of a wife who wishes to be loved!'

Nancy tried to laugh with him.

CHAPTER 8

He must be a strong man whom the sudden stare of Penury does not daunt and, in some measure, debase. Tarrant, whatever the possibilities of his nature, had fallen under a spell of indolent security, which declared its power only when he came face to face with the demand for vigorous action. The moment found him a sheer poltroon. 'What! Is it possible that I—*I*—am henceforth penniless? I, to whom the gods were so gracious? I, without warning, flung from sheltered comfort on to the bare road side, where I must either toil or beg?' The thing seemed unintelligible. He had never imagined such ruin of his hopes.

For the first time, he turned anxious thoughts upon the money to which his wife was—would be—might be—entitled. He computed the chances of success in the deception he and she were practising, and knew with shame that he must henceforth be party to a vulgar fraud. Could Nancy be trusted to carry through this elaborate imposition—difficult for the strongest-minded woman? Was it not a certainty that some negligence, or some accident, must disclose her secret? Then had he a wife and child upon his hands, to support even as common men support wife and child, by incessant labour. The prospect chilled him.

If he went to the West Indies, his absence would heighten the probability of Nancy's detection. Yet he desired to escape from her. Not to abandon her; of that thought he was incapable; but to escape the duty—repulsive to his imagination—of encouraging her through the various stages of their fraud. From the other side of the Atlantic he would write affectionate, consolatory letters; face to face with her, could he support the show of tenderness, go through an endless series of emotional interviews, always reminding himself that the end in view was hard cash? Not for love's sake; he loved her less than before she proved herself his wife in earnest. Veritable love—no man knew better—would have impelled him to save himself and her from a degrading position.

Was he committing himself to a criminality which the law would visit? Hardly that—until he entered into possession of money fraudulently obtained.

In miserable night-watchings, he fell to the most sordid calculations. Supposing their plot revealed, would Nancy in fact be left without resources? Surely not,—with her brother, her aunt, her lifelong friends the Barmbys, to take thought for her. She could not suffer extremities. And upon this he blushed relief.

Better to make up his mind that the secret must inevitably out. For the moment, Nancy believed she had resigned herself to his departure, and that she had strength to go through with the long ordeal. But a woman in her situation cannot be depended upon to pursue a consistent course. It is Nature's ordinance that motherhood shall be attained through phases of mental disturbance, which leave the sufferer scarce a pretence of responsibility. Nancy would play strange pranks, by which, assuredly, he would be driven to exasperation if they passed under his eyes. He had no mind to be called father; perhaps even his humanity might fail under the test to which, as a lover, he had given scarce a casual thought. By removing himself, and awaiting the issue afar off, he gained time and opportunity for reflection. Of course his wife could not come to want; that, after all, was the one clearly comforting thought. Her old servant would take good care of her, happen what might.

He must taste of liberty again before sinking into the humdrum of married life. The thought of an ocean voyage, of the new life amid tropic splendours, excited his imagination all the more because it blended with the thought of recovered freedom. Marriage had come upon him with unfair abruptness; for such a change as that, even the ordinary bachelor demands a season preparative; much more, then, the young man who revelled in a philosophic sense of detachment, who wrote his motto 'Vixi hodie!' For marriage he was simply unfit; forced together, he and his wife would soon be mutually detestable. A temporary parting might mature in the hearts of both that affection of which the seed was undeniably planted. With passion they had done; the enduring tenderness of a reasonable love must now unite them, were they to be united at all. And to give such love a chance of growing in him, Tarrant felt that he must lose sight of Nancy until her child was born.

Yes, it had begun already, the trial he dreaded. A letter from Nancy, written and posted only an hour or two after her return home —a long, distracted letter. Would he forgive her for seeming to be an obstacle in the way of what he had proposed? Would he promise her to be faithful? Would he—

He had hardly patience to read it through.

The next evening, on returning home about ten o'clock, he was startled by the sight of Nancy's figure at the foot of his staircase.

'What has happened?'

'Nothing—don't be frightened. But I wanted to see you tonight.'

She gripped his hand.

'How long have you waited? What! Hours? But this is downright madness—such a night as this! Couldn't you put a note for me in the letter-box?'

'Don't—don't speak so! I wanted to see you.' She hurried her words, as if afraid he would refuse to listen. 'I have told Mary— I wanted you to know—'

'Come in. But there's no fire, and you're chilled through. Do you want to be ill? What outrageous silliness!'

Her vitality was indeed at a low ebb, and reproaches made her weep. Tarrant half carried her up to his room, made a light, and fell to his knees at fire-building.

'Let me do it,' Nancy exclaimed. 'Let me wait upon you—'

'If you don't sit still and keep quiet, you'll make me angry in earnest.'

'Then you're not *really* angry with me? I couldn't help it.'

'No, I'm afraid you couldn't,' Tarrant muttered cheerlessly.

'I wanted to tell you that Mary will be our friend. She was speechless with astonishment; at first I didn't know what she would say; she looked at me as she had never looked before—as if she were the mistress, and I the servant. But see what I have come to; all I felt was a dread lest she should think it her duty to cast me off. I haven't a bit of pride left. I could have fallen on my knees before her; I almost did. But she was very good and kind and gentle at last. She'll do everything she can for me.'

The fire in a blaze, Tarrant stood up and regarded it gloomily.

'Well, did she think it possible?' he asked at length.

'Yes, she did. She said it would be very difficult, but the secret might be kept—if I were strong enough. And I *am* strong enough —I *will* be—'

'It doesn't look like it,' said Tarrant, taking the edge off his words with a smile.

'I won't come again in this way. Where have you been tonight?'

'Oh, with friends.'

'Which friends? where?'

He moved impatiently.

'People you don't know, Nancy, and wouldn't care about if you did. Do you know what time it is?'

'Do tell me where you have been. It isn't prying into your affairs. Your friends ought to be mine; at least, I mean, I ought to know their names, and something about them. Suppose I were to tell you I had been spending the evening with friends—'

'My dear girl, I shouldn't ask a question, unless you invited it. However, it's better to tell you that I have been making arrangements to sublet these chambers. I can't afford to keep them, even if there were any use in it. Harvey Munden has introduced me to a man who is likely to relieve me of the burden. I shall warehouse my books and furniture—'

'Then you are going? Really going to leave England?'

He affected astonishment; in truth, nothing now could surprise him.

'But wasn't it all decided between us? Didn't you repeat it in your letter?'

'Yes—I know—but I didn't think it would come so soon.'

'We won't talk about it to-night,' said Tarrant firmly. 'For one thing, there's no time. Come closer to the fire, and get warm through; then I must see you home.'

Nancy hung her head. When, in a few moments, she looked up again, it was to say drily:

'There's no need for you to see me home.'

'I'm going to, at all events.'

'Why? You don't care much about me. I might as well be run over— or anything—'

To this remark no sort of answer was vouchsafed. Nancy sat with her feet on the fender, and Tarrant kept up a great blaze with chips, which sputtered out their moisture before they began to crackle. He and she both seemed intent on this process of combustion.

'Now you're quite warm,' said the young man, as if speaking to a child, 'and it's time to go.'

Nancy rose obediently, gazed at him with dreaming eyes, and suffered herself to be led away by the arm. In Chancery Lane, Tarrant hailed a crawling hansom. When they were driving rapidly southward, Nancy began to question him about the date of his departure; she learnt that he might be gone in less than a week.

'If you could behave quietly and sensibly, we would have an evening to make final arrangements.'

'I can,' she answered, with a calm that surprised him. 'If you go without letting me see you again, I don't know what I might do. But I can be as sensible as you are, if I'm treated fairly.'

He grasped her hand.

'Remember, dear girl, that I have a good deal to worry me just now. Do you suppose I leave you with a light heart?'

162

'If you can persuade me that you care—'

'I care a good deal more than I can easily say. Your position is a very hard one,—harder than mine. But I'm going away to work for your future. I see clearly that it's the best thing I could do. Whether Vawdrey's ideas come to anything or not, I shall make profit out of the journey; I mean to write,—I think it's all I can do to any purpose,—and the material I shall get together over there will give me a start. Don't think I am cold-hearted because I talk in this way; if I broke down, so much the worse for both of us. The time has come for serious work.'

'But we shan't lose my money. I've made up my mind we shan't.'

'It's impossible for you to guard against every danger. We must be prepared for the worst, and that responsibility rests on me. Try and keep your mind at ease; whatever happens, to protect you is my duty, and I shall not fail in it.'

Speaking thus, Tarrant felt the glow of virtue. His words were perfectly sincere, but had reference to a future which his thoughts left comfortably vague.

They were to meet again, probably for the definite parting, three days hence. Tarrant, whose desire for escape had now become incontrollable, used the intervening time in a rush of preparations. He did not debate with himself as to the length of his sojourn in the West Indies; that must be determined by circumstances. Explicitly he had avoided a promise on the subject. What money he possessed he would take with him; it might be to his interest, for Nancy's likewise, to exceed the term of absence provided for in his stipulations with Mr. Vawdrey. But all he deliberately thought of was the getting away. Impatient with Nancy, because of the vagaries resultant from her mental and physical state, he himself exhibited a flagrant triumph of instinct over reason. Once in enjoyment of liberty, he would reflect, like a practical man, on the details of his position, review and recognise his obligations, pay his debt to honour; but liberty first of all. Not his the nature to accept bondage; it demoralised him, made him do and say things of which he was ashamed. Only let him taste the breezes of ocean, and the healthful spirit which is one with rectitude would again inspire him.

Much to his surprise, he neither saw nor heard from Nancy until the hour appointed. She came very punctually. On opening the door to her, with an air of resolute cheerfulness, he saw something in her face that removed the necessity for playing a part. It was the look which had so charmed him in their love-days, the indescribable look, characteristic of Nancy, and of her alone; a gleam between smile and laughter, a glance mingling pride with submission, a silent note of personality which thrilled the senses and touched the heart.

'What now?' he asked, holding her hand and gazing at her. 'Some good news?'

'None that I know of. How hot your room is! Why, you look glad to see me!'

'Was I ever anything else?'

She answered him with a smile.

'It's a very pleasant surprise,' he continued, watching her as she threw off her out-door things. 'I expected a doleful visage, eyes red with weeping.'

'Did you? See how much a man thinks of himself! If you choose to go away, I choose to think as little of you as possible. That's common sense—isn't it?'

'I don't want you to cry about it.'

'Oh yes, you do. It flatters you, and you like flattery. But I've been too obliging. I feel myself again, and there's no more flattery for you—till you come back. I don't ask you when that will be. I ask you nothing at all. I am independent of you.'

Tarrant grew uneasy. He feared that this mood of jest would change only too suddenly, and her collapse into feminine feebleness be the more complete.

'Be as independent as you like,' he said; 'only keep your love for me.'

'Oh, indeed! It's your experience, is it, that the two things can go together? That's the difference between man and woman, I suppose. I shall love you just as little as possible—and how little that will be, perhaps I had better not tell you.'

Still he stood gazing at her.

'You look very beautiful to-day.'

'I know. I saw it for myself before I left home. But we won't talk about that. When do you go?'

'My goods will be warehoused to-morrow, and the next day I go to Liverpool.'

'I'm glad it's so soon. We shan't need to see each other again. Smoke your pipe. I'm going to make a cup of tea.'

'Kiss me first. You forgot when you came in.'

'You get no kiss by ordering it. Beg for it prettily, and we'll see.'

'What does it all mean, Nancy? How can you have altered like this?'

'You prefer me as I was last time?'

164

'Not I, indeed. You make me feel that it will be very hard to leave you. I shall carry away a picture of you quite different from the dreary face that I had got to be afraid of.'

Nancy laughed, and of a sudden held out her hands to him.

'Haven't I thought of that? These were the very words I hoped to hear from you. Now beg for a kiss, and you shall have one.'

Never, perhaps, had they spent together so harmonious an evening. Nancy's tenderness took at length a graver turn, but she remained herself, face and speech untroubled by morbid influence.

'I won't see you again,' she said, 'because I mightn't be able to behave as I can to-day. To-day I am myself; for a long time I have been living I don't know how.'

Tarrant murmured something about her state of health.

'Yes, I know all about that. A strange thought came to me last night. When my father was alive I fretted because I couldn't be independent; I wanted to be quite free, to live as I chose; I looked forward to it as the one thing desirable. Now, I look back on that as a time of liberty. I am in bondage, now—threefold bondage.'

'How threefold?'

'To you, because I love you, and couldn't cease loving you, however I tried. Then, to my father's will, which makes me live in hiding, as if I were a criminal. And then—'

'What other tyranny?'

'You mustn't expect all my love. Before long some one else will rule over me.—- What an exchange I have made! And I was going to be so independent.'

To the listener, her speech seemed to come from a maturer mind than she had hitherto revealed. But he suffered from the thought that this might be merely a pathological phase. In reminding him of her motherhood, she checked the flow of his emotion.

'You'll remember,' Nancy went on, 'that I'm not enjoying myself whilst you are away. I don't want you to be unhappy—only to think of me, and keep in mind what I'm going through. If you do that, you won't be away from me longer than you can help.'

It was said with unforced pathos, and Tarrant's better part made generous reply.

165

'If you find it too hard, dear, write to me, and tell me, and there shall be an end of it.'

'Never. You think me wretchedly weak, but you shall see—'

'It's of your own free will you undertake it?'

'Yes, of my own free will,' she answered firmly. 'I won't come to you penniless. It isn't right I should do so. My father didn't mean that. If I had had the sense and the courage to tell him, all this misery would have been spared. That money is mine by every right, and I won't lose it. Not only for your sake and my own—there is some one else to think of.'

Tarrant gave her a kind look.

'Don't count upon it. Trust to me.'

'I like to hear you say that, but I don't wish you to be put to proof. You are not the kind of man to make money.'

'How do you mean it?'

'As you like to take it. Silly boy, don't I love you just because you are *not* one of the money-making men? If you hadn't a penny in the world, I should love you just the same; and I couldn't love you more if you had millions.'

The change which Tarrant expected did not come. To the end, she was brave and bright, her own best self. She said good-bye without a tear, refused to let him accompany her, and so, even as she had resolved, left in her husband's mind an image beckoning his return.

Part IV: The Veiled Figure

CHAPTER 1

Before his admission to a partnership in Mr. Lord's business, Samuel Barmby lived with his father and two sisters in Coldharbour Lane. Their house was small, old and crumbling for lack of repair; the landlord, his ground-lease having but a year or two to run, looked on with equanimity whilst the building decayed. Under any circumstances, the family must soon have sought a home elsewhere, and Samuel's good fortune enabled them to take a house in Dagmar Road, not far from Grove Lane; a new and most respectable house, with bay windows rising from the half-sunk basement to the second storey. Samuel, notwithstanding his breadth of mind, privately admitted the charm of such an address as 'Dagmar Road,' which looks well at the head of note-paper, and falls with sonority from the lips.

The Barmby sisters, Lucy and Amelia by name, were unpretentious young women, without personal attractions, and soberly educated. They professed a form of Dissent; their reading was in certain religious and semi-religious periodicals, rarely in books; domestic occupations took up most of their time, and they seldom had any engagements. At appointed seasons, a festivity in connection with 'the Chapel' called them forth; it kept them in a flutter for many days, and gave them a headache. In the strictest sense their life was provincial; nominally denizens of London, they dwelt as remote from everything metropolitan as though Camberwell were a village of the Midlands. If they suffered from discontent, no one heard of it; a confession by one or the other that she 'felt dull' excited the sister's surprise, and invariably led to the suggestion of 'a little medicine.'

Their brother they regarded with admiration, tempered by anxiety. 'Great talents,' they knew by report, were often perilous to the possessor, and there was reason to fear that Samuel Bennett Barmby had not resisted all the temptations to which his intellect exposed him. At the age of one-and-twenty he made a startling announcement; 'the Chapel' no longer satisfied the needs of his soul, and he found himself summoned to join the Church of England as by law established. Religious intolerance not being a family characteristic, Mr. Barmby and his daughters, though they looked grave over the young man's apostasy, admitted his freedom in this matter; their respected friend Mr. Lord belonged to the Church, and it could not be thought that so earnest-minded a man walked in the way to perdition. At the same time, Samuel began to exhibit a liking for social pleasures, which were, it might be hoped, innocent, but, as they kept him from home of evenings, gave some ground for uneasiness. He had joined a society of young men who met for intellectual debate, and his success as an orator fostered the spiritual pride already discernible in him. His next step could not be regarded without concern, for he became a member of the National Sunday League. Deceptive name! At first the Miss. Barmbys supposed this was a union for safe-guarding the Sabbath-day; it appalled them to discover that the League had quite an opposite tendency, that its adherents sallied forth together on 'Sunday excursions,' that they received tickets for Sunday admission to picture galleries, and in various other ways offended orthodox feeling. But again the father and sisters gave patient ear to Samuel's elaborate arguments. They became convinced that he had no evil intentions. The elder girl, having caught up a pregnant phrase in some periodical she approved, began to remark that Samuel had 'a modern mind;' and this eventually consoled them.

When it began to be observed that Samuel talked somewhat frequently of Miss. Lord, the implied suggestion caused a tremor of confused feeling. To the Miss. Barmbys, Nancy seemed an enigmatic person; they had tried to like her, but could not; they objected to her assumption of superiority, and were in grave doubt as to her opinions on cardinal points of faith and behaviour. Yet, when it appeared a possibility that their brother might woo Miss. Lord and win her for a wife, the girls did their best to see her in a more favourable light. Not for a moment did it occur to them that Nancy could regard a proposal from Samuel as anything but an honour; to *them* she might behave slightingly, for they were of her own sex, and not clever; but a girl who prided herself on intellectual attainments must of course look up to Samuel Bennett with reverence. In their unworldliness—of a truth they were good, simple creatures—the slight difference of social position seemed unimportant. And with Samuel's elevation to a partnership, even that one shadowy obstacle was removed. Henceforth they would meet Nancy in a conciliatory spirit, and, if she insisted upon it, bow down before her.

Mr. Barmby, senior, whose years drew nigh to three-score, had a great advantage in point of physical health over his old friend Stephen Lord, and his mind enjoyed a placidity which promised him length of days. Since the age of seventeen he had plied a pen in the office of a Life Assurance Company, where his salary, by small and slow increments, had grown at length to two hundred and fifty a year. Himself a small and slow person, he had every reason to be satisfied with this progress, and hoped for no further advance. He was of eminently sober mind, profoundly conscientious, and quite devoid of social ambition,—points of character which explained the long intimacy between him and Stephen Lord. Yet one habit he possessed which foreshadowed the intellectual composition of his son,—he loved to write letters to the newspapers. At very long intervals one of these communications achieved the honour of type, and then Mr Barmby was radiant with modest self-approval. He never signed such letters with his own name, but chose a pseudonym befitting the subject. Thus, if moved to civic indignation by pieces of orange-peel on the pavement, he styled himself 'Urban Rambler;' if anxious to protest against the overcrowding of 'bus or railway-carriage, his signature was 'Otium cum Dignitate.'

When he took a holiday at the seaside, unwonted leisure and novel circumstances prompted him to address local editors at considerable length. The preservation of decency by bathers was then his favourite topic, and he would sign 'Pudor,' or perchance 'Paterfamilias.' His public epistles, if collected, would have made an entertaining and Instructive volume, so admirably did they represent one phase of the popular mind. 'No, sir,'—this sentence frequently occurred,—'it was not thus that our fathers achieved national and civic greatness.' And again: 'All the feelings of an English parent revolt,' &c. Or: 'And now, sir, where is this to end?'—a phrase applied at one moment to the prospects of religion and morality, at another to the multiplication of muffin-bells.

On a Sunday afternoon, Mr. Barmby often read aloud to his daughters, and in general his chosen book was 'Paradise Lost.' These performances had an indescribable solemnity, but it unfortunately happened that, as his fervour increased, the reader became regardless of aspirates. Thus, at the culmination of Satanic impiety, he would give forth with shaking voice—

'Ail, orrors, ail! and thou profoundest Ell, Receive thy new possessor!'

This, though it did not distress the girls, was painful to Samuel Bennett, who had given no little care to the correction of similar lapses in his own speech.

Samuel conceived himself much ahead of his family. Quite uneducated, in any legitimate sense of the word, he had yet learnt that such a thing as education existed, and, by dint of busy perusal of penny popularities, had even become familiar with names and phrases, with modes of thought and of ambition, appertaining to a world for ever closed against him. He spoke of Culture, and imagined himself far on the way to attain it. His mind was packed with the oddest jumble of incongruities; Herbert Spencer jostled with Charles Bradlaugh, Matthew Arnold with Samuel Smiles; in one breath he lauded George Eliot, in the next was enthusiastic over a novel by Mrs. Henry Wood; from puerile facetiae he passed to speculations on the origin of being, and with equally light heart. Save for Pilgrim's Progress and Robinson Crusoe, he had read no English classic; since boyhood, indeed, he had probably read no book at all, for much diet of newspapers rendered him all but incapable of sustained attention. Whatever he seemed to know of serious authors came to him at second or third hand. Avowing his faith in Christianity when with orthodox people, in the society of sceptics he permitted himself to smile at the old faiths,—though he preferred to escape this temptation, the Nonconformist conscience still reigning within him. At home he posed as a broad-minded Anglican, and having somewhere read that Tennyson's 'In Memoriam' represented this attitude, he spoke of the poem as 'one of the books that have made me what I am.'

His circle of acquaintances lay apart from that in which the Lords moved; it consisted for the most part of young men humbly endowed in the matter of income, and making little pretence of social dignity. When others resorted to theatre or public-house, or places not so readily designated, Samuel and his friends met together to discourse on subjects of which they knew somewhat less than nothing. Some of them occasionally held audacious language, especially when topics such as the relations of the sexes invited their wisdom; they had read something somewhere which urged them to cast off the trammels of conventional thought; they 'ventured to say' that in a very few years 'surprising changes of opinion would come about.' These revolutionaries, after startling the more sober of their hearers, went quietly home to mother or landlady, supped on cheese and cocoa, and next day plied the cleric pen with exemplary zeal.

Samuel believed himself in love. That he should conceive matrimonial intentions with regard to Stephen Lord's daughter was but the natural issue of circumstance; from that conception resulted an amorous mood, so much inflamed by Nancy's presence that a young man, whose thoughts did not often transgress decorum, had every reason to suppose himself her victim. When Nancy rejected his formal offer of devotion, the desire to wed her besieged him more vigorously; Samuel was piqued at the tone of lofty trifling in which the girl answered his proposal; for assuredly he esteemed himself no less remarkable a person than he appeared in the eyes of his sisters, and his vanity had been encouraged by Mr. Lord's favour. Of his qualities as a man of business there was no doubt; in one direction or another, he would have struck the road to fortune; why Nancy should regard him with condescension, and make him feel at once that his suit was hopeless, puzzled him for many a day. He tried flattery, affecting to regard her as his superior in things of the intellect, but only with the mortifying result that Miss. Lord accepted his humility as quite natural. Then he held apart in dignified reserve, and found no difficulty in maintaining this attitude until after Mr. Lord's death. Of course he did not let his relatives know of the repulse he had suffered, but, when speaking to them of what had happened on Jubilee night, he made it appear that his estimate of Miss. Lord was undergoing modification. 'She has lost him, all through her flightiness,' said the sisters to each other. They were not sorry, and felt free again to criticise Nancy's ideas of maidenly modesty.

The provisions of Mr. Lord's will could not but trouble the intercourse between Grove Lane and Dagmar Road. Mr. Barmby, senior, undertook with characteristic seriousness the guardianship conferred upon him. He had long interviews with Horace and Nancy, in which he acquitted himself greatly to his own satisfaction. Samuel, equally a trustee, showed his delicacy by holding aloof save when civility dictated a call upon the young people. But his hopes had revived; he was quite willing to wait three years for Nancy, and it seemed to him more than probable that this period of reflection would bring the young lady to a sense of his merits. In the meantime, he would pursue with energy the business now at his sole direction, and make it far more lucrative than when managed on Mr. Lord's old-fashioned principles.

As the weeks went on, it seemed more clear than at first that Nancy resented the authority held by Samuel and his father. They were not welcome at the house in Grove Lane; the Miss. Barmbys called several times without being admitted, though they felt sure that Nancy was at home. Under these circumstances, it became desirable to discover some intermediary who would keep them acquainted with the details of Nancy's life and of her brother's. Such intermediary was at hand, in the person of Miss. Jessica Morgan.

CHAPTER 2

Until of late there had existed a bare acquaintance between Jessica and the Barmby
family. The two or three hours which she perforce spent in Samuel's company on
Jubilee night caused Jessica no little embarrassment; as a natural result, their
meetings after that had a colour of intimacy, and it was not long before Miss.
Morgan and the Miss. Barmbys began to see more of each other. Nancy, on a
motive correspondent with that which actuated her guardians, desired Jessica's
familiarity with the household in Dagmar Road; her friend could thus learn and
communicate sundry facts of importance, else hidden from her in the retirement to
which she was now condemned. How did the Barmbys regard her behaviour to
them? Did they, in their questioning, betray any suspicion fraught with danger?
Jessica, enjoying the possession of a most important secret, which she had
religiously guarded even from her mother, made time to accept the Barmbys'
invitations pretty frequently, and invited the girls to her own home as often as she
could afford a little outlay on cakes and preserves.

It made a salutary distraction in her life. As December drew near, she exhibited
alarming symptoms of over-work, and but for the romance which assured to her an
occasional hour of idleness, she must have collapsed before the date of her
examination. As it was, she frightened one of her pupils, at the end of a long lesson,
by falling to the floor and lying there for ten minutes in unconsciousness. The
warning passed unheeded; day and night she toiled at her insuperable tasks, at times
half frenzied by the strangest lapses of memory, and feeling, the more she laboured,
only the more convinced that at the last moment every fact she had acquired would
ruthlessly desert her.

Her place of abode favoured neither health nor mental tranquillity. It was one of a
row of new houses in a new quarter. A year or two ago the site had been an enclosed
meadow, portion of the land attached to what was once a country mansion; London,
devourer of rural limits, of a sudden made hideous encroachment upon the old estate,
now held by a speculative builder; of many streets to be constructed, three or four
had already come into being, and others were mapped out, in mud and inchoate
masonry, athwart the ravaged field. Great elms, the pride of generations passed
away, fell before the speculative axe, or were left standing in mournful isolation to
please a speculative architect; bits of wayside hedge still shivered in fog and wind,
amid hoardings variegated with placards and scaffolding black against the sky. The
very earth had lost its wholesome odour; trampled into mire, fouled with builders'
refuse and the noisome drift from adjacent streets, it sent forth, under the sooty rain,
a smell of corruption, of all the town's uncleanliness. On this rising locality had
been bestowed the title of 'Park.' Mrs. Morgan was decided in her choice of a
dwelling here by the euphonious address, Merton Avenue, Something-or-other Park.

The old mansion—not very old, and far from beautiful, but stoutly built—stood grim
and desolate, long dismantled, and waiting only to be torn down for the behoof of
speculative dealers in old material. What aforetime was a tree-bordered drive, now
curved between dead stumps, a mere slushy cartway; the stone pillars, which had

marked the entrance, damaged in the rending away of metal with a market value, drooped sideways, ready at a touch to bury themselves in slime.

Through summer months the Morgans had suffered sufficiently from the defects of their house; with the coming on of winter, they found themselves exposed to miseries barely endurable. At the first slight frost, cistern and water-pipes went to ruin; already so damp that unlovely vegetation had cropped up on cellar walls, the edifice was now drenched with torrents of water. Plaster fell from the ceilings; paper peeled away down the staircase; stuccoed portions of the front began to crack and moulder. Not a door that would close as a door should; not a window that would open in the way expected of it; not a fireplace but discharged its smoke into the room, rather than by the approved channel. Everywhere piercing draughts, which often entered by orifices unexplained and unexplainable. From cellar floor to chimney-pot, no square inch of honest or trustworthy workmanship. So thin were the parti-walls that conversation not only might, but must, be distinctly heard from room to room, and from house to house; the Morgans learnt to subdue their voices, lest all they said should become common property of the neighbourhood. For the privilege of occupying such a residence, 'the interior,' said advertisement, 'handsomely decorated,' they were racked with an expenditure which, away in the sweet-scented country, would have housed them amid garden graces and orchard fruitfulness.

At this time, Mr. Morgan had joined an acquaintance in the establishment of a debt-collecting agency; his partner provided the modest capital needful for such an enterprise, and upon himself fell the disagreeable work. A man of mild temper and humane instincts, he spent his day in hunting people who would not or could not pay the money they owed, straining his wits to circumvent the fraudulent, and swooping relentlessly upon the victims of misfortune. The occupation revolted him, but at present he saw no other way of supporting the genteel appearances which— he knew not why—were indispensable to his life. He subsisted like a bird of prey; he was ever on the look out for carrion which the law permitted him to seize. From the point of view forced upon him, society became a mere system of legalised rapine. 'You are in debt; behold the bond. Behold, too, my authority for squeezing out of you the uttermost farthing. You must beg or starve? I deplore it, but I, for my part, have a genteel family to maintain on what I rend from your grip.' He set his forehead against shame; he stooped to the basest chicanery; he exposed himself to insult, to curses, to threats of violence. Sometimes a whole day of inconceivably sordid toil resulted in the pouching of a few pence; sometimes his reward was a substantial sum. He knew himself despised by many of the creditors who employed him. 'Bad debts? For how much will you sell them to me?' And as often as not he took away with his bargain a glance which was equivalent to a kick.

The genteel family knew nothing of these expedients. Mrs. Morgan talked dolorously to her friends of 'commercial depression,' and gave it to be vaguely understood that her husband had suffered great losses because he conducted his affairs in the spirit of a gentleman. Her son was in an office;' her elder daughter was attempting the art of fiction, which did not promise to be lucrative; Jessica, more highly educated, would shortly matriculate at the University of London—a consoling prospect, but involving the payment of a fee that could with difficulty be afforded.

Every friend of the family held it a matter of course that Jessica would succeed in the examination. It seemed probable that she would have a place in Honours.

And, meanwhile, the poor girl herself was repenting of the indiscreet boastfulness with which she had made known her purpose. To come out in an inferior class would be painful enough; how support the possibility of absolute failure? Yet she knew only too well that in certain 'subjects' she was worse than shaky. Her Greek —her Chemistry—her Algebra—

By way of propitiating the stern fates, she began to talk with Lucy and Amelia Barmby in a tone of diffidence. Half a year ago, she would have held her head very high in such company; now the simple goodness of the old-fashioned girls made an appeal to her aching heart, and their homely talk soothed her exhausted brain.

'It's fearfully difficult,' she said to them one evening, as she sat in their parlour. 'And I lose so much time with my pupils. Really, you know, I haven't a fair chance. I was showing Nancy Lord the Algebra paper set last summer, and she confessed she could hardly do a single question.'

'She couldn't?' exclaimed one of the sisters in astonishment. 'But we always thought she was so very clever.'

'So she is—in many things. But she never dreamt of going in for such an examination as this.'

'And do you really know more than she does?'

Jessica smiled with affected modesty.

'Oh, I have studied so much more.'

It was sweet to gain this triumph over her friend, whose progress in the school of life she watched with the jealousy of a girl condemned to sterile passions.

Their talk was interrupted by the entrance of Samuel Barmby, and his elder sister, addressing him without reflection, said wonderingly:

'Sam, did you know that Nancy Lord couldn't pass the examination that Miss. Morgan is going in for?'

Jessica blushed, and hastened to extenuate this crude statement.

'Oh, I didn't say that. Only that she would have to study very hard if she went in for the matriculation.'

'Of course she would,' Samuel assented, largely, as he took his stand before the fireplace and beamed upon the female trio. 'Miss Lord goes in for broad culture; that's quite a different thing from studying for examinations.'

To the hearers, Jessica not excepted, this seemed to argue the spirit of broad culture in Samuel himself. Miss. Morgan pursued nervously:

'Examinations are nothing. I believe very stupid people often do well in them, and clever people often fail.'

Her voice sank on the last word, and she tried to read Barmby's face without meeting his look. Of late, a change had come about in her estimation of Samuel. Formerly she spoke of him with contemptuous amusement, in the tone set by Nancy; since she had become a friend of the family, his sisters' profound respect had influenced her way of thinking, and in secret she was disposed rather to admire 'the Prophet.' He had always struck her as a comely man, and, her education notwithstanding, she never perceived in his remarks that downright imbecility which excited Nancy's derision. On Jubilee night he was anything but a tedious companion; apart from her critical friend, Jessica had listened without impatience to his jests, his instructive facts, his flowing rhetoric. Now-a-days, in her enfeebled state of body and mind, she began to look forward with distinct pleasure to her occasional meetings with Samuel, pleasure which perhaps was enhanced by the air of condescension wherewith he tempered his courtesy. Morbid miseries brought out the frailty of her character. Desiring to be highly esteemed by Mr. Barmby, she found herself no less willing to join his sisters in a chorus of humbly feminine admiration, when he discoursed to them from an altitude. At moments, after gazing upon his cloquent countenance, she was beset by strange impulses which brought blood to her cheek, and made her dread the Miss. Barmbys' scrutiny.

'I look upon examinations,' Samuel was saying, 'as a professional matter. I never went in for them myself, simply because I—I turned my energies in another direction.'

'You *could* have passed them,' remarked one of his sisters, 'easily enough.'

'In Miss. Morgan's presence,'—he stroked his chin, and smiled with delicious fatuity—'I prefer to say nothing on that point.'

'Oh but of course you could, Mr. Barmby,' sounded Jessica's voice, in an unsteady falsetto, whilst her eyes were turned upon the floor. 'You would have thought nothing of this matriculation, which seems to me so dreadful.'

Profoundly flattered, Samuel addressed the girl in his suavest tones.

'I have a theory, Miss. Morgan, that young ladies ought not to undergo these ordeals. The delicacy of their nervous system unfits them for such a strain. I'm sure we shall all feel very glad when you are successfully through the trial. After it, you ought to have a long rest.'

'Oh, you ought—indeed you ought,' assented the girls.

'By the bye,' said Samuel, 'my father has heard from Miss. Lord that she is going away for a month or two. She says her health requires it.'

Jessica sat silent, still with downcast eyes.

'But it's a new thing, isn't it,' remarked Amelia, 'for Miss. Lord to be in bad health?'

'She has suffered a good deal, I'm afraid,' said Jessica, 'since her father's death. The doctor tells her she oughtn't to live in that dull house through the winter.'

'In that case,' Samuel exclaimed, 'of course she must go at once— of course!'

He never spoke of Nancy but with stress of unctuous generosity. This, if his hearers knew what he had suffered at her hands, must tell greatly to his credit; if they were not aware of the circumstances, such a tone would become him as the young lady's hopeful admirer.

'I fear her nerves are affected,' pursued Jessica. 'She can't bear society. So unlike her, isn't it? She goes out very little indeed, —sometimes not for days together. And really she sees nobody. I'm getting quite anxious about her.'

The subject was an awkward one in this house, and it soon gave place to freer conversation. On her way home, though mechanically repeating dates and formulae, Jessica could not resist the tendency of her thoughts, to dwell on Samuel's features and Samuel's eloquence. This was a new danger; she had now little more than a fortnight for her final 'cram,' and any serious distraction meant ruin.

In a day or two she took leave of Nancy, who had chosen for her winter retreat no less remote a spot than Falmouth. Horace having settled himself in lodgings, the house was to be shut up; Mary Woodruff of course went down into Cornwall. Nancy had written a letter to Mr. Barmby, senior, excusing herself for not being able to see him before her departure; it was an amiable letter, but contained frank avowal of pain and discontent at the prospect of her long pupilage. 'Of course I submit to the burden my father chose to lay upon me, and before long, I hope, I shall be able to take things in a better spirit. All I ask of you, dear Mr. Barmby, is to have forbearance with me until I get back my health and feel more cheerful. You know that I could not be in better hands whilst Mary is with me. I shall write frequently, and give you an account of myself. Let me hear sometimes, and show me that you make allowance for my very trying position.'

Jessica heard the letter discussed by its recipient and his family. Samuel spoke with his wonted magnanimity; his father took a liberal view of the matter. And in writing to her friend a few days later, Jessica was able to say: 'I think you may safely stay at Falmouth for the whole winter. You will not be interfered with if you write nicely. I shouldn't wonder if they would let you keep out of their reach *as long as it is necessary*.'

The week of Jessica's ordeal was now at hand. She had had another fainting-fit; her sleep was broken every night with hideous dreams; she ate scarce enough to keep herself alive; a perpetual fever parched her throat and burned at her temples.

On the last day of 'cram,' she sat from morning to night in her comfortless little bedroom, bending over the smoky fire, reading desperately through a pile of note-books. The motive of vanity no longer supported her; gladly she would have crept away into a life of insignificance; but the fee for the examination was paid, and she must face the terrors, the shame, that waited her at Burlington House. No hope of 'passing.' Perhaps at the last moment a stroke of mortal illness would come to her relief.

Not so. She found herself in the ghastly torture-hall, at a desk on which lay sheets of paper, not whiter than her face. Somebody gave her a scroll, stereotyped in imitation of manuscript—the questions to be answered. For a quarter of an hour she could not understand a word. She saw the face of Samuel Barmby, and heard his tones—'The delicacy of a young lady's nervous system unfits her for such a strain.'

That evening she went home with a half-formed intention of poisoning herself.

But the morrow saw her seated again before another scroll of stereotype, still thinking of Samuel Barmby, still hearing his voice. The man was grown hateful to her; he seemed to haunt her brain malignantly, and to paralyse her hand.

Day after day in the room of torture, until all was done. Then upon her long despair followed a wild, unreasoning hope. Though it rained, she walked all the way home, singing, chattering to herself, and reached the house-door without consciousness of the distance she had traversed. Her mother and sister came out into the hall; they had been watching for her.

'I did a good paper to-day—I think I've passed after all—yes, I feel sure I've passed!'

'You look dreadful,' exclaimed Mrs. Morgan. 'And you're wet through—'

'I did a good paper to-day—I feel sure I've passed!'

She sat down to a meal, but could not swallow.

'I feel sure I've passed—I feel sure—'

And she fell from the chair, to all appearances stone-dead.

They took her upstairs, undressed her, sent for the doctor. When he came, she had been lying for half-an-hour conscious, but mute. She looked gravely at him, and said, as if repeating a lesson:

'The delicacy of a young lady's nervous system unfits her for such a strain.'

'Undoubtedly,' repeated the doctor, with equal gravity.

'But,' she added eagerly, 'let Mr. Barmby know at once that I have passed.'

'He shall know at once,' said the doctor.

CHAPTER 3

A lady who lived at Kilburn, and entertained largely in a house not designed for large entertainment, was 'at home' this evening. At eleven o'clock the two drawing-rooms contained as many people as could sit and stand with semblance of comfort; around the hostess, on the landing, pressed a crowd, which grew constantly thicker by affluence from the staircase. In the hall below a 'Hungarian band' discoursed very loud music. Among recent arrivals appeared a troupe of nigger minstrels, engaged to give their exhilarating entertainment—if space could be found for them. Bursts of laughter from the dining-room announced the success of an American joker, who, in return for a substantial cheque, provided amusement in fashionable gatherings. A brilliant scene. The air, which encouraged perspiration, was rich with many odours; voices endeavouring to make themselves audible in colloquy, swelled to a tumultuous volume that vied with the Hungarian clangours.

In a corner of the staircase, squeezed behind two very fat women in very low dresses, stood Horace Lord. His heated countenance wore a look of fretful impatience; he kept rising upon his toes in an endeavour to distinguish faces down in the hall. At length his expression changed, and with eager eyes he began to force a way for himself between the fat women. Not unrewarded with glaring glances, and even with severe remarks, he succeeded in gaining the foot of the staircase, and came within reach of the persons for whom he had been waiting. These were Mrs. Damerel and Fanny French. The elder lady exhibited a toilet of opulence corresponding with her mature charms; the younger, as became a *debutante*, wore graceful white, symbol of her maiden modesty.

'You promised to be early,' said Horace, addressing Mrs. Damerel, but regarding Fanny, who stood in conversation with a florid man of uncertain age.

'Couldn't get here before, my dear boy.'

'Surely you haven't brought that fellow with you?'

'Hush! You mustn't talk in that way. We met at the door. Mrs. Dane knows him. What does it matter?'

Horace moved aside to Fanny. Flushed with excitement, her hair adorned with flowers, she looked very pretty.

'Come along,' he said, gripping her hand more violently than he intended. 'Let us get upstairs.'

'Oh, you hurt me! Don't be so silly.'

The man beside her gave Horace a friendly nod. His name was Mankelow. Horace had met him once or twice of late at Mrs. Damerel's, but did not like him, and felt still less disposed to do so now that Mankelow was acquainted with Fanny French. He suspected that the two were more familiar than Fanny pretended. With little ceremony, he interposed himself between the girl and this possible rival.

'Why didn't you make her come earlier?' he said to Fanny, as they began a slow upward struggle in the rear of Mrs. Damerel.

'It isn't fashionable to come early.'

'Nonsense! Look at the people here already.'

Fanny threw up her chin, and glanced back to see that Mankelow was following. In his vexation, Horace was seized with a cough—a cough several times repeated before he could check it.

'Your cold's no better,' said Fanny. 'You oughtn't to have come out at night.'

'It *is* better,' he replied sharply. 'That's the first time I've coughed to-day. Do you mean you would rather not have found me here?'

'How silly you are! People will hear what you're saying.'

It was Fanny's 'first season,' but not her first 'at home.' Mrs. Damerel seemed to be taking an affectionate interest in her, and had introduced her to several people. Horace, gratified in the beginning, now suffered from jealousy; it tortured him to observe Fanny when she talked with men. That her breeding was defective, mattered nothing in this composite world of pseudo-elegance. Young Lord, who did not lack native intelligence, understood by this time that Mrs. Damerel and her friends were far from belonging to a high order of society; he saw vulgarity rampant in every drawing-room to which he was admitted, and occasionally heard things which startled his suburban prejudices. But Fanny, in her wild enjoyment of these novel splendours, appeared to lose all self-control. She flirted outrageously, and before his very eyes. If he reproached her, she laughed at him; if he threatened to free himself, she returned a look which impudently bade him try. Horace had all her faults by heart, and no longer tried to think that he respected her, or that, if he married such a girl, his life could possibly be a happy one; but she still played upon his passions, and at her beck he followed like a dog.

The hostess, Mrs. Dane, a woman who looked as if she had once been superior to the kind of life she now led, welcomed him with peculiar warmth, and in a quick confidential voice bade him keep near her for a few minutes.

'There's some one I want to introduce you to—some one I'm sure you will like to know.'

180

Obeying her, he soon lost sight of Fanny; but Mrs. Dane continued to talk, at intervals, in such a flattering tone, that his turbid emotions were soothed. He had heard of the Chittles? No? They were very old friends of hers, said Mrs. Dane, and she particularly wanted him to know them. Ah, here they came; mother and daughter. Horace observed them. Mrs. Chittle was a frail, worn, nervous woman, who must once have been comely; her daughter, a girl of two-and-twenty, had a pale, thin face of much sweetness and gentleness. They seemed by no means at home in this company; but Mrs. Chittle, when she conversed, assumed a vivacious air; the daughter, trying to follow her example, strove vainly against an excessive bashfulness, and seldom raised her eyes. Why he should be expected to pay special attention to these people, Horace was at a loss to understand; but Mrs. Chittle attached herself to him, and soon led him into familiar dialogue. He learnt from her that they had lived for two or three years in a very quiet country place; they had come up for the season, but did not know many people. She spoke of her daughter, who stood just out of earshot,—her eyes cast down, on her face a sad fixed smile,—and said that it had been necessary almost to force her into society. 'She loves the country, and is so fond of books; but at her age it's really a shame to live like a nun—don't you think so, Mr. Lord?' Decidedly it was, said Horace. 'I'm doing my best,' pursued Mrs. Chittle, 'to cure her of her shyness. She is really afraid of people—and it's such a pity. She says that the things people talk about don't interest her; but *all* people are not frivolous—are they, Mr. Lord?' Horace hoped not; and presently out of mere good-nature he tried to converse with the young lady in a way that should neither alarm her shyness nor prove distasteful to her intelligence. But with very little success. From time to time the girl glanced at him with strange timidity, yet seemed quite willing to listen as long as he chose to talk.

Fanny, being at a considerable distance from home, was to return to the boarding-house where her chaperon now lived, and have a room there for the night. Horace disliked this arrangement, for the objectionable Mankelow lived in the same house. When he was able to get speech with Fanny, he tried to persuade her to go with him all the way home to Camberwell in a cab. Miss French would not listen to the suggestion.

'Who ever heard of such a thing? It wouldn't be proper.'

'Proper! Oh, I like that!' he replied, with scathing irony.

'You can either like it or not. Mrs. Damerel wouldn't dream of allowing it. I think she's quite as good a judge of propriety as you are.'

They were in a corner of the dining-room. Fanny, having supped much to her satisfaction, had a high colour, and treated her lover with more than usual insolence. Horace had eaten little, but had not refrained from beverages; he was disposed to assert himself.

'It seems to me that we ought to have an understanding. You never do as I wish in a single thing. What do you mean by it?'

'Oh, if you're going to be nasty—'

She made the gesture of a servant-girl who quarrels with her young man at the street-corner.

'I can't stand the kind of treatment you've given me lately,' said Horace, with muffled anger.

'I've told you I shall do just as I like.'

'Very well. That's as much as to say that you care nothing about me. I'm not going to be the slave of a girl who has no sense of honour —not even of decency. If you wish me to speak to you again you must speak first.'

And he left her, Fanny laughing scornfully.

It drew towards one o'clock when, having exhausted the delights of the evening, and being in a decidedly limp condition, Mrs. Damerel and her protegee drove home. Fanny said nothing of what had passed between her and Horace. The elder lady, after keeping silence for half the drive, spoke at length in a tone of indulgent playfulness.

'So you talked a good deal with Mr. Mankelow?'

'Not for long. Now and then. He took me down to supper—the first time.'

'I'm afraid somebody will be a little jealous. I shall get into trouble. I didn't foresee this.'

'Somebody must treat me in a reasonable way,' Fanny answered, with a dry laugh.

'I'm quite sure he will,' said Mrs. Damerel suavely. 'But I feel myself a little responsible, you know. Let me put you on your guard against Mr. Mankelow. I'm afraid he's rather a dangerous man. I have heard rather alarming stories about him. You see he's very rich, and very rich men, if they're rather handsome as well, say and do things —you understand?'

'Is he really very rich?'

'Well, several thousands a year, and a prospect of more when relatives die. I don't mean to say that he is a bad man. He belongs to a very good family, and I believe him perfectly honourable. He would never do any one any harm—or, if he happened to, without meaning it, I'm quite sure he'd repair it in the honourable way.'

'You said he was dangerous—'

182

'To a young lady who is already engaged. Confess that you think him rather good-looking.'

Having inflamed the girl's imagination, Mrs. Damerel presently dropped the subject, and fell again into weary silence.

At noon of the next day she received a call from Horace, who found her over tea and toast in her private sitting-room. The young man looked bilious; he coughed, too, and said that he must have caught fresh cold last night.

'That house was like an oven. I won't go to any more such places. That isn't my idea of enjoying myself.'

Mrs. Damerel examined him with affectionate solicitude, and reflected before speaking.

'Haven't you been living rather fast lately?'

He avoided her eyes.

'Not at all.'

'Quite sure? How much money have you spent this last month?'

'Not much.'

By careful interrogation—the caressing notes of her voice seemed to convey genuine feeling—Mrs. Damerel elicited the fact that he had spent not less than fifty pounds in a few weeks. She looked very grave.

'What would our little Fanny say to this?'

'I don't care what she would say.'

And he unburdened himself of his complaints against the frivolous charmer, Mrs. Damerel listening with a compassionate smile.

'I'm afraid it's all too true, dear boy. But didn't I warn you?'

'You have made her worse. And I more than half believe you have purposely put her in the way of that fellow Mankelow. Now I tell you plainly'—his voice quivered—- 'if I lose her, I'll raise all the money I can and play the very devil.'

'Hush! no naughty words! Let us talk about something else till you are quieter.—- What did you think of Mrs. Chittle?'

'I thought nothing of her, good or bad.'

'Of her daughter, then. Isn't she a sweet, quiet girl? Do you know that she is rich? It's perfectly true. Mrs. Chittle is the widow of a man who made a big fortune out of a kind of imitation velvet. It sold only for a few years, then something else drove it out of the market; but the money was made. I know all about it from Mrs. Dane.'

'It's nothing to me,' said Horace peevishly.

But Mrs. Damerel continued:

'The poor girl has been very unfortunate. In the last year of her father's life they lived in good style, town-house and country-house. And she fell in love with somebody who—who treated her badly; broke it off, in fact, just before the wedding. She had a bad illness, and since then she has lived as her mother told you.'

'How do you know she told me?'

'I—oh, I took it for granted. She said you had had a long talk. You can see, of course, that they're not ordinary people. Didn't Winifred—her name is Winifred— strike you as very refined and lady-like?'

'She hardly spoke half-a-dozen words.'

'That's her nervousness. She has quite got out of the habit of society. But she's very clever, and so good. I want you to see more of her. If she comes here to tea, will you—just to please me— look in for half-an-hour?'

She bent her head aside, wistfully. Horace vouchsafed no reply.

'Dear boy, I know very well what a disappointment you are suffering. Why not be quite open with me? Though I'm only a tiresome old aunt, I feel every bit as anxious for your happiness as if I were your mother—I do indeed, Horace. You believe me, don't you?'

'You have been very kind, in many ways. But you've done harm to Fanny—'

'No harm whatever, Horace—believe me. I have only given her an opportunity of showing what she really is. You see now that she thinks of nothing at all but money and selfish pleasures. Compare her, my dear, with such a girl as Winifred Chittle. I only mean— just to show you the difference between a lady and such a girl as Fanny. She has treated you abominably, my poor boy. And what would she bring you? Not that I wish you to marry for money. I have seen too much of the world to be so foolish, so wicked. But when there *are* sweet, clever, lady-like girls, with large incomes—! And a handsome boy like you! You may blush, but there's no harm in telling the truth. You are far too modest. You don't know how you look in the eyes of an affectionate, thoughtful girl—like Winifred, for instance. It's dreadful to think of you throwing yourself away! My dear, it may sound shocking to you, but Fanny French isn't the sort of girl that men *marry*.'

Horace showed himself startled.

'You are so young,' pursued the mature lady, with an indulgent smile. 'You need the advice of some one who knows the world. In years to come, you will feel very grateful to me. Now don't let us talk any more of that, just now; but tell me something about Nancy. How much longer does she mean to stay in Cornwall?'

He answered absently.

'She talks of another month or two.'

'But what have her guardians to say to that? Why, she has been away for nearly half a year. How can that be called living at the old house?'

'It's no business of mine.'

'Nor of mine, you mean to say. Still, it does seem rather strange. I suppose she is quite to be trusted?'

'Trusted? What harm can come to her? She's keeping out of Sam Barmby's way, that's all. I believe he plagued her to marry him. A nice husband for Nancy!'

'I wish we had taken to each other,' said Mrs. Damerel musingly. 'I think she was a little jealous of the attention I had paid to *you*. But perhaps we shall do better some day. And I'm quite content so long as *you* care a little for me, dear boy. You'll never give me up, will you?'

It was asked with unusual show of feeling; she leaned forward, her eyes fixed tenderly upon the boy's face.

'You would never let a Fanny French come between us, Horace dear?'

'I only wish you hadn't brought her among your friends.'

'Some day you will be glad of what I did. Whatever happens, I am your best friend—the best and truest friend you will ever have. You will know it some day.'

The voice impressed Horace, its emotion was so true. Several times through the day he recalled and thought of it. As yet he had felt nothing like affection for Mrs. Damerel, but before their next meeting an impulse he did not try to account for

185

caused him to write her a letter—simply to assure her that he was not ungrateful for her kindness. The reply that came in a few hours surprised and touched him, for it repeated in yet warmer words all she had spoken. 'Let me be in the place of a mother to you, dear Horace. Think of me as if I were your mother. If I were your mother indeed, I could not love you more.' He mused over this, and received from it a sense of comfort which was quite new to him.

All through the winter he had been living as a gentleman of assured independence. This was managed very simply. Acting on Mrs. Damerel's counsel he insured his life, and straightaway used the policy as security for a loan of five hundred pounds from a friend of Mrs. Damerel's. The insurance itself was not effected without a disagreeable little episode. As a result of the medical examination, Horace learnt, greatly to his surprise, that he would have to pay a premium somewhat higher than the ordinary. Unpleasant questions were asked: Was he quite sure that he knew of no case of consumption in his family? Quite sure, he answered stoutly, and sincerely. Why? Did the doctor think *him* consumptive? Oh dear no, but—a slight constitutional weakness. In fine, the higher premium must be exacted. He paid it with the indifference of his years, but said nothing to Mrs. Damerel.

And thereupon began the sowing of wild oats. At two-and-twenty, after domestic restraint and occupations that he detested, he was let loose upon life. Five hundred pounds seemed to him practically inexhaustible. He did not wish to indulge in great extravagance; merely to see and to taste the world.

Ah, the rapture of those first nights, when he revelled amid the tumult of London, pursuing joy with a pocket full of sovereigns! Theatres, music-halls, restaurants and public-houses—he had seen so little of these things, that they excited him as they do a lad fresh from the country. He drew the line nowhere. Love of a worthy woman tells for chastity even in the young and the sensual; love of a Fanny French merely debauches the mind and inflames the passions. Secure in his paganism, Horace followed where the lures of London beckoned him; he knew not reproach of conscience; shame offered but thin resistance to his boiling blood. By a miracle he had as yet escaped worse damage to health than a severe cold, caught one night after heroic drinking. That laid him by the heels for a time, and the cough still clung to him.

In less than two years he would command seven thousand pounds, and a share in the business now conducted by Samuel Barmby. What need to stint himself whilst he felt able to enjoy life? If Fanny deceived him, were there not, after all, other and better Fannys to be won by his money? For it was a result of this girl's worthlessness that Horace, in most things so ingenuous, had come to regard women with unconscious cynicism. He did not think he could be loved for his own sake, but he believed that, at any time, the show of love, perhaps its ultimate sincerity, might be won by display of cash.

Midway in the month of May he again caught a severe cold, and was confined to the house for nearly three weeks. Mrs. Damerel, who nursed him well and tenderly, proposed that he should go down for change of air to Falmouth. He wrote to Nancy, asking whether she would care to see him. A prompt reply informed him that his sister was on the point of returning to London, so that he had better choose some nearer seaside resort.

He went to Hastings for a few days, but wearied of the place, and came back to his London excitements. Nancy, however, had not yet returned; nor did she until the beginning of July.

CHAPTER 4

This winter saw the establishment of the South London Fashionable Dress Supply Association—the name finally selected by Beatrice French and her advisers. It was an undertaking shrewdly conceived, skilfully planned, and energetically set going. Beatrice knew the public to which her advertisements appealed; she understood exactly the baits that would prove irresistible to its folly and greed. In respect that it was a public of average mortals, it would believe that business might be conducted to the sole advantage of the customer. In respect that it consisted of women, it would give eager attention to a scheme that permitted each customer to spend her money, and yet to have it. In respect that it consisted of ignorant and pretentious women, this public could be counted upon to deceive itself in the service of its own vanity, and maintain against all opposition that the garments obtained on this soothing system were supremely good and fashionable.

On a basis of assumptions such as these, there was every possibility of profitable commerce without any approach to technical fraud.

By means of the familiar 'goose-club,' licensed victuallers make themselves the bankers of people who are too weak-minded to save their own money until they wish to spend it, and who are quite content to receive in ultimate return goods worth something less than half the deposit. By means of the familiar teapot, grocers persuade their customers that an excellent trade can be done by giving away the whole profit on each transaction. Beatrice French, an observant young woman, with a head for figures, had often noted and reflected upon these two egregious illustrations of human absurdity. Her dressmaking enterprise assimilated the features of both, and added novel devices that sprang from her own fruitful brain. The 'Fashion Club,' a wheel within a wheel, was merely the goose-club; strictly a goose-club, for the licensed victualler addresses himself to the male of the species. The larger net, cast for those who lacked money or a spirit of speculation, caught all who, in the realm of grocery, are lured by the teapot. Every sovereign spent with the Association carried a bonus, paid not in cash but in kind. These startling advantages were made known through the medium of hand-bills, leaflets, nicely printed little pamphlets, gorgeously designed placards; the publicity department, being in the hands of Mr. Luckworth Crewe, of Farringdon Street, was most ably and vigorously conducted.

Thanks also to Luckworth Crewe, Beatrice had allied herself with partners, who brought to the affair capital, experience, and activity. Before Christmas—an important point—the scene of operations was ready: a handsome shop, with the new and attractive appendages (so-called 'club-room,' refreshment-bar, &c.) which Crewe and Beatrice had visioned in their prophetic minds. Before the close of the year substantial business had been done, and 1888 opened with exhilarating prospects.

The ineptitude of uneducated English women in all that relates to their attire is a fact that it boots not to enlarge upon. Beatrice French could not be regarded as an exception; for though she recognised monstrosities, she very reasonably distrusted her own taste in the choice of a garment. For her sisters, monstrosities had a distinct charm, and to this class of women belonged all customers of the Association who pretended to think for themselves as to wherewithal they should be clothed. But women in general came to the shop with confessed blankness of mind; beyond the desire to buy something that was modish, and to pay for it in a minus quantity, they knew, felt, thought nothing whatever. Green or violet, cerulean or magenta, all was one to them. In the matter of shape they sought merely a confident assurance from articulate man or woman— themselves being somewhat less articulate than jay or jackdaw— that this or that was 'the feature of the season.' They could not distinguish between a becoming garment and one that called for the consuming fires of Heaven. It is often assumed as a commonplace that women, whatever else they cannot do, may be trusted to make up their minds about habiliments. Nothing more false, as Beatrice French was abundantly aware. A very large proportion of the servant-keeping females in Brixton, Camberwell, and Peckham could not, with any confidence, buy a chemise or a pair of stockings; and when it came to garments visible, they were lost indeed.

Fanny French began to regret that she had not realised her capital, and put it into the Association. Wishing at length to do so, she met with a scornful rebuff. Beatrice would have none of her money, but told her she might use the shop like any other customer, which of course Fanny did.

Mrs. Peachey, meanwhile, kept declaring to both her sisters that they must not expect to live henceforth in De Crespigny Park on the old nominal terms. Beatrice was on the way to wealth; Fanny moved in West End society, under the chaperonage of a rich woman; they ought to be ashamed of themselves for not volunteering handsome recognition of the benefits they had received beneath their sister's roof. But neither Beatrice nor Fanny appeared to see the matter in this light. The truth was, that they both had in view a change of domicile. The elder desired more comfort and more independence than De Crespigny Park could afford her; the younger desired a great many things, and flattered herself that a very simple step would put her in possession of them.

The master of the house no longer took any interest in the fortunes of his sisters-in-law. He would not bid them depart, he would not bid them stay, least of all would he demand money from them. Of money he had no need, and he was the hapless possessor of a characteristic not to be found in any other member of his household — natural delicacy.

Arthur Peachey lived only for his child, the little boy, whose newly prattling tongue made the sole welcome he expected or cared for on his return from a hard day's work. Happily the child had good health, but he never left home without dread of perils that might befall it in his absence. On the mother he counted not at all; a good-tempered cow might with more confidence have been set to watch over the little one's safety. The nurse-girl Emma, retained in spite of her mistress's malice, still seemed to discharge her duties faithfully; but, being mortal, she demanded intervals of leisure from time to time, and at such seasons, as Peachey too well knew, the child was uncared for. Had his heart been resolute as it was tender, he would long ago have carried out a project which haunted him at every moment of anger or fear. In the town of Canterbury lived a sister of his who for several years had been happily wedded, but remained childless. If the worst came to the worst, if his wife compelled him to the breaking-up of a home which was no home, this married sister would gladly take the little boy into her motherly care. He had never dared to propose the step; but Ada might perchance give ready assent to it, even now. For motherhood she had no single qualification but the physical. Before her child's coming into the world, she snarled at the restraints it imposed upon her; at its birth, she clamoured against nature for the pains she had to undergo, and hated her husband because he was the intermediate cause of them. The helpless infant gave her no pleasure, touched no emotion in her heart, save when she saw it in the nurse's care, and received female compliments upon its beauty. She rejected it at night because it broke her sleep; in the day, because she could not handle it without making it cry. When Peachey remonstrated with her, she stared in insolent surprise, and wished that *he* had had to suffer all her hardships of the past year.

Peachey could not be said to have any leisure. On returning from business he was involved forthwith in domestic troubles and broils, which consumed the dreary evening, and invaded even his sleep. Thus it happened that at long intervals he was tempted, instead of going home to dinner, to spend a couple of hours at a certain small eating-house, a resort of his bachelor days, where he could read the newspapers, have a well-cooked chop in quietude, and afterwards, if acquaintances were here, play a game of chess. Of course he had to shield this modest dissipation with a flat falsehood, alleging to his wife that business had kept him late. Thus on an evening of June, when the soft air and the mellow sunlight overcame him with a longing for rest, he despatched a telegram to De Crespigny Park, and strolled quietly about the streets until the hour and his appetite pointed him tablewards. The pity of it was that he could not dismiss anxieties; he loathed the coward falsehood, and thought more of home than of his present freedom. But at least Ada's tongue was silent.

He seated himself in the familiar corner, and turned over illustrated papers, whilst his chop hissed on the grid. Ah, if he were but unmarried, what a life he might make for himself now that the day's labour brought its ample reward! He would have rooms in London, and a still, clean lodging somewhere among the lanes and fields. His ideals expressed the homeliness of the man. On intellect he could not pride himself; his education had been but of the 'commercial' order; he liked to meditate rather than to read; questions of the day concerned him not at all. A weak man, but of clean and kindly instincts. In mercantile life he had succeeded by virtue of his intensely methodical habits—the characteristic which made him suffer so from his wife's indolence, incapacity, and vicious ill-humour.

Before his marriage he had thought of women as domestic beings. A wife was the genius of home. He knew men who thanked their wives for all the prosperity and content that they enjoyed. Others he knew who told quite a different tale, but these surely were sorrowful exceptions. Nowadays he saw the matter in a light of fuller experience. In his rank of life married happiness was a rare thing, and the fault could generally be traced to wives who had no sense of responsibility, no understanding of household duties, no love of simple pleasures, no religion.

Yes, there was the point—no religion. Ada had grown up to regard church-going as a sign of respectability, but without a shadow of religious faith. Her incredible ignorance of the Bible story, of Christian dogmas, often amazed him. Himself a believer, though careless in the practice of forms, he was not disturbed by the modern tendency to look for morals apart from faith; he had not the trouble of reflecting that an ignorant woman is the last creature to be moralised by anything but the Christian code; he saw straight into the fact—that there was no hope of impressing Ada with ideas of goodness, truthfulness, purity, simply because she recognised no moral authority.

For such minds no moral authority—merely as a moral authority— is or can be valid. Such natures are ruled only by superstition— the representative of reasoned faith in nobler beings. Rob them of their superstition, and they perish amid all uncleanliness.

Thou shalt not lie—for God consumes a liar in the flames of hell! Ada Peachey could lend ear to no admonition short of that. And, living when she did, bred as she was, only a John Knox could have impressed her with this menace—to be forgotten when the echoes of his voice had failed.

He did not enjoy his chop this evening. In the game of chess that followed he played idly, with absent thoughts. And before the glow of sunset had died from the calm heaven he set out to walk homeward, anxious, melancholy.

On approaching the house he suffered, as always, from quickened pulse and heart constricted with fear. Until he knew that all was well, he looked like a man who anticipates dread calamity. This evening, on opening the door, he fell back terror-stricken. In the hall stood a police-constable, surrounded by a group of women: Mrs. Peachey, her sisters, Emma the nurse-girl, and two other servants.

'Oh, here you are at last!' exclaimed his wife, in a voice exhausted with rage. 'You're just in time to see this beast taken off to the lock-up. Perhaps you'll believe me now!'

'What is it? What has she done?'

'Stolen money, that's what she's done—your precious Emma! She's been at it for a long time; I've told you some one was robbing me. So I marked some coins in my purse, and left it in the bedroom whilst we were at dinner; and then, when I found half-a-crown gone —and it was her evening out, too—I sent for a policeman before she knew anything, and we made her turn out her pockets. And there's the half-crown! Perhaps you'll believe it this time!'

The girl's face declared her guilt; she had hardly attempted denial. Then, with a clamour of furious verbosity, Ada enlightened her husband on other points of Emma's behaviour. It was a long story, gathered, in the last few minutes, partly from the culprit herself, partly from her fellow-servants. Emma had got into the clutches of a jewellery tallyman, one of the fellows who sell trinkets to servant-girls on the pay-by-instalment system. She had made several purchases of gewgaws, and had already paid three or four times their value, but was still in debt to the tallyman, who threatened all manner of impossible proceedings if she did not make up her arrears. Bottomless ignorance and imbecile vanity had been the girl's ruin, aided by a grave indiscretion on Peachey's part, of which he was to hear presently.

Some one must go to the police-station and make a formal charge. Ada would undertake this duty with pious eagerness, enjoying it all the more because of loud wailings and entreaties which the girl now addressed to her master. Peachey looked at his sisters-in-law, and in neither face perceived a compassionate softening. Fanny stood by as at a spectacle provided for her amusement, without rancour, but equally without pity. Beatrice was contemptuous. What right, said her countenance, had a servant-girl to covet jewellery? And how pitiable the spirit that prompted to a filching of half-crowns! For the criminals of finance, who devastate a thousand homes, Miss French had no small admiration; crimes such as the present were mean and dirty.

Ada reappeared, hurriedly clad for going forth; but no one had fetched a cab. Incensed, she ordered her husband to do so.

'Who are you speaking to?' he replied wrathfully. 'I am not your servant.'

Fanny laughed. The policeman, professionally calm, averted a smiling face.

'It's nothing to me,' said Mrs. Peachey. 'I'm quite willing to walk. Come along, constable.'

Her husband interposed.

'The girl doesn't go from my house until she's properly dressed.' He turned to the other servants. 'Please to blow the whistle at the door, or get a cab somehow. Emma, go upstairs and put your things on.'

'It was about time you behaved like a man,' fell quietly from Beatrice.

'You're right.' He looked sternly at the speaker. 'It *is* time, and that you shall all know.'

192

The culprit, suddenly silent, obeyed his order. The constable went out at the front door, and there waited whilst a cab-summoning whistle shrilled along De Crespigny Park.

Ada had ascended to the first landing, to make sure that the culprit did not escape her. Beatrice and Fanny retired into the drawing-room. After a lapse of some ten minutes two cabs rattled up to the door from opposite directions, each driver lashing his horse to gain the advantage. So nearly were they matched, that with difficulty the vehicles avoided a collision. The man who had secured a place immediately in front of the doorsteps, waved his whip and uttered a shout of insulting triumph; his rival answered with volleys of abuse, and drove round as if meditating an assault; it was necessary for the policeman to interfere. Whereupon the defeated competitor vowed that it was sanguinary hard lines; that for the sanguinary whole of this sanguinary day had he waited vainly for a sanguinary fare, and but for a sanguinary stumble of his sanguinary horse—

Tired of waiting, and suspicious of the delay, Ada went up to the room where the servant was supposed to be making ready. It was a little room, which served as night-nursery; by the girl's bed stood a cot occupied by the child. Ada, exclaiming 'Now, come along!' opened the door violently. A candle was burning; the boy, awake but silent, sat up in his cot, and looked about with sleepy, yet frightened eyes.

'Where are you?'

Emma could not be seen. Astonished and enraged, Ada rushed forward; she found the girl lying on the floor, and after bending over her, started back with a cry half of alarm, half of disgust.

'Come up here at once!' she screamed down the staircase. 'Come up! The wretch has cut her throat!'

There was a rush of feet. Peachey, the first to enter, saw a gash on the neck of the insensible girl; in her hand she held a pair of scissors.

'I hope you're satisfied,' he said to his wife.

The police-officer, animated by a brisk succession of events such as he could not hope for every day, raised the prostrate figure, and speedily announced that the wound was not mortal.

'She's fainted, that's all. Tried to do for herself with them scissors, and didn't know the way to go about it. We'll get her off sharp to the surgeon.'

'It'll be attempted suicide, now, as well as stealing,' cried Ada.

Terrified by the crowd of noisy people, the child began to cry loudly. Peachey lifted him out of the cot, wrapped a blanket about him, and carried him down to his own bedroom. There, heedless of what was going on above, he tried to soothe the little fellow, lavishing caresses and tender words.

'My little boy will be good? He'll wait here, quietly, till father comes back? Only a few minutes, and father will come back, and sit by him. Yes—he shall sleep here, all night—'

Ada burst into the room.

'I should think you'd better go and look after your dear Emma. As if I didn't know what's been going on! It's all come out, so you needn't tell me any lies. You've been giving her money. The other servants knew of it; she confessed it herself. Oh, you're a nice sort of man, you are! Men of your sort are always good at preaching to other people. You've given her money—what does *that* mean? I suspected it all along. You wouldn't have her sent away; oh no! She was so good to the child—and so good to somebody else! A dirty servant! I'd choose some one better than that, if I was a man. How much has she cost you? As much, no doubt, as one of the swell women in Piccadilly Circus—'

Peachey turned upon her, the sweat beading on his ghastly face.

'Go!—Out of this room—or by God I shall do something fearful! —Out!'

She backed before him. He seized her by the shoulders, and flung her forth, then locked the door. From without she railed at him in the language of the gutter and the brothel. Presently her shouts were mingled with piercing shrieks; they came from the would-be-suicide, who, restored to consciousness, was being carried down for removal in the cab. Peachey, looking and feeling like a man whom passion had brought within sight of murder, stopped his ears and huddled himself against the bedside. The child screamed in terror.

At length came silence. Peachey opened the door, and listened. Below, voices sounded in quiet conversation.

'Who is down there?' he called.

'All of us except Ada,' replied Beatrice. 'The policeman said she needn't go unless she liked, but she *did* like.'

'Very well.'

He ran up to the deserted bedroom, carefully gathered together his child's day-garments, and brought them down. Then, as well as he could, he dressed the boy.

'Is it time to get up?' inquired the little three-year-old, astonished at all that was happening, but soothed and amused by the thought that his father had turned nurse. 'It isn't light yet.'

'You are going somewhere with father, dear. Somewhere nice.'

The dialogue between them, in sweet broken words such as the child had not yet outgrown, and the parent did not wish to abandon for common speech, went on until the dressing was completed.

'Now, will my boy show me where his clothes are for going out? His cap, and his coat—'

Oh yes, they were up in the nursery; boy would show father—and laughed merrily that he knew something father didn't. A few minutes more, and the equipment was completed.

'Now wait for me here—only a minute. My boy won't cry, if I leave him for a minute?'

'Cry! of course not!' Peachey descended to the drawing-room, closed the door behind him, and stood facing his sisters-in-law.

'I want to tell you that I am going away, and taking the child with me. Ada needn't expect me back to-night—nor ever. As long as I live I will never again be under the same roof with her. You, Beatrice, said it was about time I behaved like a man. You were right. I've put up long enough with things such as no man ought to endure for a day. Tell your sister that she may go on living here, if she chooses, for another six months, to the end of the year— not longer. She shall be supplied with sufficient money. After Christmas she may find a home for herself where she likes; money will be paid to her through a lawyer, but from this day I will neither speak nor write to her. You two must make your own arrangements; you have means enough. You know very well, both of you, why I am taking this step; think and say about me what you like. I have no time to talk, and so I bid you good-bye.'

They did not seek to detain him, but stood mute whilst he left the room.

The little boy, timid and impatient, was at the head of the stairs. His father enveloped him warmly in a shawl, and so they went forth. It was not long before they met with a vacant cab. Half-an-hour's drive brought them to the eating-house where Peachey had had his chop that evening, and here he obtained a bedroom for the night.

By eleven o'clock the child slept peacefully. The father, seated at a table, was engaged in writing to a solicitor.

At midnight he lay softly down by the child's side, and there, until dawn, listened to the low breathing of his innocent little bedfellow. Though he could not sleep, it was joy, rather than any painful excitement, that kept him wakeful. A great and loathsome burden had fallen from him, and in the same moment he had rescued his boy out of an atmosphere of hated impurity. At length he could respect himself, and for the first time in four long years he looked to the future with tranquil hope.

Careless of the frank curiosity with which the people of the house regarded him, he went down at seven o'clock, and asked for a railway time-table. Having found a convenient train to Canterbury, he ordered breakfast for himself and the child to be laid in a private room. It was a merry meal. Sunshine of midsummer fell warm and bright upon the table; the street below was so full of busy life that the little boy must needs have his breakfast by the window, where he could eat and look forth at the same time. No such delightful holiday had he ever enjoyed. Alone with father, and going away by train into wonderful new worlds.

'Is Emma coming?' he asked.

It was significant that he did not speak of his mother.

They drove to the railway station, Peachey no less excited than the child. From here he despatched a telegram to his partners, saying that he should be absent for a day or two.

Then the train, struggling slowly out of London's welter, through the newest outposts of gloom and grime, bore them, hearts companioned in love and blamelessness, to the broad sunny meadows and the sweet hop-gardens of Kent.

CHAPTER 5

'Serves her jolly well right,' said Beatrice.

'A lot *she'll* care,' said Fanny. 'I should think myself precious lucky. She gets rid of him, and of the kid too, and has as much as she wants to live on. It's better than she deserves.—Do you believe he's been carrying on with that girl?'

Miss. French laughed contemptuously.

'Not he!'

'Well, there's been a jolly good row to-night, if we never see another. We shall all be in the papers!' The prospect had charms for Fanny. 'What are you going to do? Live here till Christmas?'

Beatrice was quietly reviewing the situation. She kept silence, and her sister also became meditative. Suddenly Fanny inquired:

'What sort of a place is Brussels?'

'Brussels? Why? I know nothing about it. Not much of a place, I think; sprouts come from there, don't they?'

'It's a big town,' said the other, 'and a lively sort of place, they say.'

'Why do you ask me, if you know? What about it?'

As usual when performing the operation which, in her, answered to thought, Fanny shuffled with her hands on her waist. At a distance from Beatrice she stood still, and said:

'Some one I know is going there. I've a good mind to go too. I want to see abroad.'

Her sister asked several searching questions, but Fanny would not make known whether the friend was male or female.

'I shouldn't be much surprised,' remarked the woman of business, indifferently, 'if you go and make a fool of yourself before long. That Mrs. Damerel is up to some game with you; any one could see it with half an eye. I suppose it isn't Lord that's going to Brussels?'

Fanny sputtered her disdain.

'If you had any common sense,' pursued her sister, 'you'd stick to him; but you haven't. Oh yes, you think you can do better. Very well, we shall see. If you find yourself in a hole one of these days, don't expect *me* to pull you out. I wouldn't give you a penny to save you from the workhouse.'

'Wait till you're asked. I know where all *your* money 'll go to. And that's into Crewe's pocket. He'll fool you out of all you have.'

Beatrice reddened with wrath. But, unlike the other members of her family, she could command her tongue. Fanny found it impossible to draw another word from her.

On returning from the police-station, haggard and faint with excitement, but supported by the anticipation of fresh attacks upon her husband, Ada immediately learnt what had happened. For the first moment she could hardly believe it. She rushed upstairs, and saw that the child was really gone; then a blind frenzy took hold upon her. Alarming and inexplicable sounds drew her sisters from below; they found her, armed with something heavy, smashing every breakable object in her bedroom—mirrors, toilet-ware, pictures, chimney-piece ornaments.

'She's gone mad!' shrieked Fanny. 'She'll kill us!'

'That beast shall pay for it!' yelled Ada, with a frantic blow at the dressing-table.

Wanton destruction of property revolted all Beatrice's instincts. Courageous enough, she sprang upon the wild animal, and flung her down.

Now indeed the last trace of veneer was gone, the last rag of pseudo-civilisation was rent off these young women; in physical conflict, vilifying each other like the female spawn of Whitechapel, they revealed themselves as born—raw material which the mill of education is supposed to convert into middle-class ladyhood. As a result of being held still by superior strength Ada fell into convulsions, foamed at the mouth, her eyes starting from their sockets; then she lay as one dead.

'You've killed her,' cried the terrified Fanny.

'No fear. Give me some water to pitch over her.'

With a full jug from another bedroom, she drenched the prostrate figure. When Ada came round she was powerless; even her rancorous lips could utter only a sound of moaning. The sisters stripped her stark naked on the floor, made a show of drying her with towels, and tumbled her into bed. Then Beatrice brewed a great jorum of hot whisky-punch, and after drinking freely to steady her shaken nerves, poured a pint or so down Mrs. Peachey's throat.

'There won't be a funeral just yet,' she remarked, with a laugh. 'Now we'll have supper; I feel hungry.'

They went to bed at something after midnight. The servants, having stolen a bottle of spirits from the cupboard, which Beatrice left open, both got drunk, and slept till morning upon the kitchen-floor.

On the morrow, Miss. French, attired as a walking advertisement of the South London Fashionable Dress Supply Association, betook herself to Farringdon Street for an interview with her commercial friend. Crewe was absent, but one of three clerks, who occupied his largest room, informed her that it could not be very long before he returned, and being so familiar a figure here, she was permitted to wait in the agent's sanctum. When the door closed upon her, the three young men discussed her character with sprightly freedom. Beatrice, the while, splendidly indifferent to the remarks she could easily divine, made a rapid examination of loose papers lying on Crewe's desk, read several letters, opened several books, and found nothing that interested her until, on turning over a slip of paper with pencilled figures upon it, she discovered a hotel-bill, the heading: Royal Hotel, Falmouth. It was for a day and night's entertainment, the debtor 'Mr. Crewe,' the date less than a week gone by. This document she considered attentively, her brows knitted, her eyes wide. But a sound caused her to drop it upon the desk again. Another moment, and Crewe entered.

He looked keenly at her, and less good-humouredly than of wont. These persons never shook hands, and indeed dispensed, as a rule, with all forms of civility.

'What are you staring at?' asked Crewe bluffly.

'What are *you* staring at?'

'Nothing, that I know.' He hung up his hat, and sat down. 'I've a note to write; wait a minute.'

The note written, and given to a clerk, Crewe seemed to recover equanimity. His visitor told him all that happened in De Crespigny Park, even to the crudest details, and they laughed together uproariously.

'I'm going to take a flat,' Beatrice then informed him. 'Just find me something convenient and moderate, will you? A bachelor's flat.'

'What about Fanny?'

'She has something on; I don't know what it is. Talks about going to Brussels—with a friend.'

Crewe looked astonished.

'You ought to see after her. I know what the end 'll be. Brussels? I've heard of English girls going there, but they don't usually come back.'

'What can I do? I'm pretty certain that Damerel woman has a game on hand. She doesn't want Fanny to marry her nephew—if Lord *is* her nephew. She wants his money, that's my idea.'

'Mine, too,' remarked the other quietly. 'Look here, old chap, it's your duty to look after your little damned fool of a sister; I tell you that plainly. I shan't think well of you if you don't.'

Beatrice displayed eagerness to defend herself. She had done her best; Fanny scorned all advice, and could not be held against her will.

'Has she given up all thought of Lord?'

'I'm not sure, but I think so. And it looks as if he was going his own way, and didn't care much. He never writes to her now. Of course it's that woman's doing.'

Crewe reflected.

'I shall have to look into Mrs. Damerel's affairs. Might be worth while. Where is she living?' He made a note of the information. 'Well, anything else to tell me?'

Beatrice spoke of business matters, then asked him if he had been out of town lately. The question sounded rather abrupt, and caused Crewe to regard her with an expression she privately interpreted.

'A few short runs. Nowhere particular.'

'Oh?—Not been down into Cornwall?'

He lost his temper.

'What are you after? What business is it of yours? If you're going to spy on me, I'll soon let you know that I won't stand that kind of thing.'

'Don't disturb yourself,' said Beatrice, with a cold smile. 'I haven't been spying, and you can go where you like for anything I care. I guessed you *had* been down there, that's all.'

Crewe kept silence, his look betraying uneasiness as well as anger. Speaking at length, he fixed her with keen eyes.

200

'If it's any satisfaction to you, you're welcome to know that I have been into Cornwall—and to Falmouth.'

Beatrice merely nodded, and still he searched her face.

'Just answer me a plain question, old chap. Come, there's no nonsense between us; we know each other—eh?'

'Oh yes, we know each other,' Miss. French answered, her lips puckering a little.

'What do you know about *her*? What has she been doing all this time?'

Beatrice laughed.

'I know just as little about her as I care.'

'You care a good deal more than you'll confess. I wouldn't be up to women's tricks, if I were you.'

She revolted.

'After all, I suppose I *am* a woman?'

'Well, I suppose so.' Crewe grinned good-naturedly. 'But that isn't in the terms of our partnership, you remember. You can be a reasonable fellow enough, when you like. Just tell me the truth. What do you know about Nancy Lord?' Beatrice assumed an air of mystery.

'I'll tell you that, if you tell me what it is you want of her. Is it her money?'

'Her money be damned!'

'It's herself, then.'

'And what if it is? What have *you* to say to it?'

Her eyes fell, and she muttered 'Nothing.'

'Just bear that in mind, then. And now that I've answered your question, answer mine. What have you heard about her? Or what have you found out?'

She raised her eyes again and again, but in a mocking voice said, 'Nothing.'

'You're telling me a lie.'

'You're a brute to say so!'

They exchanged fierce glances, but could not meet each other's eyes steadily. Crewe, mastering his irritation, said with a careless laugh:

'All right, I believe you. Didn't mean to offend you, old chap.'

'I won't be called that!' She was trembling with stormy emotions. 'You shall treat me decently.'

'Very well. Old girl, then.'

'I'm a good deal younger than you are. And I'm a good deal better than you, in every way. I'm a lady, at all events, and you can't pretend to be a gentleman. You're a rough, common fellow—'

'Holloa! Holloa! Draw it mild.'

He was startled, and in some degree abashed; his eyes, travelling to the door, indicated a fear that this singular business-colloquy might be overheard. But Beatrice went on, without subduing her voice, and, having delivered herself of much plain language, walked from the room, leaving the door open behind her.

As a rule, she returned from her day's occupations to dinner, in De Crespigny Park, at seven o'clock. To-day her arrival at home was considerably later. About three o'clock she made a call at the boarding-house where Mrs. Damerel lived, but was disappointed in her wish to see that lady, who would not be in before the hour of dining. She called again at seven, and Mrs. Damerel received her very graciously. It was the first time they had met. Beatrice, in no mood for polite grimaces, at once disclosed the object of her visit; she wanted to talk about Fanny; did Mrs. Damerel know anything of a proposed journey to Brussels? The lady professed utter ignorance of any such intention on Fanny's part. She had not seen Fanny for at least a fortnight.

'How can that be? She told me she dined here last Sunday.'

'That's very strange,' answered Mrs. Damerel, with suave concern. 'She certainly did not dine here.'

'And the Sunday before?'

'Your sister has dined here only once, Miss. French, and that was three months ago.'

'Then I don't understand it. Haven't you been taking her to theatres, and parties, and that kind of thing?'

202

'I have taken her once to a theatre, and twice to evening "at homes." The last time we were together anywhere was at Mrs. Dane's, about the middle of May. Since then I have seen her hardly at all. I'm very much afraid you are under some misconception. Thinking your sister was engaged to marry my nephew, Mr. Lord, I naturally desired to offer her a few friendly attentions. But it came out, at length, that she did not regard the engagement as serious. I was obliged to speak gravely to my young nephew, and beg him to consider his position. There is the second dinner-bell, but I am quite at your service, Miss. French, if you wish to question me further.'

Beatrice was much inclined to resent this tone, and to use her vernacular. But it seemed only too probable that Fanny had been deceiving her, and, as she really feared for the girl's safety, prudence bade her be civil with Mrs. Damerel.

'Can't you help me to find out what Fanny has really been doing?'

'I'm afraid it's quite out of my power. She never confided in me, and it is so long since I have seen anything of her at all.'

'It's best to speak plainly,' said Beatrice, in her business tone. 'Can't you think of any man, in the society you introduced her to, who may be trying to lead her astray?'

'Really, Miss. French! The society in which I move is not what you seem to suppose. If your sister is in any danger of *that* kind, you must make your inquiries elsewhere—in an inferior rank of life.'

Beatrice no longer contained herself.

'Perhaps I know rather more than you think about your kind of society. There's not much to choose between the men and the women.'

'Miss. French, I believe you reside in a part of London called Camberwell. And I believe you are engaged in some kind of millinery business. This excuses you for ill-manners. All the same, I must beg you to relieve me of your presence.' She rang the bell. 'Good evening.'

'I dare say we shall see each other again,' replied Beatrice, with an insulting laugh. 'I heard some one say to-day that it might be as well to find out *who you really are*. And if any harm comes to Fanny, I shall take a little trouble about that inquiry myself.'

Mrs. Damerel changed colour, but no movement betrayed anxiety. In the attitude of dignified disdain, she kept her eyes on a point above Miss. French's head, and stood so until the plebeian adversary had withdrawn.

Then she sat down, and for a few minutes communed with herself. In the end, instead of going to dinner, she rang her bell again. A servant appeared.

'Is Mr. Mankelow in the dining-room?'

'Yes, ma'am.'

'Ask him to be kind enough to come here for a moment.'

With little delay, Mr. Mankelow answered the summons which called him from his soup. He wore evening dress; his thin hair was parted down the middle; his smooth-shaven and rather florid face expressed the annoyance of a hungry man at so unseasonable an interruption.

'Do forgive me,' began Mrs. Damerel, in a pathetic falsetto. 'I have been so upset, I felt obliged to seek advice immediately, and no one seemed so likely to be of help to me as you—a man of the world. Would you believe that a sister of that silly little Miss. French has just been here—a downright. virago—declaring that the girl has been led astray, and that I am responsible for it? Can you imagine such impertinence? She has fibbed shockingly to the people at home —told them she was constantly here with me in the evenings, when she must have been—who knows where. It will teach me to meddle again with girls of that class.'

Mankelow stood with his hands behind him, and legs apart, regarding the speaker with a comically puzzled air.

'My dear Mrs. Damerel,'—he had a thick, military sort of voice,— 'why in the world should this interpose between us and dinner? Afterwards, we might—'

'But I am really anxious about the silly little creature. It would be extremely disagreeable if my name got mixed up in a scandal of any kind. You remember my telling you that she didn't belong exactly to the working-class. She has even a little property of her own; and I shouldn't wonder if she has friends who might make a disturbance if her—her vagaries could be in any way connected with me and my circle. Something was mentioned about Brussels. She has been chattering about some one who wanted to take her to Brussels—'

The listener arched his eyebrows more and more.

'What *can* it matter to you?'

'To be sure, I have no acquaintance with any one who could do such things—'

'Why, of course not. And even if you had, I understand that the girl is long out of her teens—'

204

'Long since.'

'Then it's her own affair—and that of the man who cares to purchase such amusement. By-the-bye, it happens rather oddly that I myself have to run over to Brussels on business; but I trust'—he laughed—'that my years and my character—'

'Oh, Mr. Mankelow, absurd! It's probably some commercial traveller, or man of that sort, don't you think? The one thing I *do* hope is, that, if anything like this happens, the girl will somehow make it clear to her friends that *I* had no knowledge whatever of what was going on. But that can hardly be hoped, I fear!—'

Their eyes crossed; they stood for a moment perusing vacancy.

'Yes, I think it might be hoped,' said Mankelow airily. 'She seemed to me a rather reckless sort of young person. It's highly probable she will write letters which release every one but herself from responsibility. In fact'—he gazed at her with a cynical smile— 'my knowledge of human nature disposes me to assure you that she certainly will. She might even, I should say, write a letter to *you*—perhaps a cheeky sort of letter, which would at once set your mind at ease.'

'Oh, if you really take that view—'

'I do indeed. Don't you think we might dismiss the matter, and dine?'

They did so.

Until noon of to-day, Mrs. Peachey had kept her bed, lying amid the wreck wrought by last night's madness. She then felt well enough to rise, and after refreshment betook herself by cab to the offices of Messrs Ducker, Blunt & Co., manufacturers of disinfectants, where she conversed with one of the partners, and learnt that her husband had telegraphed his intention to be absent for a day or two. Having, with the self-respect which distinguished her, related her story from the most calumnious point of view, she went home again to nurse her headache and quarrel with Fanny. But Fanny had in the meantime left home, and, unaccountable fact, had taken with her a large tin box and a dress-basket; heavily packed, said the servants. Her direction to the cabman was merely Westminster Bridge, which conveyed to Mrs. Peachey no sort of suggestion.

When Beatrice came back, and learnt this event, she went apart in wrathful gloom. Ada could not engage her in a quarrel. It was a wretchedly dull evening.

They talked next morning, and Beatrice announced her purpose of going to live by herself as soon as possible. But she would not quarrel. Left alone, Ada prepared to visit certain of their relatives in different parts of London, to spread among them the news of her husband's infamy.

205

CHAPTER 6

When Mary Woodruff unlocked the house-door and entered the little hall, it smelt and felt as though the damp and sooty fogs of winter still lingered here, untouched by the July warmth. She came alone, and straightway spent several hours in characteristic activity— airing, cleaning, brightening. For a few days there would be no servant; Mary, after her long leisure down in Cornwall, enjoyed the prospect of doing all the work herself. They had reached London last evening, and had slept at a family hotel, where Nancy remained until the house was in order for her.

Unhappily, their arrival timed with a change of weather, which brought clouds and rain. The glories of an unshadowed sky would have little more than availed to support Nancy's courage as she passed the creaking little gate and touched the threshold of a home to which she returned only on compulsion; gloom overhead, and puddles underfoot, tried her spirit sorely. She had a pale face, and thin cheeks, and moved with languid step.

Her first glance was at the letter-box.

'Nothing?'

Mary shook her head. During their absence letters had been re-addressed by the post-office, and since the notice of return nothing had come.

'I'm quite sure a letter has been lost.'

'Yes, it may have been. But there'll be an answer to your last very soon.'

'I don't think so. Most likely I shall never hear again.'

And Nancy sat by the window of the front room, looking, as she had looked so many a time, at the lime tree opposite and the house visible through wet branches. A view unchanged since she could remember; recalling all her old ambitions, revolts, pretences, and ignorances; recalling her father, who from his grave still oppressed her living heart.

Somewhere near sounded the wailing shout of a dustman. It was like the voice of a soul condemned to purge itself in filth.

'Mary!' She rose up and went to the kitchen. 'I can't live here! It will kill me if I have to live in this dreadful place. Why, even you have been crying; I can see you have. If *you* give way, think what it must be to me!'

'It's only for a day or two, dear,' answered Mary. 'We shall feel at home again very soon. Miss. Morgan will come this evening, and perhaps your brother.'

'I must do something. Give me some work.'

Mary could not but regard this as a healthy symptom, and she suggested tasks that called for moderate effort. Sick of reading— she had read through a whole circulating library in the past six months—Nancy bestirred herself about the house; but she avoided her father's room.

Horace did not come to-day; a note arrived from him, saying that he would call early to-morrow morning. But at tea-time Jessica presented herself. She looked less ghostly than half a year ago; the grave illness through which she had passed seemed to have been helpful to her constitution. Yet she was noticeably changed. In her letters Nancy had remarked an excessive simplicity, a sort of childishness, very unlike Jessica's previous way of writing; and the same peculiarity now appeared in her conversation. By turns she was mawkish and sprightly, tearful and giggling. Her dress, formerly neglected to the point of untidiness, betrayed a new-born taste for fashionable equipment; she suddenly drew attention to it in the midst of serious talk, asking with a bashful smirk whether Nancy thought it suited her.

'I got it at Miss. French's place—the Association, you know. It's really wonderful how cheap things are there. And the very best cut, by dressmakers from Paris.'

Nancy wondered, and felt that her diminishing regard for Miss. Morgan had suffered a fresh blow.

There was much news to receive and impart. In writing from Falmouth, Nancy had referred to the details of her own life with studied ambiguity. She regretted having taken Jessica into her confidence, and avoided penning a word which, if read by any one but her correspondent, would betray the perilous secret. Jessica, after her illness, was inclined to resent this extreme caution, which irritated her curiosity; but in vain she assured Nancy that there was not the least fear of her letters falling into wrong hands. For weeks at a time she heard nothing, and then would come a letter, long indeed, but without a syllable of the information she desired. Near the end of May she received a line or two, 'I have been really ill, but am now much better. I shall stay here only a few weeks more. Don't be anxious; I am well cared for, and the worst is over.'

She heard the interpretation from Nancy's lips, and laughed and cried over it.

'What you must have suffered, my poor dear! And to be separated from the little darling! Oh, it's too cruel! You are sure they will be kind to it?'

'Mary has every confidence in the woman. And I like the look of her; I don't feel uneasy. I shall go there very often, of course.'

'And when is *he* coming back? He oughtn't to have kept away all this time. How unkind!'

'Not at all,' Nancy replied, with sudden reserve. 'He is acting for the best. You mustn't ask me about that; you shall know more some day.'

Jessica, whose face made legible presentment of her every thought, looked disappointed and peevish.

'And you are really going in for the examination again?' Nancy asked.

'Oh, of course I am!' answered the other perkily; 'but not till summer of next year. I'm not allowed to study much yet; the doctor says I might do my brain a serious injury. I read a great deal; books that rest the mind—poetry and fiction; of course only the very best fiction. I shall soon be able to begin teaching again; but I must be very careful. Only an hour or two a day at first, and perhaps quite young children.'

Evidently the girl felt a certain pride in what she had undergone. Her failure to matriculate was forgotten in the sense that she offered a most interesting case of breakdown from undue mental exertion. The doctor had declared his astonishment that she held up until the examination was over.

'He simply wouldn't believe me when I told him the hours I worked. He said I ought to be on my trial for attempted suicide!'

And she laughed with extravagant conceit.

'You have quite made friends with the Barmbys,' said Nancy, eyeing her curiously.

'They are very nice people. Of course the girls quite understand what a difference there is between themselves and me. I like them because they are so modest; they would never think of contradicting my opinion about anything.'

'And what about the Prophet?'

'I don't think you ever quite understood him,' Jessica replied, with an obvious confusion which perplexed her friend. 'He isn't at all the kind of man you thought.'

'No doubt I was wrong,' Nancy hastened to say. 'It was prejudice. And you remember that I never had any fault to find with his—his character.'

'You disliked him,' said the other sharply. 'And you still dislike him. I'm sure you do.'

So plainly did Jessica desire a confirmation of this statement, that Nancy allowed herself to be drawn into half avowing a positive dislike for Samuel. Whereupon Jessica looked pleased, and tossed her head in a singular way.

'I needn't remind you,' fell from Nancy, after a moment of troubled reflection, 'how careful you must be in talking about me to the Barmbys.'

'Oh, don't have the slightest fear.'

'Weren't you delirious in your illness?'

'I should think I was indeed! For a long time.'

'I hope you said nothing—'

'About you? Oh, not a word; I'm quite sure. I talked all the time about my studies. The doctor heard me one day repeating a long bit of Virgil. And I kept calling for bits of paper to work out problems in Geometrical Progression. Just fancy! I don't think most girls are delirious in that way. If I had said anything about you that sounded queer, of course mother would have told me afterwards. Oh, it was quite an intellectual delirium.'

Had Jessica, since her illness, become an insufferable simpleton? or —Nancy wondered—was it she herself who, through experience and sorrows, was grown wiser, and saw her friend in a new light? It troubled her gravely that the preservation of a secret more than ever momentous should depend upon a person with so little sense. The girl's departure was a relief; but in the silence that followed upon silly talk, she had leisure to contemplate this risk, hitherto scarce taken into account. She spoke of it with Mary, the one friend to whom her heart went out in absolute trust, from whom she concealed but few of her thoughts, and whose moral worth, only understood since circumstances compelled her reliance upon it, had set before her a new ideal of life. Mary, she well knew, abhorred the deceit they were practising, and thought hard things of the man who made it a necessity; so it did not surprise her that the devoted woman showed no deep concern at a new danger.

'It's more the shame than anything else, that I fear now,' said Nancy. 'If I have to support myself and my child, I shall do it. How, I don't know; but other women find a way, and I should. If he deserts me, I am not such a poor creature as to grieve on that account; I should despise him too much even to hate him. But the shame of it would be terrible. It's common, vulgar cheating—such as you read of in the newspapers—such as people are punished for. I never thought of it in that way when he was here. Yet he felt it. He spoke of it like that, but I wouldn't listen.'

Mary heard this with interest.

'Did he wish you to give it up?' she asked. 'You never told me that.'

'He said he would rather we did. But that was when he had never thought of being in want himself. Afterwards—yes, even then he spoke in the same way; but what could we do?'

'Don't fear that he will forsake you,' said Mary. 'You will hear from him very soon. He knows the right and the wrong, and right will be stronger with him in the end.'

'If only I were sure that he has heard of his child's birth. If he *has*, and won't even write to me, then he is no man, and it's better we should never see each other again.'

She knew the hours of postal delivery, and listened with throbbing heart to the double knocks at neighbouring houses. When the last postman was gone by, she sat down, sick with disappointment.

At bedtime she said to Mary, 'My little baby is asleep; oh, if I could but see it for a moment!' And tears choked her as she turned away.

It was more than two months since she had heard from her husband.

At first Tarrant wrote as frequently as he had promised. She learnt speedily of his arrival at New York, then that he had reached Nassau, the capital of the Bahamas, then that he was with his friend Sutherland on the little island amid the coral reefs. Subsequent letters, written in buoyant spirits, contained long descriptions of the scenery about him, and of the life he led. He expressed a firm confidence in Sutherland's enterprises; beyond a doubt, there was no end of money to be made by an energetic man; he should report most favourably to Mr. Vawdrey, whose co-operation would of course be invaluable. For his own part, whether he profited or not from these commercial schemes, he had not been mistaken in foreseeing material for journalism, even for a book. Yes, he should certainly write a book on the Bahamas, if only to expose the monstrous system of misgovernment which accounted for the sterility into which these islands had fallen. The climate, in winter at all events, was superb. Sutherland and he lay about in delicious sunshine, under a marvellous sky, smoking excellent cigars, and talking over old Oxford days. He quoted Tennyson: 'Larger constellations burning,' &c.

At the end of December, when Nancy, according to their agreement, began to hope for his return, a letter in a very different tone burdened her with dismal doubts. Tarrant had quarrelled with his friend. He had discovered that Sutherland was little better than a swindler. 'I see that the fellow's professed energy was all sham. He is the laziest scamp imaginable; lazier even than his boozing old father. He schemes only to get money out of people; and his disappointment on finding that *I* have no money to lose, has shown itself at length in very gross forms. I find he is a gambler; there has just been a tremendous row between him and an American, whom he is said to have cheated at cards. Last year he was for several weeks in Mexico City, a place notorious for gambling, and there lost a large sum of money that didn't belong to him.' The upshot was that he could no longer advise Mr. Vawdrey to have anything to do with Sutherland. But he must not leave the Bahamas yet; that would be most unwise, as he was daily gathering most valuable information. Vawdrey might be induced to lend him a hundred pounds or so. But he would write again very soon.

210

It was the close of January when he dated his next letter. Vawdrey had sent him fifty pounds; this, however, was to include the cost of his return to England. 'See, then, what I have decided. I shall make a hurried tour through the West Indian Islands, then cross to the States, and travel by land to New York or Boston, seeing all I can afford to on the way. If I have to come home as a steerage passenger, never mind; that, too, will be valuable experience.' There followed many affectionate phrases, but Nancy's heart remained cold.

He wrote next from Washington, after six weeks' silence. Difficulties of which he would speak at length in another letter had caused him to postpone answering the two letters he had received. Nancy must never lose faith in him; his love was unshaken; before the birth of her child he would assuredly be back in England. Let her address to New York. He was well, but could not pretend to be very cheerful. However, courage! He had plans and hopes, of which she should soon hear.

After that, Nancy knew nothing of him, save that he was living in New York. He wrote two or three times, but briefly, always promising details in the next epistle. Then he ceased to correspond. Not even the announcement of the child's birth elicited a word from him. One subsequent letter had Nancy despatched; this unanswered, she would write no more.

She was herself surprised at the calmness with which she faced so dreadful a possibility as desertion by the man she had loved and married, the father of her baby. It meant, perhaps, that she could not believe such fate had really befallen her. Even in Tarrant's last short letter sounded a note of kindness, of truthfulness, incompatible, it seemed to her, with base cruelty. 'I dreamt of you last night, dearest, and woke up with a heart that ached for your suffering.' How could a man pen those words, and be meditating dastardly behaviour to the woman he addressed? Was he ill, then? or had fatal accident befallen him? She feared such explanation only in her weakest moments. If, long ago, he could keep silence for six weeks at a time, why not now for months? As for the news she had sent him—does a man think it important that a little child has been born into the world? Likely enough that again he merely 'postponed' writing. Of course he no longer loved her, say what he might; at most he thought of her with a feeling of compassion—not strong enough to overcome his dislike of exertion. He would come back—when it pleased him.

Nancy would not sully her mind by thinking that he might only return when her position made it worth his while. He was not a man of that stamp. Simply, he had ceased to care for her; and having no means of his own, whilst she was abundantly provided, he yielded to the temptation to hold aloof from a woman whose claim upon him grew burdensome. Her thoughts admitted no worse accusation than this. Did any grave ill befall her; if, for instance, the fact of her marriage became known, and she were left helpless; her letter to New York would not be disregarded. To reflect thus signified a mental balance rare in women, and remarkable in one situated as Nancy was. She talked with her companion far less consistently, for talk served to relieve the oppression of her heart and mind.

When, next morning, Horace entered the sitting-room, brother and sister viewed each other with surprise. Neither was prepared for the outward change wrought in both by the past half-year. Nancy looked what she in truth had become, a matronly young woman, in uncertain health, and possessed by a view of life too grave for her years; Horace, no longer a mere lad, exhibited in sunken cheeks and eyes bright with an unhappy recklessness, the acquisition of experience which corrupts before it can mature. Moving to offer her lips, Nancy was checked by the young man's exclamation.

'What on earth has been the matter with you? I never saw any one so altered.'

His voice, with its deepened note, and the modification of his very accent, due to novel circumstances, checked the hearer's affectionate impulse. If not unfeeling, the utterance had nothing fraternal. Deeply pained, and no less alarmed by this warning of the curiosity her appearance would excite in all who knew her, Nancy made a faltering reply.

'Why should you seem astonished? You know very well I have had an illness.'

'But what sort of illness? What caused it? You used always to be well enough.'

'You had better go and talk to my medical attendant,' said Nancy, in a cold, offended voice.

Horace resumed with irritability.

'Isn't it natural for me to ask such questions? You're not a bit like yourself. And what did you mean by telling me you were coming back at once, when I wanted to join you at Falmouth?'

'I meant to. But after all, I had to stay longer.'

'Oh well, it's nothing to me.'

They had not even shaken hands, and now felt no desire to correct the omission, which was at first involuntary. Horace seemed to have lost all the amiability of his nature; he looked about him with restless, excited eyes.

'Are you in a hurry?' asked his sister, head erect.

'No hurry that I know of.—You haven't heard what's been going on?'

'Where?'

'Of course it won't interest you. There's something about you I can't understand. Is it father's will that has spoilt your temper, and made you behave so strangely?'

'It is not *my* temper that's spoilt. And as for behaving strangely—.' She made an effort to command herself. 'Sit down, Horace, and let me know what is the matter with you. Why we should be unfriendly, I really can't imagine. I have suffered from ill health, that's all. I'm sorry I behaved in that way when you talked of coming to Falmouth; it wasn't meant as you seem to think. Tell me what you have to tell.'

He could not take a reposeful attitude, but, after struggling with some reluctance, began to explain the agitation that beset him.

'Mrs. Damerel has done something I didn't think any woman would be capable of. For months she has been trying to ruin Fanny, and now it has come—she has succeeded. She made no secret of wanting to break things off between her and me, but I never thought her plotting could go as far as this. Fanny has run away—gone to the Continent with a man Mrs. Damerel introduced to her.'

'Perhaps they are married,' said Nancy, with singular impulsiveness.

'Of course they're not. It's a fellow I knew to be a scoundrel the first time I set eyes on him. I warned Fanny against him, and I told Mrs. Damerel that I should hold her responsible if any harm came of the acquaintance she was encouraging between him and Fanny. She did encourage it, though she pretended not to. Her aim was to separate me and Fanny—she didn't care how.'

He spoke in a high, vehement note; his cheeks flushed violently, his clenched fist quivered at his side.

'How do you know where she is gone?' Nancy asked.

'She as good as told her sister that she was going to Brussels with some one. Then one day she disappeared, with her luggage. And that fellow—Mankelow's his name—has gone too. He lived in the same boarding-house with Mrs. Damerel.'

'That is all the evidence you have?'

'Quite enough,' he replied bitterly.

'It doesn't seem so to me. But suppose you're right, what proof have you that Mrs. Damerel had anything to do with it? If she is our mother's sister—and you say there can be no doubt of it—I won't believe that she could carry out such a hateful plot as this.'

'What does it matter who she is? I would swear fifty times that she has done it. You know very well, when you saw her, you disliked her at once. You were right in that, and I was wrong.'

'I can't be sure. Perhaps it was she that disliked me, more than I did her. For one thing, I don't believe that people make such plots. And what plotting was needed? Couldn't any one have told you what a girl like Fanny French would do if she lost her head among people of a higher class?'

'Then Mrs. Damerel must have foreseen it. That's just what I say. She pretended to be a friend to the girl, on purpose to ruin her.'

'Have you accused her of it?'

'Yes, I have.' His eyes flashed. Nancy marvelled at this fire, drawn from a gentle nature by what seemed to her so inadequate, so contemptible a cause. 'Of course she denied it, and got angry with me; but any one could see she was glad of what had happened. There's an end between us, at all events. I shall never go to see her again; she's a woman who thinks of nothing but money and fashion. I dislike her friends, every one of them I've met. I told her that what she had done ought to be a punishable crime.'

Nancy reflected, then said quietly:

'Whether you are right or wrong, I don't think you would have got any good from her. But will you tell me what you are going to do? I told you that I thought borrowing money only to live on it in idleness was very foolish.'

Her brother stiffened his neck.

'You must allow me to judge for myself.'

'But have you judged for yourself? Wasn't it by Mrs. Damerel's advice that you gave up business?'

'Partly. But I should have done it in any case.'

'Have you any plans?'

'No, I haven't,' he answered. 'You can't expect a man to have plans whose life has been thoroughly upset.'

Nancy, reminded of his youthfulness by the tone in which he called himself a 'man,' experienced a revival of natural feeling. Though revolting against the suggestion that a woman akin to them had been guilty of what her brother believed, she was glad to think that Fanny French had relinquished all legitimate claim upon him, and that his connection with 'smart' society had come to an end. Obvious enough were the perils of his situation, and she, as elder sister, recognised a duty towards him; she softened her voice, and endeavoured to re-establish the confidence of old time. Impossible at once, though with resolution she might ultimately succeed. Horace, at present, was a mere compound of agitated and inflamed senses. The life he had been leading appeared in a vicious development of his previously harmless conceit and egoism. All his characteristics had turned out, as it were, the seamy side; and Nancy with difficulty preserved her patience as he showed point after point of perverted disposition. The result of their talk was a careless promise from Horace that he would come to Grove Lane not seldomer than once a week.

He stayed only an hour, resisting Nancy's endeavour to detain him at least for the mid-day meal. To Mary he spoke formally, awkwardly, as though unable to accept her position in the house, and then made his escape like one driven by an evil spirit.

CHAPTER 7

With the clearing of the sky, Nancy's spirit grew lighter. She went about London, and enjoyed it after her long seclusion in the little Cornish town; enjoyed, too, her release from manifold restraints and perils. Her mental suffering had made the physical harder to bear; she was now recovering health of mind and body, and found with surprise that life had a new savour, independent of the timorous joy born with her child. Strangely, as it seemed to her, she grew conscious of a personal freedom not unlike what she had vainly desired in the days of petulant girlhood; the sense came only at moments, but was real and precious; under its influence she forgot everything abnormal in her situation, and—though without recognising this significance—knew the exultation of a woman who has justified her being.

A day or two of roaming at large gave her an appetite for activity. Satisfied that her child was safe and well cared for, she turned her eyes upon the life of the world, and wished to take some part in it —not the part she had been wont to picture for herself before reality supplanted dreams. Horace's example on the one hand, and that of Jessica Morgan on the other, helped her to contemn mere social excitement and the idle vanity which formerly she styled pursuit of culture. Must there not be discoverable, in the world to which she had, or could obtain, access, some honest, strenuous occupation, which would hold in check her unprofitable thoughts and soothe her self-respect?

That her fraud, up to and beyond the crucial point, had escaped detection, must be held so wonderful, that she felt justified in an assurance of impunity. The narrowest escape of which she was aware had befallen only a few weeks ago. On the sixth day after the birth of the child, there was brought to her lodgings at Falmouth a note addressed to 'Miss. Lord.' Letters bearing this address had arrived frequently, and by the people of the house were supposed to be for Mary Woodruff, who went by the name of 'Miss. Lord,' Nancy having disguised herself as 'Mrs. Woodruff;' but they had always come by post, and the present missive must be from some acquaintance actually in the town. Nancy could not remember the handwriting. Breaking open the envelope as she lay in bed, she saw with alarm the signature 'Luckworth Crewe.' He was at Falmouth on business, Crewe wrote, and, before leaving London, he had ventured to ask Miss Lord's address from her brother, whom he casually met somewhere. Would Nancy allow him to see her, were it but for a minute or two? Earnestly he besought this favour. He desired nothing more than to see Miss. Lord, and to speak with her in the way of an ordinary acquaintance. After all this time, she had, he felt sure, forgiven his behaviour at their last meeting. Only five minutes of conversation—

All seemed lost. Nancy was silent in despair. But Mary faced the perilous juncture, and, to all appearances, averted catastrophe. She dressed herself, and went straight to the hotel where Crewe had put up, and where he awaited an answer. Having made known who she was, she delivered a verbal message: Miss. Lord was not well enough to see any one to-day, and, in any case, she could not have received Mr Crewe; she begged him to pardon her; before long, they might perhaps meet in

London, but, for her own part, she wished Mr. Crewe would learn to regard her as a stranger. Of course there followed a dialogue; and Mary, seeming to speak with all freedom, convinced Crewe that his attempt to gain an interview was quite hopeless. She gave him much information concerning her mistress—none of it false, but all misleading—and in the end had to resist an offer of gold coins, pressed upon her as a bribe for her good word with Nancy.

The question was—had Crewe been content to leave Falmouth without making inquiries of other people? To a man of his experience, nothing was easier than such investigation. But, with other grounds of anxiety, this had ceased to disturb Nancy's mind. Practically, she lived as though all danger were at an end. The task immediately before her seemed very simple; she had only to resume the old habits, and guard against thoughtless self-betrayal in her everyday talk. The chance that any one would discover her habit of visiting a certain house at the distance of several miles from Camberwell, was too slight for consideration.

She wrote to Mr. Barmby, senior, informing him of her return, in improved health, to Grove Lane, and thanking him once more for his allowing her to make so long a stay in Cornwall. If he wished to see her, she would be at home at any time convenient to him. In a few days the old gentleman called, and for an hour or two discoursed well-meaning commonplace. He was sorry to observe that she looked a trifle pale; in the autumn she must go away again, and to a more bracing locality—he would suggest Broadstairs, which had always exercised the most beneficial effect upon his own health. Above all, he begged her to refrain from excessive study, most deleterious to a female constitution. Then he asked questions about Horace, and agreed with Nancy that the young man ought to decide upon some new pursuit, if he had definitely abandoned the old; lack of steady occupation was most deleterious at his age. In short, Mr. Barmby rather apologised for his guardianship than sought to make assertion of it; and Nancy, by a few feminine devices, won a better opinion than she had hitherto enjoyed. On the day following, Samuel Barmby and his sisters waited upon Miss. Lord; all three were surprisingly solemn, and Samuel talked for the most part of a 'paragraph' he had recently read, which stated that the smoke of London, if properly utilised, would be worth a vast sum of money. 'The English are a wasteful people,' was his conclusion; to which Nancy assented with a face as grave as his own.

Not a little to her astonishment, the next day brought her a long letter in Samuel's fair commercial hand. It began by assuring her that the writer had no intention whatever of troubling her with the renewal of a suit so firmly rejected on more than one occasion; he wished only to take this opportunity of her return from a long absence to express the abiding nature of his devotion, which years hence would be unbroken as to-day. He would never distress her by unwelcome demonstrations; possibly she might never again hear from his lips what he now committed to paper. Enough for him, Samuel, to cherish a love which could not but exalt and purify him, which was indeed, 'in the words of Shakespeare, "a liberal education."' In recompense of his self-command, he only besought that Miss. Lord would allow him, from time to time, to look upon her face, and to converse with her of intellectual subjects. 'A paper,' he added, 'which I read last week at our Society, is now being printed— solely at the request of friends. The subject is one that may interest you, "The Influence of Culture on Morality." I beg that you will accept the copy I shall have the pleasure of sending you, and that, at some future date, you will honour me with your remarks thereon.'

Which epistle Nancy cruelly read aloud to Mary, with a sprightliness and sarcastic humour not excelled by her criticisms of 'the Prophet' in days gone by. Mary did not quite understand, but she saw in this behaviour a proof of the wonderful courage with which Nancy faced her troubles.

A week had passed, and no news from America.

'I don't care,' said Nancy. 'Really and truly, I don't care. Yesterday I never once thought of it—never once looked for the postman. The worst is over now, and he may write or not, as he likes.'

Mary felt sure there would be an explanation of such strange silence.

'Only illness or death would explain it so as to make me forgive him. But he isn't ill. He is alive, and enjoying himself.'

There was no bitterness in her voice. She seemed to have outlived all sorrows and anxieties relative to her husband.

Mary suggested that it was always possible to call at Mr. Vawdrey's house and make inquiries of Mrs. Baker.

'No, I won't do that. Other women would do it, but I won't. So long as I mayn't tell the truth, I should only set them talking about me; you know how. I see the use, now, of having a good deal of pride. I'm only sorry for those letters I wrote when I wasn't in my senses. If he writes now, I shall not answer. He shall know that I am as independent as he is. What a blessed thing it is for a woman to have money of her own! It's because most women haven't, that they're such poor, wretched slaves.'

'If he knew you were in want,' said her companion, 'he would never have behaved like this.'

'Who can say?—No, I won't pretend to think worse of him than I do. You're quite right. He wouldn't leave his wife to starve. It's certain that he hears about me from some one. If I were found out, and lost everything, some one would let him know. But I wouldn't accept support from him, now. He might provide for his child, but he shall never provide for me, come what may—never!'

It was in the evening, after dinner. Nancy had a newspaper, and was reading the advertisements that offered miscellaneous employment.

218

'What do you think this can be?' she asked, looking up after a long silence. '"To ladies with leisure. Ladies desiring to add to their income by easy and pleasant work should write"'—&c. &c.

'I've no faith in those kind of advertisements,' said Mary.

'No; of course it's rubbish. There's no easy and pleasant way of earning money; only silly people expect it. And I don't want anything easy or pleasant. I want honest hard work. Not work with my hands—I'm not suited for that, but real work, such as lots of educated girls are doing. I'm quite willing to pay for learning it; most likely I shall have to. Who could I write to for advice?'

They were sitting upstairs, and so did not hear a visitor's knock that sounded at the front door. The servant came and announced that Miss. French wished to see Miss. Lord.

'Miss. French? Is it the younger Miss. French?'

The girl could not say; she had repeated the name given to her. Nancy spoke to her friend in a low voice.

'It may be Fanny. I don't think Beatrice would call, unless it's to say something about her sister. She had better come up here, I suppose?'

Mary retired, and in a few moments there entered, not Fanny, but Beatrice. She was civilly, not cordially, welcomed. Her eye, as she spoke the words natural at such a meeting, dwelt with singular persistency on Nancy's face.

'You are quite well again?'

'Quite, thank you.'

'It has been a troublesome illness, I'm afraid.'

Nancy hesitated, detecting a peculiarity of look and tone which caused her uneasiness.

'I had a sort of low fever—was altogether out of sorts—"below par," the doctor said. Are you all well?'

Settling herself comfortably, as if for a long chat, Beatrice sketched with some humour the course of recent events in De Crespigny Park.

'I'm out of it all, thank goodness. I prefer a quiet life. Then there's Fanny. You know all about *her*, I dare say?'

'Nothing at all,' Nancy replied distantly.

'But your brother does. Hasn't he been to see you yet?'

Nancy was in no mood to submit to examination.

'Whatever I may have heard, I know nothing about Fanny's, affairs, and, really, they don't concern me.

'I should have thought they might,' rejoined the other, smiling absently. 'She has run away from her friends'—a pause—'and is living somewhere rather mysteriously'—another pause—'and I think it more than likely that she's *married*.'

The listener preserved a face of indifference, though the lines were decidedly tense.

'Doesn't that interest you?' asked Beatrice, in the most genial tone.

'If it's true,' was the blunt reply.

'You mean, you are glad if she has married somebody else, and not your brother?'

'Yes, I am glad of that.'

Beatrice mused, with wrinkles at the corner of her eye. Then, fixing Nancy with a very keen look, she said quietly:

'I'm not sure that she's married. But if she isn't, no doubt she ought to be.'

On Nancy's part there was a nervous movement, but she said nothing. Her face grew rigid.

'I have an idea who the man is,' Miss. French pursued; 'but I can't be quite certain. One has heard of similar cases. Even *you* have, no doubt?'

'I don't care to talk about it,' fell mechanically from Nancy's lips, which had lost their colour.

'But I've come just for that purpose.'

The eyes of mocking scrutiny would not be resisted. They drew a gaze from Nancy, and then a haughty exclamation.

'I don't understand you. Please say whatever you have to say in plain words.'

'Don't be angry with me. You were always too ready at taking offence. I mean it in quite a friendly way; you can trust me; I'm not one of the women that chatter. Don't you think you ought to sympathise a little with Fanny? She has gone to Brussels, or somewhere about there. But she *might* have gone down into Cornwall —to a place like Falmouth. It was quite far enough off—don't you think?'

Nancy was stricken mute, and her countenance would no longer disguise what she suffered.

'No need to upset yourself,' pursued the other in smiling confidence. 'I mean no harm. I'm curious, that's all; just want to know one or two things. We're old friends, and whatever you tell me will go no further, depend upon that.'

'What do you mean?'

The words came from lips that moved with difficulty. Beatrice, still smiling, bent forward.

'Is it any one that I know?'

'Any one—? Who—?'

'That made it necessary for you to go down into Cornwall, my dear.'

Nancy heaved a sigh, the result of holding her breath too long. She half rose, and sat down again. In a torture of flashing thoughts, she tried to determine whether Beatrice had any information, or spoke conjecturally. Yet she was able to discern that either case meant disaster; to have excited the suspicions of such a person, was the same as being unmasked; an inquiry at Falmouth, and all would at once be known.

No, not all. Not the fact of her marriage; not the name of her husband.

Driven to bay by such an opponent, she assumed an air wholly unnatural to her—one of cynical effrontery.

'You had better say what you know.'

'All right. Who was the father of the child born not long ago?'

'That's asking a question.'

'And telling what I know at the same time. It saves breath.'

Beatrice laughed; and Nancy, become a mere automaton, laughed too.

'That's more like it,' said Miss. French cheerfully. 'Now we shall get on together. It's very shocking, my dear. A person of my strict morality hardly knows how to look you in the face. Perhaps you had rather I didn't try. Very well. Now tell me all about it, comfortably. I have a guess, you know.'

'What is it?'

'Wait a little. I don't want to be laughed at. Is it any one I know?'

'You have never seen him, and I dare say never heard of him.'

Beatrice stared incredulously.

'I wouldn't tell fibs, Nancy.'

'I'm telling the truth.'

'It's very queer, then.'

'Who did you think—?'

The speaking automaton, as though by defect of mechanism, stopped short.

'Look straight at me. I shouldn't have been surprised to hear that it was Luckworth Crewe.'

Nancy's defiant gaze, shame in anguish shielding itself with the front of audacity, changed to utter astonishment. The blood rushed back into her cheeks; she voiced a smothered exclamation of scorn.

'The father of my child? Luckworth Crewe?'

'I thought it not impossible,' said Beatrice, plainly baffled.

'It was like you.' Nancy gave a hard laugh. 'You judged me by yourself. Have another guess!'

Surprised both at the denial, so obviously true, and at the unexpected tone with which Nancy was meeting her attack, Miss. French sat meditative.

'It's no use guessing,' she said at length, with complete good-humour. 'I don't know of any one else.'

'Very well. You can't expect me to tell you.'

222

'As you please. It's a queer thing; I felt pretty sure. But if you're telling the truth, I don't care a rap who the man is.'

'You can rest in peace,' said Nancy, with careless scorn.

'Any way of convincing me, except by saying it?'

'Yes. Wait here a moment.'

She left the room, and returned with the note which Crewe had addressed to her from the hotel at Falmouth.

'Read that, and look at the date.'

Beatrice studied the document, and in silence canvassed the possibilities of trickery. No; it was genuine evidence. She remembered the date of Crewe's journey to Falmouth, and, in this new light, could interpret his quarrelsome behaviour after he had returned. Only the discovery she had since made inflamed her with a suspicion which till then had never entered her mind.

'Of course, you didn't let him see you?'

'Of course not.'.

'All right. Don't suppose I wanted to insult you. I took it for granted you were married. Of course it happened before your father's death, and his awkward will obliged you to keep it dark?'

Again Nancy was smitten with fear. Deeming Miss. French an unscrupulous enemy, she felt that to confess marriage was to abandon every hope. Pride appealed to her courage, bade her, here and now, have done with the ignoble fraud; but fear proved stronger. She could not face exposure, and all that must follow.

She spoke coldly, but with down-dropt eyes.

'I am not married.'

The words cost her little effort. Practically, she had uttered them before; her overbold replies were an admission of what, from the first, she supposed Beatrice to charge her with—not secret wedlock, but secret shame. Beatrice, however, had adopted that line of suggestion merely from policy, hoping to sting the proud girl into avowal of a legitimate union; she heard the contrary declaration with fresh surprise.

'I should never have believed it of Miss. Lord,' was her half ingenuous, half sly comment.

Nancy, beginning to realise what she had done, sat with head bent, speechless.

'Don't distress yourself,' continued the other. 'Not a soul will hear of it from me. If you like to tell me more, you can do it quite safely; I'm no blabber, and I'm not a rascal. I should never have troubled to make inquiries about you, down yonder, if it hadn't been that I suspected Crewe. That's a confession, you know; take it in return for yours.'

Nancy was tongue-tied. A full sense of her humiliation had burst upon her. She, who always condescended to Miss. French, now lay smirched before her feet, an object of vulgar contempt.

'What does it matter?' went on Beatrice genially. 'You've got over the worst, and very cleverly. Are you going to marry him when you come in for your money?'

'Perhaps—I don't know—'

She faltered, no longer able to mask in impudence, and hardly restraining tears. Beatrice ceased to doubt, and could only wonder with amusement.

'Why shouldn't we be good friends, Nancy? I tell you, I am no rascal. I never thought of making anything out of your secret—not I. If it had been Crewe, marriage or no marriage—well, I might have shown my temper. I believe I have a pretty rough side to my tongue; but I'm a good enough sort if you take me in the right way. Of course I shall never rest for wondering who it can be—'

She paused, but Nancy did not look up, did not stir.

'Perhaps you'll tell me some other time. But there's one thing I should like to ask about, and it's for your own good that I should know it. When Crewe was down there, don't you think he tumbled to anything?'

Perplexed by unfamiliar slang, Nancy raised her eyes.

'Found out anything, you mean? I don't know.'

'But you must have been in a jolly fright about it?'

'I gave it very little thought,' replied Nancy, able now to command a steady voice, and retiring behind a manner of frigid indifference.

'No? Well, of course I understand that better now I know that you can't lose anything. Still, it is to be hoped he didn't go asking questions. By-the-bye, you may as well just tell me: he has asked you to marry him, hasn't he?'

'Yes.'

Beatrice nodded.

'Doesn't matter. You needn't be afraid, even if he got hold of anything. He isn't the kind of man to injure you out of spite.'

'I fear him as little as I fear you.'

'Well, as I've told you, you needn't fear me at all. I like you better for this—a good deal better than I used to. If you want any help, you know where to turn; I'll do whatever I can for you; and I'm in the way of being useful to my friends. You're cut up just now; it's natural. I won't bother you any longer. But just remember what I've said. If I can be of any service, don't be above making use of me.'

Nancy heard without heeding; for an anguish of shame and misery once more fell upon her, and seemed to lay waste her soul.

Part V: Compassed Round

CHAPTER 1

There needed not Mary Woodruff's suggestion to remind Nancy that no further away than Champion Hill were people of whom, in extremity, she might inquire concerning her husband. At present, even could she have entertained the thought, it seemed doubtful whether the Vawdrey household knew more of Tarrant's position and purposes than she herself; for, only a month ago, Jessica Morgan had called upon the girls and had ventured a question about their cousin, whereupon they answered that he was in America, but that he had not written for a long time. To Mrs. Baker, Jessica did not like to speak on the subject, but probably that lady could have answered only as the children did.

Once, indeed, a few days after her return, Nancy took the familiar walk along Champion Hill, and glanced, in passing, at Mr. Vawdrey's house; afterwards, she shunned that region. The memories it revived were infinitely painful. She saw herself an immature and foolish girl, behaving in a way which, for all its affectation of reserve and dignity, no doubt offered to such a man as Lionel Tarrant a hint that here, if he chose, he might make a facile conquest. Had he not acted upon the hint? It wrung her heart with shame to remember how, in those days, she followed the lure of a crude imagination. A year ago? Oh, a lifetime!

Unwilling, now, to justify herself with the plea of love; doubtful, in very truth, whether her passion merited that name; she looked back in the stern spirit of a woman judging another's frailty. What treatment could she have anticipated at the hands of her lover save that she had received? He married her—it was much; he forsook her —it was natural. The truth of which she had caught troublous glimpses in the heyday of her folly now stood revealed as pitiless condemnation. Tarrant never respected her, never thought of her as a woman whom he could seriously woo and wed. She had a certain power over his emotions, and not the sensual alone; but his love would not endure the test of absence. From the other side of the Atlantic he saw her as he had seen her at first, and shrank from returning to the bondage which in a weak moment he had accepted.

One night about this time she said to herself:

'I was his mistress, never his wife.'

And all her desperate endeavours to obscure the history of their love, to assert herself as worthy to be called wife, mother, had fallen fruitless. Those long imploring letters, despatched to America from her solitude by the Cornish sea, elicited nothing but a word or two which sounded more like pity than affection. Pity does not suffice to recall the wandering steps of a man wedded against his will.

In her heart, she absolved him of all baseness. The man of ignoble thought would have been influenced by her market value as a wife. Tarrant, all the more because he was reduced to poverty, would resolutely forget the crude advantage of remaining faithful to her.

Herein Nancy proved herself more akin to her father than she had ever seemed when Stephen Lord sought eagerly in her character for hopeful traits.

The severity of her self-judgment, and the indulgence tempering her attitude towards Tarrant, declared a love which had survived its phase of youthful passion. But Nancy did not recognise this symptom of moral growth. She believed herself to have become indifferent to her husband, and only wondered that she did not hate him. Her heart seemed to spend all its emotion on the little being to whom she had given life—a healthy boy, who already, so she fancied, knew a difference between his mother and his nurse, and gurgled a peculiar note of contentment when lying in her arms. Whether wife or not, she claimed every privilege of motherhood. Had the child been a weakling, she could not have known this abounding solace: the defect would have reproached her. But from the day of his birth he manifested so vigorous a will to live, clung so hungrily to the fountain-breast, kicked and clamoured with such irresistible self-assertion, that the mother's pride equalled her tenderness. 'My own brave boy! My son!' Wonderful new words: honey upon the lips and rapture to the ear. She murmured them as though inspired with speech never uttered by mortal.

The interval of a day between her journeys to see the child taxed her patience; but each visit brought a growth of confidence. No harm would befall him: Mary had chosen wisely.

Horace kept aloof and sent no message. When at length she wrote to him a letter all of sisterly kindness, there came a stinted reply. He said that he was going away for a holiday, and might be absent until September. 'Don't bother about me. You shall hear again before long. There's just a chance that I may go in for business again, with prospect of making money. Particulars when I see you.'

Nancy found this note awaiting her after a day's absence from home, and with it another. To her surprise, Mrs. Damerel had written. 'I called early this afternoon, wishing particularly to see you. Will you please let me know when I should find you at home? It is about Horace that I want to speak.' It began with 'My dear Nancy,' and ended, 'Yours affectionately.' Glad of the opportunity thus offered, she answered at once, making an appointment for the next day.

When Mrs. Damerel came, Nancy was even more struck than at their former meeting with her resemblance to Horace. Eyes and lips recalled Horace at every moment. This time, the conversation began more smoothly. On both sides appeared a disposition to friendliness, though Nancy only marked her distrust in the hope of learning more about this mysterious relative and of being useful to her brother.

'You have a prejudice against me,' said the visitor, when she had inquired concerning Nancy's health. 'It's only natural. I hardly seem to you a real relative,

I'm afraid—you know so little about me; and now Horace has been laying dreadful things to my charge.'

'He thinks you responsible for what has happened to Fanny French,' Nancy replied, in an impartial voice.

'Yes, and I assure you he is mistaken. Miss. French deceived him and her own people, leading them to think that she was spending her time with me, when really she was—who knows where? To you I am quite ready to confess that I hoped something might come between her and Horace; but as for plotting—really Iam not so melodramatic a person. All I did in the way of design was to give Horace an opportunity of seeing the girl in a new light. You can imagine very well, no doubt, how she conducted herself. I quite believe that Horace was getting tired and ashamed of her, but then came her disappearance, and that made him angry with me.'

Even the voice suggested Horace's tones, especially when softened in familiar dialogue. Nancy paid closer attention to the speaker's looks and movements than to the matter of what she said. Mrs. Damerel might possibly be a well-meaning woman—her peculiarities might result from social habits, and not from insincerity; yet Nancy could not like her. Everything about her prompted a question and a doubt. How old was she? Probably much older than she looked. What was her breeding, her education? Probably far less thorough than she would have one believe. Was she in good circumstances? Nancy suspected that her fashionable and expensive dress signified extravagance and vanity rather than wealth.

'I have brought a letter to show you which she has sent me from abroad. Read it, and form your own conclusion. Is it the letter of an injured innocent?'

A scrawl on foreign note-paper, which ran thus:

DEAR MRS DAMEREL,—Just a word to console you for the loss of my society. I have gone to a better world, so dry your tears. If you see my masher, tell him I've met with somebody a bit more like a man. I should advise him to go to school again and finish his education. I won't trouble you to write. Many thanks for the kindness you *didn't* mean to do me.—Yours in the best of spirits (I don't mean Cognac),

FANNY (*nee*) FRENCH.

Nancy returned the paper with a look of disgust, saying, 'I didn't think she was as bad as that.'

'No more did I. It really gave me a little shock of surprise.'

'Do you think it likely she is married?'

Mrs. Damerel pursed her lips and arched her eyebrows with so unpleasant an effect on Nancy that she looked away.

'I have no means whatever of forming an opinion.'

'But there's no more fear for Horace,' said Nancy.

'I hope not—I think not. But my purpose in coming was to consult with you about the poor boy. He has renounced me; he won't answer my letters; and I am so dreadfully afraid that a sort of despair—it sounds ridiculous, but he is so very young—may drive him into reckless living. You have taken part with him against me, I fear—'

'No, I haven't. I told him I was quite sure the girl had only herself to blame, whatever happened.'

'How kind of you!' Mrs. Damerel sank her voice to a sort of cooing, not unmelodious, but to Nancy's ear a hollow affectation. 'If we could understand each other! I am so anxious for your dear brother's happiness—and for yours, believe me. I have suffered greatly since he told me I was his enemy, and cast me off.'

Here sounded a note of pathos which impressed the critical listener. There was a look, too, in Mrs. Damerel's eyes quite unlike any that Nancy had yet detected.

'What do you wish him to do?' she asked. 'If I must tell you the truth, I don't think he'll get any good in the life of society.'

Society's representative answered in a tone of affectionate frankness:

'He won't; I can see that. I don't wish him to live idly. The question is, What ought he to do? I think you know a gentleman of his acquaintance, Mr. Crewe?'

The question was added rather abruptly, and with a watchful gaze.

'I know him a little.'

'Something has been said, I believe, about Horace investing money in Mr. Crewe's business. Do you think it would be advisable?'

Surprise kept Nancy silent.

'Is Mr. Crewe trustworthy? I understand he has been in business for himself only a short time.'

Nancy declared herself unable to judge Mr. Crewe, whether in private or in commercial life. And here she paused, but could not refrain from adding the question whether Mrs. Damerel had personal knowledge of him.

'I have met him once.'

Immediately, all Nancy's suspicions were revived. She had felt a desire to talk of intimate things, with mention of her mother's name; but the repulsion excited in her by this woman's air of subtlety, by looks, movements, tones which she did not understand, forbade it. She could not speak with satisfaction even of Horace, feeling that Mrs. Damerel's affection, however genuine, must needs be baleful. From this point her part in the dialogue was slight.

'If any of Miss. French's relatives,' said the visitor presently, 'should accuse me to you, you will be able to contradict them. I am sure I can depend upon you for that service?'

'I am not likely to see them; and I should have thought you would care very little what was said about you by people of that kind.'

'I care little enough,' rejoined Mrs. Damerel, with a curl of the lips. 'It's Horace I am thinking of. These people will embitter him against me, so long as they have any ground to go upon.'

'But haven't you let him know of that letter?'

Mrs. Damerel seemed to fall into abstraction, answered with a vague 'Yes,' and after surveying the room, said softly:

'So you must live here alone for another two or three years?'

'It isn't compulsory: it's only a condition.'

Another vague 'Yes.' Then:

'I do so wish Horace would come back and make his home here.'

'I'm afraid you have spoilt him for that,' said Nancy, with relief in this piece of plain speaking.

Mrs. Damerel did not openly resent it. She looked a mild surprise, and answered blandly:

'Then I must undo the mischief. You shall help me. When he has got over this little trouble, he will see who are his true friends. Let us work together for his good.'

Nancy was inclined, once more, to reproach herself, and listened with patience whilst her relative continued talking in grave kindly tones. Lest she should spoil the effect of these impressive remarks, Mrs. Damerel then took leave. In shaking hands, she bent upon the girl a gaze of affection, and, as she turned away, softly sighed.

Of what had passed in the recent interview with Beatrice French, Nancy said nothing to her faithful companion. This burden of shame must be borne by herself alone. It affected profoundly the courageous mood which had promised to make her life tolerable; henceforth, she all but abandoned the hope of gaining that end for which she had submitted to so deep a humiliation. Through Beatrice, would not her secret, coloured shamefully, become known to Luckworth Crewe, and to others? Already, perchance, a growing scandal attached to her name. Fear had enabled her to endure dishonour in the eyes of one woman, but at any moment the disgrace might front her in an intolerable shape; then, regardless of the cost, she would proclaim her marriage, and have, in return for all she had suffered, nothing but the reproach of an attempted fraud.

To find employment, means of honourable support, was an urgent necessity.

She had written in reply to sundry advertisements, but without result. She tried to draw up an advertisement on her own account, but found the difficulty insuperable. What was there she could do? Teach children, perhaps; but as a visiting governess, the only position of the kind which circumstances left open to her, she could hope for nothing more than the paltriest remuneration. Be somebody's 'secretary'? That sounded pleasant, but very ambitious: a sense of incompetency chilled her. In an office, in a shop, who would dream of giving her an engagement?

Walking about the streets of London in search of suggestions, she gained only an understanding of her insignificance. In the battle of life every girl who could work a sewing-machine or make a matchbox was of more account than she. If she entered a shop to make purchases, the young women at the counter seemed to smile superiority. Of what avail her 'education,' her 'culture'? The roar of myriad industries made mocking laughter at such futile pretensions. She shrank back into her suburban home.

A little book on 'employments for women,' which she saw advertised and bought, merely heightened her discouragement. Here, doubtless, were occupations she might learn; but, when it came to choosing, and contemplating the practical steps that must be taken, her heart sank. She was a coward; she dreaded the world; she saw as never yet the blessedness of having money and a secure home.

The word 'home' grew very sweet to her ears. A man, she said to herself, may go forth and find his work, his pleasure, in the highways; but is not a woman's place under the sheltering roof? What right had a mother to be searching abroad for tasks and duties? Task enough, duty obvious, in the tending of her child. Had she but a little country cottage with needs assured, and her baby cradled beside her, she would ask no more.

How idle all the thoughts of her girlhood! How little she knew of life as it would reveal itself to her mature eyes!

Fatigued into listlessness, she went to the lending-library, and chose a novel for an hour's amusement. It happened that this story was concerned with the fortunes of a young woman who, after many an affliction sore, discovered with notable suddenness the path to fame, lucre, and the husband of her heart: she became at a bound a successful novelist. Nancy's cheek flushed with a splendid thought. Why should not *she* do likewise? At all events—for modesty was now her ruling characteristic—why should she not earn a little money by writing Stories? Numbers of women took to it; not a few succeeded. It was a pursuit that demanded no apprenticeship, that could be followed in the privacy of home, a pursuit wherein her education would be of service. With imagination already fired by the optimistic author, she began to walk about the room and devise romantic incidents. A love story, of course—and why not one very like her own? The characters were ready to her hands. She would begin this very evening.

Mary saw the glow upon her face, the delightful frenzy in her eyes, and wondered.

'I have an idea,' said Nancy. 'Don't ask me about it. Just leave me alone. I think I see my way.'

Daily she secluded herself for several hours; and, whatever the literary value of her labour, it plainly kept her in good spirits, and benefited her health. Save for the visits to her baby, regular as before, she hardly left home.

Jessica Morgan came very often, much oftener than Nancy desired; not only was her talk wearisome, but it consumed valuable time. She much desired to see the baby, and Nancy found it difficult to invent excuses for her unwillingness. When importunity could not be otherwise defeated, she pretended a conscientious scruple.

'I have deceived my husband in telling him that no one knows of our marriage but Mary. If I let you see the child, I should feel that I was deceiving him again. Don't ask me; I can't.'

Not unnaturally this struck Jessica as far-fetched. She argued against it, and became petulant. Nancy lost patience, but remembered in time that she was at Jessica's mercy, and, to her mortification, had to adopt a coaxing, almost a suppliant, tone, with the result that Miss. Morgan's overweening conceit was flattered into arrogance. Her sentimental protestations became strangely mixed with a self-assertiveness very galling to Nancy's pride. Without the slightest apparent cause for ill-humour, she said one day:

'I do feel sorry for you; it must be a dreadful thing to have married a man who has no sense of honour.'

Nancy fired up.

'What do you mean?'

'How can he have, when he makes you deceive people in this way for the sake of the money he'll get?'

'He doesn't! It's my own choice.'

'Then he oughtn't let you do it. No honourable man would.'

'That has nothing to do with you,' Nancy exclaimed, anger blanching her cheek. 'Please don't talk about my husband. You say things you ought to be ashamed of.'

'Oh, don't be angry!' The facile tears started in Jessica's eyes. 'It's because I feel indignant on your account, dear.'

'I don't want your indignation. Never mention this subject again, or I shall feel sure you do it on purpose to annoy me.'

Jessica melted into mawkishness; none the less, Nancy felt a slave to her former friend, who, for whatever reason, seemed to have grown hypocritical and spiteful. When next the girl called, she was told that Miss. Lord had left home for the day, a fiction which spared Nancy an hour's torment. Miss. Morgan made up for it by coming very early on the next Sunday afternoon, and preparing herself avowedly for a stay until late in the evening. Resolute to avoid a long *tete-a-tete*, which was sure to exasperate her temper, Nancy kept Mary in the room, and listened to no hint from Jessica that they should retire for the accustomed privacy.

At four o'clock they were joined by Samuel Barmby, whom, for once, Nancy welcomed with pleasure. Samuel, who had come in the hope of finding Miss. Lord alone, gave but the coldest attention to Jessica; Mary, however, he greeted with grave courtesy, addressing to her several remarks which were meant as a recognition of social equality in the quondam servant. He was dressed with elaborate care. Snowy cuffs concealed half his hands; his moustache, of late in training, sketched the graceful curl it would presently achieve; a faint perfume attended the drawing forth of his silk handkerchief.

Samuel never lacked a subject for the display of eloquence. Today it was one that called for indignant fervour.

'A most disgraceful fact has come under my notice, and I am sorry to say, Miss. Lord, that it concerns some one with whom you are acquainted.'

'Indeed?' said Nancy, not without tremor. 'Who is that?'

'Mr. Peachey, of De Crespigny Park. I believe you are on terms of friendship with the family.'

'Oh, you can hardly call it friendship. I know them.'

'Then I may speak without fear of paining you. You are aware that Mr Peachey is a member of the firm of Ducker, Blunt & Co., who manufacture disinfectants. Now, if any manufacture should be carried on in a conscientious spirit—as of course *all* manufactures should—surely it is that of disinfectants. Only think what depends upon it! People who make disinfectants ought to regard themselves as invested with a sacred trust. The whole community looks to them for protection against disease. The abuse of such confidence cannot be too severely condemned, all the more so, that there is absolutely no legal remedy against the adulteration of disinfectants. Did you know that, Miss. Lord? The law guards against adulteration of food, but it seems—I have been making inquiry into the matter—that no thought has ever been given by the legislature to the subject of disinfectants!'

Nancy saw that Jessica was watching the speaker with jealous eyes, and, in spite of prudence, she could not help behaving to Mr. Barmby more graciously than usual; a small revenge for the treatment she had suffered at the hands of Miss. Morgan.

'I could point out a great number of such anomalies,' pursued Samuel. 'But this matter of disinfectants is really one of the gravest. My father has written to *The Times* about it, and his letter will probably be inserted to-morrow. I am thinking of bringing it before the attention of our Society.'

'Do Mr. Peachey's people adulterate their disinfectants?' inquired Nancy.

'I was going to tell you. Some acquaintances of ours have had a severe illness in their house, and have been using disinfectants made by Ducker, Blunt & Co. Fortunately they have a very good medical man, and through him it has been discovered that these pretended safeguards are all but absolutely worthless. He had the stuff analysed. Now, isn't this shameful? Isn't this abominable? For my own part, I should call it constructive murder.'

The phrase came by haphazard to Samuel's tongue, and he uttered it with gusto, repeating it twice or thrice.

'Constructive murder—nothing short of that. And to think that these people enjoy a positive immunity—impunity.' He corrected himself quickly; then, uncertain whether he had really made a mistake, reddened and twisted his gloves. 'To think'—he raised his voice—'that they are capable of making money out of disease and death! It is one of the worst illustrations of a corrupt spirit in the commercial life of our times that has yet come under my observation.'

He remained for a couple of hours, talking ceaselessly. A glance which he now and then cast at Miss. Morgan betrayed his hope that she would take her leave before the necessary time of his own departure. Jessica, perfectly aware of this desire, sat as though no less at home than Nancy. Every remark she made was a stroke of malice at her friend, and in her drawn features appeared the passions by which she was tormented.

As soon as Mr. Barmby had regretfully withdrawn, Nancy turned upon the girl with flashing eyes.

'I want to speak to you. Come downstairs.'

She led the way to the dining-room. Jessica followed without a word.

'Why are you behaving like this? What has come to you?'

The feeble anæmic creature fell back before this outbreak of wholesome wrath; her eyes stared in alarm.

'I won't put up with it,' cried Nancy. 'If you think you can insult me because I trusted you when you were my only friend, you'll find your mistake. A little more, and you shall see how little your power over me is worth. Am I to live at *your* mercy! I'd starve rather. What do you mean by it?'

'Oh—Nancy—to think you should speak to me like this.'

'You are to be allowed to spit poison at me—are you? And I must bear it? No, that I won't! Of course I know what's the matter with you. You have fallen in love with Samuel Barmby.—You have! Any one can see it. You have no more command of yourself than a child. And because he prefers me to you, you rage against me. Idiot! What is Samuel Barmby to me? Can I do more to keep him off? Can I say to him, "Do have pity on poor Miss. Morgan, who—"'

She was interrupted by a scream, on which followed a torrent of frenzied words from Jessica.

'You're a bad-hearted woman! You've behaved disgracefully yourself —oh! I know more than you think; and now you accuse me of being as bad. Why did you get married in such a hurry? Do you think I didn't understand it? It's you who have no command over yourself. If the truth were known, no decent woman would ever speak to You again. And you've got your reward. Pretend as you like, I know your husband has deserted you. What else could you expect? That's what makes you hate every one that hasn't fallen into the mud. I wouldn't have such a character as yours! All this afternoon you've been looking at that man as no married woman could who respected herself. You encourage him; he comes here often—'

Hysterical passion strangled her voice, and before she could recover breath, Nancy, terrible in ire, advanced upon her.

'Leave this house, and never dare to show yourself here again! Do what you like, I'll endure you no longer—be off!'

Jessica retreated, her bloodless lips apart, her eyes starting as in suffocation. She stumbled against a chair, fell to the ground, and, with a cry of anguish, threw herself upon her knees before Nancy.

'What did I say? I didn't mean it—I don't know what I have been saying—it was all madness. Oh, do forgive me! That isn't how I really think of you—you know it isn't—I'm not so wicked as that. We have been friends so long—I must have gone mad to speak such words. Don't drive me away from you, dear, dear Nancy! I implore you to forgive me! Look, I pray to you on my knees to forget it. Despise me for being such a weak, wicked creature, but don't drive me away like that! I didn't mean one word I said.'

'Rubbish! Of course you meant it. You have thought it every day, and you'll say it again, behind my back, if not to my face. Stand up, and don't make yourself sillier than you are.'

'You can't call me anything too bad—but don't drive me away. I can't bear it. You are the only friend I have in the world—the only, only friend. No one was ever kind and good to me but you, and this is how I have repaid you. Oh, I hate myself! I could tear my tongue out for saying such things. Only say that you'll try to forgive me—dear Nancy—dear—'

She fell with face upon the carpet, and grovelled there in anguish of conflicting passions, a lamentable object. Unable to bear the sight of her, Nancy moved away, and stood with back turned, perforce hearing the moans and sobs and half-articulate words which lasted until the fit of hysteria left its victim in mute exhaustion. Then, contemptuously pitiful, she drew near again to the prostrate figure.

'Stand up at once, and let us have an end of this vulgar folly. Stand up, or I'll leave you here, and never speak to you again.'

'Nancy—can you forgive me?'

'I believe you have never got over your illness. If I were you, I should see the doctor again, and try to be cured. You'll end in an asylum, if you don't mind.'

'I often feel almost mad—I do really. Will you forget those dreadful words I spoke? I know you can't forgive me at once—'

'Only stand up, and try to behave like a reasonable being. What do I care for your words?'

The girl raised herself, threw her arms over a chair, and wept miserably.

CHAPTER 2

On an afternoon at the end of October, Samuel Barmby, returned from business, found Miss. Morgan having tea with his sisters. For a month or two after Midsummer the Barmbys had scarcely seen her; now their friendly intercourse was renewed, and Jessica came at least once a week. She had an engagement at a girls' school in this neighbourhood, and, though her health threatened another collapse, she talked of resuming study for the Matriculation of next year.

Samuel, perfectly aware of the slavish homage which Miss. Morgan paid him, took pleasure in posing before her. It never entered his mind to make any return beyond genial patronage, but the incense of a female devotee was always grateful to him, and he had come to look upon Jessica as a young person peculiarly appreciative of intellectual distinction. A week ago, walking with her to the omnibus after an evening she had spent in Dagmar Road, he had indulged a spirit of confidence, and led her to speak of Nancy Lord. The upshot of five minutes' conversation was a frank inquiry, which he could hardly have permitted himself but for the shadow of night and the isolating noises around them. As an intimate friend, did she feel able to tell him whether or not Miss. Lord was engaged to be married? Jessica, after a brief silence, answered that she did *not* feel at liberty to disclose what she knew on the subject; but the words she used, and her voice in uttering them, left no doubt as to her meaning. Samuel said no more. At parting, he pressed the girl's hand warmly.

This afternoon, they began by avoiding each other's look. Samuel seemed indisposed for conversation; he sipped at a cup of tea with an abstracted and somewhat weary air, until Miss. Morgan addressed him.

'To-morrow is the evening of your lecture, isn't it, Mr. Barmby?'

'To-morrow.'

By the agency of a friend who belonged to a society of mutual improvement at Pentonville, Samuel had been invited to go over and illumine with his wisdom the seekers after culture in that remote district, a proposal that flattered him immensely, and inspired him with a hope of more than suburban fame. For some months he had spoken of the engagement. He was to discourse upon 'National Greatness: its Obligations and its Dangers.'

'Of course it will be printed afterwards?' pursued the devotee.

'Oh, I don't know. It's hardly worth that.'

'Oh, I'm sure it will be!'

And Jessica appealed to the sisters, who declared that certain passages they had been privileged to hear seemed to them very remarkable.

Ladies were to be admitted, but the Miss. Barmbys felt afraid to undertake so long a journey after dark.

'I know some one who would very much like to go,' said Jessica, steadying her voice. 'Could you spare me a ticket to give away, Mr Barmby?'

Samuel smiled graciously, and promised the ticket.

Of course it was for Jessica's own use. On the following evening, long before the hour which would have allowed her ample time to reach Pentonville by eight o'clock, she set forth excitedly. Unless Samuel Barmby were accompanied by some friend from Camberwell,— only too probable,—she might hope to make the return journey under his protection. Perhaps he would speak again of Nancy Lord, and this time he should be answered with less reserve. What harm if she even told him the name of the man whom Nancy was 'engaged' to marry?

Nancy was no longer her friend. A show of reconciliation had followed that scene on the Sunday afternoon three months ago; but Jessica well knew that she had put herself beyond forgiveness, nor did she desire it. Even without the memory of her offence, by this time she must needs have regarded Nancy with steadfast dislike. Weeks had gone by since their last meeting, which was rendered so unpleasant by mutual coldness that a renewal of intercourse seemed out of the question.

She would not be guilty of treachery. But, in justice to herself, she might give Samuel Barmby to understand how hopeless was his wooing.

To her disappointment, the lecture-room was small and undignified; she had imagined a capacious hall, with Samuel Bennett Barmby standing up before an audience of several hundred people. The cane-bottomed chairs numbered not more than fifty, and at eight o'clock some of them were still unoccupied. Nor did the assembly answer to her expectation. It seemed to consist of young shopmen, with a few females of their kind interspersed. She chose a place in the middle of the room, where the lecturer could hardly fail to observe her presence.

With Barmby's entrance disillusion gave way before the ardours of flesh and spirit. The whole hour through she never took her eyes from him. His smooth, pink face, with its shining moustache, embodied her ideal of manly beauty; his tall figure inflamed her senses; the words that fell from his lips sounded to her with oracular impressiveness, conveying a wisdom before which she bowed, and a noble enthusiasm to which she responded in fervent exaltation. And she had been wont to ridicule this man, to join in mockery of his eloquence with a conceited wanton such as Nancy Lord! No, it never came from her heart; it was moral cowardice; from the first she had recognised Samuel Barmby's infinite superiority to the ignoble, the impure girl who dared to deride him.

240

He saw her; their eyes met once, and again, and yet again. He knew that she alone in the audience could comprehend his noble morality, grasp the extent of his far-sighted speculations. To her he spoke. And in his deep glowing heart he could not but thank her for such evidence of sympathy.

There followed a tedious debate, a muddy flow of gabble and balderdash. It was over by ten o'clock. With jealous eyes she watched her hero surrounded by people who thought, poor creatures, that they were worthy of offering him congratulations. At a distance she lingered. And behold, his eye once more fell upon her! He came out from among the silly chatterers, and walked towards her.

'You played me a trick, Miss. Morgan. I should never have allowed you to come all this way to hear me.'

'If I had come ten times the distance, I should have been repaid!'

His round eyes gloated upon the flattery.

'Well, well, I mustn't pretend that I think the lecture worthless. But you might have had the manuscript to read. Are you quite alone? Then I must take care of you. It's a wretched night; we'll have a cab to King's Cross.'

He said it with a consciousness of large-handed generosity. Jessica's heart leapt and throbbed.

She was by his side in the vehicle. Her body touched his. She felt his warm breath as he talked. In all too short a time they reached the railway station.

'Did you come this way? Have you a ticket? Leave that to me.'

Again largely generous, he strode to the booking-office.

They descended and stood together upon the platform, among hurrying crowds, in black fumes that poisoned the palate with sulphur. This way and that sped the demon engines, whirling lighted waggons full of people. Shrill whistles, the hiss and roar of steam, the bang, clap, bang of carriage-doors, the clatter of feet on wood and stone —all echoed and reverberated from a huge cloudy vault above them. High and low, on every available yard of wall, advertisements clamoured to the eye: theatres, journals, soaps, medicines, concerts, furniture, wines, prayer-meetings—all the produce and refuse of civilisation announced in staring letters, in daubed effigies, base, paltry, grotesque. A battle-ground of advertisements, fitly chosen amid subterranean din and reek; a symbol to the gaze of that relentless warfare which ceases not, night and day, in the world above.

For the southward train they had to wait ten minutes. Jessica, keeping as close as possible to her companion's side, tried to converse, but her thoughts were in a tumult like to that about her. She felt a faintness, a quivering in her limbs.

'May I sit down for a moment?' she said, looking at Barmby with a childlike appeal.

'To be sure.'

She pointed in a direction away from the crowd.

'I have something to say—it's quieter—'

Samuel evinced surprise, but allowed himself to be led towards the black mouth of the tunnel, whence at that moment rushed an engine with glaring lights upon its breast.

'We may not be alone in the train,' continued Jessica. 'There's something you ought to know I must tell you to-night. You were asking me about Nancy Lord.'

She spoke with panting breath, and looked fixedly at him. The eagerness with which he lent ear gave her strength to proceed.

'You asked me if she was engaged.'

'Yes—well?'

He had even forgotten his politeness; he saw in her a mere source of information. Jessica moved closer to him on the bench.

'Had you any reason for thinking she was?'

'No particular reason, except something strange in her behaviour.'

'Would you like to know the whole truth?'

It was a very cold night, and a keen wind swept the platform; but Jessica, though indifferently clad, felt no discomfort from this cause. Yet she pressed closer to her companion, so that her cheek all but touched his shoulder.

'Of course I should,' Barmby answered. 'Is there any mystery?'

'I oughtn't to tell.'

'Then you had better not. But why did you begin?'

242

'You ought to know.'

'Why ought I to know?'

'Because you—.' She broke off. A sudden chill made her teeth chatter.

'Well—why?' asked Samuel, with impatience.

'Are you—are you in love with her?'

Voice and look embarrassed him. So did the girl's proximity; she was now all but leaning on his shoulder. Respectable Mr. Barmby could not be aware that Jessica's state of mind rendered her scarcely responsible for what she said or did.

'That's a very plain question,' he began; but she interrupted him.

'I oughtn't to ask it. There's no need for you to answer. I know you have wanted to marry her for a long time. But you never will.'

'Perhaps not—if she has promised somebody else.'

'If I tell you—will you be kind to me?'

'Kind?'

'I didn't mean that,' she added hurriedly. 'I mean—will you understand that I felt it a duty? I oughtn't to tell a secret; but it's a secret that oughtn't to be kept. Will you understand that I did it out of—out of friendship for you, and because I thought it right?'

'Oh, certainly. After going so far, you had better tell me and have done with it.'

Jessica approached her lips to his ear, and whispered:

'She is married.'

'What? Impossible!'

'She was married at Teignmouth, just before she came back from her holiday, last year.'

'Well! Upon my word! And that's why she has been away in Cornwall?'

Again Jessica whispered, her body quivering the while:

'She has a child. It was born last May.'

'Well! Upon my word! Now I understand. Who could have imagined!'

'You see what she is. She hides it for the sake of the money.'

'But who is her husband?' asked Samuel, staring at the bloodless face.

'A man called Tarrant, a relative of Mr. Vawdrey, of Champion Hill. She thought he was rich. I don't know whether he is or not, but I believe he doesn't mean to come back to her. He's in America now.'

Barmby questioned, and Jessica answered, until there was nothing left to ask or to tell,—save the one thing which rose suddenly to Jessica's lips.

'You won't let her know that I have told you?'

Samuel gravely, but coldly, assured her that she need not fear betrayal.

CHAPTER 3

It was to be in three volumes. She saw her way pretty clearly to the end of the first; she had ideas for the second; the third must take care of itself—until she reached it. Hero and heroine ready to her hand; subordinate characters vaguely floating in the background. After an hour or two of meditation, she sat down and dashed at Chapter One.

Long before the end of the year it ought to be finished.

But in August came her baby's first illness; for nearly a fortnight she was away from home, and on her return, though no anxiety remained, she found it difficult to resume work. The few chapters completed had a sorry look; they did not read well, not at all like writing destined to be read in print. After a week's disheartenment she made a new beginning.

At the end of September baby again alarmed her. A trivial ailment as before, but she could not leave the child until all was well. Again she reviewed her work, and with more repugnance than after the previous interruption. But go on with it she must and would. The distasteful labour, slow, wearisome, often performed without pretence of hope, went on until October. Then she broke down. Mary Woodruff found her crying by the fireside, feverish and unnerved.

'I can't sleep,' she said. 'I hear the clock strike every hour, night after night.'

But she would not confess the cause. In writing her poor novel she had lived again through the story enacted at Teignmouth, and her heart failed beneath its burden of hopeless longing. Her husband had forsaken her. Even if she saw him again, what solace could be found in the mere proximity of a man who did not love her, who had never loved her? The child was not enough; its fatherless estate enhanced the misery of her own solitude. When the leaves fell, and the sky darkened, and the long London winter gloomed before her, she sank with a moan of despair.

Mary's strength and tenderness were now invaluable. By sheer force of will she overcame the malady in its physical effects, and did wonders in the assailing of its moral source. Her appeal now, as formerly, was to the nobler pride always struggling for control in Nancy's character. A few days of combat with the besieging melancholy that threatened disaster, and Nancy could meet her friend's look with a smile. She put away and turned the key upon her futile scribbling; no more of that. Novel-writing was not her vocation; she must seek again.

Early in the afternoon she made ready to go forth on the only business which now took her from home. It was nearly a week since she had seen her boy.

Opening the front door, she came unexpectedly under two pairs of eyes. Face to face with her stood Samuel Barmby, his hand raised to signal at the knocker, just withdrawn from him. And behind Barmby was a postman, holding a letter, which in another moment would have dropped into the box.

Samuel performed the civil salute.

'Ha!—How do you do, Miss. Lord?—You are going out, I'm afraid.'

'Yes, I am going out.'

She replied mechanically, and in speaking took the letter held out to her. A glance at it sent all her blood rushing upon the heart.

'I want to see you particularly,' said Samuel. 'Could I call again, this afternoon?'

Nancy gazed at him, but did not hear. He saw the sudden pallor of her cheeks, and thought he understood it. As she stood like a statue, he spoke again.

'It is very particular business. If you could give me an appointment—'

'Business?—Oh, come in, if you like.'

She drew back to admit him, but in the passage stood looking at her letter. Barmby was perplexed and embarrassed.

'You had rather I called again?'

'Called again? Just as you like.'

'Oh, then I will stay,' said Samuel bluntly. For he had things in mind which disposed him to resent this flagrant discourtesy.

His voice awakened Nancy. She opened the door of the dining-room.

'Will you sit down, Mr. Barmby, and excuse me for a few minutes?'

'Certainly. Don't let me inconvenience you, Miss. Lord.'

At another time Nancy would have remarked something very unusual in his way of speaking, especially in the utterance of her name. But for the letter in her hand she must have noticed with uneasiness a certain severity of countenance, which had taken the place of Barmby's wonted smile. As it was, she scarcely realised his presence; and, on closing the door of the room he had entered, she forthwith forgot that such a man existed.

Her letter! His handwriting at last. And he was in England.

She flew up to her bedroom, and tore open the envelope. He was in London; 'Great College Street, S. W.' A short letter, soon read.

DEAREST NANCY,—I am ashamed to write, yet write I must. All your letters reached me; there was no reason for my silence but the unwillingness to keep sending bad news. I have still nothing good to tell you, but here I am in London again, and you must know of it.

When I posted my last letter to you from New York, I meant to come back as soon as I could get money enough to pay my passage. Since then I have gone through a miserable time, idle for the most part, ill for a few weeks, and occasionally trying to write something that editors would pay for. But after all I had to borrow. It has brought me home (steerage, if you know what that means), and now I must earn more.

If we were to meet, I might be able to say something else. I can't write it. Let me hear from you, if you think me worth a letter.— Yours ever, dear girl,

L.

For a quarter of an hour she stood with this sheet open, as though still reading. Her face was void of emotion; she had a vacant look, cheerless, but with no more decided significance.

Then she remembered that Samuel Barmby was waiting for her downstairs. He might have something to say which really concerned her. Better see him at once and get rid of him. With slow step she descended to the dining-room. The letter, folded and rolled, she carried in her hand.

'I'm sorry to have kept you waiting, Mr. Barmby.'

'Don't mention it. Will you sit down?'

'Yes, of course.' She spoke abstractedly, and took a seat not far from him. 'I was just going out, but—there's no hurry.'

'I hardly know how to begin. Perhaps I had better prepare you by saying that I have received very strange information.'

His air was magisterial; he subdued his voice to a note of profound solemnity.

'What sort of information?' asked Nancy vaguely, her brows knitted in a look rather of annoyance than apprehension.

'Very strange indeed.'

'You have said that already.'

Her temper was failing. She felt a nervous impulse to behave rudely, to declare the contempt it was always difficult to disguise when talking with Barmby.

'I repeat it, because you seem to have no idea what I am going to speak of. I am the last person to find pleasure in such a disagreeable duty as is now laid upon me. In that respect, I believe you will do me justice.'

'Will you speak plainly? This roundabout talk is intolerable.'

Samuel drew himself up, and regarded her with offended dignity. He had promised himself no small satisfaction from this interview, had foreseen its salient points. His mere aspect would be enough to subdue Nancy, and when he began to speak she would tremble before him. Such a moment would repay him for the enforced humility of years. Perhaps she would weep; she might even implore him to be merciful. How to act in that event he had quite made up his mind. But all such

248

anticipations were confused by Nancy's singular behaviour. She seemed, in truth, not to understand the hints which should have overwhelmed her.

More magisterial than ever, he began to speak with slow emphasis.

'Miss. Lord,—I will still address you by that name,—though for a very long time I have regarded you as a person worthy of all admiration, and have sincerely humbled myself before you, I cannot help thinking that a certain respect is due to me. Even though I find that you have deceived me as to your position, the old feelings are still so strong in me that I could not bear to give you needless pain. Instead of announcing to my father, and to other people, the strange facts which I have learnt, I come here as a friend,—I speak with all possible forbearance,—I do my utmost to spare you. Am I not justified in expecting at least courteous treatment?'

A pause of awful impressiveness. The listener, fully conscious at length of the situation she had to face, fell into a calmer mood. All was over. Suspense and the burden of falsehood had no longer to be endured. Her part now, for this hour at all events, was merely to stand by whilst Fate unfolded itself.

'Please say whatever you have to say, Mr. Barmby,' she replied with quiet civility. 'I believe your intention was good. You made me nervous, that was all.'

'Pray forgive me. Perhaps it will be best if I ask you a simple question. You will see that the position I hold under your father's will leaves me no choice but to ask it. Is it true that you are married?'

'I will answer if you tell me how you came to think that I was married.'

'I have been credibly informed.'

'By whom?'

'You must forgive me. I can't tell you the name.'

'Then I can't answer your question.'

Samuel mused. He was unwilling to break a distinct promise.

'No doubt,' said Nancy, 'you have undertaken not to mention the person.'

'I have.'

'If it is some one who used to be a friend of mine, you needn't have any scruples. She as good as told me what she meant to do. Of course it is Miss. Morgan?'

'As you have yourself spoken the name—'

'Very well. She isn't in her senses, and I wonder she has kept the secret so long.'

'You admit the truth of what she has told me?'

'Yes. I am married.'

She made the avowal in a tone very like that in which, to Beatrice French, she had affirmed the contrary.

'And your true name is Mrs. Tarrant?'

'That is my name.'

The crudely masculine in Barmby prompted one more question, but some other motive checked him. He let his eyes wander slowly about the room. Even yet there was a chance of playing off certain effects which he had rehearsed with gusto.

'Can you imagine,'—his voice shook a little,—'how much I suffer in hearing you say this?'

'If you mean that you still had the hopes expressed in your letter some time ago, I can only say, in my defence, that I gave you an honest answer.'

'Yes. You said you could never marry me. But of course I couldn't understand it in this sense. It is a blow. I find it very hard to bear.'

He rose and went to the window, as if ashamed of the emotion he could not command. Nancy, too much occupied with her own troubles to ask or care whether his distress was genuine, laid Tarrant's letter upon a side-table, and began to draw off her gloves. Then she unbuttoned her jacket. These out-of-door garments oppressed her. Samuel turned his head and came slowly back.

'There are things that might be said, but I will not say them. Most men in my position would yield to the temptation of revenge. But for many years I have kept in view a moral ideal, and now I have the satisfaction of conquering my lower self. You shall not hear one word of reproach from my lips.'

He waited for the reply, the expected murmur of gratitude. Nancy said nothing.

'Mrs. Tarrant,'—he stood before her,—'what do you suppose must be the result of this?'

'There can only be one.'

'You mean the ruin of your prospects. But do you forget that all the money you have received since Mr. Lord's death has been obtained by false pretences? Are you not aware that this is a criminal offence?'

Nancy raised her eyes and looked steadily at him.

'Then I must bear the punishment.'

For a minute Barmby enjoyed her suffering. Of his foreseen effects, this one had come nearest to succeeding. But he was not satisfied; he hoped she would beseech his clemency.

'The punishment might be very serious. I really can't say what view my father may take of this deception.'

'Is there any use in talking about it? I am penniless—that's all you have to tell me. What else I have to bear, I shall know soon enough.'

'One thing I must ask. Isn't your husband in a position to support you?'

'I can't answer that. Please to say nothing about my husband.'

Barmby caught at hope. It might be true, as Jessica Morgan believed, that Nancy was forsaken. The man Tarrant might be wealthy enough to disregard her prospects. In that case an assiduous lover, one who, by the exercise of a prudent generosity, had obtained power over the girl, could yet hope for reward. Samuel had as little of the villain in his composition as any Camberwell householder. He cherished no dark designs. But, after the manner of his kind, he was in love with Nancy, and even the long pursuit of a lofty ideal does not render a man proof against the elementary forces of human nature.

'We will suppose then,' he said, with a certain cheerfulness, 'that you have nothing whatever to depend upon but your father's will. What is before you? How can you live?'

'That is my own affair.'

It was not said offensively, but in a tone of bitter resignation. Barmby sat down opposite to her, and leaned forward.

'Do you think for one moment,'—his voice was softly melodious,— 'that I—I who have loved you for years—could let you suffer for want of money?'

He had not skill to read her countenance. Trouble he discerned, and shame; but the half-veiled eyes, the quivering nostril, the hard, cold lips, spoke a language beyond

Samuel's interpretation. Even had he known of the outrages previously inflicted upon her pride, and that this new attack came at a moment when her courage was baffled, her heart cruelly wounded, he would just as little have comprehended the spirit which now kept her mute.

He imagined her overcome by his generosity. Another of his great effects had come off with tolerable success.

'Put your mind at rest,' he pursued mellifluously. 'You shall suffer no hardships. I answer for it.'

Still mute, and her head bowed low. Such is the power of nobility displayed before an erring soul!

'You have never done me justice. Confess that you haven't!'

To this remarkable appeal Nancy perforce replied:

'I never thought ill of you.'

When she had spoken, colour came into her cheeks. Observing it, Samuel was strangely moved. Had he impressed her even more profoundly than he hoped to do? Jessica Morgan's undisguised subjugation had flattered him into credulity respecting his influence over the female mind.

'But you didn't think me capable of—of anything extraordinary?' Even in her torment, Nancy marvelled at this revelation of fatuity. She did not understand the pranks of such a mind as Barmby's when its balance is disturbed by exciting circumstance.

'What are you offering me?' she asked, in a low voice. 'How could I take money from you?'

'I didn't mean that you should. Your secret has been betrayed to me. Suppose I refuse to know anything about it, and leave things as they were?'

Nancy kept her eyes down.

'Suppose I say: Duty bids me injure this woman who has injured *me*; but no, I will not! Suppose I say: I can make her regret bitterly that she married that other man; but no, I will not! Suppose, instead of making your secret known, I do my utmost to guard it! What would be your opinion of this behaviour?'

'I should think it was kindly meant, but useless.'

252

'Useless? Why?'

'Because it isn't in your power to guard the secret. Jessica Morgan won't leave her work half done.'

'If that's all, I say again that you can put your mind at rest. I answer for Miss. Morgan. With her my will is law.'

Samuel smiled. A smile ineffable. The smile of a suburban deity.

'Why should you take any trouble about me?' said Nancy. 'I can do nothing for you in return.'

'You can.'

She looked anxiously at him, for his voice sounded ominous.

'What?'

'You can acknowledge that you never did me justice.'

'It's true that I didn't,' she answered languidly; speaking as though the concession mattered little.

Barmby brightened. His hands were upon his knees; he raised his chin, and smiled at vacancy.

'You thought me unworthy of you. You can confess to me that you were mistaken.'

'I didn't know you as I do now,' fell from the expressionless lips.

'Thank you for saying that! Well, then, your anxiety is at an end. You are not in the hands of a mercenary enemy, but of a man whose principles forbid him to do anything ignoble, who has an ideal of life, the result of much study and thought. You have never heard me speak about religion, but you would be gravely mistaken if you thought I had no religious convictions. Some day I shall treat that subject before our Society, and it is probable that my views will give rise to a good deal of discussion. I have formed a religion for myself; when I write my essay, I think I shall call it "The Religion of a Man of Business." One of the great evils of the day is the vulgar supposition that commerce has nothing to do with religious faith. I shall show how utterly wrong that is. It would take too long to explain to you my mature views of Christianity. I am not sure that I recognise any of the ordinary dogmas; I think I have progressed beyond them. However, we shall have many opportunities of talking about these things.'

Nancy uttered a mere 'Yes.' She was looking at Tarrant's letter on the side-table, and wishing to be alone that she might read it again.

'In the meantime,' Samuel pursued, 'whatever difficulty arises, confide it to me. Probably you will wish to tell me more before long; you know that I am not unworthy to be your adviser. And so let us shake hands, in sign of genuine friendship.'

Nancy gave her fingers, which felt very cold upon Barmby's warm, moist palm.

'This conversation has been trying to you,' he said, 'but relief of mind will soon follow. If anything occurs to me that may help to soothe you, I will write.'

'Thank you.'

'At the beginning of our interview you didn't think it would end like this?'

There was something of the boy in Samuel, perhaps the wholesomest part of him. Having manifested his admirable qualities, he felt a light-hearted pleasure in asking for renewed assurance of the good opinion he had earned.

'I hardly cared,' said Nancy, as she rose with a sigh of weariness.

'But you have got over that. You will be quite cheerful now?'

'In time, no doubt.'

'I shall call again—let us say on Wednesday evening. By that time I shall be able to put you entirely at ease with regard to Miss Morgan.'

Nancy made no reply. In shaking hands, she regarded the radiant Samuel with a dreamy interest; and when he had left her, she still gazed for a few moments at the door.

CHAPTER 4

The habit of confidence prompted Nancy to seek Mary Woodruff, and show her the long-expected letter. But for Barmby's visit she would have done so. As it was, her mind sullenly resisted the natural impulse. Forlorn misery, intensified by successive humiliations, whereof the latest was the bitterest, hardened her even against the one, the indubitable friend, to whom she had never looked in vain for help and solace. Of course it was not necessary to let Mary know with what heart-breaking coldness Tarrant had communicated the fact of his return; but she preferred to keep silence altogether. Having sunk so low as to accept, with semblance of gratitude, pompous favours, dishonouring connivance, at the hands of Samuel Barmby, she would now stand alone in her uttermost degradation. Happen what might, she would act and suffer in solitude.

Something she had in mind to do which Mary, if told of it, would regard with disapproval. Mary was not a deserted and insulted wife; she could reason and counsel with the calmness of one who sympathised, but had nothing worse to endure. Even Mary's sympathy was necessarily imperfect, since she knew not, and should never know, what had passed in the crucial interviews with Beatrice French, with Jessica Morgan, and with Samuel Barmby. Bent on indulging her passionate sense of injury, hungering for a taste of revenge, however poor, Nancy executed with brief delay a project which had come into her head during the hour of torture just elapsed.

She took a sheet of notepaper, and upon it wrote half-a-dozen lines, thus:

'As your reward for marrying me is still a long way off, and as you tell me that you are in want, I send you as much as I can spare at present. Next month you shall hear from me again.'

Within the paper she folded a five-pound note, and placed both in an envelope, which she addressed to Lionel Tarrant, Esq., at his lodgings in Westminster. Having posted this at the first pillar-box she walked on.

Her only object was to combat mental anguish by bodily exercise, to distract, if possible, the thoughts which hammered upon her brain by moving amid the life of the streets. In Camberwell Road she passed the place of business inscribed with the names 'Lord and Barmby'; it made her think, not of the man who, from being an object of her good-natured contempt, was now become a hated enemy, but of her father, and she mourned for him with profounder feeling than when her tears flowed over his new-made grave. But for headstrong folly, incredible in the retrospect, that father would have been her dear and honoured companion, her friend in every best sense of the word, her guide and protector. Many and many a time had he invited her affection, her trust. For long years it was in her power to make him happy, and, in doing so, to enrich her own life, to discipline her mind as no study of books, even had it been genuine, ever could. Oh, to have the time back again—the despised privilege—the thwarted embittered love! She was beginning to understand her father, to surmise with mature intelligence the causes of his seeming harshness. To her own boy, when he was old enough, she would talk of him and praise him. Perhaps, even thus late, his spirit of stern truthfulness might bear fruit in her life and in her son's.

The tender memory and pure resolve did not long possess her. They soon yielded before the potency of present evil, and for an hour or more she walked along the sordid highway, nursing passions which struck their venom into her heart.

It was one of those cold, dry, clouded evenings of autumn, when London streets affect the imagination with a peculiar suggestiveness. New-lit lamps, sickly yellow under the dying day, stretch in immense vistas, unobscured by fog, but exhibit no detail of the track they will presently illumine; one by one the shop-fronts grow radiant on deepening gloom, and show in silhouette the figures numberless that are hurrying past. By accentuating a pause between the life of daytime and that which will begin after dark, this grey hour excites to an unwonted perception of the city's vastness and of its multifarious labour; melancholy, yet not dismal, the brooding twilight seems to betoken Nature's compassion for myriad mortals exiled from her beauty and her solace. Noises far and near blend into a muffled murmur, sound's equivalent of the impression received by the eye; it seems to utter the weariness of unending ineffectual toil.

Nancy had now walked as far as Newington, a district unfamiliar to her, and repulsive. By the Elephant and Castle she stood watching the tumultuous traffic which whirls and roars at this confluence of six highways; she had neither a mind to go on, nor yet to return. The conductor of an omnibus close at hand kept bellowing 'London Bridge!' and her thoughts wandered to that day of meeting with Luckworth Crewe, when he took her up the Monument. She had never felt more than an idle interest in Crewe, and whenever she remembered him nowadays, it was only to reflect with bitterness that he doubtless knew a part of her secret,—the part that was known to Beatrice French,—and on that account had ceased to urge his suit; yet at this moment she wished that she had pledged herself to him in good faith. His behaviour argued the steadfast devotion of an honest man, however lacking in refinement. Their long engagement would have been brightened with many hopes; in the end she might have learned to love him, and prosperity would have opened to her a world of satisfactions, for which she could no longer hope.

It grew cold. She allowed the movements of a group of people to direct her steps, and went eastward along New Kent Road. But when the shops were past, and only a dreary prospect of featureless dwellings lay before her, she felt her heart sink, and paused in vacillating wretchedness.

From a house near by sounded a piano; a foolish jingle, but it smote her with a longing for companionship, for friendly, cheerful talk. And then of a sudden she determined that this life of intolerable isolation should come to an end. Her efforts to find employment that would bring her among people had failed simply because she applied to strangers, who knew nothing of her capabilities, and cared nothing for

256

her needs. But a way offered itself if she could overcome the poor lingering vestiges of pride and shame which hitherto had seemed to render it impossible. In this hour her desolate spirit rejected everything but the thought of relief to be found in new occupation, fresh society. She had endured to the limit of strength. Under the falling night, before the grey vision of a city which, by its alien business and pleasure, made her a mere outcast, she all at once found hope in a resource which till now had signified despair.

Summoning the first empty cab, she gave an address known to her only by hearsay, that of the South London Fashionable Dress Supply Association, and was driven thither in about a quarter of an hour. The shop, with its windows cunningly laid out to allure the female eye, spread a brilliant frontage between two much duller places of business; at the doorway stood a commissionaire, distributing some newly printed advertisements to the persons who entered, or who paused in passing. Nancy accepted a paper without thinking about it, and went through the swing doors held open for her by a stripling in buttons; she approached a young woman at the nearest counter, and in a low voice asked whether Miss. French was on the premises.

'I'm not sure, madam. I will inquire at once.'

'She calls me "madam,"' said Nancy to herself whilst waiting. 'So do shopkeepers generally. I suppose I look old.'

The young person (she honeyed a Cockney twang) speedily came back to report that Miss. French had left about half-an-hour ago, and was not likely to return.

'Can you give me her private address?'

Not having seen Miss. French since the latter's unwelcome call in Grove Lane, she only knew that Beatrice had left De Crespigny Park to inhabit a flat somewhere or other.

'I wish to see her particularly, on business.'

'Excuse me a moment, madam.'

On returning, the young person requested Nancy to follow her up the shop, and led into a glass-partitioned office, where, at a table covered with fashion-plates, sat a middle-aged man, with a bald head of peculiar lustre. He rose and bowed; Nancy repeated her request.

'Could I despatch a message for you, madam?'

'My business is private.'

The bald-headed man coughed urbanely, and begged to know her name.

'Miss. Lord—of Grove Lane.'

Immediately his countenance changed from deprecating solemnity to a broad smile of recognition.

'Miss. Lord! Oh, to be sure; I will give you the address at once. Pray pardon my questions; we have to be so very careful. So many people desire private interviews with Miss. French. I will jot down the address.'

He did so on the back of an advertisement, and added verbal directions. Nancy hurried away.

Another cab conveyed her to Brixton, and set her down before a block of recently built flats. She ascended to the second floor, pressed the button of a bell, and was speedily confronted by a girl of the natty parlour-maid species. This time she began by giving her name, and had only a moment to wait before she was admitted to a small drawing-room, furnished with semblance of luxury. A glowing fire and the light of an amber-shaded lamp showed as much fashionable upholstery and bric-a-brac as could be squeezed into the narrow space. Something else was perceptible which might perhaps have been dispensed with; to wit, the odour of a very savoury meal, a meal in which fried onions had no insignificant part. But before the visitor could comment to herself upon this disadvantage attaching to flats, Beatrice joined her.

'I could hardly believe it! So you have really looked me up? Awfully jolly of you! I'm quite alone; we'll have a bit of dinner together.'

Miss. French was in her most expansive mood. She understood the call as one of simple friendliness.

'I wasn't sure that you knew the address. Got it at the shop? They don't go telling everybody, I hope—'

'Some one there seemed to know my name,' said Nancy, whom the warmth and light and cheery welcome encouraged in the step she had taken. And she explained.

'Ah, Mr. Clatworthy—rum old cove, when you get to know him. Yes, yes; no doubt he has heard me speak of you—in a general way, you know. Come into my snooze-corner, and take your things off.'

The snooze-corner, commonly called a bedroom, lacked one detail of comfort—pure air. The odour of dinner blending with toilet perfumes made an atmosphere decidedly oppressive. Beatrice remarked on the smallness of the chamber, adding archly, 'But I sleep single.'

258

'What's your brother doing?' she asked, while helping to remove Nancy's jacket. 'I passed him in Oxford Street the other day, and he either didn't see me, or didn't want to. Thought he looked rather dissipated.'

'I know very little about him,' answered the visitor, who spoke and acted without reflection, conscious chiefly at this moment of faintness induced by fatigue and hunger.

'Fanny's in Paris,' pursued Miss. French. 'Writes as if she was amusing herself. I think I shall run over and have a look at her. Seen Ada? She's been playing the fool as usual. Found out that Arthur had taken the kid to his sister's at Canterbury; went down and made a deuce of a kick-up; they had to chuck her out of the house. Of course she cares no more about the child than I do; it's only to spite her husband. She's going to law with him, she says. She won't leave the house in De Crespigny Park, and she's running up bills—you bet!'

Nancy tried to laugh. The effort, and its semi-success, indicated surrender to her companion's spirit rather than any attention to the subject spoken of.

They returned to the drawing-room, but had not time to begin a conversation before the servant summoned them to dinner. A very satisfying meal it proved; not badly cooked, as cooking is understood in Brixton, and served with more of ceremony than the guest had expected. Fried scallops, rump steak smothered in onions, an apple tart, and very sound Stilton cheese. Such fare testified to the virile qualities of Beatrice's mind; she was above the feminine folly of neglecting honest victuals. Moreover, there appeared two wines, sherry and claret.

'Did you ever try this kind of thing?' said the hostess finally, reaching a box of cigarettes.

'I?—Of course not,' Nancy replied, with a laugh.

'It's expected of a sensible woman now-a-days. I've got to like it. Better try; no need to make yourself uncomfortable. Just keep the smoke in your mouth for half-a-minute, and blow it out prettily. I buy these in the Haymarket; special brand for women.'

'And you dine like this, by yourself, every day?'

'Like this, but not always alone. Some one or other drops in. Luckworth Crewe was here yesterday.'

Speaking, she watched Nancy, who bore the regard with carelessness, and replied lightly:

'It's an independent sort of life, at all events.'

'Just the kind of life that suits me. I'm my own mistress.'

There was a suggested allusion in the sly tone of the last phrase; but Nancy, thinking her own thoughts, did not perceive it. As the servant had left them alone, they could now talk freely. Beatrice, by her frequent glance of curiosity, seemed to await some explanation of a visit so unlooked-for.

'How are things going with you?' she asked at length, tapping the ash of her cigarette over a plate.

'I want something to do,' was the blunt reply.

'Too much alone—isn't that it?'

'Yes.'

'Just what I thought. You don't see him often?'

Nancy had ceased her pretence of smoking, and leaned back. A flush on her face, and something unwonted in the expression of her eyes, —something like a smile, yet touched with apathy,—told of physical influences which assisted her resolve to have done with scruple and delicacy. She handled her wine-glass, which was half full, and, before answering, raised it to her lips.

'No, I don't see him often.'

'Well, I told you to come to me if I could be any use. What's your idea?'

'Do you know of anything I could do? It isn't so much to earn money, as to—to be occupied, and escape from loneliness. But I must have two afternoons in the week to myself.'

Beatrice nodded and smiled.

'No,—not for that,' Nancy added hastily. 'To see my boy.'

The other appeared to accept this correction.

'All right. I think I can find you something. We're opening a branch.' She mentioned the locality. 'There'll be a club-room, like at headquarters, and we shall want some one ladylike to sit there and answer questions. You wouldn't be likely to see any one that knows you, and you'd get a good deal of fun out of it. Hours from ten to five, but Saturday afternoon off, and Wednesday after three, if that would do?'

'Yes, that would do very well. Any payment, at first?'

'Oh, we wouldn't be so mean as all that. Say ten shillings a week till Christmas, and afterwards we could see'—she laughed— 'whether you're worth more.'

'I know nothing about fashions.'

'You can learn all you need to know in an hour. It's the ladylike appearance and talk more than anything else.'

Nancy sipped again from her wine-glass.

'When could I begin?'

'The place 'll be ready on Monday week. Next week you might put in a few hours with us. Just sit and watch and listen, that's all; to get the hang of the thing.'

'Thank you for being so ready to help me.'

'Not a bit of it. I haven't done yet. There's a condition. If I fix up this job for you, will you tell me something I want to know?'

Nancy turned her eyes apprehensively.

'You can guess what it is. I quite believe what you told me some time ago, but I shan't feel quite easy until I know—'

She finished the sentence with a look. Nancy's eyes fell.

'Curiosity, nothing else,' added the other. 'Just to make quite sure it isn't anybody I've thought of.'

There was a long silence. Leaning forward upon the table, Nancy turned her wine-glass about and about. She now had a very high colour, and breathed quickly.

'Is it off, then?' said Beatrice, in an indifferent tone.

Thereupon Nancy disclosed the name of her husband—her lover, as Miss. French thought him. Plied with further questions, she told where he was living, but gave no account of the circumstances that had estranged them. Abundantly satisfied, Beatrice grew almost affectionate, and talked merrily.

Nancy wished to ask whether Luckworth Crewe had any knowledge of her position. It was long before her lips could utter the words, but at length they were spoken. And Beatrice assured her that Crewe, good silly fellow, did not even suspect the truth.

CHAPTER 5

'For a man,' said Tarrant, 'who can pay no more than twelve and sixpence a week, it's the best accommodation to be found in London. There's an air of civilisation about the house. Look; a bath, and a little book-case, and an easy-chair such as can be used by a man who respects himself. You feel you are among people who tub o' mornings and know the meaning of leisure. Then the view!'

He was talking to his friend Harvey Munden, the journalist. The room in which they stood might with advantage have been larger, but as a bed-chamber it served well enough, and only the poverty of its occupant, who put it to the additional use of sitting-room and study, made the lack of space particularly noticeable. The window afforded a prospect pleasant enough to eyes such as theirs. Above the lower houses on the opposite side of the way appeared tall trees, in the sere garb of later autumn, growing by old Westminster School; and beyond them, grey in twilight, rose the towers of the Abbey. From this point of view no vicinage of modern brickwork spoilt their charm; the time-worn monitors stood alone against a sky of ruddy smoke-drift and purple cloud.

'The old Adam is stronger than ever in me,' he pursued. 'If I were condemned for life to the United States, I should go mad, and perish in an attempt to swim the Atlantic.'

'Then why did you stay so long?'

'I could have stayed with advantage even longer. It's something to have studied with tolerable thoroughness the most hateful form of society yet developed. I saw it at first as a man does who is living at his ease; at last, as a poor devil who is thankful for the institution of free lunches. I went first-class, and I came back as a steerage passenger. It has been a year well spent.'

It had made him, in aspect, more than a twelve-month older. His lounging attitude, the spirit of his talk, showed that he was unchanged in bodily and mental habits; but certain lines new-graven upon his visage, and an austerity that had taken the place of youthful self-consciousness, signified a more than normal progress in experience.

'Do you know,' said Munden slyly, 'that you have brought back a trans-Atlantic accent?'

'Accent? The devil! I don't believe it.'

'Intonation, at all events.'

Tarrant professed a serious annoyance.

'If that's true, I'll go and live for a month in Limerick.'

'It would be cheaper to join a Socialist club in the East End. But just tell me how you stand. How long can you hold out in these aristocratic lodgings?'

'Till Christmas. I'm ashamed to say how I've got the money, so don't ask. I reached London with empty pockets. And I'll tell you one thing I have learnt, Munden. There's no villainy, no scoundrelism, no baseness conceivable, that isn't excused by want of money. I understand the whole "social question." The man who has never felt the perspiration come out on his forehead in asking himself how he is going to keep body and soul together, has no right to an opinion on the greatest question of the day.'

'What particular scoundrelism or baseness have you committed?' asked the other.

Tarrant averted his eyes.

'I said I could understand such things.'

'One sees that you have been breathed upon by democracy.'

'I loathe the word and the thing even more than I did, which is saying a good deal.'

'Be it so. You say you are going to work?'

'Yes, I have come back to work. Even now, it's difficult to realise that I must work or starve. I understand how fellows who have unexpectedly lost their income go through life sponging on relatives and friends. I understand how an educated man goes sinking through all the social grades, down to the common lodging-house and the infirmary. And I honestly believe there's only one thing that saves me from doing likewise.'

'And what's that?'

'I can't tell you—not yet, at all events.'

'I always thought you a very fine specimen of the man born to do nothing,' said Munden, with that smile which permitted him a surprising candour in conversation.

'And you were quite right,' returned Tarrant, with a laugh. 'I am a born artist in indolence. It's the pity of pities that circumstances will frustrate Nature's purpose.'

'You think you can support yourself by journalism?'

'I must try.—Run your eye over that.'

263

He took from the table a slip of manuscript, headed, 'A Reverie in Wall Street.' Munden read it, sat thoughtful for a moment, and laughed.

'Devilish savage. Did you write it after a free lunch?'

'Wrote it this morning. Shall I try one of the evening papers with it,—or one of the weeklies?'

Munden suggested a few alterations, and mentioned the journal which he thought might possibly find room for such a bit of satire.

'Done anything else?'

'Here's a half-finished paper—"The Commercial Prospects of the Bahamas."'

'Let me look.'

After reading a page or two with critically wrinkled forehead, Munden laid it down.

'Seems pretty solid,—libellous, too, I should say. You've more stuff in you than I thought. All right: go ahead.—Come and dine with me to-morrow, to meet a man who may be useful.'

'To-morrow I can't. I dine at Lady Pollard's.'

'Who is she?'

'Didn't you know Pollard of Trinity?—the only son of his mother, and she a widow.'

'Next day, then.'

'Can't. I dine with some people at Bedford Park.'

Munden lifted his eyebrows.

'At this rate, you may live pretty well on a dress suit. Any more engagements?'

'None that I know of. But I shall accept all that offer. I'm hungry for the society of decent English people. I used to neglect my acquaintances; I know better now. Go and live for a month in a cheap New York boarding-house, and you'll come out with a wholesome taste for English refinement.'

To enable his friend to read, Tarrant had already lit a lamp. Munden, glancing about the room, said carelessly:

'Do you still possess the furniture of the old place?'

'No,' was the answer, given with annoyance. 'Vawdrey had it sold for me.'

'Pictures, books, and all the nick-nacks?'

'Everything.—Of course I'm sorry for it; but I thought at the time that I shouldn't return to England for some years.'

'You never said anything of that kind to me.'

'No, I didn't,' the other replied gloomily. And all at once he fell into so taciturn a mood, that his companion, after a few more remarks and inquiries, rose from his chair to leave.

From seven to nine Tarrant sat resolutely at his table, and covered a few pages with the kind of composition which now came most easily to him,—a somewhat virulent sarcasm. He found pleasure in the work; but after nine o'clock his thoughts strayed to matters of personal interest, and got beyond control. Would the last post of the evening bring him an answer to a letter he had despatched this morning? At length he laid down his pen, and listened nervously for that knock which, at one time or another, is to all men a heart-shaking sound.

It came at the street door, and was quickly followed by a tap at his own. Nancy had lost no time in replying. What her letter might contain he found it impossible to conjecture. Reproaches? Joyous welcome? Wrath? Forgiveness? He knew her so imperfectly, that he could not feel sure even as to the probabilities of the case. And his suspense was abundantly justified. Her answer came upon him with the force of a shock totally unexpected.

He read the lines again and again; he stared at the bank-note. His first sensation was one of painful surprise; thereupon succeeded fiery resentment. Reason put in a modest word, hinting that he had deserved no better; but he refused to listen. Nothing could excuse so gross an insult. He had not thought Nancy capable of this behaviour. Tested, she betrayed the vice of birth. Her imputation upon his motive in marrying her was sheer vulgar abuse, possible only on vulgar lips. Well and good; now he knew her; all the torment of conscience he had suffered was needless. And for the moment he experienced a great relief.

In less than ten minutes letter and bank-note were enclosed in a new envelope, and addressed back again to the sender. With no word of comment; she must interpret him as she could, and would. He went out, and threw the offensive packet into the nearest receptacle for such things.

Work was over for to-night. After pacing in the obscurity of Dean's Yard until his pulse had recovered a normal beat, he issued into the peopled ways, and turned towards Westminster Bridge.

Despite his neglect of Nancy, he had never ceased to think of her with a tenderness which, in his own judgment, signified something more than the simple fidelity of a married man. Faithful in the technical sense he had not been, but the casual amours of a young man caused him no self-reproach; Nancy's image remained without rival in his mind; he had continued to acknowledge her claims upon him, and, from time to time, to think of her with a lover's longing. As he only wrote when prompted by such a mood, his letters, however unsatisfying, were sincere. Various influences conflicted with this amiable and honourable sentiment. The desire of independence which had speeded him away from England still accompanied him on his return; he had never ceased to regret his marriage, and it seemed to him that, without this legal bondage, it would have been much easier to play a manly part at the time of Nancy's becoming a mother. Were she frankly his mistress, he would not be keeping thus far away when most she needed the consolation of his presence. The secret marriage condemned him to a course of shame, and the more he thought of it, the more he marvelled at his deliberate complicity in such a fraud. When poverty began to make itself felt, when he was actually hampered in his movements by want of money, this form of indignity, more than any galling to his pride, intensified the impatience with which he remembered that he could no longer roam the world as an adventurer. Any day some trivial accident might oppress him with the burden of a wife and child who looked to him for their support. Tarrant the married man, unless he were content to turn simple rogue and vagabond, must make for himself a place in the money-earning world. His indolence had no small part in his revolt against the stress of such a consideration. The climate of the Bahamas by no means tended to invigorate him, and in the United States he found so much to observe,—even to enjoy,—that the necessity of effort was kept out of sight as long as, by one expedient and another, he succeeded in procuring means to live upon without working.

During the homeward voyage—a trial such as he had never known, amid squalid discomforts which enraged even more than they disgusted him—his heart softened in anticipation of a meeting with Nancy, and of the sight of his child. Apart from his fellow-travellers,— in whom he could perceive nothing but coarseness and vileness,—he spent the hours in longing for England and for the home he would make there, in castigating the flagrant faults of his character, moderating his ambitions, and endeavouring to find a way out of the numerous grave difficulties with which his future was beset.

Landed, he rather forgot than discarded these wholesome meditations. What he had first to do was so very unpleasant, and taxed so rudely his self-respect, that he insensibly fell back again into the rebellious temper. Choice there was none; reaching London with a few shillings in his pocket, of necessity he repaired forthwith to Mr Vawdrey's office in the City, and made known the straits into which he had fallen.

'Now, my dear fellow,' said Mr. Vawdrey, with his usual good-humour, 'how much have you had of me since you started for the Bahamas?'

'That is hardly a fair question,' Tarrant replied, endeavouring not to hang his head like an everyday beggar. 'I went out on a commission—'

'True. But after you ceased to be a commissioner?'

'You have lent me seventy pounds. Living in the States is expensive. What I got for my furniture has gone as well, yet I certainly haven't been extravagant; and for the last month or two I lived like a tramp. Will you make my debt to you a round hundred? It shall be repaid, though I may be a year or two about it.'

The loan was granted, but together with a great deal of unpalatable counsel. Having found his lodging, Tarrant at once invested ten pounds in providing himself with a dress suit, and improving his ordinary attire,—he had sold every garment he could spare in New York. For the dress suit he had an immediate use; on the very platform of Euston Station, at his arrival, a chance meeting with one of his old college friends resulted in an invitation to dine, and, even had not policy urged him to make the most of such acquaintances, he was in no mood for rejecting a summons back into the world of civilisation. Postponing the purposed letter to Nancy (which, had he written it sooner, would have been very unlike the letter he subsequently sent), he equipped himself once more as a gentleman, and spent several very enjoyable hours in looking up the members of his former circle—Hodiernals and others. Only to Harvey Munden did he confide something of the anxieties which lay beneath his assumed lightheartedness. Munden was almost the only man he knew for whom he had a genuine respect.

Renewal of intercourse with people of good social standing made him more than ever fretful in the thought that he had clogged himself with marriage. Whatever Nancy's reply to his announcement that he was home again, he would have read it with discontent. To have the fact forced upon him (a fact he seriously believed it) that his wife could not be depended upon even for elementary generosity of thought, was at this moment especially disastrous; it weighed the balance against his feelings of justice and humanity, hitherto, no matter how he acted, always preponderant over the baser issues of character and circumstance.

He stood leaning upon the parapet of Westminster Bridge, his eyes scanning the dark façade of the Houses of Parliament.

How would the strong, unscrupulous, really ambitious man act in such a case? What was to prevent him from ignoring the fact that he was married, and directing his course precisely as he would have done if poverty had come upon him before his act of supreme foolishness? Journalism must have been his refuge then, as now; but Society would have held out to him the hope of every adventurer—a marriage with some woman whose wealth and connections would clear an upward path in whatever line he chose to follow. Why not abandon to Nancy the inheritance it would degrade him to share, and so purchase back his freedom? The bargain might be made; a strong man would carry it through, and ultimately triumph by daring all risks.

Having wrought himself to this point of insensate revolt, he quitted his musing-station on the bridge, and walked away.

Nancy did not write again. There passed four or five days, and Tarrant, working hard as well as enjoying the pleasures of Society, made up his mind not to see her. He would leave events to take their course. A heaviness of heart often troubled him, but he resisted it, and told himself that he was becoming stronger.

After a long day of writing, he addressed a packet to a certain periodical, and went out to post it. No sooner had he left the house than a woman, who had been about to pass him on the pavement, abruptly turned round and hurriedly walked away. But for this action, he would not have noticed her; as it was, he recognised the figure, and an impulse which allowed of no reflection brought him in a moment to her side. In the ill-lighted street a face could with difficulty be observed, but Nancy's features were unmistakable to the eye that now fell upon them.

'Stop, and let me speak to you,' he exclaimed.

She walked only the more quickly, and he was obliged to take her by the arm.

'What do you want?'

She spoke as if to an insolent stranger, and shook off his grasp.

'If you have nothing to say to me, why are you here?'

'Here? I suppose the streets are free to me?'

'Nothing would bring you to Great College Street if you didn't know that I was living here. Now that we have met, we must talk.'

'I have nothing at all to say to you.'

'Well, then *I* will talk.—Come this way; there's a quiet place where no one will notice us.'

Nancy kept her eyes resolutely averted from him; he, the while, searched her face with eagerness, as well as the faint rays of the nearest lamp allowed it.

'If you have anything to say, you must say it here.'

'It's no use, then. Go your way, and I'll go mine.'

268

He turned, and walked slowly in the direction of Dean's Yard. There was the sound of a step behind him, and when he had come into the dark, quiet square, Nancy was there too.

'Better to be reasonable,' said Tarrant, approaching her again. 'I want to ask you why you answered a well-meant letter with vulgar insult?'

'The insult came from you,' she answered, in a shaking voice.

'What did I say that gave you offence?'

'How can you ask such a question? To write in that way after never answering my letter for months, leaving me without a word at such a time, making me think either that you were dead or that you would never let me hear of you again—'

'I told you it was a mere note, just to let you know I was back. I said you should hear more when we met.'

'Very well, we have met. What have you to say for yourself?'

'First of all, this. That you are mistaken in supposing I should ever consent to share your money. The thought was natural to you, no doubt; but I see things from a different point of view.'

His cold anger completely disguised the emotion stirred in him by Nancy's presence. Had he not spoken thus, he must have given way to joy and tenderness. For Nancy seemed more beautiful than the memory he had retained of her, and even at such a juncture she was far from exhibiting the gross characteristics attributed to her by his rebellious imagination.

'Then I don't understand,' were her next words, 'why you wrote to me again at all.'

'There are many things in me that you don't understand, and can't understand.'

'Yes, I think so. That's why I see no use in our talking.'

Tarrant was ashamed of what he had said—a meaningless retort, which covered his inability to speak as his heart prompted.

'At all events I wanted to see you, and it's fortunate you passed just as I was coming out.'

Nancy would not accept the conciliatory phrase.

'I hadn't the least intention of seeing you,' she replied. 'It was a curiosity to know where you lived, nothing else. I shall never forgive you for the way in which you have behaved to me, so you needn't try to explain yourself.'

'Here and now, I should certainly not try. The only thing I will say about myself is, that I very much regret not having made known that you were married to me when plain honesty required it. Now, I look upon it as something over and done with, as far as I am concerned. I shall never benefit by the deception—'

She interrupted him.

'How do you know that *I* shall benefit by it? How can you tell what has been happening since you last heard from me in America?'

'I have taken it for granted that things are the same.'

'Then you didn't even take measures to have news of me from any one else?'

'What need? I should always have received any letter you sent.'

'You thought it likely that I should appeal to you if I were in difficulties.'

He stood silent, glad of the obscurity which made it needless for him to command his features. At length:

'What is the simple fact? Has your secret been discovered, or not?'

'How does it concern you?'

'Only in this way: that if you are to be dependent upon any one, it must be upon me.'

Nancy gave a scornful laugh.

'That's very generous, considering your position. But happily you can't force me to accept your generosity, any more than I can compel you to take a share of my money.'

'Without the jibe at my poverty,' Tarrant said, 'that is a sufficient answer. As we can't even pretend to be friendly with each other, I am very glad there need be no talk of our future relations. You are provided for, and no doubt will take care not to lose the provision. If ever you prefer to forget that we are legally bound, I shall be no obstacle.'

'I have thought of that,' replied Nancy, after a pause, her voice expressing satisfaction. 'Perhaps we should do better to make the understanding at once. You are quite free; I should never acknowledge you as my husband.'

'You seriously mean it?'

'Do I seem to be joking?'

'Very well. I won't say that I should never acknowledge you as my wife; so far from that, I hold myself responsible whenever you choose to make any kind of claim upon me. But I shall not dream of interfering with your liberty. If ever you wish to write to me, you may safely address to the house at Champion Hill.—And remember always,' he added sternly, 'that it was not I who made such a parting necessary.'

Nancy returned his look through the gloom, and said in like tone:

'I shall do my best never to think of it at all. Fortunately, my time and my thoughts are occupied.'

'How?' Tarrant could not help asking, as she turned away; for her tone implied some special significance in the words.

'You have no right to ask anything whatever about me,' came from Nancy, who was already moving away.

He allowed her to go.

'So it is to be as I wished,' he said to himself, with mock courage. 'So much the better.'

And he went home to a night of misery.

CHAPTER 6

Not long after the disappearance of Fanny French, Mrs. Damerel called one day upon Luckworth Crewe at his office in Farringdon Street. Crewe seldom had business with ladies, and few things could have surprised him more than a visit from this lady in particular, whom he knew so well by name, and regarded with such special interest. She introduced herself as a person wishing to find a good investment for a small capital; but the half-hour's conversation which followed became in the end almost a confidential chat. Mrs. Damerel spoke of her nephew Horace Lord, with whom, she understood, Mr. Crewe was on terms of intimacy; she professed a grave solicitude on his account, related frankly the unhappy circumstances which had estranged the young man from her, and ultimately asked whether Crewe could not make it worth his own while to save Horace from the shoals of idleness, and pilot him into some safe commercial haven. This meeting was the first of many between the fashionable lady and the keen man of affairs. Without a suspicion of how it had come about, Horace Lord presently found himself an informal partner in Crewe's business; he invested only a nominal sum, which might be looked upon as a premium of apprenticeship; but there was an understanding that at the close of the term of tutelage imposed by his father's will, he should have the offer of a genuine partnership on very inviting terms.

Horace was not sorry to enter again upon regular occupation. He had considerably damaged his health in the effort to live up to his ideal of thwarted passion, and could no longer entertain a hope that Fanny's escapade was consistent with innocence. Having learnt how money slips through the fingers of a gentleman with fastidious tastes, he welcomed a prospect of increased resources, and applied himself with some energy to learning his new business. But with Mrs. Damerel he utterly refused to be reconciled, and of his sister he saw very little. Nancy, however, approved the step he had taken, and said she would be content to know that all was well with him.

Upon a Sunday morning, when the church bells had ceased to clang, Luckworth Crewe, not altogether at his ease in garb of flagrant respectability, sat by the fireside of a pleasant little room conversing with Mrs. Damerel. Their subject, as usual at the beginning of talk, was Horace Lord.

'He won't speak of you at all,' said Crewe, in a voice singularly subdued, sympathetic, respectful. 'I have done all I could, short of telling him that I know you. He's very touchy still on that old affair.'

'How would he like it,' asked the lady, 'if you told him that we are acquaintances?'

'Impossible to say. Perhaps it would make no difference one way or another.'

Mrs. Damerel was strikingly, yet becomingly, arrayed. The past year had dealt no less gently with her than its predecessors; if anything, her complexion had gained in brilliancy, perhaps a consequence of the hygienic precautions due to her fear of becoming stout. A stranger, even a specialist in the matter, might have doubted whether the fourth decade lay more than a month or two behind her. So far from seeking to impress her visitor with a pose of social superiority, she behaved to him as though his presence honoured as much as it delighted her; look, tone, bearing, each was a flattery which no obtuseness could fail to apprehend, and Crewe's countenance proved him anything but inappreciative. Hitherto she had spoken and listened with her head drooping in gentle melancholy; now, with a sudden change intended to signify the native buoyancy of her disposition, she uttered a rippling laugh, which showed her excellent teeth, and said prettily:

'Poor boy! I must suffer the penalty of having tried to save him from one of my own sex.—Not,' she added, 'that I foresaw how that poor silly girl would justify my worst fears of her. Perhaps,' her head drooping again, 'I ought to reproach myself with what happened.'

'I don't see that at all,' replied Crewe, whose eyes lost nothing of the exhibition addressed to them. 'Even if you had been the cause of it, which of course you weren't, I should have said you had done the right thing. Every one knew what Fanny French must come to.'

'Isn't it sad? A pretty girl—but so ill brought up, I fear. Can you give me any news of her sister, the one who came here and frightened me so?'

'Oh, she's going on as usual.'

Crewe checked himself, and showed hesitation.

'She almost threatened me,' Mrs. Damerel pursued, with timid sweetness. 'Do you think she is the kind of person to plot any harm against one?'

'She had better not try it on,' said Crewe, in his natural voice. Then, as if recollecting himself, he pursued more softly: 'But I was going to speak of her. You haven't heard that Miss. Lord has taken a position in the new branch of that Dress Supply Association?'

Mrs. Damerel kept an astonished silence.

'There can't be any doubt of it; I have been told on the best authority. She is in what they call the "club-room," a superintendent. It's a queer thing; what can have led her to it?'

'I must make inquiries,' said Mrs. Damerel, with an air of concern. 'How sad it is, Mr. Crewe, that these young relatives of mine,— almost the only relatives I have,—should refuse me their confidence and their affection. Pray, does Horace know of what his sister is doing?'

'I thought I wouldn't speak to him about it until I had seen you.'

'How very kind! How grateful I am to you for your constant thoughtfulness!'

Why Crewe should have practised such reticence, why it signified kindness and thoughtfulness to Mrs. Damerel, neither he nor she could easily have explained. But their eyes met, with diffident admiration on the one side, and touching amiability on the other. Then they discussed Nancy's inexplicable behaviour from every point of view; or rather, Mrs. Damerel discussed it, and her companion made a pretence of doing so. Crewe's manner had become patently artificial; he either expressed himself in trivial phrases, which merely avoided silence, or betrayed an embarrassment, an abstraction, which caused the lady to observe him with all the acuteness at her command.

You haven't seen her lately?' she asked, when Crewe had been staring at the window for a minute or two.

'Seen her?—No; not for a long time.'

'I think you told me you haven't called there since Mr. Lord's death?'

'I never was there at all,' he answered abruptly.

'Oh, I remember your saying so. Of course there is no reason why she shouldn't go into business, if time is heavy on her hands, as I dare say it may be. So many ladies prefer to have an occupation of that kind now-a-days. It's a sign of progress; we are getting more sensible; Society used to have such silly prejudices. Even within my recollection—how quickly things change!—no lady would have dreamt of permitting her daughter to take an engagement in a shop or any such place. Now we have women of title starting as milliners and modistes, and soon it will be quite a common thing to see one's friends behind the counter.'

She gave a gay little laugh, in which Crewe joined unmelodiously,— for he durst not be merry in the note natural to him,—then raised her eyes in playful appeal.

'If ever I should fall into misfortune, Mr. Crewe, would you put me in the way of earning my living.'

'You couldn't. You're above all that kind of thing. It's for the rough and ready sort of women, and I can't say I have much opinion of them.'

'That's a very nice little compliment; but at the same time, it's rather severe on the women who are practical.—Tell me frankly: Is my—my niece one of the people you haven't much opinion of?'

274

Crewe shuffled his feet.

'I wasn't thinking of Miss. Lord.'

'But what is really your opinion of her?' Mrs. Damerel urged softly.

Crewe looked up and down, smiled in a vacant way, and appeared very uncomfortable.

'May I guess the truth?' said his playful companion.

'No, I'll tell you. I wanted to marry her, and did my best to get her to promise.'

'I thought so!' She paused on the note of arch satisfaction, and mused. 'How nice of you to confess!—And that's all past and forgotten, is it?'

Never man more unlike himself than the bold advertising-agent in this colloquy. He was subdued and shy; his usual racy and virile talk had given place to an insipid mildness. He seemed bent on showing that the graces of polite society were not so strange to him as one might suppose. But under Mrs. Damerel's interrogation a restiveness began to appear in him, and at length he answered in his natural blunt voice:

'Yes, it's all over—and for a good reason.'

The lady's curiosity was still more provoked.

'No,' she exclaimed laughingly, 'I am *not* going to ask the reason. That would be presuming too far on friendship.'

Crewe fixed his eyes on a corner of the room, and seemed to look there for a solution of some difficulty. When the silence had lasted more than a minute, he began to speak slowly and awkwardly.

'I've half a mind to—in fact, I've been thinking that you ought to know.'

'The good reason?'

'Yes. You're the only one that could stand in the place of a mother to her. And I don't think she ought to be living alone, like she is, with no one to advise and help her.'

'I have felt that very strongly,' said Mrs. Damerel. 'The old servant who is with her can't be at all a suitable companion—that is, to be treated on equal terms. A very strange arrangement, indeed. But you don't mean that you thought less well of her because she is living in that way?'

'Of course not. It's something a good deal more serious than that.'

Mrs. Damerel became suddenly grave.

'Then I certainly ought to know.'

'You ought. I think it very likely she would have been glad enough to make a friend of you, if it hadn't been for this—this affair, which stood in the way. There can't be any harm in telling you, as you couldn't wish anything but her good.'

'That surely you may take for granted.'

'Well then, I have an idea that she's trying to earn money because some one is getting all he can out of her—leaving her very little for herself; and if so, it's time you interfered.'

The listener was so startled that she changed colour.

'You mean that some man has her in his power?'

'If I'm not mistaken, it comes to that. But for her father's will, she would have been married long ago, and—she ought to be.'

Having blurted out these words, Crewe felt much more at ease. As Mrs. Damerel's eyes fell, the sense of sexual predominance awoke in him, and he was no longer so prostrate before the lady's natural and artificial graces.

'How do you know this?' she asked, in an undertone.

'From some one who had it from Miss. Lord herself.'

'Are you quite sure that it isn't a malicious falsehood?'

'As sure as I am that I sit here. I know the man's name, and where he lives, and all about him. And I know where the child is at nurse.

'The child?—Oh—surely—never!'

A genuine agitation possessed her; she had a frightened, pain-stricken look, and moved as if she must act without delay.

276

'It's nearly six months old,' Crewe continued. 'Of course that's why she was away so long.'

'But why haven't you told me this before? It was your duty to tell me—your plain duty. How long have you known?'

'I heard of it first of all about three months ago, but it was only the other day that I was told the man's name, and other things about him.'

'Is it known to many people? Is the poor girl talked about?'

'No, no,' Crewe replied, with confidence. 'The person who told me is the only one who has found it out; you may depend upon that.'

'It must be a woman,' said Mrs. Damerel sharply.

'Yes, it's a woman. Some one *I* know very well. She told me just because she thought I was still hoping to marry Miss. Lord, and— well, the truth is, though we're good friends, she has a little spite against me, and I suppose it amused her to tell me something disagreeable.'

'I have no doubt,' said Mrs. Damerel, 'that the secret has been betrayed to a dozen people.'

'I'll go bail it hasn't!' returned Crewe, falling into his vernacular.

'I can hardly believe it at all. I should never have dreamt that such a thing was possible. What is the man's name? what is his position?'

'Tarrant is his name, and he's related somehow to a Mr. Vawdrey, well known in the City, who has a big house over at Champion Hill. I have no notion how they came together, or how long it was going on. But this Mr. Tarrant has been in America for a year, I understand; has only just come back; and now he's living In poorish lodgings,— Great College Street, Westminster. I've made a few inquiries about him, but I can't get at very much. A man who knows Vawdrey tells me that Tarrant has no means, and that he's a loafing, affected sort of chap. If that's true,—and it seems likely from the way he's living,—of course he will be ready enough to marry Miss. Lord when the proper time has come; I'm only afraid that's all he had in view from the first. And I can't help suspecting, as I said, that she's supporting him now. If not, why should she go and work in a shop? At all events, a decent man wouldn't allow her to do it.'

'A decent man,' said the listener, 'would never have allowed her to fall into disgrace.'

'Certainly not,' Crewe assented with energy. 'And as for my keeping quiet about it, Mrs. Damerel, you've only to think what an awkward affair it was to mention. I'm quite sure you'll have a little feeling against me, because I knew of it—'

'I beg you not to think that!' She returned to her manner of suave friendliness. 'I shall owe you gratitude for telling me, and nothing but gratitude. You have behaved with very great delicacy; I cannot say how highly I appreciate your feeling on the poor girl's behalf.'

'If I can be of any use, I am always at your service.'

'Thank you, dear Mr. Crewe, thank you! In you I have found a real friend,—and how rarely they are met with! Of course I shall make inquiries at once. My niece must be protected. A helpless girl in that dreadful position may commit unheard-of follies. I fear you are right. He is making her his victim. With such a secret, she is absolutely at his mercy. And it explains why she has shunned me. Oh, do you think her brother knows it?'

'I'm quite sure he doesn't; hasn't the least suspicion.'

'Of course not. But it's wonderful how she has escaped. Your informant—how did she find it out? You say she had the story from the girl's own lips. But why? She must have shown that she knew something.'

Crewe imparted such details as had come to his knowledge; they were meagre, and left many obscurities, but Mrs. Damerel rewarded him with effusive gratitude, and strengthened the spell which she had cast upon this knight of Farringdon Street.

CHAPTER 7

Every day Tarrant said to himself: 'I am a free man; I was only married in a dream.' Every night he thought of Nancy, and suffered heartache.

He thought, too, of Nancy's child, his own son. That Nancy was a tender mother, he knew from the letter she had written him after the baby's birth,—a letter he would have liked to read again, but forbore. Must not the separation from her child be hard? If he saw the poor little mortal, how would the sight affect him? At moments he felt a longing perhaps definable as the instinct of paternity; but he was not the man to grow sentimental over babies, his own or other people's. Irony and sarcasm—very agreeable to a certain class of newspaper readers—were just now his stock-in-trade, and he could not afford to indulge any softer mode of meditation.

His acquaintances agreed that the year of absence had not improved him. He was alarmingly clever; he talked well; but his amiability, the poetry of his mind, seemed to have been lost in America. He could no longer admire or praise.

For his own part, he did not clearly perceive this change. It struck him only that the old friends were less interesting than he had thought them; and he looked for reception in circles better able to appreciate his epigrams and paradoxes.

A few weeks of such life broke him so completely to harness, that he forgot the seasonable miseries which had been wont to drive him from London at the approach of November. When the first fog blackened against his windows, he merely lit the lamp and wrote on, indifferent. Two years ago he had declared that a London November would fatally blight his soul; that he must flee to a land of sunshine, or perish. There was little time, now, to think about his soul.

One Monday morning arrived a letter which surprised and disturbed him. It ran thus:

'Mrs. Eustace Damerel presents her compliments to Mr. Tarrant, and would take it as a great favour if he could call upon her, either to-morrow or Tuesday, at any hour between three and seven. She particularly desires to see Mr. Tarrant on a private matter of mutual interest.'

Now this could have but one meaning. Mrs. Eustace Damerel was, of course, Nancy's relative; from Nancy herself, or in some other way, she must have learnt the fact of his marriage. Probably from Nancy, since she knew where he lived. He was summoned to a judicial interview. Happily, attendance was not compulsory.

Second thoughts advised him that he had better accept the invitation. He must know what measures were in progress against him. If Nancy had already broken her word, she might be disposed to revenge herself in every way that would occur to an angry woman of small refinement; she might make life in London impossible for him.

He sat down and penned a reply, saying that he would call upon Mrs. Damerel at five to-morrow. But he did not post this. After all, a day's delay would only irritate him; better to go this afternoon, in which case it was not worth while sending an answer.

It seemed to him very probable that Nancy would be with her aunt, to confront him. If so,—if indeed she were going to act like any coarse woman, with no regard but for her own passions and Interests, —he would at least have the consolation of expelling from his mind, at once and for ever, her haunting image.

Mrs. Damerel, who during the past twelve months had changed her abode half-a-dozen times, now occupied private lodgings in Tyburnia. On his admittance, Tarrant sat alone for nearly five minutes in a pretentiously furnished room—just the room in which he had expected to find Nancy's relative; the delay and the surroundings exasperated his nervous mood, so that, when the lady entered, he behaved with slighter courtesy than became his breeding. Nothing in her appearance surprised or interested him. There was a distant facial resemblance to Nancy, natural in her mother's sister; there was expensive, though not particularly tasteful dress, and a gait, a manner, distinguishable readily enough from what they aimed at displaying— the grace of a woman born to social privilege.

It would be a humiliating conversation; Tarrant braced himself to go through with it. He stood stiffly while his hostess regarded him with shrewd eyes. She had merely bent her head.

'Will you sit down, Mr. Tarrant?'

He took a chair without speaking.

'I think you know me by name?'

'I have heard of a Mrs. Damerel.'

'Some time ago, I suppose? And in that you have the advantage of me. I heard your name yesterday for the first time.'

It was the sharp rejoinder of a woman of the world. Tarrant began to perceive that he had to do with intelligence, and would not be allowed to perform his share of the talking *de haut en bas*.

'In what can I be of service to you?' he asked with constrained civility.

'You can tell me, please, what sort of connection there is between you and my niece, Miss. Lord.'

Mrs. Damerel was obviously annoyed by his demeanour, and made little effort to disguise her feeling. She gave him the look of one who does not mean to be trifled with.

'Really,' answered the young man with a smile, 'I don't know what authority you have to make such inquiries. You are not, I believe, Miss. Lord's guardian.'

'No, but I am her only relative who can act on her behalf where knowledge of the world is required. As a gentleman, you will bear this in mind. It's quite true that I can't oblige you to tell me anything; but when I say that I haven't spoken even to my niece of what I have heard, and haven't communicated with the gentlemen who *are* her guardians, I think you will see that I am not acting in a way you ought to resent.'

'You mean, Mrs. Damerel, that what passes between us is in confidence?'

'I only mean, Mr. Tarrant, that I am giving you an opportunity of explaining yourself—so that I can keep the matter private if your explanation is satisfactory.'

'You have a charge of some kind to bring against me,' said Tarrant composedly. 'I must first of all hear what it is. The prisoner at the bar can't be prosecuting counsel at the same time.'

'Do you acknowledge that you are on intimate terms with Miss. Lord?'

'I have known her for a year or two.'

Tarrant began to exercise caution. Nancy had no hand in this matter; some one had told tales about her, that was all. He must learn, without committing himself, exactly how much had been discovered.

'Are you engaged to her?'

'Engaged to marry her? No.'

He saw in Mrs. Damerel's clear eye that she convicted him of ambiguities.

'You have not even made her a promise of marriage?'

'How much simpler, if you would advance a clear charge. I will answer it honestly.'

Mrs. Damerel seemed to weigh the value of this undertaking. Tarrant met her gaze with steady indifference.

'It may only be a piece of scandal,—a mistake, or a malicious invention. I have been told that—that you are in everything but law my niece's husband.'

They regarded each other during a moment's silence. Tarrant's look indicated rapid and anxious thought.

'It seems,' he said at length, 'that you have no great faith in the person who told you this.'

'It is the easiest matter in the world to find out whether the story is true or not. Inquiries at Falmouth would be quite sufficient, I dare say. I give you the opportunity of keeping it quiet, that's all.'

'You won't care to let me know who told you?'

'There's no reason why I shouldn't,' said Mrs. Damerel, after reflection. 'Do you know Mr. Luckworth Crewe?'

'I don't think I ever heard the name.'

'Indeed? He is well acquainted with Miss. Lord. Some one he wouldn't mention gave him all the particulars, having learnt them from Miss Lord herself, and he thought it his duty to inform me of my niece's very painful position.'

'Who is this man?' Tarrant asked abruptly.

'I am rather surprised you have never heard of him. He's a man of business. My nephew, Mr. Horace Lord, is shortly to be in partnership with him.'

'Crewe? No, the name is quite strange to me.'

Tarrant's countenance darkened; he paused for an instant, then added impatiently:

'You say he had "all the particulars." What were they, these particulars?'

'Will one be enough? A child was born at Falmouth, and is now at a place just outside London, in the care of some stranger.'

The source of this information might, or might not, be Nancy herself. In either case, there was no further hope of secrecy. Tarrant abandoned his reserve, and spoke quietly, civilly.

'So far, you have heard the truth. What have you to ask of me, now?'

'You have been abroad for a long time, I think?'

'For about a year.'

282

'Does that mean that you wished to see no more of her?'

'That I deserted her, in plain words? It meant nothing of the kind.'

'You are aware, then, that she has taken a place in a house of business, just as if she thought it necessary to earn her own living?'

Tarrant displayed astonishment.

'I am aware of no such thing. How long has that been going on?'

'Then you don't see her?'

'I have seen her, but she told me nothing of that.'

'There's something very strange in this, Mr. Tarrant. You seem to me to be speaking the truth. No, please don't take offence. Before I saw you, you were a total stranger to me, and after what I had heard, I couldn't think very well of you. I may as well confess that you seem a different kind of man from what I expected. I don't wish to offend you, far from it. If we can talk over this distressing affair in a friendly way, so much the better. I have nothing whatever in view but to protect my niece—to do the best that can be done for her.'

'That I have taken for granted,' Tarrant replied. 'I understand that you expected to meet a scoundrel of a very recognisable type. Well, I am not exactly that. But what particular act of rascality have you in mind? Something worse than mere seduction, of course.'

'Will you answer a disagreeable question? Are you well-to-do?'

'Anything but that.'

'Indeed? And you can form no idea why Nancy has gone to work in a shop?'

Tarrant raised his eyebrows.

'I see,' he said deliberately. 'You suspect that I have been taking money from her?'

'I *did* suspect it; now it seems to me more unlikely.'

'Many thanks,' he answered, with cold irony. 'So the situation was this: Miss. Lord had been led astray by a rascally fellow, who not only left her to get on as best she could, but lived on her income, so that she had at length to earn money for her own needs. There's something very clear and rounded, very dramatic, about that. What I should like to know is, whether Miss. Lord tells the story in this way.'

'I can't say that she does. I think it was Mr. Crewe who explained things like that.'

'I am obliged to Mr. Crewe. But he may, after all, only repeat what he has heard. It's a pity we don't know Miss. Lord's actual confidante.'

'Of course you have *not* received assistance from her?'

Tarrant stared for a moment, then laughed unpleasantly.

'I have no recollection of it.'

'Another disagreeable question. Did you really go away and leave her to get on as best she could?'

He looked darkly at her.

'And if I did?'

'Wasn't it rather unaccountable behaviour—in a gentleman?'

'Possibly.'

'I can't believe it. There is something unexplained.'

'Yes, there *is* something unexplained.—Mrs. Damerel, I should have thought you would naturally speak first to your niece. Why did you send for me before doing so?'

'To find out what sort of man you were, so that I should be able to form my own opinion of what Nancy chose to tell me. Perhaps she may refuse to tell me anything at all—we are not like ordinary relatives, I am sorry to say. But I dare say you know better than I do how she thinks of me.'

'I have heard her speak of you only once or twice. At all events, now that you are prepared, you will go and see her?'

'I must. It would be wrong to stand by and do nothing.'

'And you will see her guardians?'

'That must depend. I certainly shall if she seems to be suffering hardships. I must know why she goes out to work, as if she were pinched for money. There is her child to support, of course, but that wouldn't make any difference to her; she is well provided for.'

284

'Yes. There's no choice but to fall back upon the villain theory.'

He rose, and took up his hat.

'You mustn't go yet, Mr. Tarrant,' said his hostess firmly. 'I have said that I can't believe such things of you. If you would only explain—'

'That's just what I can't do. It's as much a mystery to me as to you —her wishing to earn money.'

'I was going to say—if you would only explain your intentions as to the future—'

'My intentions will depend entirely on what I hear from your niece. I shall see her as soon as possible. Perhaps you can tell me at what hour she returns from business?'

'No, I can't. I wish you would talk a little longer.'

His eyes flashed angrily.

'Mrs. Damerel, I have said all that I am willing to say. What you have heard is partly true; you probably won't have to wait very long for the rest of the story, but I have no time and no inclination to tell it. Go and see your niece to-morrow by all means,—or her guardians, if it seems necessary.'

'I am very sorry we are parting in this way.'

'You must remember how difficult it is to keep one's temper under certain kinds of accusation.'

'I don't accuse you.'

'Well, then, to explain calmly that one couldn't commit this or that sordid rascality;—it comes to the same thing. However, I am obliged to you for opening my eyes. I have got into a very foolish position, and I promise you I will get out of it as quickly as may be.'

Whereupon he bowed his leave-taking, and withdrew.

CHAPTER 8

It was not yet dark, but street-lamps had begun to flare and flicker in the gust of a cold, damp evening. A thin and slippery mud smeared the pavement. Tarrant had walked mechanically as far as to the top of Park Lane before he began to consider his immediate course. Among the people who stood waiting for omnibuses, he meditated thus:

'She may not get home until seven or half-past; then she will have a meal. I had better put it off till about half-past eight. That leaves me some four hours to dispose of. First of all I'll walk home, and—yes, by all the devils! I'll finish that bit of writing. A year ago I could no more have done it, under such circumstances, than have built a suspension bridge. To-day I will— just to show that I've some grit in me.'

Down Park Lane, and by Buckingham Palace across to Westminster, he kept his thoughts for the most part on that bit of writing. Only thus could he save himself from an access of fury which would only have injured him—the ire of shame in which a man is tempted to beat his head against stone walls. He composed aloud, balancing many a pretty antithesis, and polishing more than one lively paradox.

In his bedroom-study the fire had gone out. No matter; he would write in the cold. It was mere amanuensis work, penning at the dictation of his sarcastic demon. Was he a sybarite? Many a poor scribbler has earned bed and breakfast with numb fingers. The fire in his body would serve him for an hour or two.

So he sat down, and achieved his task to the last syllable. He read it through, corrected it, made it up for post, and rose with the plaudits of conscience. 'Who shall say now that I am a fop and a weakling?'

Half-past seven. Good; just time enough to appease his hunger and reach Grove Lane by the suitable hour. He went out to the little coffee-shop which was his resort in Spartan moods, ate with considerable appetite, and walked over Westminster Bridge to the Camberwell tram. To kill time on the journey he bought a halfpenny paper.

As he ascended Grove Lane his heart throbbed more than the exercise warranted. At the door of the house, which he had never yet entered, and which he had not looked upon for more than a year, he stood to calm himself, with lips set and cheek pale in the darkness. Then a confident peal at the knocker.

It was Mary who opened. He had never seen her, but knew that this grave, hard-featured person, not totally unlike a born gentlewoman, must be Mary Woodruff. And in her eyes he read a suspicion of his own identity.

'Is Miss. Lord at home?' he asked, in a matter-of-fact way.

'Yes.—What name shall I mention?'

'Mr. Tarrant.'

Her eyes fell, and she requested him to enter, to wait in the hall for a moment; then went upstairs. She was absent for a few minutes, and on returning asked him to follow her. She led to the dawing-room: on the way, Tarrant felt a surprise that in so small a house the drawing-room should be correctly situated on the upper floor.

Here he had again to wait. A comfortable room, he thought, and with a true air of home about it. He knew how significant is this impression first received on entering a strange abode; home or encampment, attraction or repulsion, according to the mind of the woman who rules there. Was it Nancy, or Mary, who made the atmosphere of the house?

The door opened, and he faced towards it.

Nancy's dress had an emphasis of fashion formerly unknown to it; appropriate enough considering her new occupation. The flush upon her cheeks, the light of doubtful meaning in her eyes, gave splendour to a beauty matured by motherhood. In the dark street, a fortnight ago, Tarrant could hardly be said to have seen her; he gazed in wonder and admiration.

'What has brought you here?'

'A cause quite sufficient.—This is a little house; can we talk without being overheard?'

'You can shout if you wish to,' she answered flippantly. 'The servant is Out, and Mary is downstairs.'

Nancy did not seat herself, and offered no seat to the visitor.

'Why have you made yourself a shop-girl?'

'I didn't know that I had.'

'I am told you go daily to some shop or other.'

'I am engaged at a place of business, but I don't.—However, that doesn't matter. What business is it of yours?'

'Who is Mr. Luckworth Crewe?'

Nancy kept her eyes still more resolutely fronting his severe look.

'A man I used to know.'

'You don't see him now-a-days?'

'It's many months since I saw him.'

'Who, then, is the woman who has told him your whole story—with embellishments, and who says she has had it from you yourself?'

Nancy was speechless.

'I don't say there is any such person,' Tarrant continued. 'The man may have lied in that particular. But he has somehow got to know a good deal about you,—where and when your child was born, where it is now, where I live, and so on. And all this he has reported to your aunt, Mrs. Damerel.'

'To her?—How do you know?'

For answer he held out Mrs. Damerel's note of invitation, then added:

'I have been with her this afternoon. She is coming to offer you her protection against the scoundrel who has ruined you, and who is now living upon you.'

'What do you mean?'

'That's the form the story has taken, either in Mr. Crewe's mind, or in that of the woman who told it to him.'

'Don't they know that I am married?'

'Evidently not.'

'And they think you—are having money from me?'

'That's how they explain your taking a place in a shop.'

Nancy laughed, and laughed again.

'How ridiculous!'

'I'm glad you can get amusement out of it. Perhaps you can suggest how the joke began?'

She moved a few steps, then turned again to him.

288

'Yes, I know who the woman must be. It's Beatrice French.'

'A bosom friend of yours, of course.'

'Nothing of the kind.'

'But you have taken her into your confidence—up to a certain point?'

'Yes, I have told her. And she told Mr. Crewe? I understand that. Well, what does it matter?'

Tarrant was at a loss to interpret this singular levity. He had never truly believed that reading of Nancy's character by means of which he tried to persuade himself that his marriage was an unmitigated calamity, and a final parting between them the best thing that could happen. His memories of her, and the letters she had written him, coloured her personality far otherwise. Yet was not the harsh judgment after all the true one?

'It doesn't matter to you,' he said, 'that people think you an unmarried mother,—that people are talking about you with grins and sneers?'

Nancy reddened in angry shame.

'Let them talk!' she exclaimed violently. 'What does it matter, so long as they don't know I'm married?'

'So long as they don't know?—How came you to tell this woman?'

'Do you suppose I told her for amusement? She found out what had happened at Falmouth,—found out simply by going down there and making inquiries; because she suspected me of some secret affair with a man she wants to marry herself—this Mr. Crewe. The wonder of wonders is that no one else got to know of it in that way. Any one who cared much what happened to me would have seen the all but impossibility of keeping such a secret.'

It is a notable instance of evolutionary process that the female mind, in wrath, flies to just those logical ineptitudes which most surely exasperate the male intelligence. Tarrant gave a laugh of irate scorn.

'Why, you told me the other day that I cared particularly whether your secret was discovered or not—that I only married you in the hope of profiting by it?'

'Wouldn't any woman think so?'

'I hope not. I believe there are some women who don't rush naturally to a base supposition.'

'Did I?' Nancy exclaimed, with a vehement passion that made her breast heave. 'Didn't I give you time enough—believe in you until I could believe no longer?'

The note of her thrilling voice went to Tarrant's heart, and his head drooped.

'That may be true,' he said gravely. 'But go on with your explanation. This woman came to you, and told you what she had discovered?'

'Yes.'

'And you allowed her to think you unmarried?'

'What choice had I? How was my child to be brought up if I lost everything?'

'Good God, Nancy! Did you imagine I should leave you to starve?'

His emotion, his utterance of her name, caused her to examine him with a kind of wonder.

'How did I know?—How could I tell, at that time, whether you were alive or dead?—I had to think of myself and the child.'

'My poor girl!'

The words fell from him involuntarily. Nancy's look became as scornful and defiant as before.

'Oh, that was nothing. I've gone through a good deal more than that.'

'Stop. Tell me this. Have you in your anger—anger natural enough —allowed yourself to speak to any one about me in the way I should never forgive? In the spirit of your letter, I mean. Did you give this Beatrice French any ground for thinking that I made a speculation of you?'

'I said nothing of that kind.'

'Nor to any one else?'

'To no one.'

290

'Yet you told this woman where I was living, and that I had been abroad for a long time. Why?'

'Yes, I told her so much about you,' Nancy replied. 'Not when she first came to me, but afterwards—only the other day. I wanted employment, and didn't know how to get it, except through her. She promised me a place if I would disclose your name; not that she knew or cared anything about *you*, but because she still had suspicions about Mr. Crewe. I was desperate, and I told her.'

'Desperate? Why?'

'How can I make you understand what I have gone through? What do you care? And what do *I* care whether you understand or not? It wasn't for money, and Beatrice French knew it wasn't.'

'Then it must have been that you could not bear the monotony of your life.'

Her answer was a short, careless laugh.

'Where is this shop? What do you do?'

'It's a dress-supply association. I advise fools about the fashions, and exhibit myself as a walking fashion-plate. I can't see how it should interest you.'

'Whatever concerns you, Nancy, interests me more than anything else in the world.'

Again she laughed.

'What more do you want to know?'

She was half turned from him, leaning at the mantelpiece, a foot on the fender.

'You said just now that you have gone through worse things than the shame of being thought unmarried. Tell me about it all.'

'Not I, indeed. When I was willing to tell you everything, you didn't care to hear it. It's too late now.'

'It's not too late, happily, to drag you out of this wretched slough into which you are sinking. Whatever the cost, *that* shall be done!'

'Thank you, I am not disposed to let any one drag me anywhere. I want no help; and if I did, you would be the last person I should accept it from. I don't know why you came here after the agreement we made the other night.'

Tarrant stepped towards her.

'I came to find out whether you were telling lies about me, and I should never have thought it possible but for my bad conscience. I know you had every excuse for being embittered and for acting revengefully. It seems you have only told lies about yourself. As, after all, you are my wife, I shan't allow that.'

Once more she turned upon him passionately.

'I am *not* your wife! You married me against your will, and shook me off as soon as possible. I won't be bound to you; I shall act as a free woman.'

'Bound to me you are, and shall be—as I to you.'

'You may say it fifty times, and it will mean nothing.—How bound to you? Bound to share my money?'

'I forgive you that, because I have treated you ill. You don't mean it either. You know I am incapable of such a thought. But that shall very soon be put right. Your marriage shall be made known at once.'

'Known to whom?'

'To the people concerned—to your guardians.'

'Don't trouble yourself,' she answered, with a smile. 'They know it already.'

Tarrant half closed his eyes as he looked at her.

'What's the use of such a silly falsehood?'

'I told you I had gone through a good deal more than you imagined. I have struggled to keep my money, in spite of shames and miseries, and I will have it for myself—- and my child! If you want to know the truth, go to Samuel Barmby, and ask him what he has had to do with me. I owe no explanation to *you*.'

Tarrant could see her face only in profile. Marvelling at the complications she gradually revealed, he felt his blood grow warm with desire of her beauty. She was his wife, yet guarded as by maidenhood. A familiar touch would bring the colour to her cheeks, the light of resentment to her eyes. Passion made him glad of the estrangement which compelled a new wooing, and promised, on her part, a new surrender.

'You don't owe it me, Nancy; but if I beg you to tell me all— because I have come to my senses again—because I know how foolish and cruel I have been—'

292

'Remember what we agreed. Go your way, and let me go mine.'

'I had no idea of what I was agreeing to. I took it for granted that your marriage was strictly a secret, and that you might be free in the real sense if you chose.'

'Yes, and you were quite willing, because it gave you your freedom as well. I am as free as I wish to be. I have made a life for myself that satisfies me—and now you come to undo everything. I won't be tormented—I have endured enough.'

'Then only one course is open to me. I shall publish your marriage everywhere. I shall make a home for you, and have the child brought to it; then come or not, as you please.'

At mention of the child Nancy regarded him with cold curiosity.

'How are you to make a home for me? I thought you had difficulty enough in supporting yourself.'

'That is no concern of yours. It shall be done, and in a day or two. Then make your choice.'

'You think I can be forced to live with a man I don't love?'

'I shouldn't dream of living with a woman who didn't love me. But you are married, and a mother, and the secrecy that is degrading you shall come to an end. Acknowledge me or not, I shall acknowledge *you*, and make it known that I am to blame for all that has happened.'

'And what good will you do?'

'I shall do good to myself, at all events. I'm a selfish fellow, and shall be so to the end, no doubt.'

Nancy glanced at him to interpret the speech by his expression. He was smiling.

'What good will it do you to have to support me? The selfishness I see in it is your wishing to take me from a comfortable home and make me poor.'

'That can't be helped. And, what's more, you won't think it a hardship.'

'How do you know that? I have borne dreadful degradations rather than lose my money.'

'That was for the child's sake, not for your own.'

He said it softly and kindly, and for the first time Nancy met his eyes without defiance.

'It was; I could always have earned my own living, somehow.'

Tarrant paused a moment, then spoke with look averted.

'Is he well, and properly cared for?'

'If he were not well and safe, I shouldn't be away from him.'

'When will you let me see him, Nancy?'

She did not smile, but there was a brightening of her countenance, which she concealed. Tarrant stepped to her side.

'Dear—my own love—will you try to forgive me? It was all my cursed laziness. It would never have happened if I hadn't fallen into poverty. Poverty is the devil, and it overcame me.'

'How can you think that *I* shall be strong enough to face it?' she asked, moving half a step away. 'Leave me to myself; I am contented; I have made up my mind about what is before me, and I won't go through all that again.'

Tired of standing, she dropped upon the nearest chair, and lay back.

'You can't be contented, Nancy, in a position that dishonours you. From what you tell me, it seems that your secret is no secret at all. Will you compel me to go to that man Barmby and seek information from him about my own wife?'

'I have had to do worse things than that.'

'Don't torture me by such vague hints. I entreat you to tell me at once the worst that you have suffered. How did Barmby get to know of your marriage? And why has he kept silent about it? There can't be anything that you are ashamed to say.'

'No. The shame is all yours.'

'I take it upon myself, all of it; I ought never to have left you; but that baseness followed only too naturally on the cowardice which kept me from declaring our marriage when honour demanded it. I have played a contemptible part in this story; don't refuse to help me now that I am ready to behave more like a man. Put your hand in mine, and let us be friends, if we mayn't be more.'

She sat irresponsive.

294

'You were a brave girl. You consented to my going away because it seemed best, and I took advantage of your sincerity. Often enough that last look of yours has reproached me. I wonder how I had the heart to leave you alone.'

Nancy raised herself, and said coldly:

'It was what I might have expected. I had only my own folly to thank. You behaved as most men would.'

This was a harder reproach than any yet. Tarrant winced under it. He would much rather have been accused of abnormal villainy.

'And I was foolish,' continued Nancy, 'in more ways than you knew. You feared I had told Jessica Morgan of our marriage, and you were right; of course I denied it. She has been the cause of my worst trouble.'

In rapid sentences she told the story of her successive humiliations, recounted her sufferings at the hands of Jessica and Beatrice and Samuel Barmby. When she ceased, there were tears in her eyes.

'Has Barmby been here again?' Tarrant asked sternly.

'Yes. He has been twice, and talked in just the same way, and I had to sit still before him—'

'Has he said one word that—?'

'No, no,' she interrupted hastily. 'He's only a fool—not man enough to—'

'That saves me trouble,' said Tarrant; 'I have only to treat him like a fool. My poor darling, what vile torments you have endured! And you pretend that you would rather live on this fellow's interested generosity—for, of course, he hopes to be rewarded— than throw the whole squalid entanglement behind you and be a free, honest woman, even if a poor one?'

'I see no freedom.'

'You have lost all your love for me. Well, I can't complain of that. But bear my name you shall, and be supported by me. I tell you that it was never *possible* for me actually to desert you and the little one—never possible. I shirked a duty as long as I could; that's all it comes to. I loafed and paltered until the want of a dinner drove me into honesty. Try to forget it, dear Nancy. Try to forgive me, my dearest!'

She was dry-eyed again, and his appeal seemed to have no power over her emotions.

'You are forgetting,' she said practically, 'that I have lived on money to which I had no right, and that I—or you—can be forced to repay it.'

'Repaid it must be, whether demanded or not. Where does Barmby live? Perhaps I could see him to-night.'

'What means have you of keeping us all alive?'

'Some of my work has been accepted here and there; but there's something else I have in mind. I don't ask you to become a poverty-stricken wife in the ordinary way. I can't afford to take a house. I must put you, with the child, into as good lodgings as I can hope to pay for, and work on by myself, just seeing you as often as you will let me. Even if you were willing, it would be a mistake for us to live together. For one thing, I couldn't work under such conditions; for another, it would make you a slave. Tell me: are you willing to undertake the care of the child, if nothing else is asked of you?'

Nancy gave him a disdainful smile, a smile like those of her girlhood.

'I'm not quite so feeble a creature as you think me.'

'You would rather have the child to yourself, than be living away from him?'

'If you have made up your mind, why trouble to ask such questions?'

'Because I have no wish to force burdens upon you. You said just now that you could see little prospect of freedom in such a life as I have to offer you. I thought you perhaps meant that the care of the child would—'

'I meant nothing,' Nancy broke in, with fretful impatience.

'Where is he—our boy?'

'At Dulwich. I told you that in my last letter.'

'Yes—yes. I thought you might have changed.'

'I couldn't have found a better, kinder woman. Can you guess how many answers I had to the advertisement? Thirty-two.'

'Of course five-and-twenty of them took it for granted you would pay so much a week and ask no questions. They would just not have starved the baby,—unless you had hinted to them that you were willing to pay a lump sum for a death-certificate, in which case the affair would have been more or less skilfully managed.'

296

'Mary knew all about that. She came from Falmouth, and spent two days in visiting people. I knew I could rely on her judgment. There were only four or five people she cared to see at all, and of these only one that seemed trustworthy.'

'To be sure. One out of two-and-thirty. A higher percentage than would apply to mankind at large, I dare say. By-the-bye, I was afraid you might have found a difficulty in registering the birth.'

'No. I went to the office myself, the morning that I was leaving Falmouth, and the registrar evidently knew nothing about me. It isn't such a small place that everybody living there is noticed and talked of.'

'And Mary took the child straight to Dulwich?'

'Two days before I came,—so as to have the house ready for me.

'Perhaps it was unfortunate, Nancy, that you had so good a friend. But for that, I should have suffered more uneasiness about you.'

She answered with energy:

'There is no husband in the world worth such a friend as Mary.'

At this Tarrant first smiled, then laughed. Nancy kept her lips rigid. It happened that he again saw her face in exact profile, and again it warmed the current of his blood.

'Some day you shall think better of that.'

She paid no attention. Watching her, he asked:

'What are you thinking of so earnestly?'

Her answer was delayed a little, but she said at length, with an absent manner:

'Horace might lend me the money to pay back what I owe.'

'Your brother?—If he can afford it, there would be less objection to that than to any other plan I can think of. But I must ask it myself; you shall beg no more favours. I will ask it in your presence.'

'You will do nothing of the kind,' Nancy replied drily. 'If you think to please me by humiliating yourself, you are very much mistaken. And you mustn't imagine that I put myself into your hands to be looked after as though I had no will of my own. With the past you have nothing to do,—with *my* past, at all events. Care for the future as you like.'

'But I must see your guardians.'

'No. I won't have that.'

She stood up to emphasise her words.

'I must. It's the only way in which I can satisfy myself—'

'Then I refuse to take a step,' said Nancy. 'Leave all that to me, and I will go to live where you please, and never grumble, however poor I am. Interfere, and I will go on living as now, on Samuel Barmby's generosity.'

There was no mistaking her resolution. Tarrant hesitated, and bit his lip.

'How long, then, before you act?' he inquired abruptly.

'When my new home is found, I am ready to go there.'

'You will deal honestly with me? You will tell every one, and give up everything not strictly yours?'

'I have done with lies,' said Nancy.

'Thank heaven, so have I!'

Part VI: A Virtue of Necessity

CHAPTER 1

Upon the final tempest in De Crespigny Park there followed, for Arthur Peachey, a calmer and happier season than he had ever known. To have acted with stern resolve is always a satisfaction, especially to the man conscious of weak good-nature, and condemned for the most part to yield. In his cheap lodging at Clapham, Peachey awoke each morning with a vague sense of joy, which became delight as soon as he had collected his senses. He was a free man. No snarl greeted him as he turned his head upon the pillow; he could lie and meditate, could rise quietly when the moment sounded, could go downstairs to a leisurely meal, cheered perhaps by a letter reporting that all was well with his dear little son. Simple, elementary pleasures, but how he savoured them after his years of sordid bondage!

It was the blessedness of divorce, without squalid publicity. It was the vast relief of widowerhood, without dreary memories of death and burial.

In releasing himself from such companionship, the man felt as though he had washed and become clean.

Innocent of scientific speculation, he had the misfortune about this time to read in paper or magazine something on the subject of heredity, the idle verbiage of some half-informed scribbler. It set him anxiously thinking whether his son would develop the vices of the mother's mind, and from that day he read all the printed chatter regarding natural inheritance that he could lay his hands on. The benefit he derived from this course of study was neither more nor less than might have been expected; it supplied him with a new trouble, which sometimes kept him wakeful. He could only resolve that his boy should have the best education procurable for money, if he starved himself in providing it.

He had begun to live with the utmost economy, and for a twofold reason: the business of Messrs Ducker, Blunt & Co. threatened a decline, and, this apart, he desired to get out of it, to obtain an interest in some more honourable concern. For a long time it had been known to him that the disinfectants manufactured by his firm were far from trustworthy, and of late the complaints of purchasers had become frequent. With the manufacturing department he had nothing to do; he tried to think himself free from responsibility; for, in spite of amiable qualities, he was a man of business, and saw a great part of life through the commercial spectacles commonly worn now-a-days. Nevertheless conscience unsettled him. One day he heard his partners joking over the legislative omission by virtue of which they were able to adulterate their disinfectants to any extent without fear of penalty; their laughter grated upon him, and he got out of the way. If he could lay aside a few thousands of pounds, assuredly his connection with the affair should be terminated. So he lived, for his own part, on a pound a week, and informed Ada through his solicitor that she must be satisfied with a certain very moderate allowance.

Mrs. Peachey naturally laid herself out to give every one as much trouble as possible. Insulting post-cards showered upon her husband at his place of business.

300

After a few weeks she discovered his lodging, and addressed the post-cards thither; but she made no attempt at personal molestation. The loss of her child gave her not the slightest concern, yet she determined to find out where the boy was living. She remembered that Peachey had relatives at Canterbury, and after a troublesome search succeeded in her purpose. An interview with her husband's married sister proved so unsatisfactory to Ada, that she had recourse to her familiar weapons, rage, insult, and menace; with the result that she was forcibly removed, and made a scandal in the quiet street.

Then she consulted men of law, and found one who encouraged her to sue for restitution of conjugal rights. It came to nothing, however; for in the meantime she was growing tired of her solitary existence, —friends of course she had none,—and the spirit moved her to try a change of tactics.

She wrote a long, long letter, penitent, tear-bestained. 'I have behaved outrageously to you, dearest Arthur; I must have been mad to say and do such things. The doctor tells me that my health has been in a very bad state for a long time, and I really don't remember half that has happened. You were quite right when you told me that I should be better if I didn't live such an idle life, and I have quite, quite made up my mind to be an industrious and a *good* woman. All yesterday I spent in needlework and crying. Oh, the tears that I have shed! My darling husband, what can I do to win your forgiveness? Do consider how lonely I am in this house. Beatrice has been horrid to me. If I said all I think about *her*, she wouldn't like to hear it; but I am learning to control my tongue. She lives alone in a flat, and has men to spend every evening with her; it's disgraceful! And there's Fanny, who I am sure is leading an immoral life abroad. Of course I shall never speak to her again. You were quite right when you said my sisters were worthless.'—Peachey had never permitted himself any such remark.—'I will have no one but you, my dear, good, sweet husband.'

So on, over several pages. Reading it, the husband stood aghast at this new revelation of female possibilities; at the end, he hurriedly threw it into the fire, fearing, and with good reason, that weakness in his own character to which the woman addressed herself.

Every day for a week there arrived a replica of this epistle, and at length he answered. It was the fatal concession. Though he wrote with almost savage severity, Ada replied in terms of exuberant gratitude. Oh, how delighted she was to see his dear handwriting once more! How it reminded her of happy days, when they loved each other so tenderly! Then came two strophes of a sentimental drawing-room song, and lastly, an impassioned appeal to be allowed to see her husband, were it only for five minutes.

Another week of such besieging, and the poor fellow's foolish heart gave way. He would see the wretched woman, and tell her that, though never could he consent to live with her again, he had no malicious feeling, and was willing to be her friend at a distance. So, at six o'clock one evening, behold him tremulously approaching the house in De Crespigny Park,—tremulously, because he dreaded the assault upon his emotions to which he so recklessly exposed himself. He was admitted by a very young servant, in a very clean cap and apron. Silence possessed the dwelling; he did not venture to tread with natural step. He entered the drawing-room, and there, from amid a heap of household linen which required the needle, rose the penitent wife. Ostentatiously she drew from her finger a thimble, then advanced with head bent.

'How kind of you, Arthur! How—how very—'

And she was dissolved in tears—so genuine, that they marked pale rillets across the bloom of her cheeks.

About a month after that the furniture was removed from De Crespigny Park to a much smaller house at Brixton, where Mr. and Mrs. Peachey took up their abode together. A medical man shortly called, and Ada, not without secret disgust, smilingly made known to her husband that she must now be very careful of her health.

On one point only the man had held to a rational resolve; he would not allow his little son to be brought back to London, away from the home where he was happy and thriving. Out of mere self-will Ada strove for a long time to overcome this decision; finding argument and artifice of no avail, she dropped the matter. Peachey owed this triumph largely to the firm commonsense of his sister, who plainly refused to let the little fellow quit her care for that of such a woman as he was unfortunate enough to call mother.

Christmas came, and with it an unanticipated call from Miss. Fanny French, who said she had lately recovered from a serious illness in Paris; the nature of her malady she did not specify; it had left her haggard and thin, but by no means deficient in vivacity. She was dressed with tawdry extravagance, wore a mass of false yellow hair, had her eyebrows dyed black,—piquant contrast,—and her cheeks and lips richly carmined. No veritable information as to her past and present could be gleaned from the mixture of French and English which she ceaselessly gabbled. She had come over for Christmas, that was all; could not dream of returning to live in wretched England. At Brussels and in Paris she had made hosts of friends, just the right sort of people.

Ada told her all the news. Of most interest was that which related to Nancy Lord. Only a month ago it had become known that Nancy was married, and the mother of a child.

'The Barmbys found it out somehow,' Ada narrated. 'She was married to a man called Tarrant, some one we never heard of, on the very day of her father's death, and, of course, before she knew anything about his will. Then, of course, it had to be kept dark, or she'd lose all her money. Her husband hadn't a farthing. She supported him, and they say he lived most of the time in her house. He's a regular scamp, a drinking, betting fellow. Well, it all came out, and the Barmbys turned her into the street at a moment's notice— serve her right!'

Fanny shrieked with merriment.

'And what is she doing?'

'She went on her knees to Beatrice, and begged for a place at the shop, if it was only a few shillings a week. Nice come-down for Nancy Lord, wasn't it? Of course Beatrice sent her off with a flea in her ear. I don't know where she's living, but I've heard that her husband has gone to America, and left her to shift for herself, now there's nothing more to be got out of her.'

For supplementary details of this racy narrative, Fanny sought out Beatrice; but to her astonishment and annoyance Beatrice would tell nothing. The elder sister urged Fanny to give an account of herself, and used some very plain speech of the admonitory kind.

'What has become of that jackanapes, Horace Lord?' asked Fanny, after a contemptuous remark about 'sermons.'

'I don't know. The question is, what's going to become of *you*?'

Whereupon the girl grew vituperative in two languages, and made off. Her relatives saw no more of her for a long time.

To Mrs. Peachey was born a daughter. Naturally, the months preceding this event had been, for her husband, a renewal of martyrdom; his one supporting solace lay in the thought of the little lad at Canterbury. All the old troubles were revived; from morning to night the house rang with brawls between mistress and servants; in the paroxysms favoured by her physical condition, Ada behaved like a candidate for Bedlam, and more than once obliged her husband to seek temporary peace in lodgings. He left home at eight o'clock every morning, and returned as late as possible. The necessity of passing long evenings made him haunt places of entertainment, and he sometimes had recourse to drink,—he by nature the soberest of men,—in fear of what awaited him on his tardy appearance at Brixton. A month after Ada's confinement he once more acted a sane part, and announced by letter that he would die rather than continue living with his wife. As it was fine autumn weather he went down to a seaside place, where his Canterbury relatives and the little boy joined him for a holiday of several weeks. Again Ada was to receive an allowance. She despatched a few very virulent post-cards, but presently grew quiet, and appeared to accept the situation.

In early winter Fanny French came over to England. She had again been ill, and this time with results obviously graver. Her first call was upon Beatrice, who still occupied the flat at Brixton, and here she unbosomed herself of a dolorous story. All her money had vanished; stolen, most of it, Fanny declared; she was without resources, and, as any one could see, in a wretched state of health. Would Beatrice have compassion on her? Would she lend her money till she was well enough to 'look round'?

Miss. French at once took the girl into her own home, and had her looked after. Fanny coughed in an alarming way; the doctor, speaking privately with Beatrice, made an unpleasant report; was it possible to send the patient to a mild climate for the winter months? Yes, Miss. French could manage that, and would. A suitable attendant having been procured, Fanny was despatched to Bournemouth, whence, in a day or two, she wrote to her sister thus:

'You've been awfully kind to me, and I shan't forget it when I'm well again. Feel a good deal fitter already. Dullish place this, but I've got to put up with it. I've had a letter from Ada. If you see her, tell her she's a beast, and I wish Arthur would wring her scraggy neck. She says it's all my own fault; wait till I'm back again, and I'll pay her a call. My own fault indeed! It seems to me I'm very much to be pitied.'

Walking one day along the sea-front by herself, Fanny observed a young man's figure a few paces in advance of her, which seemed to awaken recollections. Presently the young man turned and showed, beyond doubt, the countenance of Horace Lord. He met her eyes, gave a doubtful, troubled look, and was going past when Fanny accosted him.

'Well, don't you know me?'

'Why, it *is*—it really *is*! How glad I am to see you! But what on earth are you doing here?'

'Amusing myself—*comme vous voyez*; and you?'

'Oh, doing the same.'

They had shaken hands, and were sauntering on together.

'Anything wrong with your health?' Fanny asked, scrutinising the pale thin face, with its touch of warmth on the cheeks.

'Oh, I've had a bit of a cold; nothing to speak of. You been out of sorts?'

'A little run down. Over-study, they say.'

Horace looked his surprise.

'Why, I didn't know you went in for that kind of thing.'

304

'Didn't you? I've been studying abroad for a long time. Thinking of taking a place as French teacher in some tip-top high school.'

'I am very glad to hear it. Capital idea. Sure I hope you'll be successful.'

'Thanks awf'ly. Tell me something about yourself. Why, it's two years since we saw each other, isn't it? Are you married yet?'

Horace smiled and coloured.

'No, no—not yet. I'm in business with Luckworth Crewe,—sort of sleeping partner just now.'

'Are you really? And how's your sister?'

The young man bent his brows uncomfortably.

'Don't you know anything about her?' he asked.

'I've heard she's married.'

'Yes, a man called Tarrant. Very clever fellow; he writes for the papers.—I say, Miss. French, I generally have a glass of wine and a biscuit, at the confectioner's, about this time. Will you give me the pleasure of your company?'

'*Charmee, Monsieur*! I generally go in for the same kind of thing.'

So they repaired to the cake-shop, and sat talking for half-an-hour of trifles which made them laugh.

'And you really didn't know me?' said Fanny, when her glass of wine was finished. 'Have I changed so much?'

'A good deal. Not for the worse, oh dear no!'

The girl giggled.

'Well, I don't mind saying that *you* have changed a good deal for the better.'

Horace flushed at the compliment.

'I'm much older,' he answered with a sigh, as though the years of a sexagenarian weighed upon him.

'That's just what I like in you. You're so much more of a man. Don't be offended.'

They went forth again into the sunshine. At the door both coughed, and both pretended that it wasn't a cough at all, but a voluntary little hem.

CHAPTER 2

Mrs. Damerel was younger than ever. She had spent October abroad, with her friends Mrs. and Miss. Chittle, and the greater part of November at Brighton, with other friends. Back in town she established herself at one of the various boarding-houses honoured by her patronage, and prepared to enjoy the social life of winter.

Half a year ago an unwonted depression had troubled her serene existence. At the close of the London season she seemed weary and spiritless, very unlike herself; having no invitation for the next two months, she withdrew to Whitsand, and there spent some cheerless weeks.

Whitsand was the as yet unfashionable seaside place which had attracted the speculative eye of Luckworth Crewe. For the past two years he had been trying to inspire certain men of capital with his own faith in the possibilities of Whitsand; he owned a share in the new hotel just opened; whenever his manifold affairs allowed him a day's holiday, he spent it at Whitsand, pacing the small esplanade, and meditating improvements. That these 'improvements' signified the conversion of a pretty little old-world spot into a hideous brand new resort of noisy hordes, in no degree troubled Mr. Crewe's conscience. For his own part, he could appreciate the charms of Whitsand as it stood; he was by no means insensible to natural beauty and the ancient peace which so contrasted with his life of every day; but first and foremost in his mind came the necessity of making money; and to fill his pockets he would no more hesitate about destroying the loveliest spot on earth, than the starving hunter would stay his hand out of admiration for bird or beast.

It was with much delight that he heard of Mrs. Damerel's retreat to Whitsand. To the note in which she acquainted him with her arrival there he replied effusively. 'The patronage of a few really fashionable people, such as yourself, would soon do wonders. We must have a special paragraph in the local paper, drawing attention to your being there'—and so on. An answer by return of post rather disappointed him. On no account, wrote Mrs. Damerel, must her name be specially mentioned in the paper. She had taken very simple lodgings, very inexpensive, and wished to live as quietly as possible. But, after seeing the place, she quite agreed with Mr Crewe that it had a future, and if he could run down some day, whilst she was here, it would give her great pleasure to hear his projects explained on the spot.

Crewe ran down. In speaking of Mrs. Damerel as a 'really fashionable' person, he used no insincerity; from their first meeting he had seen in this lady his ideal of social distinction; she was, in fact, the only woman of skilfully pretentious demeanour with whom he had ever spoken. Her distant likeness to Nancy Lord interested and attracted him; her suave superiority awed his conscious roughness; she seemed to him exquisitely gracious, wonderfully sweet. And as, little by little, he attained the right to think of her almost as a friend, his humble admiration became blended with feelings he took particular care not to betray, lest he should expose himself to ridicule. That her age exceeded his own by some years he was of course aware, but this fact soon dropped out of his mind, and never returned to it. Not only did he think Mrs. Damerel a type of aristocratic beauty, he saw in her countenance all the freshness and the promise of youth.

The slight mystery attaching to her position only increased his susceptibility to her charms. It seemed to him very probable that she had but a moderate income; perhaps she was not free from anxieties on that score. But such a woman would of course marry again, and marry well. The thought grew troublesome, and presently accounted for ebullitions of wrath, accompanied by more than usually vigorous language, when business matters went wrong.

At Whitsand, Mrs. Damerel showed herself more than ever sweetly affable. The season, she said, had been rather too much for her; she must take care of her health; besides—and her smile played upon Crewe's pulses—there were troubles, cares, of which she could not speak *even* to so valued a friend.

'I'm afraid you're anxious about your nephew,' murmured the man of business; though at the same time he suspected other things, for the lodgings in which he found Mrs. Damerel were certainly modest.

'Yes, I trouble a good deal about him. If only dear Horace would be reconciled to me. It seems such a long, long time. You know that we have corresponded, but he refuses to see me. It pains me deeply, Mr Crewe.'

And, after a silence:

'There's a special reason why I wish he would be friends with me,— a reason that concerns his own future. Why should I not tell you? I am sure you will respect my confidence.—He will very soon become independent, and then I do so fear he may make a foolish marriage. Yet all the time there is a chance waiting for him which would establish his fortune and his happiness for life. Did he ever speak to you of Miss. Chittle?'

'I don't remember the name.'

'Such a dear, sweet girl, and with really large means. He was introduced to her during the happy time when we saw so much of each other, and she at once became interested in him. Her dear mother assured me of it. She is a very shy, retiring girl, and has refused many offers, before and since then. Isn't it a pity? But I am losing all hope, and I so fear he may have formed some other attachment.'

Crewe went back to London resolved that Horace Lord should no longer 'play the fool.' And he was successful. Horace had all but lost his resentment against Mrs. Damerel; he kept aloof out of stubborn conceit—it had not dignity enough to be called pride; the same feeling that still estranged him from Nancy, though he would gladly have welcomed his sister's offer of affection. Persuaded, or commanded, by Luckworth Crewe, he took the train to Whitsand, and remained there for several days. Mrs. Damerel wrote her friend in Farringdon Street a letter of gratitude, which acted upon him like champagne. In a postscript she said: 'Mrs. Chittle and her daughter have consented to come here for a week or two. They will take rooms at the Imperial.'

Before the end of September, Horace Lord was engaged to Winifred Chittle.

Two years had made very little change in Miss. Chittle's appearance. She was still colourless and abnormally shy, still had the look of one who sheds secret tears, and her repugnance to Society had, if possible, increased. Horace thought her pretty, was impressed by her extreme gentleness and refinement, but she obtained no power over his emotions such as that formerly exercised by Fanny French. It struck him, too, as a very strange thing, that a young lady with a large fortune should be willing to marry a man of his social insignificance. 'My dear,' said Mrs. Damerel, 'it was a case of love at first sight.' But Horace, who had gained some experience of life, could not believe this. He wooed, and won; yet even when Winifred accepted him, he felt that she did it under some constraint. Her pale face declared no happiness.

Had she chosen, Mrs. Damerel could have explained the mystery. She knew that, several years ago, Winifred's name had been blighted by a scandal, and that the girl's shrinking from every proposal of marriage was due, in part perhaps, to the memory of love betrayed, in part to a sense of honour, and to the suspicion that men, knowing her disgrace, condoned it for the sake of her wealth. Interest made Mrs. Damerel generous; she admitted every excuse for Winifred, and persuaded herself that in procuring Horace such a wife she was doing him only a nominal wrong. The young people could live apart from that corner of Society in which Miss. Chittle's name gave occasion to smiles or looks of perfunctory censure. If Winifred, after marriage, chose to make confession, why, that was her own affair, and Horace would be wise enough, all advantages considered, to take the matter philosophically.

That was the view of a practical-minded observer. To read Winifred perfectly, there needed a much more subtle and sympathetic intelligence. The girl had, in truth, conceived a liking for Horace Lord, and it grew stronger when she learnt that neither by birth nor present circumstances did he belong to her own world. To please her mother she was willing to take a husband, but the husband must be of her own choice. She wished to enter upon a wholly new life, remote from the social conditions which of late years had crushed her spirit. From the men who had hitherto approached her, she shrank in fear. Horace Lord, good-looking and not uneducated, yet so far from formidable, suggested a new hope; even though he might be actuated by the ordinary motives, she discerned in him a softness, a pliability of nature, which would harmonise with her own timid disposition. To the thought of deceiving him on the subject of her past, she was reconciled by a resolve to make his happiness the sole object of her existence in the future. Horace was amiability itself, and seemed, if not to love her ardently (which, perhaps, she did not even desire), at least to regard her with an increasing affection.

Nothing was said about the condition of the prospective bridegroom's health, though Horace had confided to Mrs. Damerel that he suffered from a troublesome cough, accompanied now and then by an alarming symptom. In her boundless exultation at the end achieved, Mrs. Damerel made light of this complaint. Horace was not free to marry until nearly the end of the year; for, though money would henceforth be no matter of anxiety, he might as well secure the small inheritance presently due to him. November and December he should spend at Bournemouth under the best medical care, and after that, if needful, his wife would go with him to Madeira or some such place.

No wonder Mrs. Damerel could think of nothing but the great fact that Horace had secured a fortune. Her own resources were coming to an end, and but for the certainty that Horace would not grudge her an ample provision, she must at this moment have been racking her brains (even as through the summer) for help against the evil that drew near. Constitutional lightness of heart had enabled her to enjoy life on a steadily, and rapidly, diminishing fund. There had been hope in Nancy's direction, as well as in her brother's; but the disclosure of Nancy's marriage, and Horace's persistency in unfriendliness, brought Mrs. Damerel to a sense of peril. One offer of marriage she had received and declined; it came from a man of advanced years and small property. Another offer she might, or thought she might, at any moment provoke; but only in direst extremity could she think of bestowing her hand upon Luckworth Crewe. Crewe was in love with her, an amusing fact in itself, and especially so in regard to his former relations with Nancy Lord. He might become a wealthy man; on the other hand, he might not; and in any case he was a plebeian.

All such miseries were now dismissed from her mind. She went abroad with the Chittles, enjoyed herself at Brighton, and came home to prepare for Horace's wedding, Horace himself being at Bournemouth. After her letter of gratitude to Crewe she had ceased to correspond with him; she did not trouble to acquaint him with Horace's engagement; and when Crewe, having heard the news from his partner, ventured to send her a letter of congratulation, Mrs. Damerel replied in two or three very civil but cold sentences. Back in London, she did not invite the man of projects to call upon her. The status she had lost when fears beset her must now be recovered. Let Crewe cherish a passion for her if he liked, but let him understand that social reasons made it laughably hopeless.

Horace was to come up to London in the third week of December, and to be married on New Year's Day; the honeymoon would be spent at Ventnor, or somewhere thereabout. Afraid to lose sight of her relative for more than a week or two, Mrs. Damerel had already been twice to Bournemouth, and now she decided to go for a third time, just to talk quietly over the forthcoming event, and, whether Horace broached the subject or not, to apprise him of the straits into which she was drifting. Unannounced by letter, she reached Bournemouth early in the afternoon, and went straight to Horace's lodgings. The young man had just finished luncheon, and, all things considered, including the fact that it was a remarkably bright and warm day for the time of year, he might have been expected to welcome Mrs. Damerel cheerfully. Yet on seeing her his countenance fell; he betrayed an embarrassment which the lady noted with anxious suspicion.

'Aren't you glad to see me, dear boy?' she began, with a kiss upon his cheek.

'Yes—oh yes. I never dreamt of your appearing just now, that was all.'

'I couldn't resist the temptation. Such a morning in London! Almost as fine as it is here. And how is your cough?'

Even as she made the inquiry, he answered it by coughing very badly.

'I don't think this place suits you, Horace,' said Mrs. Damerel gravely. 'You're not imprudent, I hope? Don't go out after dark?'

Oh, it was nothing, Horace maintained; for several days he had hardly coughed at all. But with every word he uttered, Mrs. Damerel became more convinced of something unusual in his state of mind; he could not keep still, and, in trying to put himself at ease, assumed strange postures.

'When did you hear from Winifred?' she asked.

'Yesterday—no, the day before.'

He shrank from her scrutiny, and an expression of annoyance began to disturb his features. Mrs. Damerel knew well enough the significance of that particular look; it meant the irritation of his self-will, the summoning of forces to resist something he disliked.

'There has been no difference between you, I hope?'

'No—oh no,' Horace replied, wriggling under her look.

At that moment a servant opened the door.

'Two ladies have called in a carriage, sir, and would like to see you.'

'I'll go down. Excuse me for a moment, aunt.'

'Who are they, Horace?' asked Mrs. Damerel, rising with an ill-concealed look of dismay.

'Some friends I have made here. I'll just go and speak to them.'

He hurried away. No sooner was he gone than Mrs. Damerel sprang to the window, where she could look down upon the carriage standing before the house; it was open, and in it sat two ladies, one middle-aged, the other much younger. To her vexation she could not, from this distance, clearly discern their faces; but on glancing rapidly round the room, she saw Horace's little binocular. An instant brought it into focus upon the carriage, and what she then saw gave Mrs. Damerel such a shock, that an exclamation escaped her. Still she gazed through the glasses, and only turned away when the vehicle drove on.

Horace came up flushed and panting.

'It's all right. They wanted me to go for a drive, but I explained—'

He saw the binocular in Mrs. Damerel's hand, and at the same moment read detection on her countenance. She gazed at him; he answered the look with lowering challenge.

'Horace, that was Fanny French.'

'So it was, aunt.'

'What is going on between you?'

The young man took a seat on the edge of the table, and swung his leg. He looked suddenly obstinate.

'We met by accident—here—the other day.'

'How can I believe that, Horace?' said Mrs. Damerel, in a voice of soft reproach. And she drew near to him. 'Be truthful with me, dear. Do tell me the truth!—Is she anything to you?'

'I have told you the truth, aunt. She came here, as I have done, for her health. I haven't seen her for two years.'

'And you don't wish to renew acquaintance with her,—I'm sure you don't.'

He looked away, and said nothing.

'My dear, do you know her character?'

'What about her?'

The tone was startling, but Mrs. Damerel kept firm, though agitated.

312

'She has led the most disgraceful life. I heard about her half a year after she ran away, but of course I wouldn't tell you such painful things.'

Horace reddened with anger.

'And who is to blame for it?' he cried passionately. 'Who drove her to it?'

'Oh, don't, don't come back to that again, Horace!' pleaded the other. 'How can any one drive a girl into a life of scandalous immorality? It was in herself, dear. She took to it naturally, as so many women do. Remember that letter she wrote from Brussels, which I sent you a copy of—'

'It was a forgery!' thundered Horace. 'I have asked her. She says she never wrote any such letter.'

'Then she lies, as such creatures always do.'

Bitterness of apprehension overcame Mrs. Damerel's prudence. With flashing eyes, she faced the young man and dared his wrath. As they stood thus, the two were astonishingly like each other, from forehead to chin.

'It's no use, I'm not going to quarrel with you, aunt. Think what you like of Miss. French, *I* know the truth about her.'

He slipped from the table, and moved away.

'I will say no more, Horace. You are independent, and must have your own acquaintances. But after you are married—'

The other voice interrupted.

'I had better tell you at once. I shall not marry Miss. Chittle. I am going to write this afternoon to break it off.'

Mrs. Damerel went pale, and stood motionless.

'Horace, you can't be so wicked as that!'

'It's better,' he pursued recklessly, 'to break it off now, than to marry her and make her miserable. I don't love her, and I have never really thought I did. I was going to marry her only for her money. Why she wants to marry me, I don't know. There's something wrong; she doesn't really care for me.'

'She does! I assure you she does!'

'Then I can't help it.'

Mrs. Damerel went close to him, and touched his arm.

'My dear,'—her voice was so low that it seemed terror-stricken, —'you don't mean to marry—any one else?'

He drew apart, she followed him.

'Oh, that would be terrible! What can I say to open your eyes and show you what you are doing? Horace, have you no sense of honour? Can you find it in your heart to cast off a girl who loves you, and thinks that in so short a time she will be your wife?'

'This again is your fault,' he replied, with a violence which proved the conflict of emotions in him. 'But for you, I should never have proposed to Winifred—never dreamt of such a thing. What do I want with her money? I have enough of my own, and I shall make more in business. Why have you driven me into this? Did you expect to get some profit out of it?'

The blow struck home, and Mrs. Damerel flinched.

'I had your happiness in view, my dear.'

'My happiness! that's your view of things; that's why I couldn't really like you, from the first. You think of nothing but money. Why you objected to Fanny French at first was because you wished me to marry some one richer. I don't thank you for that kind of happiness; I had rather marry a woman I can love.'

'And you can love such a creature as that?'

Again she lost her self-command; the mere thought of Fanny's possible triumph exasperated her.

'I won't hear her abused,' cried Horace, with answering passion. 'You are the last person who ought to do it. Comparing her and you, I can't help saying—'

An exclamation of pain checked his random words; he looked at Mrs. Damerel, and saw her features wrung with anguish.

'You mustn't speak to me like that!' Once more she approached him. 'If you only knew—I can't bear it—I've always been a worldly woman, but you are breaking my heart, Horace! My dear, my dear, if only out of pity for me—'

'Why should I pity you?' he cried impatiently.

314

'Because—Horace—give me your hand, dear; let me tell you something.—I am your mother.'

She sobbed and choked, clinging to his arm, resting her forehead against it. The young man, stricken with amazement, stared at her, speechless.

'I am your own mother, dear,' she went on, in a quivering voice. 'Your mother and Nancy's. And neither of you can love me.'

'How can that be?' Horace asked, with genuine perplexity. 'How could you have married some one else?'

She passed an arm about his neck, and hid her face against him.

'I left your father—and he made me free to marry again.'

'You were divorced?'

Horace did not mean to speak brutally; in his wonderment he merely pressed for a complete explanation. The answer was a sob, and for some moments neither of them spoke. Then the mother, her face still hidden, went on in a thick voice:

'I married because I was poor—for no other reason—and then came the temptation. I behaved wickedly, I deserted my little children. Don't revenge yourself upon me now, darling! If only I could have told you this before—I did so want to, but I was afraid. I had to conceal half my love for you. You can't imagine how I have suffered from your anger, and from Nancy's coldness. You don't know me; I have never been able to let you see what I really think and feel. I am worldly; I can't live without luxuries and society and amusements; but I love you, my dear son, and it will break my heart if you ruin yourself. It's true I thought of Winifred's money, but she is very fond of you, Horace; her mother has told me she is. And it was because of my own position. I have spent nearly all my husband left me; it wasn't enough to supply me with an income; I could only hope that something—that you, dear, would forgive your poor mother, and help her. If you cast me off, what shall I do?'

There was a silence. Then the young man spoke gravely:

'You are welcome, mother, to half my income. But you must leave me free to marry as I like.'

'Then I can't take a penny from you,' she answered, weeping. 'If you ruin yourself, you ruin me as well.'

'The ruin would come if I married Winifred. I love Fanny; I love her with all my heart and soul, and have never ceased to love her. Tell me what you like about her, it will make no difference.'

A fit of violent coughing stopped his speech; he turned away, and stood by the window, holding his handkerchief to his mouth.

Mrs. Damerel sank upon a chair in mute misery.

CHAPTER 3

Below the hill at Harrow, in a byway which has no charm but that of quietness, stands a row of small plain houses, built not long ago, yet at a time when small houses were constructed with some regard for soundness and durability. Each contains six rooms, has a little strip of garden in the rear, and is, or was in 1889, let at a rent of six-and-twenty pounds. The house at the far end of the row (as the inhabitants described it) was then tenanted by Mary Woodruff, and with her, as a lodger, lived Mrs. Tarrant.

As a lodger, seeing that she paid a specified weekly sum for her shelter and maintenance; in no other respect could the wretched title apply to her. To occupy furnished lodgings, is to live in a house owned and ruled by servants; the least tolerable status known to civilisation. From her long experience at Falmouth, Nancy knew enough of the petty miseries attendant upon that condition to think of it with dread when the stress of heroic crisis compelled her speedy departure from the old home. It is seldom that heroic crisis bears the precise consequence presumed by the actors in it; supreme moments are wont to result in some form of compromise. So Nancy, prepared to go forth into the wilderness of landladies, babe in arm, found that so dreary a self-sacrifice neither was exacted of her, nor would indeed be permitted; she had to reckon with Mary Woodruff. Mary, thanks to her old master, enjoyed an income more than sufficient to her needs; if Nancy must needs go into lodgings,—inevitable, perhaps, as matters stood,—her friend was ready with kind and practical suggestion; to wit, that she should take and furnish a house for herself, and place a portion of it at Mrs. Tarrant's disposal. To this even Tarrant could offer no objection; he stipulated only that his wife should find a temporary refuge from the home she had occupied on false pretences until Mary had her new house in readiness. This was managed without difficulty. Nancy went to Dulwich, and for several weeks dwelt with the honest woman who took care of her child.

Of the dealings between Nancy and her legal guardians Tarrant learned nothing, save the bare fact that her marriage was avowed, and all benefit under her father's will renounced. He did not visit the house at Dulwich, and only saw his child after the removal to Harrow. On this occasion he asked Nancy what arrangements had been made concerning the money that must be reimbursed to the Messrs Barmby; she replied that justice would be done, but the affair was hers alone, and to her must be left.

Tarrant himself suggested the neighbourhood of Harrow for Nancy's abode. It united the conditions of being remote from Camberwell, of lying beyond the great smoke-area, and of permitting him, poor as he was, to visit his wife whenever he thought fit.

In December, Nancy had lived thus for all but a twelvemonth, seeing the while none of her old acquaintances, and with very little news from her old world. What she heard came through Horace, who, after learning with astonishment the secret in his sister's life, came by degrees to something like the old terms of affection with her, and went over to Harrow pretty frequently. Of his engagement to Winifred Chittle he at once informed Nancy, who tried to be glad of it, but could have little faith in anything traceable to the influence of Mrs. Damerel. With that lady the Harrow household had no direct communication; Tarrant had written to her on the night of crisis, civilly requesting her to keep aloof, as her advice and assistance were m nowise needed. She answered him with good temper, and wrote kindly to Nancy; after that, silence on both sides.

It wanted a few days to Christmas; with nightfall had come a roaring wind and sleety rain; the house-door was locked; within, lamps and fires burned cheerily. At half-past six, Nancy—she occupied the two front rooms—sat in her parlour, resting after the exertion of putting her son to bed. To judge from her countenance, she was well and happy. The furniture about her aimed at nothing but homely comfort; the pictures and books, being beyond dispute her own, had come from Grove Lane.

Save when Tarrant was here, Nancy and Mary of course lived like friends who share a house, eating together and generally sitting together. During an hour or two each day the younger woman desired solitude, for a reason understood by her companion, who then looked after the baby. This present evening Nancy had proposed to spend alone; but, after sitting idly for a few minutes, she opened the door and called Mary—just then occupied in teaching a young servant how to iron.

'I shall not write, after all,' she said, when her friend came. 'I'm too tired. Bring your sewing, or your book, here.'

Mary was never talkative; Nancy kept a longer silence than usual.

'How,' she exclaimed at length, 'do poor women with a lot of children manage? It really is a mystery to me. Here am I with one baby, and with the constant help of two people; yet he tires me out. Not a troublesome baby, either; healthy and good-tempered. Yet the thought and anxiety and downright hard labour for a good twelve hours out of the twenty-four! I feel that a second child would be too much for me.'

She laughed, but looked seriously for the reply.

'Poor mothers,' said Mary, 'can't give the same care to their children that you give to baby. The little ones grow up, or they don't grow up—that's what it comes to.'

'Yes; that is to say, only the fit survive. A very good thing— when other people's children are in question. But I should kill myself in taking care of them, if I had a large family.'

'I have known mothers who did,' Mary remarked.

'It comes to this. Nature doesn't intend a married woman to be anything *but* a married woman. In the natural state of things, she must either be the slave of husband and children, or defy her duty. She can have no time to herself, no thoughts for herself. It's a hard saying, but who can doubt that it is Nature's law? I should like to revolt against it, yet I feel revolt to be silly. One might as well'I revolt against being born a woman instead of a man.'

Mary reflected, but held her peace.

'Then comes in money,' pursued Nancy, 'and that alters the state of the case at once. The wife with money says to people: Come here, and be my slaves. Toil for me, whilst I am enjoying myself in ways that Dame Nature wouldn't allow. I want to read, to play music, to see my friends, to see the world. Unless you will slave for me, I can't budge from nursery and kitchen.—Isn't it a queer thing?'

The less sophisticated woman had a difficulty in catching Nancy's point of view. She began to argue that domestic service was no slavery.

'But it *comes* to that,' Nancy insisted. 'And what I mean is, that the thought has made me far more contented than I was at first. After all, one can put up with a great deal, if you feel you're obeying a law of Nature. Now, I have brains, and I should like to use them; but Nature says that's not so important as bringing up the little child to whom I have given life. One thought that troubles me is, that every generation of women is sacrificed to the generation that follows; and of course that's why women are so inferior to men. But then again, Nature says that women are born *only* to be sacrificed. I always come round to that. I don't like it, but I am bound to believe it.'

'Children grow up,' said Mary, 'and then mothers are free.'

'Free to do what? To think of what they *might* have done in the best years of their life.'

It was not said discontentedly; Nancy's mood seemed to be singularly calm and philosophical. She propped her chin on her hand, and gazed at the fire.

'Well,' remarked Mary, with a smile, 'you, at all events, are not one of the poorest women. All seems to be going well, and you will be able, I am sure, to get all the help you need.'

'Perhaps. But I shall never feel quiet in my conscience. I shall feel as if I had defeated Nature by a trick, and fear that she'll somehow be revenged on me.'

This was quite beyond Mary's scope of thought, and she frankly said so.

'One thing I'm quite sure of, Nancy,' she added, 'and that is, that education makes life very much harder to live. That's why I don't hold with educating the poor—not beyond reading and writing. Without education, life is very plain, though it may be a struggle. But from what I have seen of highly-taught people, I'm very sure they suffer worse in their minds than the poor ever do in their bodies.'

Nancy interrupted her.

'Hush! Was that baby?'

'Only the wind, I think.'

Not content, Nancy went to the foot of the stairs. Whilst she stood there listening, Mary came out, and said in a low voice:

'There's a tap at the window.'

'No!—You must have been mistaken.'

'I'm sure it was a tap on the glass.'

She withdrew to the back sitting-room, and Nancy, with quick step, went to open the house-door. A great gust of wind forced it against her as soon as she turned the handle; standing firm, she peeped into darkness.

'Any one there?'

'No enemy but winter and rough weather,' chanted a familiar voice.

'Why, what brings you here, frightening lone women at this time of night? Shut and lock the door for me. The house will be blown out of the windows.'

Nancy retreated to her parlour, and stood there in an attitude of joyous expectation. Without hurry Tarrant hung up his coat and hat in the passage, then came forward, wiping rain from his moustache. Their eyes met in a smile, frank and confident.

'Why have you come, Lionel?'

'No reason in particular. The fancy took me. Am I unwelcome?'

For answer, his wife's arms were thrown about him. A lovers' meeting, with more of tenderness, and scarcely less of warmth, than when Nancy knocked at the door in Staple Inn.

'Are you hungry?'

'Only for what you have given me.'

320

'Some tea, then, after that wretched journey.'

'No. How's the boy?'

He drew her upon his knee, and listened laughingly whilst the newest marvels of babyhood were laughingly related.

'Anything from Horace?'

'Not a word. He must be in London now; I shall write tomorrow.'

Tarrant nodded carelessly. He had the smallest interest in his wife's brother, but could not help satisfaction in the thought that Horace was to be reputably, and even brilliantly, married. From all he knew of Horace, the probability had seemed that his marriage would be some culmination of folly.

'I think you have something to tell me,' Nancy said presently, when her hand had been fondled for a minute or two.

'Nothing much, but good as far as it goes. Bunbury has asked me to write him an article every week for the first six months of '90. Column and a half, at two guineas a column.'

'Three guineas a week.'

'O rare head!'

'So there's no anxiety for the first half of next year, at all events,' said Nancy, with a sigh of relief.

'I think I can count on a margin of fifty pounds or so by midsummer —towards the debt, of course.'

Nancy bit her lip in vexation, but neither made nor wished to make any protest. Only a week or two ago, since entering upon his patrimony, Horace Lord had advanced the sum necessary to repay what Nancy owed to the Barmbys. However rich Horace was going to be, this debt to him must be cancelled. On that, as on most other points, Tarrant and his wife held a firm agreement of opinion. Yet they wanted money; the past year had been a time of struggle to make ends meet. Neither was naturally disposed to asceticism, and if they did not grumble it was only because grumbling would have been undignified.

'Did you dine with the great people on Thursday?' Nancy asked.

'Yes, and rather enjoyed it. There were one or two clever women.'

'Been anywhere else?'

'An hour at a smoking-concert the other evening. Pippit, the actor, was there, and recited a piece much better than I ever heard him speak anything on the stage. They told me he was drunk; very possibly that accounted for it.'

To a number of such details Nancy listened quietly, with bent head. She had learned to put absolute faith in all that Tarrant told her of his quasi-bachelor life; she suspected no concealment; but the monotony of her own days lay heavy upon her whilst he talked.

'Won't you smoke?' she asked, rising from his knee to fetch the pipe and tobacco-jar kept for him upon a shelf. Slippers also she brought him, and would have unlaced his muddy boots had Tarrant permitted it. When he presented a picture of masculine comfort, Nancy, sitting opposite, cautiously approached a subject of which as yet there had been no word between them.

'Oughtn't you to get more comfortable lodgings?'

'Oh, I do very well. I'm accustomed to the place, and I like the situation.'

He had kept his room in Great College Street, though often obliged to scant his meals as the weekly rent-day approached.

'Don't you think we might make some better—some more economical arrangement?'

'How?'

Nancy took courage, and spoke her thoughts.

'It's more expensive to live separately than if we were together.'

Tarrant seemed to give the point his impartial consideration.

'H'm—no, I think not. Certainly not, with our present arrangements. And even if it were we pay for your comfort, and my liberty.'

'Couldn't you have as much liberty if we were living under the same roof? Of course I know that you couldn't live out here; it would put a stop to your work at once. But suppose we moved. Mary might take a rather larger house—it needn't be much larger—in a part convenient for you. We should be able to pay her enough to set off against her increased expenses.'

Smoking calmly, Tarrant shook his head.

322

'Impracticable. Do you mean that this place is too dull for you?'

'It isn't lively, but I wasn't thinking of the place. If *you* lived here, it would be all I should wish.'

'That sounds so prettily from your lips, Nancy, that I'm half ashamed to contradict it. But the truth is that you can only say such things because we live apart. Don't deceive yourself. With a little more money, this life of ours would be as nearly perfect as married life ever can be.'

Nancy remembered a previous occasion when he spoke to the same purpose. But it was in the time she did not like to think of, and in spite of herself the recollection troubled her.

'You must have more variety,' he added. 'Next year you shall come into town much oftener—'

'I'm not thinking of that. I always like going anywhere with you; but I have plenty of occupations and pleasures at home.—I think we ought to be under the same roof.'

'Ought? Because Mrs. Tomkins would cry *haro*! if her husband the greengrocer wasn't at her elbow day and night?'

'Have more patience with me. I didn't mean *ought* in the vulgar sense—I have as little respect for Mrs. Tomkins as you have. I don't want to interfere with your liberty for a moment; indeed it would be very foolish, for I know that it would make you detest me. But I so often want to speak to you—and—and then, I can't quite feel that you acknowledge me as your wife so long as I am away.'

Tarrant nodded.

'I quite understand. The social difficulty. Well, there's no doubt it is a difficulty; I feel it on your account. I wish it were possible for you to be invited wherever I am. Some day it will be, if I don't get run over in the Strand; but—'

'I should like the invitations,' Nancy broke in, 'but you still don't understand me.'

'Yes, I think I do. You are a woman, and it's quite impossible for a woman to see this matter as a man does. Nancy, there is not one wife in fifty thousand who retains her husband's love after the first year of marriage. Put aside the fools and the worthless; think only of women with whom you might be compared—brave, sensible, pure-hearted; they can win love, but don't know how to keep it.'

'Why not put it the other way about, and say that men can love to begin with, but so soon grow careless?'

'Because I am myself an instance to the contrary.'

Nancy smiled, but was not satisfied.

'The only married people,' Tarrant pursued, 'who can live together with impunity, are those who are rich enough, and sensible enough, to have two distinct establishments under the same roof. The ordinary eight or ten-roomed house, inhabited by decent middle-class folk, is a gruesome sight. What a huddlement of male and female! They are factories of quarrel and hate—those respectable, brass-curtain-rodded sties—they are full of things that won't bear mentioning. If our income never rises above that, we shall live to the end of our days as we do now.'

Nancy looked appalled.

'But how can you hope to make thousands a year?'

'I have no such hope; hundreds would be sufficient. I don't aim at a house in London; everything there is intolerable, except the fine old houses which have a history, and which I could never afford. For my home, I want to find some rambling old place among hills and woods,—some house where generations have lived and died,—where my boy, as he grows up, may learn to love the old and beautiful things about him. I myself never had a home; most London children don't know what is meant by home; their houses are only more or less comfortable lodgings, perpetual change within and without.'

'Your thoughts are wonderfully like my father's, sometimes,' said Nancy.

'From what you have told me of him, I think we should have agreed in a good many things.'

'And how unfortunate we were! If he had recovered from that illness, —if he had lived only a few months,—everything would have been made easy.'

'For me altogether too easy,' Tarrant observed.

'It has been a good thing for you to have to work,' Nancy assented. 'I understand the change for the better in you. But'—she smiled —'you have more self-will than you used to have.'

'That's just where I have gained.—But don't think that I find it easy or pleasant to resist your wish. I couldn't do it if I were not so sure that I am acting for your advantage as well as my own. A man who finds himself married to a fool, is a fool himself if he doesn't take his own course regardless of his wife. But I am in a very different position; I love you more and more, Nancy, because I am learning more and more to respect you; I think of your happiness most assuredly as much as I think of my own. But even if my own good weighed as nothing against yours, I should be

324

wise to resist you just as I do now. Hugger-mugger marriage is a defilement and a curse. We know it from the experience of the world at large,— which is perhaps more brutalised by marriage than by anything else. —No need to test the thing once more, to our own disaster.'

'What I think is, that, though you pay me compliments, you really have a very poor opinion of me. You think I should burden and worry you in endless silly ways. I am not such a simpleton. In however small a house, there could be your rooms and mine. Do you suppose I should interfere with your freedom in coming and going?'

'Whether you meant to or not, you would—so long as we are struggling with poverty. However self-willed I am, I am not selfish; and to see you living a monotonous, imprisoned life would be a serious hindrance to me in my own living and working. Of course the fact is so at present, and I often enough think in a troubled way about you; but you are out of my sight, and that enables me to keep you out of mind. If I am away from home till one or two in the morning, there is no lonely wife fretting and wondering about me. For work such as mine, I must live as though I were not married at all.'

'But suppose we got out of our poverty,' urged Nancy, 'you would be living the same life, I suppose; and how would it be any better for you or me that we had a large house instead of a small one?'

'Your position will be totally changed. When money comes, friends come. You are not hiding away from Society because you are unfit for it, only because you can't live as your social equals do. When you have friends of your own, social engagements, interests on every hand, I shall be able to go my own way without a pang of conscience. When we come together, it will be to talk of your affairs as well as of mine. Living as you do now, you have nothing on earth but the baby to think about—a miserable state of things for a woman with a mind. I know it is miserable, and I'm struggling tooth and nail to help you out of it.'

Nancy sighed.

'Then there are years of it still before me.'

'Heaven forbid! Some years, no doubt, before we shall have a home; but not before I can bring you in contact with the kind of people you ought to know. You shall have a decent house—socially possible—somewhere out west; and I, of course, shall still go on in lodgings.'

He waited for Nancy's reply, but she kept silence.

'You are still dissatisfied?'

She looked up, and commanded her features to the expression which makes whatever woman lovely—that of rational acquiescence. On the faces of most women such look is never seen.

'No, I am content. You are working hard, and I won't make it harder for you.'

'Speak always like that!' Tarrant's face was radiant. 'That's the kind of thing that binds man to woman, body and soul. With the memory of that look and speech, would it be possible for me to slight you in my life apart? It makes you my friend; and the word friend is better to my ear than wife. A man's wife is more often than not his enemy. Harvey Munden was telling me of a poor devil of an author who daren't be out after ten at night because of the fool-fury waiting for him at home.'

Nancy laughed.

'I suppose she can't trust him.'

'And suppose she can't? What is the value of nominal fidelity, secured by mutual degradation such as that? A rational woman would infinitely rather have a husband who was often unfaithful to her than keep him faithful by such means. Husband and wife should interfere with each other not a jot more than two friends of the same sex living together. If a man, under such circumstances, worried his friend's life out by petty prying, he would get his head punched. A wife has no more justification in worrying her husband with jealousies.'

'How if it were the wife that excited suspicion?' asked Nancy.

'Infidelity in a woman is much worse than in a man. If a man really suspects his wife, he must leave her, that's all; then let her justify herself if she can.'

Nancy cared little to discuss this point. In argument with any one else, she would doubtless have maintained the equality of man and woman before the moral law; but that would only have been in order to prove herself modern-spirited. Tarrant's dictum did not revolt her.

'Friends are equals,' she said, after a little thought. 'But you don't think me your equal, and you won't be satisfied with me unless I follow your guidance.'

Tarrant laughed kindly.

'True, I am your superior in force of mind and force of body. Don't you like to hear that? Doesn't it do you good—when you think of the maudlin humbug generally talked by men to women? We can't afford to disguise that truth. All the same, we are friends, because each has the other's interest at heart, and each would be ashamed to doubt the other's loyalty.'

326

The latter part of the evening they spent with Mary, in whom Tarrant always found something new to admire. He regarded her as the most wonderful phenomenon in nature—an uneducated woman who was neither vulgar nor foolish.

Baby slept in a cot beside Nancy's bed. For fear of waking him, the wedded lovers entered their room very softly, with a shaded candle. Tarrant looked at the curly little head, the little clenched hand, and gave a silent laugh of pleasure.

On the breakfast-table next morning lay a letter from Horace. As soon as she had opened it, Nancy uttered an exclamation which prepared her companion for ill news.

'Just what I expected—though I tried not to think so. "I write aline only to tell you that my marriage is broken off. You will know the explanation before long. Don't trouble yourself about it. I should never have been happy with Winifred, nor she with me. We may not see each other for some time, but I will write again soon." He doesn't say whether he or she broke it off. I hope it was Winifred.'

'I'm afraid not,' said Tarrant, 'from the tone of that letter.'

'I'm afraid not, too. It means something wretched. He writes from his London lodgings. Lionel, let me go back with you, and see him.'

'By all means.'

Her gravest fear Nancy would not communicate. And it hit the truth.

CHAPTER 4

They parted at Baker Street, Tarrant for his lodgings and the work that awaited him there, Nancy to go westward by another train.

When she reached the house from which her brother had dated his letter, it was half-past ten. At the door stood a cab, and a servant was helping the driver to hoist a big trunk on to the top.

'Is Mr. Lord still here?' Nancy asked of the girl.

'He's just this minute a-goin', miss. This is his luggage.'

She sent her name, and was quickly led up to the first floor. There stood Horace, ready for departure.

'Why have you come?' he asked, with annoyance.

'What else could I do on hearing such news?'

'I told you I should write again, and I said plainly that it was better we shouldn't see each other for some time.—Why will people pester me out of my life?—I'm not a child to be hunted like this!'

On the instant, he had fallen into a state of excitement which alarmed his sister. There were drops of sweat on his forehead, and tears in his eyes; the blood had rushed to his cheeks, and he trembled violently.

'I am so troubled about you,' said Nancy, with anxious tenderness. 'I have been looking forward with such hope to your marriage,—and now—'

'I can't tell you anything about it just now. It was all Mrs. Damerel's doing; the engagement, I mean. It's a good thing I drew back in time.—But I have a train to catch; I really mustn't stay talking.'

'Are you going far, Horace?'

'To Bournemouth again,—for the present. I've given up these rooms, and I'm taking all my things away. In a month or two I may go abroad; but I'll let you know.'

Already he was out of the room; his sister had no choice but to follow him downstairs. He looked so ill, and behaved with such lack of self-restraint, that Nancy kept her eyes upon him in an awestricken gaze, as though watching some one on the headlong way to destruction. Pouring rain obliged her to put up her umbrella as she stepped down on to the pavement. Horace, having shouted a direction to the driver, entered the cab.

'You haven't even shaken hands with me, Horace,' Nancy exclaimed, standing at the window.

'Good-bye, dear; good-bye! You shouldn't have come in weather such as this. Get home as fast as you can. Good-bye!—Tell the fellow to drive sharp.'

And the cab clattered away, sending spurts of mud on to Nancy's waterproof.

She walked on for a few paces without reflection, until the vehicle disappeared round a corner. Coming to herself, she made for the railway again, which was at only a few minutes' distance, and there she sat down by the fire in the waiting-room. Her health for the last year had been sound as in the days of girlhood; it was rarely that she caught cold, and weather would have been indifferent to her but for the discomfort which hindered her free movement.

Vexed at so futile a journey, she resolved not to return home without making another effort to learn something about Horace. The only person to whom she could apply was the one who would certainly be possessed of information,—Mrs. Damerel. At the time of Horace's engagement, Nancy had heard from Mrs. Damerel, and replied to the letter; she remembered her aunt's address, and as the distance was not great, the temptation to go there now proved irresistible. Her husband would dislike to hear of such a step, but he had never forbidden communication with Mrs. Damerel.

By help of train and omnibus she reached her new destination in half-an-hour, and felt a relief on learning that Mrs. Damerel was at home. But it surprised her to be conducted into a room where lamps were burning, and blinds drawn close; she passed suddenly from cheerless day to cosy evening. Mrs. Damerel, negligently attired, received her with a show of warm welcome, but appeared nervous and out of spirits.

'I am not very well,' she admitted, 'and that's why I have shut out the dreadful weather. Isn't it the most sensible way of getting through the worst of a London winter? To pretend that there is daylight is quite ridiculous, so one may as well have the comforts of night.'

'I have come to speak about Horace,' said Nancy, at once. In any case, she would have felt embarrassment, and it was increased by the look with which Mrs. Damerel kept regarding her,—a look of confusion, of shrinking, of intense and painful scrutiny.

'You know what has happened?'

'I had a letter from him this morning, to say that his marriage was broken off—— nothing else. So I came over from Harrow to see him. But he had hardly a minute to speak to me. He was just starting for Bournemouth.'

'And what did he tell you?' asked Mrs. Damerel, who remained standing,—or rather had risen, after a pretence of seating herself.

'Nothing at all. He was very strange in his manner. He said he would write.'

'You know that he is seriously ill?'

'I am afraid he must be.'

'He has grown much worse during the last fortnight. Don't you suspect any reason for his throwing off poor Winifred?'

'I wondered whether he had met that girl again. But it seemed very unlikely.'

'He has. She was at Bournemouth for her health. She, too, is ill; consumptive, like poor Horace,—of course a result of the life she has been leading. And he is going to marry her.'Nancy's heart sank. She could say nothing. She remembered Horace's face, and saw in him the victim of ruthless destiny.

'I have done my utmost. He didn't speak of me?'

'Only to say that his engagement with Winifred was brought about by you.'

'And wasn't I justified? If the poor boy must die, he would at least have died with friends about him, and in peace. I always feared just what has happened. It's only a few months ago that he forgave me for being, as he thought, the cause of that girl's ruin; and since then I have hardly dared to lose sight of him. I went down to Bournemouth unexpectedly, and was with him when that creature came to the door in a carriage. You haven't seen her. She looks what she is, the vilest of the vile. As if any one can be held responsible for that! She was born to be what she is. And if I had the power, I would crush out her hateful life to save poor Horace!'

Nancy, though at one with the speaker in her hatred of Fanny French, found it as difficult as ever to feel sympathetically towards Mrs. Damerel. She could not credit this worldly woman with genuine affection for Horace; the vehemence of her speech surprised and troubled her, she knew not how.

'He said nothing more about me?' added Mrs. Damerel, after a silence.

'Nothing at all.'

330

It seemed to Nancy that she heard a sigh of relief. The other's face was turned away. Then Mrs. Damerel took a seat by the fire.

'They will be married to-morrow, I dare say, at Bournemouth—no use trying to prevent it. I don't know whether you will believe me, but it is a blow that will darken the rest of my life.'

Her voice sounded slightly hoarse, and she lay back in the chair, with drooping head.

'You have nothing to reproach yourself with,' said Nancy, yielding to a vague and troublous pity. 'And you have done as much as any one could on his behalf.'

'I shall never see him again—that's the hardest thought. She will poison him against me. He told me I had lied to him about a letter that girl wrote from Brussels; she has made him think her a spotless innocent, and he hates me for the truth I told about her.'

'However short his life,' said Nancy, 'he is only too likely to find out what she really is.'

'I am not sure of that. She knows he is doomed, and it's her interest to play a part. He will die thinking the worst of me.— Nancy, if he writes to you, and says anything against me, you will remember what it means?'

'My opinion of people is not affected by hearsay,' Nancy replied.

It was a remark of dubious significance, and Mrs. Damerel's averted eyes seemed to show that she derived little satisfaction from it. As the silence was unbroken, Nancy rose.

'I hope you will soon get rid of your cold.'

'Thank you, my dear. I haven't asked how the little boy is. Well, I hope?'

'Very well, I am glad to say.'

'And your husband—he is prospering?'

'I shouldn't like to say he is prospering; it seems to mean so much; but I think he is doing good work, and we are satisfied with the results.'

'My dear, you are an admirable wife.'

Nancy coloured; for the first time, a remark of Mrs. Damerel's had given her pleasure. She moved forward with hand offered for leave-taking. They had never kissed each other, but, as if overcoming diffidence, Mrs. Damerel advanced her lips; then, as suddenly, she drew back.

'I had forgotten. I may give you my sore throat.'

Nancy kissed her cheek.

That night Mrs. Damerel was feverish, and the next day she kept her bed. The servant who waited upon her had to endure a good many sharp reproofs; trouble did not sweeten this lady's temper, yet she never lost sight of self-respect, and even proved herself capable of acknowledging that she was in the wrong. Mrs. Damerel possessed the elements of civilisation.

This illness tried her patience in no slight degree. Something she had wished to do, something of high moment, was vexatiously postponed. A whole week went by before she could safely leave the house, and even then her mirror counselled a new delay. But on the third day of the new year she made a careful toilette, and sent for a cab,—the brougham she had been wont to hire being now beyond her means.

She drove to Farringdon Street, and climbed to the office of Mr Luckworth Crewe. Her knowledge of Crewe's habits enabled her to choose the fitting hour for this call; he had lunched, and was smoking a cigar.

'How delightful to see you here!' he exclaimed. 'But why did you trouble to come? If you had written, or telegraphed, I would have saved you the journey. I haven't even a chair that's fit for you to sit down on.'

'What nonsense! It's a most comfortable little room. Haven't you improved it since I called?'

'I shall have to look out for a bigger place. I'm outgrowing this.'

'Are you really? That's excellent news. Ah, but what sad things have been happening!'

'It's a bad business,' Crewe answered, shaking his head.

'I thought I should have heard from you about it.'

The reason of his silence she perfectly understood. Since Horace's engagement, there had been a marked change in her demeanour towards the man of business; she had answered his one or two letters with such cold formality, and, on the one occasion of his venturing to call, had received him with so marked a reserve, that Crewe, as he expressed it to himself, 'got his back up.' His ideas of chivalrous devotion were anything but complex; he could not bend before a divinity who snubbed him; if the once gracious lady chose to avert her countenance, he would let her know that it didn't matter much to him after all. Moreover, Mrs. Damerel's behaviour was too suggestive; he could hardly be wrong in explaining it by the fact that her nephew, about to be enriched by marriage, might henceforth be depended upon for all the assistance she needed. This, in the Americanism which came naturally to Crewe's lips, was 'playing it rather low down,' and he resented it.

The sudden ruin of Horace Lord's prospects (he had learnt the course of events from Horace himself) amused and gratified him. How would the high and mighty Mrs. Damerel relish this catastrophe? Would she have the 'cheek' to return to her old graciousness? If so, he had the game in his hands; she should see that he was not to be made a fool of a second time.

Yet the mere announcement of her name sufficed to shatter his resolve. Her smile, her soft accents, her polished manners, laid the old spell upon him. He sought to excuse himself for having forsaken her in her trial.

'It really floored me. I didn't know what to say or do. I was afraid you might think I was meddling with what didn't concern me.'

'Oh, how could I have thought that? It has made me ill; I have suffered more than I can tell you.'

'You don't look quite the thing,' said Crewe, searching her face.

'Have you heard all?'

'I think so. He is married, and that's the end of it, I suppose.'

Mrs. Damerel winced at this blunt announcement.

'When was it?' she asked, in an undertone. 'I only knew he had made up his mind.'

Crewe mentioned the date; the day after Nancy's call upon her.

'And are they at Bournemouth?'

'Yes. Will be for a month or so, he says.'

'Well, we won't talk of it. As you say, that's the end. Nothing worse could have happened. Has he been speaking of me again like he used to?'

'I haven't heard him mention your name.'

She heaved a sigh, and began to look round the office.

'Let us try to forget, and talk of pleasanter things. It seems such a long time since you told me anything about your business. You remember how we used to gossip. I suppose I have been so absorbed in that poor boy's affairs; it made me selfish—I was so overjoyed, I really could think of nothing else. And now—! But I must and will drive it out of my mind. I have been moping at home, day after day, in wretched solitude. I wanted to write to you, but I hadn't the heart—scarcely the strength. I kept hoping you might call—if only to ask howl was. Of course everything had to be explained to inquisitive people—how I hate them all! It's the nature of the world to mock at misfortunes such as this. It would really have done me good to speak for a few minutes with such a friend as you—a real friend. I am going to live a quiet, retired life. I am sick of the world, its falsity, and its malice, and its bitter, bitter disappointments.'

Crewe's native wit and rich store of experience availed him nothing when Mrs. Damerel discoursed thus. The silvery accents flattered his ear, and crept into the soft places of his nature. He felt as when a clever actress in a pathetic part wrought upon him in the after-dinner mood.

'You must bear up against it, Mrs. Damerel. And I don't think a retired life would suit you at all. You are made for Society.'

'Don't seek for compliments. I am speaking quite sincerely. Ah, those were happy days that I spent at Whitsand! Tell me what you have been doing. Is there any hope of the pier yet?'

'Why, it's as good as built!' cried the other. 'Didn't you see the advertisements, when we floated the company a month ago? I suppose you don't read that kind of thing. We shall begin at the works in early spring.—Look here!'

He unrolled a large design, a coloured picture of Whitsand pier as it already existed in his imagination. Not content with having the mere structure exhibited, Crewe had persuaded the draughtsman to add embellishments of a kind which, in days to come, would be his own peculiar care; from end to end, the pier glowed with the placards of advertisers. Below, on the sands, appeared bathing-machines, and these also were covered with manifold advertisements. Nay, the very pleasure-boats on the sunny waves declared the glory of somebody's soap, of somebody's purgatives.

'I'll make that place one of the biggest advertising stations in England—see if I don't! You remember the caves? I'm going to have them lighted with electricity, and painted all round with advertisements of the most artistic kind.'

'What a brilliant idea!'

'There's something else you might like to hear of. It struck me I would write a Guide to Advertising, and here it is.' He handed a copy of the book. 'It advertises *me*, and brings a little grist to the mill on its own account. Three weeks since I got it out, and we've sold three thousand of it. Costs nothing to print; the advertisements more than pay for that. Price, one shilling.'

'But how you do work, Mr. Crewe! It's marvellous. And yet you look so well,—you have really a seaside colour!'

'I never ailed much since I can remember. The harder I work, the better I feel.'

'I, too, have always been rather proud of my constitution.' Her eyes dropped. 'But then I have led a life of idleness. Couldn't you make me useful in some way? Set me to work! I am convinced I should be so much happier. Let me help you, Mr. Crewe. I write a pretty fair hand, don't I?'

Crewe smiled at her, made a sound as if clearing his throat, grasped his knee, and was on the very point of momentous utterance, when the door opened. Turning his head impatiently, he saw, not the clerk whose duty it was to announce people, but a lady, much younger than Mrs. Damerel, and more fashionably dressed, who for some reason had preferred to announce herself.

'Why do you come in like that?' Crewe demanded, staring at her. 'I'm engaged.'

'Are you indeed?'

'You ought to send in your name.'

'They said you had a lady here, so I told them another would make no difference.—How do you do, Mrs. Damerel? It's so long since I had the pleasure of seeing you.'

Beatrice French stepped forward, smiling ominously, and eyeing first Crewe then his companion with curiosity of the frankest impertinence. Mrs. Damerel stood up.

'We will speak of our business at another time, Mr. Crewe.'

Crewe, red with anger, turned upon Beatrice.

'I tell you I am engaged—'

'To Mrs. Damerel?' asked the intruder airily.

'You might suppose,'—he addressed the elder lady,—'that this woman has some sort of hold upon me—'

'I'm sure I hope not,' said Mrs. Damerel, 'for your own sake.'

'Nothing of the kind. She has pestered me a good deal, and it began in this way.'

Beatrice gave him so fierce a look, that his tongue faltered.

'Before you tell that little story,' she interposed, 'you had better know what I've come about. It's a queer thing that Mrs. Damerel should be here; happens more conveniently than things generally do. I had something to tell you about her. You may know it, but most likely you don't.—You remember,' she faced the other listener, 'when I came to see you a long time ago, I said it might be worth while to find out who you really were. I haven't given much thought to you since then, but I've got hold of what I wanted, as I knew I should.'

Crewe did not disguise his eagerness to hear the rest. Mrs. Damerel stood like a statue of British respectability, deaf and blind to everything that conflicts with good-breeding; stony-faced, she had set her lips in the smile appropriate to one who is braving torture.

'Do you know who she is—or not?' Beatrice asked of Crewe.

He shuffled, and made no reply.

'Fanny has just told me in a letter; she got it from her husband. Our friend here is the mother of Horace Lord and of Nancy. She ran away from her first husband, and was divorced. Whether she really married afterwards, I don't quite know; most likely not. At all events, she has run through her money, and wants her son to set her up again.'

For a few seconds Mrs. Damerel bore the astonished gaze of her admirer, then, her expression scarcely changing, she walked steadily to the door and vanished. The silence was prolonged till broken by Beatrice's laugh.

'Has she been bamboozling you, old man? I didn't know what was going on. You had bad luck with the daughter; shouldn't wonder if the mother would suit you better, all said and done.'

Crewe seated himself and gave vent to his feelings in a phrase of pure soliloquy: 'Well, I'm damned!'

'I cut in just at the right time, did I?—No malice. I've had my hit back at her, and that's enough.'

As the man of business remained absorbed in his thoughts, Beatrice took a chair. Presently he looked up at her, and said savagely:

'What the devil do you want?'

'Nothing.'

336

'Then take it and go.'

But Beatrice smiled, and kept her seat.

CHAPTER 5

Nancy stood before her husband with a substantial packet in brown paper. It was after breakfast, at the moment of their parting.

'Here is something I want you to take, and look at, and speak about the next time you come.'

'Ho, ho! I don't like the look of it.' He felt the packet. 'Several quires of paper here.'

'Be off, or you'll miss the train.'

'Poor little girl! *Et tu!*'

He kissed her affectionately, and went his way. In the ordinary course of things Nancy would not have seen him again for ten days or a fortnight. She expected a letter very soon, but on the fourth evening Tarrant's fingers tapped at the window-pane. In his hand was the brown paper parcel, done up as when he received it.

Nancy searched his face, her own perturbed and pallid.

'How long have you been working at this?'

'Nearly a year. But not every day, of course. Sometimes for a week or more I could get no time. You think it bad?'

'No,'—puff—'not in any sense'—puff—'bad. In one sense, it's good. But'—puff—'that's a private sense; a domestic sense.'

'The question is, dear, can it be sold to a publisher.'

'The question is nothing of the kind. You mustn't even try to sell it to a publisher.'

'Why not? You mean you would be ashamed if it came out. But I shouldn't put my own name to it. I have written it only in the hope of making money, and so helping you. I'll put any name to it you like.'

Tarrant smoked for a minute or two, until his companion gave a sign of impatience. He wore a very good-humoured look.

'It's more than likely you might get the thing accepted—'

'Oh, then why not?' she interrupted eagerly, with bright eyes.

338

'Because it isn't literature, but a little bit of Nancy's mind and heart, not to be profaned by vulgar handling. To sell it for hard cash would be horrible. Leave that to the poor creatures who have no choice. You are not obliged to go into the market.'

'But, Lionel, if it is a bit of my mind and heart, it must be a good book. You have often praised books to me just on that account because they were genuine.'

'The books I praised were literature. Their authors came into the world to write. It isn't enough to be genuine; there must be workmanship. Here and there you have a page of very decent English, and you are nowhere on the level of the ordinary female novelist. Indeed —don't take it ill—I was surprised at what you had turned out. But—'

He finished the sentence in smoke wreaths.

'Then I'll try again. I'll do better.'

'Never *much* better. It will never be literature.'

'What does that matter? I never thought myself a Charlotte Bronte or a George Eliot. But so many women make money out of novels, and as I had spare time I didn't see why I shouldn't use it profitably. We want money, and if it isn't actually disgraceful—and if I don't use my own name—'

'We don't want money so badly as all that. I am writing, because I must do something to live by, and I know of nothing else open to me except pen-work. Whatever trash I turned out, I should be justified; as a man, it's my duty to join in the rough-and-tumble for more or less dirty ha'pence. You, as a woman, have no such duty; nay, it's your positive duty to keep out of the beastly scrimmage.'

'It seemed to me that I was *doing* something. Why should a woman be shut out from the life of the world?'

'It seems to me that your part in the life of the world is very considerable. You have given the world a new inhabitant, and you are shaping him into a man.'

Nancy laughed, and reflected, and returned to her discontent.

'Oh, every woman can do that.'

'Not one woman in a thousand can bear a sound-bodied child; and not one in fifty thousand can bring up rightly the child she has borne. Leisure you must have; but for Heaven's sake don't waste it. Read, enjoy, sit down to the feast prepared for you.'

'I wanted to *do* something,' she persisted, refusing to catch his eye. 'I have read enough.'

'Read enough? Ha, then there's no more to be said.'

His portentous solemnity overcame her. Laughter lighted her face, and Tarrant, laying down his pipe, shouted extravagant mirth.

'Am I to burn it then?'

'You are not. You are to seal it with seven seals, to write upon it *peche de jeunesse*, and to lay it away at the back of a very private drawer. And when you are old, you shall some day bring it out, and we'll put our shaky heads together over it, and drop a tear from our dim old eyes.—By-the-bye, Nancy, will you go with me to a music-hall to-morrow night?'

'A music-hall?'

'Yes. It would do us both good, I think. I feel fagged, and you want a change.—-Here's the end of March; please Heaven, another month shall see us rambling in the lanes somewhere; meantime, we'll go to a music-hall. Each season has its glory; if we can't hear the lark, let us listen to the bellow of a lion-comique.—Do you appreciate this invitation? It means that I enjoy your company, which is more than one man in ten thousand can say of his wife. The ordinary man, when he wants to dissipate, asks—well, not his wife. And I, in plain sober truth, would rather have Nancy with me than anyone else.'

'You say that to comfort me after my vexation.'

'I say it because I think it.—The day after to-morrow I want you to come over in the morning to see some pictures in Bond Street. And the next day we'll go to the theatre.'

'You can't afford it.'

'Mind your own business. I remembered this morning that I was young, and that I shall not be so always. Doesn't that ever come upon you?'

The manuscript, fruit of such persevering toil, was hidden away, and its author spoke of it no more. But she suffered a grave disappointment. Once or twice a temptation flashed across her mind; if she secretly found a publisher, and if her novel achieved moderate success (she might alter the title), would not Tarrant forgive her for acting against his advice? It was nothing more than advice; often enough he had told her that he claimed no coercive right; that their union, if it were to endure, must admit a genuine independence on both sides. But herein, as on so many other points, she subdued her natural impulse, and conformed to her husband's idea of wifehood. It

340

made her smile to think how little she preserved of that same 'genuine independence;' but the smile had no bitterness.

Meanwhile, nothing was heard of Horace. The winter passed, and June had come before Nancy again saw her brother's handwriting. It was on an ordinary envelope, posted, as she saw by the office-stamp, at Brighton; the greater her surprise to read a few lines which coldly informed her that Horace's wife no longer lived. 'She took cold one evening a fortnight ago, and died after three days' illness.'

Nancy tried to feel glad, but she had little hope of any benefit to her brother from this close of a sordid tragedy. She answered his letter, and begged that, as soon as he felt able to do so, he would come and see her. A month's silence on Horace's part had led her to conclude that he would not come, when, without warning, he presented himself at her door. It was morning, and he stayed till nightfall, but talked very little. Sitting in the same place hour after hour, he seemed overcome with a complete exhaustion, which made speech too great an effort and kept his thoughts straying idly. Fanny's name did not pass his lips; when Nancy ventured an inquiry concerning her, he made an impatient gesture, and spoke of something else.

His only purpose in coming, it appeared, was to ask for information about the Bahamas.

'I can't get rid of my cough, and I'm afraid it may turn to something dangerous. You said, I remember, that people with weak chests wintered in the Bahamas.'

'Lionel can tell you all about it. He'll be here to-morrow. Come and have a talk with him.'

'No.' He moved pettishly. 'Tell me as much as you know yourself. I don't feel well enough to meet people.'

Looking at him with profound compassion, Nancy thought it very doubtful whether he would see another winter. But she told him all she could remember about Nassau, and encouraged him to look forward with pleasure and hopefulness to a voyage thither.

'How are you going to live till then?'

'What do you mean?' he answered, with a startled and irritated look. 'I'm not so bad as all that.'

'I meant—how are you going to arrange your life?' Nancy hastened to explain.

'Oh, I have comfortable lodgings.'

'But you oughtn't to be quite alone.—I mean it must be so cheerless.'

She made a proposal that he should have a room in this little house, and use it as a home whenever he chose; but Horace so fretted under the suggestion, that it had to be abandoned. His behaviour was that of an old man, enfeebled in mind and body. Once or twice his manner of speaking painfully reminded Nancy of her father during the last days of his life.

With a peevish sort of interest he watched his little nephew toddling about the room, but did not address a word to the child.

A cab was sent for to convey him to the railway station. Nancy had known few such melancholy days as this.

On the morning when, by agreement, she was to go into town to see her brother, there arrived a note from him. He had been advised to try a health-resort in Switzerland, and was already on the way. Sorry he could not let Nancy know before; would visit her on his return. Thus, in the style of telegraphy, as though he wrote in hot haste.

From Switzerland came two letters, much more satisfactory in tone and contents. The first, written in July, announced a distinct improvement of health. No details being supplied, Nancy could only presume that her brother was living alone at the hotel from which he dated. The second communication, a month later, began thus: 'I think I forgot to tell you that I came here with Mrs. Damerel. She will stay till the end of the summer, and then, perhaps, go with me to the Bahamas, if that seems necessary. But I am getting wonderfully well and strong. Mrs. Damerel is kinder to me than any one in the world ever was. I shall tell you more about her some day.' The writer went on to describe a project he had of taking a small farm in Devonshire, and living upon it as a country gentleman.

Tarrant warned his wife not to build hopes upon this surprising report, and a few weeks brought news that justified him. Horace wrote that he had suffered a very bad attack, and was only now sufficiently recovered to hold a pen. 'I don't know what we shall do, but I am in good hands. No one was ever better nursed, night and day— More before long.'

Indeed, it was not long. A day or two after Nancy's return from a seaside holiday, Mary brought in a telegram. It came from Mrs. Damerel. 'Your brother died at ten o'clock last night, suddenly, and without pain. I am posting a letter he had written for you.'

When the promised letter arrived, it was found to bear a date two months ago. An unwonted tenderness marked the opening words.

MY DEAREST SISTER—What I am going to write is not to be sent to you at once. Sometimes I feel afraid that I can't live very long, so I have been making a will, and I want you to know why I have left you only half of what I have to leave. The other half will go to some one who has an equal claim on me, though you don't know it. She has asked me to tell you. If I get thoroughly well again, there will be no need of this letter, and I shall tell you in private something that will astonish you very much. But if I were to die, it will be best for you to learn in this way that Mrs. Damerel is much more to us than our mother's sister; she is our own mother. She told me at the time when I was behaving like an idiot at Bournemouth. It ought to have been enough to stop me. She confessed that she had done wrong when you and I were little children; that was how she came to marry again whilst father was still alive. Though it seemed impossible, I have come to love her for her great kindness to me. I know that I could trust you, dearest Nancy, to let her share whatever you have; but it will be better if I provide for her in my will. She has been living on a small capital, and now has little left. What I can give her is little enough, but it will save her from the worst extremities. And I beg you, dear sister, to forgive her fault, if only for my sake, because she has been so loving to a silly and useless fellow.

I may as well let you know about my wife's death. She was consumptive, but seemed to get much better at Bournemouth; then she wanted to go to Brighton. We lived there at a boardinghouse, and she behaved badly, very badly. She made acquaintances I didn't like, and went about with them in spite of my objections. Like an obstinate fool, I had refused to believe what people told me about her, and now I found it all out for myself. Of course she only married me because I had money. One evening she made up her mind to go with some of her friends in a boat, by moonlight. We quarrelled about it, but she went all the same. The result was that she got inflammation of the lungs, and died. I don't pretend to be sorry for her, and I am thankful to have been released from misery so much sooner than I deserved.

And now let me tell you how my affairs stand—

At the first reading, Nancy gave but slight attention to this concluding paragraph. Even the thought of her brother's death was put aside by the emotions with which she learnt that her mother still lived. After brooding over the intelligence for half a day, she resolved to question Mary, who perhaps, during so long a residence in Grove Lane, had learnt something of the trouble that darkened her master's life. The conversation led to a disclosure by Mary of all that had been confided to her by Mr. Lord; the time had come for a fulfilment of her promise to the dead man.

CHAPTER 6

Horace's letter Nancy sent by post to her husband, requesting him to let her know his thoughts about it in writing before they again met. Of her own feeling she gave no sign. 'I want you to speak of it just as if it concerned a stranger, plainly and simply. All I need say is, that I never even suspected the truth.'

Tarrant did not keep her long in suspense, and his answer complied in reasonable measure with the desire she had expressed.

'The disclosure has, of course, pained you. Equally, of course, you wish it were not necessary to let me know of it; you are in doubt as to how it will affect me; you perhaps fear that I shall—never mind about phrasing. First, then, a word on that point. Be assured once for all that nothing external to yourself can ever touch the feeling which I now have for you. "One word is too often profaned"; I will say simply that I hold you in higher regard that any other human being.

'Try not to grieve, my dearest. It is an old story, in both senses. You wish to know how I view the matter. Well, if a wife cannot love her husband, it is better she should not pretend to do so; if she love some one else, her marriage is at an end, and she must go. Simple enough—provided there be no children. Whether it is ever permissible for a mother to desert her children, I don't know. I will only say that, in you yourself, I can find nothing more admirable than the perfect love which you devote to your child. Forsake it, you could not.

'In short, act as feeling dictates. Your mother lives; that fact cannot be ignored. In your attitude towards her, do not consult me at all; whatever your heart approves, I shall find good and right. Only, don't imagine that your feeling of to-day is final—I would say, make no resolve; they are worth little, in any concern of life.

'Write to me again, and say when you wish to see me.

After reading this, Nancy moved about with the radiance of a great joy on her countenance. She made no haste to reply; she let a day elapse; then, in the silence of a late hour, took pen and paper.

'When do I wish to see you? Always; in every moment of my day. And yet I have so far conquered "the unreasonable female"—do you remember saying that?—that I would rather never see you again than bring you to my side except when it was your pleasure to be with me. Come as soon as you can—as soon as you will.

'My mother—how shall I word it? She is nothing to me. I don't feel that Nature bids me love her. I could pardon her for leaving my father; like you, I see nothing terrible in that; but, like you, I *know* that she did wrong in abandoning her little children, and her kindness to Horace at the end cannot atone for it. I don't think she has any love for *me*. We shall not see each other; at all events, that is how I feel

344

about it at present. But I am very glad that Horace made provision for her—that of course was right; if he had not done it, it would have been my duty.

'I had better tell you that Mary has known my mother's story for a long time—but not that she still lived. My father told her just before his death, and exacted her promise that, if it seemed well, she would repeat everything to me. You shall know more about it, though it is bad all through. My dear father had reason bitterly to regret his marriage long before she openly broke it.

'But come and see me, and tell me what is to be done now that we are free to look round. There is no shame in taking what poor Horace has given us. You see that there will be at least three thousand pounds for our share, apart from the income we shall have from the business.'

He was sure to come on the evening of the morrow. Nancy went out before breakfast to post her letter; light-hearted in the assurance that her husband's days of struggle were over, that her child's future no longer depended upon the bare hope that its father would live and thrive by a profession so precarious as that of literature, she gave little thought to the details of the new phase of life before her. Whatever Tarrant proposed would be good in her sight. Probably he would wish to live in the country; he might discover the picturesque old house of which he had so often spoken. In any case, they would now live together. He had submitted her to a probation, and his last letter declared that he was satisfied with the result.

Midway in the morning, whilst she was playing with her little boy, —rain kept them in the house,—a knock at the front door announced some unfamiliar visit. Mary came to the parlour, with a face of surprise.

'Who is it?'

'Miss. Morgan.'

'What? Jessica?'

Mary handed an envelope, addressed to 'Mrs. Tarrant.' It contained a sheet of paper, on which was written in pencil: 'I beg you to see me, if only for a minute.'

'Yes, I will see her,' said Nancy, when she had frowned in brief reflection.

Mary led away the little boy, and, a moment after, introduced Jessica Morgan. At the appearance of her former friend, Nancy with difficulty checked an exclamation; Miss. Morgan wore the garb of the Salvation Army. Harmonious therewith were the features shadowed by the hideous bonnet: a face hardly to be recognised, bloodless, all but fleshless, the eyes set in a stare of weak-minded fanaticism. She came hurriedly forward, and spoke in a quick whisper.

'I was afraid you would refuse to see me.'

'Why have you come?'

'I was impelled—I had a duty to perform.'

Coldly, Nancy invited her to sit down, but the visitor shook her head.

'I mustn't take a seat in your house. I am unwelcome; we can't pretend to be on terms of friendliness. I have come, first of all,' —her eyes wandered as she spoke, inspecting the room,—'to humble myself before you—to confess that I was a dishonourable friend,—to make known with my lips that I betrayed your secret—'

Nancy interrupted the low, hurrying, panting voice, which distressed her ear as much as the facial expression that accompanied it did her eyes.

'There's no need to tell me. I knew it at the time, and you did me no harm. Indeed, it was a kindness.'

She drew away, but Jessica moved after her.

'I supposed you knew. But it is laid upon me to make a confession before you. I have to ask your pardon, most humbly and truly.'

'Do you mean that some one has told you to do this?'

'Oh no!' A gleam of infinite conceit shot over the humility of Jessica's countenance. 'I am answerable only to my own soul. In the pursuit of an ideal which I fear you cannot understand, I subdue my pride, and confess how basely I behaved to you. Will you grant me your forgiveness?'

She clasped her gloveless hands before her breast, and the fingers writhed together.

'If it is any satisfaction to you,' replied Nancy, overcome with wonder and pity, 'I will say those words. But don't think that I take upon myself—'

'Only say them. I ask your pardon—say you grant it.'

Nancy uttered the formula, and with bowed head Jessica stood for a minute in silence; her lips moved.

'And now,' she said at length, 'I must fulfil the second part of the duty which has brought me here.' Her attitude changed to one of authority, and her eyes fixed themselves on Nancy's, regarding her with the mild but severe rebuke of a spiritual superior. 'Having acknowledged my wrong-doing, I must remind you of your own. Let me ask you first of all—have you any religious life?'

Nancy's eyes had turned away, but at these words they flashed sternly upon the speaker.

'I shall let you ask no such question.'

'I expected it,' Jessica sighed patiently. 'You are still in the darkness, out of which *I* have been saved.'

'If you have nothing more to say than this, I must refuse to talk any longer.'

'There is a word I must speak,' pursued Jessica. 'If you will not heed it now, it will remain in your memory, and bear fruit at the appointed time. I alone know of the sin which poisons your soul, and the experiences through which I have passed justify me in calling you to repentance.'

Nancy raised her hand.

'Stop! That is quite enough. Perhaps you are behaving conscientiously; I will try to believe it. But not another word, or I shall speak as I don't wish to.'

'It is enough. You know very well what I refer to. Don't imagine that because you are now a married woman—'

Nancy stepped to the door, and threw it open.

'Leave the house,' she said, in an unsteady tone. 'You said you were unwelcome, and it was true. Take yourself out of my sight!'

Jessica put her head back, murmured some inaudible words, and with a smile of rancorous compassion went forth into the rain.

On recovering from the excitement of this scene, Nancy regretted her severity; the poor girl in the hideous bonnet had fallen very low, and her state of mind called for forbearance. The treachery for which Jessica sought pardon was easy to forgive; not so, however, the impertinent rebuke, which struck at a weak place in Nancy's conscience. Just when the course of time and favour of circumstances seemed to have completely healed that old wound, Jessica, with her crazy malice grotesquely disguised, came to revive the half-forgotten pangs, the shame and the doubt that had seemed to be things gone by. It would have become her, Nancy felt, to treat her hapless friend of years ago in a spirit of gentle tolerance; that she could not do so proved her—and she recognised the fact— still immature, still a backward pupil in the school of life.— 'And in the Jubilee year I thought myself a decidedly accomplished person!'

Never mind. Her husband would come this evening. Of him she could learn without humiliation.

His arrival was later than of wont. Only at eleven o'clock, when with disappointment she had laid aside her book to go to bed, did Tarrant's rap sound on the window.

'I had given you up,' said Nancy.

'Yet you are quite good-tempered.'

'Why not?'

'It is the pleasant custom of wives to make a husband uncomfortable if he comes late.'

'Then I am no true wife!' laughed Nancy.

'Something much better,' Tarrant muttered, as he threw off his overcoat.

He began to talk of ordinary affairs, and nearly half-an-hour elapsed before any mention was made of the event that had bettered their prospects. Nancy looked over a piece of his writing in an evening paper which he had brought; but she could not read it with attention. The paper fell to her lap, and she sat silent. Clearly, Tarrant would not be the first to speak of what was in both their minds. The clock ticked; the rain pattered without; the journalist smoked his pipe and looked thoughtfully at the ceiling.

'Are you sorry,' Nancy asked, 'that I am no longer penniless?'

'Ah—to be sure. We must speak of that. No, I'm not sorry. If I get run over, you and the boy—'

'Can make ourselves comfortable, and forget you; to be sure. But for the present, and until you do get run over?'

'You wish to make changes?'

'Don't you?'

348

'In one or two respects, perhaps. But leave me out of the question. You have an income of your own to dispose of; nothing oppressively splendid, I suppose. What do you think of doing?'

'What do you advise?'

'No, no. Make your own suggestion.

Nancy smiled, hesitated, and said at length:

'I think we ought to take a house.'

'In London?'

'That's as you wish.'

'Not at all. As *you* wish. Do you want society?'

'In moderation. And first of all, yours.

Tarrant met her eyes.

'Of my society, you have quite as much as is good for you,' he answered amiably. 'That you should wish for acquaintances, is reasonable enough. Take a house somewhere in the western suburbs. One or two men I know have decent wives, and you shall meet them.'

'But you? You won't live with me?'

'You know my view of that matter.'

Nancy kept her eyes down, and reflected.

'Will it be known to everybody that we don't live together?'

'Well,' answered Tarrant, with a laugh, 'by way of example, I should rather like it to be known; but as I know *you* wouldn't like it, let the appearances be as ordinary as you please.'

Again Nancy reflected. She had a struggle with herself.

'Just one question,' she said at length. 'Look me in the face. Are you—ever so little—ashamed of me?'

He regarded her steadily, smiling.

'Not in the least.'

'You were—you used to be?'

'Before I knew you; and before I knew myself. When, in fact, *you* were a notable young lady of Camberwell, and *I*—'

He paused to puff at his pipe.

'And you?'

'A notable young fool of nowhere at all.'

5876932R0

Made in the USA
Charleston, SC
15 August 2010